Augusta H. Leypoldt, George Iles

List of books for girls and women and their clubs

Augusta H. Leypoldt, George Iles

List of books for girls and women and their clubs

ISBN/EAN: 9783743306974

Manufactured in Europe, USA, Canada, Australia, Japa

Cover: Foto ©Andreas Hilbeck / pixelio.de

Manufactured and distributed by brebook publishing software (www.brebook.com)

Augusta H. Leypoldt, George Iles

List of books for girls and women and their clubs

LIST OF

Books for Girls and Women

And Their Clubs

WITH DESCRIPTIVE AND CRITICAL NOTES AND A LIST OF PERIODICALS AND HINTS FOR GIRLS' AND WOMEN'S CLUBS

EDITED BY

AUGUSTA H. LEYPOLDT AND GEORGE ILES

BOSTON
Published for the American Library Association Publishing Section by
THE LIBRARY BUREAU
1895
Price, Fifty Cents in Paper ; $1.00 in Cloth

COPYRIGHT, 1895,
BY THE AMERICAN LIBRARY ASSOCIATION

"I am sometimes asked by young people to recommend a course of reading. My advice would be that they should confine themselves to the supreme books in whatever literature, or better still, to choose some one great author, and make themselves thoroughly familiar with him. For, as all roads lead to Rome, so do they likewise lead away from it, and you will find that, in order to understand perfectly and weigh exactly any vital piece of literature, you will be gradually and pleasantly persuaded to excursions of which you little dreamed when you began, and will find yourselves scholars before you are aware. For remember that there is nothing less profitable than scholarship for the mere sake of scholarship, nor anything more wearisome in the attainment. But the moment you have a definite aim, attention is quickened, the mother of memory, and all that you acquire groups and arranges itself in an order that is lucid, because everywhere and always it is in intelligent relation to a central object of constant and growing interest. This method also forces upon us the necessity of thinking, which is, after all, the highest result of all education. For what we want is not learning, but knowledge; that is, the power to make learning answer its true end as a quickener of intelligence and a widener of the intellectual sympathies."—JAMES RUSSELL LOWELL: *Opening the Free Public Library, Chelsea, Mass.* (Democracy and other addresses).

PREFACE.

This LIST tells of some twenty-one hundred books worthy to be read or studied by girls and women. Men and women who know have chosen the books and said about them just what they would tell an inquirer face to face. In some cases trustworthy reviews have been condensed and cited. The selection especially includes books setting forth the manifold new opportunities for bread-winning, education, and culture opened to women within recent years. These new opportunities are notably furthered by the clubs and associations multiplying on every hand in America. To promote their formation, and to render them service, are among the purposes of this LIST. Although the LIST is thus adapted to girls and women, most of its books are as well suited to boys and men as to girls and women—for great literature appeals to all mankind. In planning courses of reading for the young of either sex, librarians, teachers, and parents will find the LIST very helpful.

The American Library Association intends to follow this comparatively short LIST with others, which shall be full and detailed enough to aid the comprehensive reader and the advanced student. During 1896 it is probable that it will issue handbooks on the literature of FINE ART, by Mr. Russell Sturgis ; and on that of MUSIC, by Mr. Henry E. Krehbiel ; both these authorities are contributors to this LIST. It is hoped that from this beginning the whole round of the working literature of education, science, and art will be passed upon by critics of mark for the behoof of readers and students. Notes condensed for the purpose by contributors may be printed directly on the catalogue-cards of a public library, so that in running over the department of American geology, of electricity, of photography, of engraving, one may be enabled to choose a book as intelligently as if there stood at one's side an authority on the subject—a service this of great importance in an age when books, good, bad, and indifferent, abound and superabound. In the present LIST a good many notes are available for direct transfer to catalogue-cards.

While books in general are in plentiful supply there are some subjects of importance to girls and women upon which no books exist. Co-operative housekeeping is such a subject ; throughout the United States diverse experiments are being tried, which, if rightly described and criticised, would be informing to many inquirers ; the chapters should be extended to include plans of the best apartment-houses and country-clubs, and to outline the most recent labor-saving appliances, electrical and other, introduced in city hotels. Another theme of interest to women, on which a useful book might be written, is investment. The rate of interest on sound securities is low and tends to become lower. Any method by which women have increased their incomes from investment by exercise of good judgment and wise supervision, deserves to be known to other women with a little property from which returns grow smaller and smaller. Typical cases of gain and of loss would be of very great value for encouragement or warning. In a totally different field England has given us an example worth copying. Sixty years ago Miss Martineau wrote her "Tales of Political Economy"; twenty years ago the same field was entered by Mrs. Fawcett. Both authors showed that the principles underlying the right management of a national household are much akin to those which rule the duty and the work of an industrious and sensible family. Questions of currency, taxation, and international trade, as now debated in this country, could readily be made intelligible if cast in the form of stories. With skill, these stories might easily develop a public interest in economic righteousness, now scant enough.

The editions given in this list are usually the cheapest of fair quality. At the end of this volume publishers' addresses are printed in full.

The figures which follow the notes are those of the Decimal Classification.

CONTENTS.

	PAGE
FICTION: chosen and annotated by a reviewer for *The Nation*	1–40
BIOGRAPHY: Assistant Librarians New York Free Circulating Library	41–46
HISTORY: Reuben Gold Thwaites	47–54
TRAVEL AND EXPLORATION: Adelaide R. Hasse	55–59
LITERATURE: a selection of the best English and American authors in the departments of Poetry and Belles-lettres: G. Mercer Adam	60–77
MYTHOLOGY AND FOLK-LORE: Stewart Culin	78–79
FINE ART: Part I., General, Archæology, Glossaries, and Dictionaries; Part II., Painting and Sculpture; Part III., Architecture; Part IV., Minor Decorative Arts: Russell Sturgis	80–90
MUSIC: Henry E. Krehbiel	91–93
EDUCATION: the Kindergarten: Angeline Brooks	94–95
EDUCATION AS A SCIENCE AND AN ART: Drawing, Penmanship, Shorthand, Grammar, Composition, Rhetoric, Elocution, Language, Mathematics, Book-keeping, Astronomy, Physics (including Electricity): Edward R. Shaw	96–100
CHEMISTRY: H. Carrington Bolton	101
GEOGRAPHY: Edward R. Shaw	102
GEOLOGY: E. S. Burgess	103–104
BOTANY: D. P. Penhallow	105–107
NATURAL HISTORY AND HUMAN EVOLUTION: Olive Thorne Miller	108–111
PSYCHOLOGY: E. W. Scripture	112
ECONOMIC, SOCIAL, AND POLITICAL SCIENCE: George Iles	113–116
PHILOSOPHY: J. Clark Murray	117–118
PHYSICAL CULTURE: Hygiene, Sanitation, Nursing, Emergencies: Augusta H. Leypoldt	119–120
SELF-CULTURE: Etiquette, Clubs for women and girls: Augusta H. Leypoldt	121–122
USEFUL ARTS, LIVELIHOODS: Augusta H. Leypoldt	123–125
COUNTRY OCCUPATIONS: the Farm, Orchard, Kitchen and Market Garden, Dairy, Poultry, Bee-keeping, Flower-garden, Landscape Gardening: L. H. Bailey and B. M. Watson, Jr.	126–128
DOMESTIC ECONOMY: Augusta H. Leypoldt	129–132
AMUSEMENTS AND SPORTS: Alice B. Kroeger	133–134
WORKS OF REFERENCE: Helen Kendrick Johnson	135–138
LIST OF PERIODICALS	139–140
HINTS FOR A GIRLS' CLUB WITH A HOME OF ITS OWN	141–142
OUTLINE CONSTITUTION AND BY-LAWS FOR A GIRLS' CLUB	143
A LITERARY CLUB OF GIRLS OR WOMEN	144
A WOMAN'S CLUB	145
NOTES	145
PUBLISHERS' ADDRESSES	146–147
INDEX	149

FICTION

CHOSEN AND ANNOTATED BY A REVIEWER FOR "THE NATION."

IN preparing this list the choice has been limited to two hundred and fifty American, British and Canadian authors and their principal works. While the object has been to select novels and tales of interest to girls and women, great literature appeals to all mankind, and many of the books here named are as attractive to boys and men as to their sisters and mothers. Besides the acknowledged masters of fiction, the present list includes the writers who, without being great, have founded schools or led fashions, also the authors who have passed on from generation to generation the chief traditions of novel-writing, and gradually developed the art. Unfortunately, many writers of fiction enjoy wide popularity without deserving it; of this class the vicious and depraved are unmentioned; others, without being vicious, are frivolous in ideas and defective in taste and skill; of these a few representatives are introduced with a word of warning.

The plan in drawing up this list is, for leading authors, first, to offer brief general characterizations; to follow with a selection of their best works, giving a short note to each book; lastly, to name without comment a few more of their works. With other authors a single note is the rule; in no case is there mention of all an author's volumes. In many cases a wide variety of editions of popular novels are published; from among these editions in one volume, in cloth, at low prices, have been chosen; and also fair editions in paper. The publishers' addresses have been abbreviated. The figures in brackets following a living author's name give the year of birth; in the case of an author not living, also the year of death; in some cases no information has been found. The first note after an author's name is followed by the number for her or his books in the Decimal Classification.

Readers who desire complete lists of novels, including translations, may refer to "The best reading," by F. B. Perkins, with its supplements, published by Putnam, New York. Wm. M. Griswold, Cambridge, Mass., issues various Lists of Fiction, American and foreign, with citations from leading critical reviews. The American Library Association, through the Library Bureau, publishes "Reading for the young," compiled by John F. Sargent, with short descriptive notes; its department of fiction is comprehensive.

New York, June, 1895.

Aguilar, Grace. [1816-1847.]
An English writer of Spanish-Hebrew extraction, who had at heart the interests of her race in all that she wrote. Her power of description is excellent, and, although her dialogue seems often old-fashioned, her novels retain decided interest. Some of them are based on the persecutions of the Jews, as recorded in history, others describe English domestic life. Her style is graceful, her characterization sympathetic, her moral tone elevated. **823.80.**

VALE OF CEDARS. N. Y., Appleton, $1.
Expulsion of Jews from Spain in the 15th century.

HOME INFLUENCE. N. Y., Appleton, $1.
English home life.

MOTHER'S RECOMPENSE. N. Y., Appleton, $1.
Sequel to "Home influence."

HOME SCENES AND HEART STUDIES. N. Y., Appleton, $1.
Short stories.

Alcott, Louisa May. [1832-1888.]
A New England writer of stories for young girls. Her wide popularity has been earned by her power of depicting real life, her sensible and stirring inculcation of truth, kindness and courage. Her style is sometimes careless, as if she had worked too hurriedly. Among her best books are the following: **813.41.**

LITTLE WOMEN, or Meg, Joe, Beth, and Amy. Bost., Roberts, $1.50.
  About Miss Alcott's three sisters and herself in their Concord home. The book that made the author famous.
LITTLE MEN: Life at Plumfield with Joe's boys. Bost., Roberts, $1.50.
  Sequel to "Little Women."
EIGHT COUSINS, or the aunt-hill. Bost., Roberts, $1.50.
AN OLD-FASHIONED GIRL. Bost., Roberts, $1.50.
  About a pleasant, sensible country girl visiting the city and afterwards becoming a music teacher.
WORK: A story of experience. Bost., Roberts, $1.50.
  How a girl supported herself and found happiness in her work.

Aldrich, Thomas Bailey. [1836- .]
  A New England poet, novelist and writer of tales. His short stories are among the best in the English language. Each episode is complete, ingeniously developed and generally ended with a surprise, which is however a logical inference from incident and character. His power for sketching a single incident is greater than for sustained narrative, and his novels are therefore more noticeable for brilliant episodes than for continuous interest. **813.44.**
MARGERY DAW, and other people. Bost., Houghton, $1.50.
  Short stories.
THE STORY OF A BAD BOY. Bost., Houghton, $1.25.
  Story of a mischievous but truly good, natural New England boy. Puritanism is characterized.
PRUDENCE PALFREY. Bost., Houghton, $1.50.
  Describes New England people with humor and satire.
THE QUEEN OF SHEBA. Bost., Houghton, $1.50.
  Scene, a New Hampshire village, afterwards Switzerland. Fine comparisons of natural scenery.
THE STILLWATER TRAGEDY. Bost., Houghton, $1.50.
  The tragedy is a murder. Deals with the labor problem.
TWO BITES AT A CHERRY. Bost., Houghton, 1893, $1.25.
  Short stories.

Alexander, *Mrs.* *(pseudonym).* *See* Hector, Mrs. Annie French.

Allen, James Lane.
  A Kentuckian story writer of rare merit, whose stories, local though they are in scene, are excellent in plot, construction and style. His diction is always refined and polished, and altogether his work may be characterized as admirable, and is worthy of even wider acceptance than it has found. His reputation was made by his descriptive work, "The Blue grass Region of Kentucky." **813.40.**
A KENTUCKY CARDINAL. N. Y., Harper, $1.
  The story revolves round a beautiful red breasted bird, "the Kentucky cardinal." Much appreciation of nature.
FLUTE AND VIOLIN, and other Kentucky tales and romances. N. Y., Harper, $1.50.
JOHN GRAY: a Kentuckian tale of the olden time. Phila., Lippincott, $1.

Anstey, F. *(pseudonym).* *See* Guthrie, Thomas A.

Arblay, *Mme.* **Frances (Burney) d'.** [1752-1840.]
  English 18th century novelist. She modelled her style and manner on the famous contemporary realistic novelists, Richardson and Fielding, though less sentimental and more humorous than the former, and not comparable with the latter for force and versatility. She confined herself to delineations of small groups in their social relations, and may be said to have invented the domestic and society novel. She observed keenly, had original insight, much ironical humor and a strong sense for comedy. At twenty-six she sprang from obscurity to fame, became the pet of London society, and for over half a century remained a conspicuous figure in both literary and fashionable circles. **823.66.**
EVELINA. N. Y., Macmillan, 2 vols., $2.
  The author's first and best book. The theme is the annoyance caused by vulgar relations to a fashionable young lady, noble on one side of the house. Some of the situations are admirably comic and the characters, though now appearing a little formal, survive very fairly the wear and tear of a century. Contemporary society pronounced this representation of itself delightful and its verdict has been accepted by posterity, which also accepts Miss Burney as the first of English women worthy to sit among the classics.
CECILIA. N. Y., Macmillan, 2 vols., $2.

Argles, *Mrs.* **Margaret (H.).** *See* Hungerford, Mrs. Margaret (Hamilton).

Aristocracy: an anonymous novel. N. Y., Appleton, paper, 50 c.
  Was written as a satire upon the many flattering pictures of society now offered the public. The characters are said to be well-known people. "Aristocracy" delineates stupid and wicked men and women. It depicts barely one decent character, and the panorama of English life is, to say the least, depressing. The style is very pointed, but the novel, while entertaining, must be said to be essentially false and unsatisfactory. **823.89.**

Atherton, *Mrs.* **Gertrude Franklin.**
  A Western novelist who has specially sketched California life. About ten years ago she had decided, but short-lived popularity. Her stories are romantic and interesting, but are imperfect in form and careless in style. **813.40.**
BEFORE THE GRINGO CAME. N. Y., J. Selwin Tait, $1; paper, 50 c.
  Eleven stories of California life before the Gringo or American came, when affairs of the heart were more urgent than those of the pocket.
LOS CERRITOS: a romance of modern times. N. Y., Lovell, Coryell, $1; paper, 50 c.
  "Los Cerritos" is an abandoned ranch in Southern California, on which poor whites and Mexican half-breds have "squatted." The wealthy owner attempts to eject these squatters, and the consequences are exciting.
WHAT DREAMS MAY COME. Chic., Belford, Clarke, $1; paper, 50 c.

Austen, Jane. [1775-1817.]
  English novelist of domestic and social life in the early days of the 19th century. The first of the three great English women in fiction, and, as an artist in letters, more finished than either Charlotte Brontë or George Eliot. The only notable predecessor in her sphere was Frances Burney, the author of "Evelina." Miss Austen's novels reproduce with singular vividness and detail the minds and manners of her period and locality. She clung closely to what she knew and saw, or divined from observation. A great world, a

popular movement, a political upheaval, had no attraction for her. The private life of the middle-class people among whom she lived was her only material. So scrupulously did she avoid the exceptional in episode or character, so studiously shun dramatic surprise, that her capacity for investing her lengthy narratives with interest seems marvellous. During the twenty years of her literary life her style knew neither development nor deterioration. It was always absolutely fitted to her theme. Her world was commonplace, rather shallow; living always in awe of the neighbors' opinions; mostly prone to trivial deceits, hypocrisy and spite, not largely loving or sympathetic. Miss Austen saw it, saw through it and laughed at it, showed it all up with keen but not unkindly satire. Modern enthusiasts for realism declare that Jane Austen alone has achieved that in English fiction, but it is wise to remember her limitation, the regions of actual life of thought and feelings which she neither could nor would touch. Perhaps no one of her novels is really better than another. They are all good, with the same characteristics. 823.74.

PRIDE AND PREJUDICE. N. Y., Ward, $1.
This novel, within strictly defined limits of action and motive, is almost perfect in scheme, grouping and expression.

SENSE AND SENSIBILITY. N. Y. Ward, 75 c.

MANSFIELD PARK. N. Y., Ward, 75 c.

EMMA. N. Y., Ward, 75 c.

NORTHANGER ABBEY. N. Y Ward, 75 c.

PERSUASION. N. Y., Macmillan, $1.
"Northanger Abbey" and "Persuasion" together in 1 vol. N. Y., Stokes, $1.

Austin, Mrs. Jane Goodwin. [1831-1894.]
New England writer of historical novels and tales, especially of the Puritan colonists of Massachusetts. She had not that great imagination which reproduces the spirit of the past, and was a trifle too conscientious about the letter to give unity and an appearance of actuality to her work. Nevertheless she was much in sympathy with her chosen period and wrote entertainingly of the struggles, physical and spiritual, of her colonial ancestors. 813.40.

A NAMELESS NOBLEMAN. Bost., Houghton, $1.25; paper, 50 c.
Scene a New England village preparing for the reception of a clergyman who is bringing home his wife. Distinctly religious in tone.

STANDISH OF STANDISH. Bost., Houghton, $1.25.
A story of the pilgrims of Plymouth Colony in the 17th century.

BETTY ALDEN. Bost., Houghton, $1.25.
Sequel to "Standish of Standish."

DAVID ALDEN'S DAUGHTER. Bost., Houghton, $1.25.
Twelve stories, each representing some noteworthy character or history of colonial times.

DOCTOR LE BARON AND HIS DAUGHTERS. Bost., Houghton, $1.25.
Relates to Plymouth Colony and gives further details about Standish of Standish and his friend Betty Alden.

THE DESMOND HUNDRED. Bost., Houghton, $1; paper, 50 c.

Balestier, Charles Wolcott. [1861-1891.]
A New Yorker who wrote fresh and vigorous tales of Western life. He had an excellent notion of a story and how to tell it, and his works indicated fine ability which, had he lived longer, would doubtless have expanded in many directions. 813.40.

THE AVERAGE WOMAN. N. Y., United States Book Co., $1.25.

BENEFITS FORGOT. N. Y., Appleton, $1.50.

NAULAHKA. N. Y., Macmillan, $1.50; paper, 50 c.
Written in collaboration with Rudyard Kipling.

Bangs, John Kendrick. [1862-.]
A New York humorous author of delightfully absurd stories and sketches, who, however, has a tendency to over-elaboration and dwells too continuously on the grotesque or merely droll. His stories, nevertheless, are bright and entertaining. 813.40.

COFFEE AND REPARTEE. N. Y., Harper, 50 c.

THE WATER GHOST, and others. N. Y., Harper, $1.25.

Barlow, Jane.
An Irish writer of vivid sketches of peasant life in Connaught villages. Her characterization is picturesque and delicate, both in humor and pathos; and her descriptions of surroundings are minute and circumstantial. Altogether a very rare and unusual artist in a homely field. 823.80.

IRISH IDYLLS. N. Y., Dodd, $1.25.

KERRIGAN'S QUALITY. N. Y., Dodd, $1.25.

Barr, Mrs. Amelia Edith. [1831-.]
An Anglo-American writer of novels and tales historical and modern. Her scenes include the Scotch Highlands and Western Isles and several States of the Union. Her plan is simple and well developed and her manner unpretentious and sincere. Whatever trials her people endure they generally survive them, and the distribution of happiness at the end, if old-fashioned and not strictly in agreement with the facts of life, is eminently satisfactory. 813.40.

JAN VEDDER'S WIFE. N. Y., Dodd, $1.25; paper, 25 c.
A very pretty story and one of the author's best. The characters of the careless, unstable sailor and his cold, self-righteous wife, are cleverly contrasted and the primitive life of the inhabitants of a Shetland village vividly described.

THE BOW OF ORANGE RIBBON. N. Y., Dodd, $1.25; paper, 25 c.
A story of New York in 1756, with a romance between a Dutch maiden and one of King George's officers. A picturesque, natural and amusing story.

REMEMBER THE ALAMO. N. Y., Dodd, $1.25.
A romantic and dramatic tale of the revolt of Americans in Texas against Mexican rule. Davy Crockett, Sam Houston and Santa Anna figure prominently and the storming of the Alamo is the great incident.

A DAUGHTER OF FIFE. N. Y., Dodd, $1.25.

LAST OF THE MCALLISTERS. N. Y., Dodd, $1.25.

Barrie, James Matthew. [1860-.]
Scotch novelist and writer of tales, plays and sketches. His rapidly achieved reputation rests on his delineation of poor, plain Scotch people, in which he shows clear understanding both of the poverty of their external life and the richness of their spiritual and mental life—a combination far from rare in Scotland. His characters are never sentimentalized or caricatured, but whether the situation be pathetic, tragic or humorous, he manages to touch the right note in the right way and produces an effect at once recognized as just. 823.80.

A WINDOW IN THRUMS. N. Y., Lovell, Coryell, $1; paper, 50 c.
> Jess Hendry, from whose window the village of Thrums is painted, is one of the author's most delicately drawn figures. Her family and friends abound in variety of force and fun, but in Jess there is an ideal of beauty that gives the book moral dignity and permanent literary worth.

AULD LICHT IDYLLS. N. Y., Lovell, Coryell, $1; paper, 50 c.
> Sketches of members of a seceding branch of the Scotch Church — very small and austere. An admirable work, full of ironical humor.

THE LITTLE MINISTER. N. Y., Lovell, Coryell, $1.25; paper, 50 c.
> The author's best novel; very romantic in plot and realistic in presentation of scene and character. The incidents take place in and about Thrums, and many of the people introduced in the sketches of Thrums re-appear.

WHEN A MAN'S SINGLE. N. Y., Lovell, Coryell, $1.25.
> Sketches, perhaps autobiographically, the early struggles of a journalist and literary man. Full of uncommon sense.

Baylor, Frances Courtenay (*Mrs.* Belger). [1848- .]   813.49.

ON BOTH SIDES. Phila., Lippincott, $1.25.
> Really two stories, one of an American family in London, the other of an English family in America. The author (a Southern novelist) has lived several years in England, and writes intelligently and amusingly of British peculiarities, while her knowledge of American character is thorough.

JUAN AND JUANITA. Bost., Houghton, $1.50.
> Mexico and Texas are the background of this story, which sketches the Indian graphically.

CLAUDIA HYDE. Bost., Houghton, $1.25.
> A capital tale of life in Virginia.

Beaconsfield, Benjamin Disraeli, Earl of. *See* Disraeli, B.

Beckford, William. [1759-1844.]

VATHEK: an Oriental tale. N. Y., Ward, Lock, 75 c.
> The author was a very rich and eccentric Englishman, with a passion for seclusion and luxury. His name is inseparably connected with palaces built at Fonthill in Wiltshire, and Cintra in Portugal. Though published in 1784, "Vathek" shows little influence either from the 18th century realists or romanticists. It is unique in prose as the "Ancient Mariner" is in poetry. It is splendidly imagined and sustain'd, even to the final doom of the wicked caliph and his monstrous mother in the immortal Hall of Eblis.   823.70.

Bell, Currer (*pseudonym*). *See* Brontë, Charlotte.

Bell, Ellis (*pseudonym*). *See* Brontë, Emily.

Bellamy, Edward. [1850- .]

LOOKING BACKWARD, 2000-1887. Bost., Houghton, $1; paper, 50 c.
> A vision of life after existing forms of government have been overturned and socialism has been long established. It made an immense sensation on account of its interesting presentation of the attractive fallacy that equality of wealth and leisure would mean universal content. It is worth reading, but not worth believing. The author is a New Englander; his interest in economics and social reform is clearly stronger than his story-telling power.   813.40.

Besant, *Sir* Walter.
[See note on Besant, Walter, and Rice, James, following.]

ALL SORTS AND CONDITIONS OF MEN. N. Y. Harper, $1.25; paper, 50 c.
> Interesting plots and scenes among the poor in London. The illustrations of how the rich might improve and amuse the poor suggested the building of the People's Palace. Characterized by sincerity and enthusiasm.

CHILDREN OF GIBEON. N. Y., Harper, $1.25; paper, 50 c.; Munro, paper, 25 c.
> Similar in motive to "All Sorts and Conditions of Men."

DOROTHY FORSTER. Lond., Chatto, 3s. 6d.; N. Y., Munro, paper, 25 c.
> Historical romance, founded on the Stuart rising in 1715, and narrating the tragic history and death of the Earl of Derwentwater. A very fine story, but unduly long.

FOR FAITH AND FREEDOM. Lond., Chatto, 3s. 6d.; N. Y., Harper, paper, 50 c.; Munro, paper, 25 c.
> A good romantic and dramatic story of the Monmouth rising in the reign of James II. The train of events includes the judicial murders authorized by Justice Jeffreys after the battle of Sedgemoor and the selling of rebels into slavery across seas.

ST. KATHERINE'S BY THE TOWER. N. Y., Harper, paper, 60 c.
> Deals with the French Revolution.

THE REBEL QUEEN. N. Y., Harper, $1.50.
> Concerned with woman's rights and wrongs.

BEYOND THE DREAMS OF AVARICE. N. Y., Harper, $1.50.
> Mr. Besant's latest story and one of his best. Wills and law-suits are the theme.

ARMOREL OF LYONNESSE. N. Y., Harper, $1.25; paper, 50 c.; Munro, paper, 25 c.

HERR PAULUS. Lond., Chatto, 3s. 6d.; N. Y., Harper, paper, 35 c.; Munro, paper, 25 c.

THE WORLD WENT VERY WELL THEN. N. Y., Harper, $1.25; Munro, paper, 25 c.

Besant, *Sir* Walter, and **Rice, James.** [Besant, 1838- .] [Rice, 1846-1882.]
> English novelists, historical and modern. They made a reputation when writing in collaboration. Their novels had more go, more strength and wit than Mr. Besant's individual productions. He, however, since Mr. Rice's death, has continued to grow in popularity. He concerns himself considerably with modern social problems, and is profusely sentimental in his solutions rather than practical. Thanks to constructive ability, an inexhaustible supply of stories and a smooth and pleasant manner, all his books are fairly agreeable and many entertaining.   823.80.

THE GOLDEN BUTTERFLY. N. Y., Lovell, Coryell, $1.
> A first-rate modern novel, well constructed, dramatic and spirited. The scenes are laid in America and England. Mr. Gilead P. Heak is as typical an American of the commercially adventurous variety as we have in fiction.

READY MONEY MORTIBOY. N. Y., Lovell, Coryell, $1.

Bishop, William Henry. [1847- .]
> A New England writer of great artistic strength. A close observer of society life, he constructs his story skilfully, and presents an organic whole which leaves a distinct impression on the reader. His characters are clearly outlined, his pathos natural, his descriptive passages graphic.   813.40.

DETMOLD. Bost., Houghton, $1.25.
> Describes an American architect pursuing studies in Europe.

THE GOLDEN JUSTICE. Bost., Houghton, $1.25; paper, 50 c.
> A vivid picture of politics and industry in a bustling

Western city. The description of the havoc wrought by a tornado is powerful.

THE HOUSE OF A MERCHANT PRINCE. Bost., Houghton, $1.25.
New York society life, a pungent, well-sustained story.

CHOY SUSAN. Bost., Houghton, $1.25.
Short stories.

Black, William. [1841-.]
Scotch novelist. His best work is descriptive of life and character in Scotch Highlands and Western Isles. His descriptions of scenery and color in those regions are frequently vivid and poetical but marred by elaboration. His plots are not strong and revolve round a central love affair. Sometimes his narratives have great sentiment and sweetness; the best appeal strongly to imagination and emotion. His later books are inferior to his earlier and are a rather tiresome exhibition of fatal fluency in composition. 823.89.

A PRINCESS OF THULE. N. Y., Harper, 80 c.; Munro, paper, 25 c.
Made Mr. Black's reputation and introduced the Isle of Skye to novel-readers. The character of the Princess Sheila is very fresh and fascinating and her whole story most touching. This ranks among the best modern English novels.

Mr. Black's best novels after this are:

A DAUGHTER OF HETH. N. Y., Harper, 80 c.; paper, 35 c.

IN SILK ATTIRE. N. Y., Harper 80 c.; paper, 35 c.; Munro, paper, 25 c.

MACLEOD OF DARE. N. Y., Harper, 80 c.; paper, 60 c.; Munro, paper, 25 c.

STRANGE ADVENTURES OF A PHAETON. N. Y., Harper, 80 c.; paper, 50 c.; Munro, paper, 25 c.

Blackmore, Richard Doddridge. [1825-.]
English novelist. His favorite time is between ancient and modern; his best-loved scene the County of Devon. His design is romantic and his characterization, especially of rustics, very real. His style is serious, with a touch of quaintness, and his humor grave and excellent. He ranks among the first of living novelists. 823.89.

LORNA DOONE. N. Y., Harper, $1; paper, 40 c.; Munro, paper, 25 c.
The author's most famous and romantic novel. It abounds in thrilling adventures, is quite intensely exciting throughout. The scenes described in Devon are visited and explored by tourists from far and near.

SPRINGHAVEN. N. Y., Harper, $1.50; paper, 25 c.
A tale of the contemplated invasion of England by Napoleon in 1805. Both Napoleon and Nelson appear on the scene, and their great fortunes are well woven with the small interests of the little seaside village.

PERLYCROSS. N. Y., Harper, $1.75.
An excellent novel of sixty years ago in Devonshire The central incident is improbable, but the descriptions and characters are delightful.

ALICE LORRAINE. N. Y., Burt, 75 c.; Munro, paper, 25 c.
Regarded by the author as his best novel.

KIT AND KITTY. N. Y., Harper, $1.25; paper, 35 c.; Munro, paper, 25 c.

EREMA. N. Y., Harper, paper, 50 c.

THE FORTUNES OF SIR THOMAS UPMORE (TOMMY UPMORE). N. Y., Harper, 50 c.; paper, 35 c.

Boldrewood, Rolf (*pseudonym*). *See* Browne, T. A.

Boyesen, Hjalmar Hjorth. [1848-.]
A New York writer of novels and tales. A Norwegian by birth. His composition is fluent and natural, and his observation of American life pretty accurate and comprehensive. He is a devoted disciple of the realistic school, and has little imagination or fancy. 813.40.

THE MAMMON OF UNRIGHTEOUSNESS. N. Y., Lovell, Coryell, $1.25; paper, 50 c.

THE LIGHT OF HER COUNTENANCE. N. Y., Appleton, 75 c.

Braddon, M. E. *See* Maxwell, Mrs. M. E.

BREAD-WINNERS, THE. N. Y., Harper, $1; paper, 50 c.
An anonymous novel of rather remarkable force. One of the first works of fiction in which the antagonism of capital and labor was discussed. After ten years it remains one of the best. The scene is in Ohio, and the tragedy turns on the iron-workers' strike. The story is pre-eminently realistic and perfectly frank in characterization. 813.40.

Brontë, Charlotte ("Currer Bell"). [1821-1855.]
English novelist of middle period of 19th century. One of the most striking personalities in English fiction; her novels are wholly an expression of that personality. Her actual experience was very limited, and of a kind that distorted an impetuous and fiery spirit. She poured her soul out in her books with painful bitterness and tremendous passion. She broke up the literary convention which represented women as tame, passionless beings, and showed them conscious of an independent existence, hopelessly battling against circumstances. The modern reader is most surprised by the submissive attitude towards men assumed to be the correct one, by the almost ridiculous qualities ascribed to men, and believed by the author to be natural and admirable, and by the readiness of her real, thinking, feeling women to fall madly in love with these imaginary and generally detestable gods. Nevertheless, her purely subjective novels have all the excitement of those dependent on thrilling plot and incident. In delineating the manners of people of whom she had no actual knowledge (her heroes included), her inexperience is evident; her style is direct and keen, but too poignant for modern taste. Her books are simply the cry of a soul for something that life refused, and will probably be read as long as humanity is capable of the sensation of passionate pity. 823.81.

JANE EYRE. N. Y., Lovell, Coryell, 50 c.; Warne, paper, 25 c.
The author's first published work. The subject is the love of a governess Jane Eyre, for her employer, Rochester. As a lover Rochester is magnificent; as a man execrable and a little ludicrous. At the time of the publication the book was widely described as immoral, many British critics being so horrified by Jane Eyre's passion of love that they quite overlooked the nobility of her renunciation. Times have changed. Immorality is now the last charge which one would think of making against Miss Brontë.

SHIRLEY. Phila., Lippincott, 50 c.; Warne, paper, 25 c.
The fidelity of description of places and people in Yorkshire revealed the identity of "Currer Bell" with Charlotte Brontë. The introduction of machinery with its effects for good and evil suggested much of this story. The portraits of the clergy are among the most striking results of the author's penetrating observation.

VILLETTE. Phila., Lippincott, 50 c.
The story is founded on Miss Brontë's experience as

a teacher in a school in Brussels. Such splendidly drawn characters as Mme. Beck and Monsieur Paul indicate the greatness Miss Brontë might have achieved had her life been fuller and wider. Monsieur Paul is her only real man minutely portrayed, but even he is given the benefit of the author's devout belief in the God-given superiority of the male sex. The original ending of "Villette" was so painful to the public that a paragraph was added in subsequent editions which suggests a mitigation of tragedy.

Brontë, Emily ("Ellis Bell"). [1819-1849.]
WUTHERING HEIGHTS. Harper, $1; Routledge, 80 c.
The only novel of the younger sister of Charlotte Brontë. A remarkable production of a gloomy imagination. The chief character, Heathcliffe, is probably the most monstrous in fiction, too inhuman even to excite hatred. The power of the book is as indisputable as its repulsiveness; and in several ways it shows creative ability superior to that of the more famous sister. No pleasure can be derived from reading it, and its only claim for continued existence is that of a curiosity in literature. **823.80.**

Broughton, Rhoda. [1840-.]
English society novelist, frequently as silly as any other of her class, but not so worthless as many. Her early stories, chiefly about impoverished girls of great beauty, good birth and bad manners, are vivacious, funny, with moments of intense and genuine passion, and not infrequent wit. Her ideas of morals are generally sentimental and wrong, but her conduct of a love-story often shows natural talent and rather uncommon skill. **823.89.**

COMETH UP AS A FLOWER. N. Y., Appleton, $1; paper, 30 c.
NOT WISELY BUT TOO WELL. N. Y., Appleton, $1; paper, 30 c.
GOOD-BYE, SWEETHEART. N. Y., Appleton, $1; paper, 30 c.
RED AS A ROSE IS SHE. N. Y., Appleton, $1; paper, 30 c.

Brown, Charles Brockden. [1771-1810.]
The first American who adopted literature as his profession. His romances, written towards the close of the eighteenth century, hold a high place in the early development of American fiction. His plots are impossible, his diction stilted, and yet he has art enough to hold and keep the interest of his reader. **813.23.**

WIELAND, or the transformation. Phila., McKay, 75 c.
ARTHUR MERVYN, or memoirs of the year 1793. Phila., McKay, 75 c.

Browne, Thomas Alexander ("Rolf Boldrewood"). [1827-.]
An Australian writer of stirring stories of adventure in the mines and bush country. His style, vigorous and rapid, befits his themes. The most original of his tales is "Robbery Under Arms." **823.80.**

ROBBERY UNDER ARMS. N. Y., Macmillan, $1.25.
THE SQUATTER'S DREAM. Macmillan, $1.25.
A MODERN BUCCANEER. N. Y., Macmillan, $1.25.

Buchanan, Robert (Williams). [1841-.]
A Scotch poet and novelist of somewhat melodramatic tendency. He is uneven in excellence: an able delineator of character. His descriptive passages are often overwrought and wordy. **823.80.**

THE MASTER OF THE MINE. Lond., Chatto, 3s. 6d.; N. Y., Munro, paper, 25 c.

THE SHADOW OF THE SWORD. Lond., Chatto, 3s. 6d.; N. Y., Munro, paper, 25 c.
A story of the Napoleonic conscriptions.

FOXGLOVE MANOR. Lond., Chatto, 3s. 6d.
GOD AND THE MAN. N. Y., Harper, paper, 20 c.

Bulwer-Lytton, Edward George Earle Lytton. [1803-1873.]
English novelist, dramatist and poet of middle period of 19th century. The generally good level of his work, its variety and quantity are perhaps not equalled by any other English novelist, yet not one of his books takes rank with the best. He had a romantic imagination, worldly wisdom, literary cultivation, distinguished elegance and facile eloquence, yet he never convinced the mind or very deeply touched the feelings. The best reason for this failure is perhaps because he lacked sincerity and penetration, always conveying the impression that his people could never have been and done exactly what he said they were and did. Some critics deny him originality, but that is not quite fair. He had wonderful aptitude for following the public's fickle fancy, and his whole work, extending over fifty years, represents a dozen different and transient fashions in fiction. His novels may be roughly divided into historical, social, and fanciful or mystical. Of the historical group the best are:

THE LAST DAYS OF POMPEII.
HAROLD, THE LAST OF THE SAXONS.
RIENZI, THE LAST OF THE TRIBUNES. N. Y., Routledge, 60 c., $1, or $1.25 each; paper, 25 c. each.

Of the social novels, also representing stages of the author's literary development, the best are:

PELHAM, OR THE ADVENTURES OF A GENTLEMAN. 1 vol.
PAUL CLIFFORD. 1 vol.
EUGENE ARAM. 1 vol.
THE CAXTONS. 1 vol.
MY NOVEL. 2 vols., $1.25 each; 3 vols., 60 c. or $1 each; 2 vols., paper, 25 c. each.
WHAT WILL HE DO WITH IT? 2 vols.
KENELM CHILLINGLY. 1 vol. N. Y., Routledge, all the preceding 60 c., $1, or $1.25 per vol.; paper, 25 c. per vol.

Of the fanciful or mystical books the best are:

ZANONI.
A STRANGE STORY.
THE COMING RACE. N. Y., Routledge, 60 c., $1, or $1.25 each; paper, 25 c. each
"The Coming Race" is hardly a novel but a vision of a future state of society, some portions of which now appear prophetic.

Bunner, Henry Cuyler. [1855-.]
New York journalist and writer of verse and tales. The form in which he embodies an incident humorous, pathetic, or sentimental is admirable and his style particularly light, neat and happy. **813.49.**

THE MIDGE. N. Y., Scribner, $1; paper, 50 c.
A charming story of the French quarter in New York.

STORY OF A NEW YORK HOUSE. N. Y., Scribner, $1.25.

ZADOC PINE, and other stories. N. Y., Scribner, $1; paper, 50 c.

SHORT SIXES. N. Y., Keppler, $1; paper, 50 c.

MORE SHORT SIXES. N. Y., Keppler, $1; paper, 50 c.

Bunyan, John. [1628-1688.]

PILGRIM'S PROGRESS. Good editions in large type are published by the American Tract Society, by Routledge, and others, from 50 c. up. Also, N. Y., Munro, paper, 25 c. Written in Bedford Jail and published in 1678. One of the greatest of imaginative prose-works. Everybody should read it and persist in admiring it. 823.42.

Burnett, *Mrs.* Frances Hodgson. [1849-.]

Anglo-American novelist and story-writer. Her work has some dramatic strength with vivacity in description and dialogue. The motive is often feeble but the interest in events well sustained. 813.48

THAT LASS O' LOWRIES. N. Y., Scribner, $1.25; paper, 50 c.
A story of Lancashire coal-miners. Much stronger than the author's later work; well imagined and sustained.

LITTLE LORD FAUNTLEROY. N. Y., Scribner, $2.
Story of a boy born in America of poor parents, who turned out to be a lord. The idea is not original, but the child is engaging, and the circumstances are prettily narrated. The book was and continues to be very popular.

THROUGH ONE ADMINISTRATION. N. Y., Scribner, $1.50.
A prolix unnatural story of Washington life, neither artistically written nor truthfully observed.

A FAIR BARBARIAN. N. Y., Scribner, $1.25; paper, 50 c.

LOUISIANA. N. Y., Scribner, $1.25.

Burney, Frances. *See* Arblay, Mme. F. B. d'.

Burnham, *Mrs.* Clara Louise. [1854-.]

A New England writer of graceful love-stories characterized by naturalness and clearness of plot and dialogue. Her style is fresh and her stories wholes me and entertaining. 813.49.

DEARLY BOUGHT. Bost., Houghton, $1.25.

NEXT DOOR. Bost., Houghton, $1.25; paper, 50 c.

NO GENTLEMEN. Bost., Houghton, $1.25; paper, 50 c.

YOUNG MAIDS AND OLD. Bost., Houghton, $1.25; paper, 50 c.

Bynner, Edwin Lassetter. [1852-.]

American historical novelist. His scenes are in Colonial times, or in the early days of the Republic. He holds his narrative well together and draws pictures of bygone manners and historical incidents skilfully and pleasantly. 813.49.

THE BEGUM'S DAUGHTER. Bost., Houghton, $1.25.
A tale of New Amsterdam in 1689. The plot is not coherent, but the episode of the Leisler rebellion in New York is admirably told.

PENELOPE'S SUITORS. Bost., Houghton, boards, 50 c.
A very pretty tale told by Penelope Pelham, and setting forth her love-story with that of Richard Bellingham, Governor of Massachusetts.

ZACHARY PHIPS. Bost., Houghton, $1.25; paper, 50 c.
Story of a Boston boy who took part in the mysterious Western expedition of Aaron Burr. Exciting and picturesque.

Cable, George Washington. [1844-.]

Southern novelist. His scenes are mostly in New Orleans or those parts of Louisiana where the Creole element is large and the ideas of the French régime are not quite forgotten. Whether or not his representation is truthful is a matter of dispute. The strange dialect used in conversation detracts for many from the pleasures of his narratives, which are picturesque and agreeably imagined, but rather formless and discursive. 813.40.

DR. SEVIER. N. Y., Scribner, $1.25; paper, 50 c.

THE GRANDISSIMES. N. Y., Scribner, $1.25; paper, 50 c.

MADAME DELPHINE. N. Y., Scribner, 75 c.
Short stories.

OLD CREOLE DAYS. N. Y., Scribner, $1.25; paper, 2 vols., 60 c.

STRANGE TRUE STORIES OF LOUISIANA. N. Y., Scribner, $1.25.

Caine, Thomas (Henry) Hall. [1853-.]

English romantic novelist, whose particular domain is the Isle of Man. He interprets primitive people whose emotional nature is stronger than reason; he develops them through circumstances always dramatic and frequently tragic. With a fine, poetical imagination, he combines constructive ability, and can so group his people and events as to give unity and force to long and involved narration. His chief fault is a tendency to melodrama and exaggeration of sentiment. 823.89.

THE SCAPEGOAT. N. Y., U. S. Book Co., $1.25; paper, 50 c.
Morocco and its people are portrayed. The character of Israel is drawn with uncommon force.

THE SHADOW OF A CRIME. Bost., Joseph Knight Co., $1.50; N. Y., Harper, paper, 20 c.
Less sombre than usual with the author. As good for descriptions of Cumberland as "Lorna Doone" for Devon.

THE DEEMSTER. N. Y., Appleton, 75 c.; paper, 50 c.; Munro, paper, 25 c.
A strong, tragic novel, of which the scene is laid in the Isle of Man about the beginning of the 18th century. The sternness of the tragedy is relieved by comedy, but the lasting impression is a sense of desolation and wreck after a war of passion.

SHE'S ALL THE WORLD TO ME. N. Y., Harper, paper, 25 c.
A poetical and beautiful story of love and friendship. The heroic devotion of Danny Fayle is one of the most touching episodes in modern fiction.

THE MANXMAN. N. Y., Appleton, $1.50.
Mr. Caine's most elaborate novel. The scheme includes all kinds and conditions of Manxmen. Interest is well sustained even to the painful but logical finish. The Manxman, Pete, is a tiresome person, noisy and too primitive. The woman for whom two lives are wrecked is worthless, and there is a fundamental improbability in the assumption at the end that there could ever be happiness for Philip Christian in his union with her.

Calmire. N. Y., Macmillan, 4th edition, revised, $1.50.
An anonymous novel, treating current questions of

Fiction.

religion and social reform from a rationalistic point of view. Rather crudely written, with lively epigram here and there. **813.49.**

Cambridge, Ada.
Australian novelist. Her scenes are in Australia and England and her stories descriptive of social and domestic life in both countries. A simple love plot, nice descriptions, and amusing dialogue are smoothly and agreeably woven together. **823.89.**

THE THREE MISS KINGS. N. Y., Appleton, $1; paper, 50 c.

MY GUARDIAN. N. Y., Appleton, $1; paper, 50 c.; Munro, paper, 25 c.

NOT ALL IN VAIN. N. Y., Appleton, $1; paper, 50 c.

Carey, Rosa Nouchette.
Popular English writer of stories for young girls. Her manner is easy and pleasant, and, though she has nothing startling to tell, she invests simple affairs with interest. **823.89.**

NOT LIKE OTHER GIRLS. Phila., Lippincott, $1; N. Y., Munro, paper, 25 c.

AUNT DIANA. Phila., Lippincott, $1.25; N. Y., Munro, paper, 25 c.

MERLE'S CRUSADE. Phila., Lippincott, $1.25; N. Y., Munro, paper, 25 c.

Carroll, Lewis (*pseudonym*). *See* Dodgson, C. L.

Catherwood, *Mrs.* **Mary Hartwell.** [1847-.]
Western writer of tales founded on heroic and picturesque incidents of the French settlement of Canada in the 17th century. If she does not always give events and personages their real historic significance, she at least introduces them readably to the public. **813.40.**

ROMANCE OF DOLLARD. N. Y., Century Co., $1.25.

LADY OF FORT ST. JOHN. Bost., Houghton, $1.25; paper, 50 c.

STORY OF TONTY. Chic., McClurg, $1.25.

Chanler, *Mrs.* **Amélie (Rives).** [1863-.]
Virginian novelist. **813.40.**

A BROTHER TO DRAGONS, and other stories. N. Y., Harper, $1.
Stories which show imagination and genuine literary force, indicating but slightly the tendency to ridiculous extravagance in the representation of passion which characterizes the author's later books, and dooms them to well-deserved oblivion.

Charles, *Mrs.* **Elizabeth (Rundell).** [1828-.]
An English writer. **823.80.**

CHRONICLES OF THE SCHÖNBERG-COTTA FAMILY. N. Y., Dodd, $1.
An interesting but somewhat tedious story of Luther and the Reformation in Germany. The pictures of manners and religious strife are thoughtful and informed. Most of the author's works deal with historical episodes involving social and political revolution, in which religious emotion has been a prominent factor.

THE DRAYTONS AND THE DAVENANTS. N. Y., Dodd, $1.

DIARY OF KITTY TREVELYAN. N. Y., Dodd, $1.

WINIFRED BERTRAM. N. Y., Dodd, $1.

Church *Mrs.* **Ross.** *See* Lean, Mrs. Florence (Marryat).

Clemens, Samuel Langhorne ("Mark Twain"). [1835-.]

THE PRINCE AND THE PAUPER. Hartford, American Pub. Co., $1.
A charming little tale, fundamentally serious, though, of course, touched with the author's irrepressible fun. The real worth of this story has been rather lost sight of—a pity—for greater popularity might have inspired the author to further effort in a similar vein. **813.40.**

Cobbleigh, Tom (*pseudonym*). *See* Raymond, W.

Collins, William Wilkie. [1824-1889.]
English novelist of middle period of 19th century. He was a master in construction of intricate plots and direct, convincing narrative. In developing the awfullest mystery, or untying the hardest knots, his method was marvellously clear and his vision of the end unclouded. Some of his people are rather impressive villains, but mostly they count only as figures for carrying on the action. He was really a great story-teller, independent of school, or fashion, or fad. **823.89.**

THE MOONSTONE. N. Y., Harper, $1.25; Burt, 75 c.; Munro, paper, 25 c.
This story of the adventures of a jewel of fabulous worth is the best example of the author's genius for inventing a puzzle, and solving it with extraordinary patience and precision. It fascinates attention and is the best story of its kind in the language.

MAN AND WIFE. N. Y., Harper, $1.25; Burt, 75 c.; Munro, paper, 2 vols., each 25 c.
The plot turns on the complications arising from lax Scotch marriage laws. By some good critics considered the author's best book.

THE WOMAN IN WHITE. N. Y., Harper, $1.25; Burt, 75 c.; Munro, paper, 2 vols., each 25 c.

NO NAME. N. Y., Harper, $1.25; paper, 60 c.; Burt, 75 c.; Munro, paper, 2 vols., each 25 c.

THE DEAD SECRET. N. Y., Harper, $1.25; Munro, paper, 25 c.

ARMADALE. N. Y., Harper, $1.25; paper, 60 c.; Burt, 75 c.; Munro, paper, 2 vols., each 25 c.

Conway, Hugh (*pseudonym*). *See* Fargus, F. J.

Cooke, Rose Terry. [1827-1892.]
A New England writer of tales of farm life with its picturesque idiom. She dwells on the more sombre aspects of the past, and her stories are often gloomy. She is a close observer of character and manners. **813.49.**

SOMEBODY'S NEIGHBORS. Bost., Houghton, $1.25.; paper, 50 c.
Short stories.

STEADFAST. Bost., Houghton, $1.25; paper, 50 c.

THE SPHINX'S CHILDREN. Bost., Houghton, $1.25.
Short stories, including "The Deacon's Week," one of her best.

HAPPY DODD. Bost., Houghton, $1.25.

THE DEACON'S WEEK. N. Y., Putman, paper, 25 c.

HUCKLEBERRIES GATHERED FROM NEW ENGLAND HILLS. Bost., Houghton, $1.25.

Cooper, James Fenimore. [1789-1851.]

New York novelist of early part of the 19th century. He created the romantic ideal of the North American Indian. His stories are, of course, full of thrilling adventure, and his descriptions of forest life and scenery fresh and enchanting. Leather-Stocking, the prince of pioneers, appears in several of the novels. The best of the Indian stories are: 813.24.

THE DEERSLAYER. THE LAST OF THE MOHICANS. THE PATHFINDER. THE PIONEERS. N. Y., Appleton, each $1 ; Lovell, Coryell, each 75 c.; Munro, paper, each 25 c.

Sea tales:
THE PILOT. THE WATER-WITCH. WING AND WING. THE RED ROVER. THE TWO ADMIRALS. N. Y., Appleton, each $1 ; Lovell, Coryell, each 75 c.; Munro, paper, each 25 c.

His sea tales are less popular than the forest stories, but are almost as good and drawn equally from the author's experience. Long Tom Coffin (in " The Pilot ") is among the famous people in fiction.

THE SPY. N. Y., Appleton, $1; Munro, paper, 25 c.

A story of the American Revolution, in which Gen. Washington and one of his trusted spies play prominent parts.

THE BRAVO. N. Y., Appleton, $1; Munro, paper, 25 c.

WORKS. N. Y., Appleton, 32 vols., $32.

Corelli, Marie (*pseudonym*). See Mackay, M.

Cotes, *Mrs.* **Sara Jeannette (Duncan).** [1862-.] 813.49.

Canadian writer of travels and tales. Her perception of weakness and eccentricity is quick and her observation of things original ; so without imagination or sentiment, she writes a pleasant and lively tale. 813.49. [For her " A Social Departure," see Travel.]

AN AMERICAN GIRL IN LONDON. N. Y., Appleton, $1.50 ; paper, 75 c.; Munro, paper, 25 c.

THE SIMPLE ADVENTURES OF A MEM SAHIB. N. Y., Appleton, $1.50.

A DAUGHTER OF TO-DAY. N. Y., Appleton, $1.50.

VERNON'S AUNT. N. Y., Appleton, $1.25.

Couch, Arthur Thomas Quiller (" Q ").

An English novelist and story writer of considerable cleverness. He has a peculiarly happy faculty of hitting off the traits of middle-class folk. Detached episodes are especially vivid, and hence he succeeds best in short stories, of which he has published many. His work shows much humor and is always picturesque. Cornwall is the scene of most of his writing. 823.89.

THE BLUE PAVILIONS. N. Y., Cassell, $1.25 ; paper, 50 c.

THE SPLENDID SPUR. N. Y., Cassell, 75 c.; paper, 50 c.; Harper, paper, 35 c.

THE DELECTABLE DUCHY. N. Y., Macmillan, $1; paper, 50 c.

Craddock, Charles Egbert (*pseudonym*). See Murfree, Mary N.

Craigie, *Mrs.* ***** ("John Oliver Hobbes").

Novelist of American birth but English by adoption. She writes light sketches of English aristocratic and artistic society, involving a short intrigue. Her people are flimsy, but attractive, and their talk is too brilliant to be natural. Their frivolity seems generally to be an assumption of people bent upon concealing emotion and fighting off seriousness. Thus, in spite of an appearance of cynicism and pessimism, the author really recognizes the sorrow and folly of sin, the existence and beauty of goodness, so, if read aright, she gives a deeper impression of the unsatisfactoriness of a merely worldly life than of its delights. She is very witty, and indulges in a frankness of speech which a few years ago would have been qualified as indelicate and is really far from elegant. 813.40.

SOME EMOTIONS AND A MORAL. N. Y., Cassell, 50 c.

THE SINNER'S COMEDY. N. Y., Cassell 50 c.

A STUDY IN TEMPTATIONS. N. Y., Cassell, 50 c.

A BUNDLE OF LIFE. N. Y., J. S. Tait, 50 c.

THE GODS, SOME MORTALS, AND LORD WICKENHAM. N. Y., Appleton, $1.50.

Craik, *Mrs.* **Dinah Maria (Mulock).** [1826-1887.]

English novelist of middle period of 19th century. Her characters were generally drawn from the middle class and her plots centred on the occasional emotional crises of common life. She often touched prominent social movements but never palmed off a tract as a story. Her best figures have striking moral worth, and she avoided delineation of the base and ignoble. She managed love affairs gracefully and naturally. 823.89.

JOHN HALIFAX, GENTLEMAN. N. Y., Harper, 90 c.; paper, 15 c; Munro, paper, 25 c.

An admirable novel for dramatic movement, characterization and sentiment. The picture of the revolt of factory hands against the substitution of machinery for manual labor is very vivid, and the hero's career is narrated with skill and infectious sympathy.

A LIFE FOR A LIFE. N. Y., Harper, 90 c.; paper, 40 c.

A BRAVE LADY. N. Y., Harper, 90 c.

AGATHA'S HUSBAND. N. Y., Harper, 90 c.

MISTRESS AND MAID. N. Y., Harper, 90 c.; paper, 30 c.; Munro, paper, 25 c.

Crawford, Francis Marion. [1845-.]

Novelist, American by birth and cosmopolitan by education. Whether his scenes be in India, England, Italy or even Turkey, he manages to give the note of race and nation. His plots are excellent and, though sometimes a trifle long-winded, he is entertaining and satisfactory. All his books show talent and training, and most of them may be read with very great pleasure. 813.40.

DR. CLAUDIUS. N. Y., Macmillan, $1.

MR. ISAACS. N. Y., Macmillan, $1; paper, 50 c.

A ROMAN SINGER. N. Y., Macmillan, $1.

MARZIO'S CRUCIFIX. N. Y., Macmillan, $1.

SARACINESCA. N. Y., Macmillan, $1; Bost., De Wolfe, paper, 50 c.

SANT' ILARIO. A sequel to "Saracinesca." N. Y., Macmillan, $1; paper, 50 c.

DON ORSINO. A sequel to "Sant' Ilario." N. Y., Macmillan, $1.

PAUL PATOFF. N. Y., Macmillan, $1.

GREIFENSTEIN. N. Y., Macmillan, $1.

A CIGARETTE MAKER'S ROMANCE. N. Y., Macmillan, $1.

A TALE OF A LONELY PARISH. N. Y., Macmillan, $1; paper, 50 c.

Crockett, S. R. [1859-.]

Scotch clergyman. Writer of novels and tales. His plots are romantic and his perception of character keen. It is too soon to say whether his work will last, but for the hour, at least, it is interesting and amusing.

823.80.

THE STICKIT MINISTER. N. Y., Macmillan, $1.50; paper, 50 c.

The author's first and best book. A collection of short incidents and character sketches. They appear to be true to life, and show skill and decision. Many are in Scotch dialect.

THE RAIDERS. N. Y., Macmillan, $1.50.

A romantic novel of love and adventure. The raiding gypsies and Highlanders carry off the hero's sweetheart, whence ensue many thrilling exploits. The gypsy king is well imagined, and, though the plot is not very firm, the story goes with a good swing.

THE LILAC SUNBONNET. N. Y., Appleton, $1.50.

THE PLAY ACTRESS. N. Y., Putnam, $1.

Cross, *Mrs.* **Marian Evans.** *See* Eliot, George.

Cruger, *Mrs.* **Julia Grinnell (Storrow)** ("Julien Gordon").

A New York writer of some of the brightest society novels of the day. Her style is flowing and readable, occasionally witty. The life of the fashionable set, especially, is described elaborately and vivaciously. She awakens and sustains a lively interest in her characters, which are drawn from all ranks, and afford powerful contrasts. 813.49

A DIPLOMAT'S DIARY. Phila., Lippincott, $1.

A PURITAN PAGAN. N. Y., Appleton, $1.

MARIONETTES. N. Y., Cassell, $1; paper, 50 c.

A SUCCESSFUL MAN. Phila., Lippincott, $1.

POPPÆA. Phila., Lippincott, $1.

Cummins, Maria Susanna. [1827-1866.]

A New England writer of sentimental stories of a moral cast—very popular in their day with young girls. 813.49.

THE LAMPLIGHTER. Bost., Houghton, $1; paper, 25 c.; N. Y., Burt, 75 c.

MABEL VAUGHAN. Bost., Houghton, $1.

Considered superior to "The Lamplighter."

Curtis, George William. [1824-1892.]

PRUE AND I. N. Y., Harper, $1.50.

A most fascinating book, hardly to be called a story. It is more properly a series of sketches, light in touch, strongly characteristic of the author's kindly genius, and likely to remain a favorite among those who love pure sentiment in graceful and classical English.

813.49.

D'Arblay, *Mme.* **F. B.** *See under* Arblay.

Davis, Richard Harding. [1864-.]

New York writer of short stories. An original and witty observer of New York life. His incidents are short and swiftly narrated in a light, brilliant style. In his best characterizations, the dude and the street Arab, he shows that creative ability which gathers the many into one, and makes a vivid impression on the memory. 813.49

VAN BIBBER, and others. N. Y., Harper, $1; paper, 60 c.

THE EXILES, and other stories. N. Y., Harper, $1.50.

THE PRINCESS ALINE. N. Y., Harper, $1.25.

Defoe, Daniel. [1661-1731.]

ROBINSON CRUSOE. N. Y., Routledge, $1 to $3; Cassell, 75 c.; Munro, paper, 25 c., and in many other editions.

One word of comment on this highly respectable cast-away would be an insult to fame won nearly two centuries ago, and growing as we increase and multiply upon the earth. The author was distinctly the father of English realistic fiction. No matter how romantic and improbable his conception, his aim was to make it appear perfectly true by a matter-of-fact statement, supported by minutely detailed circumstantial evidence. He succeeded so well that many of his contemporaries mistook his ironical theological disquisitions for serious arguments. To this day no presumably authentic historical document commands half as many faithful believers as does "The Life and Surprising Adventures of Robinson Crusoe of York, Mariner." 823.51.

Deland, *Mrs.* **Margaret.** [1857-.]

A Pennsylvania novelist. She represents people struggling with principles and moral ideas. The scenes are generally in Pennsylvania, and the drama which is subjective shows the Puritan conscience in relation to modern freedom of thought. The arguments and story are very well combined. 813.40

JOHN WARD, PREACHER. Bost., Houghton, $1.25; paper, 50 c.

SIDNEY. Bost., Houghton, $1.25, paper, 50 c.

PHILIP AND HIS WIFE. Bost., Houghton, $1.25.

THE STORY OF A CHILD. Bost., Houghton, $1.

Delineates with skill a child of uncontrolled imagination, whose little heart was hungry.

De la Ramé, Louisa ("Ouida"). [1840-.]

English novelist. Her powerful and picturesque imagination runs riot in the delineation of extravagantly splendid and generally immoral nobles, contrasted with improbable peasants, who are endowed by nature with either phenomenal beauty or talent. No representation of any kind of life could be more ridiculously remote from truth. Nevertheless there are single episodes and scenes in many of her books that are described in a rarely beautiful way, exciting enthusiasm for physical courage, or touching deeply the emotions of pity for misfortune. Her good qualities are most evident and her defects least conspicuous in: 823.89.

UNDER TWO FLAGS. Phila., Lippincott. $1; paper, 40 c.; N. Y., Munro, paper, 25 c.

BÉBÉE, OR TWO LITTLE WOODEN SHOES. Phila., Lippincott, $1; paper, 40 c.

De Mille, James. [1837-1880.]

Canadian novelist. For tales of adventure, mystery and puzzling complication his talent was similar but not equal to that of Wilkie Collins. He sometimes lost his grip on the plot and floated about aimlessly. His stories, however, hold the attention, and, given a little more cohesion and precision of detail, would have been first rate of their kind. 823.80.

THE CRYPTOGRAM. N. Y., Harper, paper, 75 c.

CORD AND CREESE. N. Y., Harper, paper, 60 c.

THE LADY OF THE ICE. N. Y., Appleton, $1.25; paper, 75 c.

Deming, Philander. [1829-.]

ADIRONDACK STORIES. Bost., Houghton, 75 c.

Show fidelity to nature and wholesome humanity. Neat in literary expression. 813.49.

TOMPKINS AND OTHER FOLKS. Bost., Houghton, $1.

Democracy. N. Y., Holt, $1, paper, 30 c.

An anonymous novel of American political life and society at the national capital. The style is piquant and vigorous, and the handling of the plot able. One of the famous novels of the day. **813.49.**

Dickens, Charles. [1812-1870.]

English novelist of middle period of 19th century. For extravagant comedy and caricature he is unequalled. He created hosts of people who for his contemporaries, at least, were as real as most of their acquaintances, and far more amusing. His genius was essentially British, expressing physical health and high spirits with a serious attachment for home and homely virtues. This excellent sentiment frequently led him into effusive sentimentality, and made him tiresome and dull. His serious object was to exhibit virtue and purity existing in most difficult conditions, and to expose the grievances of the poor. Thus his works effected decisive public reforms. In only one or two of his later books did he achieve a firm, coherent plot, and he never had any notion of literary form. In spite of technical imperfection he remains one of the great figures in the literature of his century. **823.83.**

THE PICKWICK PAPERS. N. Y., Crowell, $1; Macmillan, $1; Lovell, Coryell, 50 c.; Munro, paper, 25 c.

Inimitable for broad British fun. Mr. Pickwick and his valet, Sam Weller, number among the immortals. The whole book expresses exuberant youth, force and a mind abandoned to the comic view.

DAVID COPPERFIELD. N. Y., Crowell, $1; Macmillan, $1; Lovell, Coryell, 50 c.; Munro, paper, 2 vols., each 25 c.

Said to contain descriptions of the author's youth. It embodies a sentimental and rather tragic tale which has been frequently dramatized. The great comic characters are the Micawbers, Uriah Heap, hypocrite and sneak, illustrates one of the author's faults—the personification of a single virtue, or vice, set forth as the portrait of an actual man or woman.

MARTIN CHUZZLEWIT. N. Y., Crowell, $1; Macmillan, $1; Lovell, Coryell, 50 c.; Munro, paper, 25 c.

Some scenes laid in the Southern States gave great offence to Americans, but American manners at that time, at least, were not exactly perfect, and there may have been an excessive sensitiveness to criticism. The plot is involved and uninteresting. The most famous characters are Sarah Gamp, the Pecksniffs and Mark Tapley.

A TALE OF TWO CITIES. N. Y., Crowell, $1; Macmillan, $1; Lovell, Coryell, 50 c.; Munro, paper, 25 c.

The scenes are in London and Paris, partly during the French Revolution. The best example of the author's serious work. Madame Defarge is a tragic figure, and the sacrifice of Sidney Carton is fine, both from a human and literary point of view.

OUR MUTUAL FRIEND. N. Y., Crowell, $1; Macmillan, $1; Lovell, Coryell, 50 c.; Munro, paper, 2 vols., each 25 c.

NICHOLAS NICKLEBY. N. Y., Crowell, $1; Macmillan, $1; Lovell, Coryell, 50 c.; Munro, paper, 25 c.

BLEAK HOUSE. N. Y., Crowell, $1; Macmillan, $1; Lovell, Coryell, 75 c.; Munro, paper, 2 vols., each 25 c.

BARNABY RUDGE. N. Y., Crowell, $1; Macmillan, $1; Lovell, Coryell, 50 c.; Munro, paper, 25 c.

WORKS. Lippincott, 30 vols., $45, and other editions.

These are all fiction but two volumes—"Child's History of England" and "Pictures from Italy and American Notes."

Also, N. Y., Appleton, 22 vols., including "Child's History of England," "American Notes and Pictures from Italy," and "The Life of Charles Dickens," by John Forster, $33.50; paper, $22.50, and other editions.

Disraeli, Benjamin, Earl of Beaconsfield. [1805-1881.]

Posterity perhaps gets its clearest notion of the great English Jew from his novels, the writing of which was for him diversion from political enterprises. Under fictitious names they eulogize or satirize celebrated statesmen (from 1830 to 1870), describe the rise and fall of governments and the reasons thereof. They express intellectual brilliancy, intimate knowledge of the superficial life of a great world, sympathy with the strong, a barbaric love of and reverence for power, rank, luxury, and a keen eye for theatrical spectacle. At the time of publication the identification of Disraeli's characters with personages prominent in social and political life was easily made. His books abound in epigrams and phrases which have passed into common speech. **823.86.**

VIVIAN GREY. N. Y., Crowell, 75 c.; Munro, paper, 25 c.

The author's first novel, believed to describe his own youthful conditions and ambitions.

LOTHAIR. N. Y., Appleton, $1.25; paper, 50 c.; Crowell, 75 c.

Supposed to be inspired by the conversion to Catholicism of a Scotch nobleman. After much hesitation the hero lands in the Church of England. This shows more humanity and also more devotion to material splendor than any other of Disraeli's works.

ENDYMION. N. Y., Appleton, $1; paper, 75 c.

The author's latest novel. The scenes run from 1830-40. Louis Napoleon (Napoleon III.), as Prince Florestan, is conspicuous, and there are fine descriptions of some historical pageants.

Dodgson, Charles Lutwidge ("Lewis Carroll"). [1832-1890.]

An English clergyman, whose world-wide reputation rests on two very droll books. A genius for nonsense verse and comic invention account for the popularity of the books with grown people, if not with children. **823.89.**

ALICE'S ADVENTURES IN WONDERLAND. N. Y., Macmillan, $1; Lovell, Coryell, 75 c.; Munro, paper, 25 c.

THROUGH THE LOOKING-GLASS. N. Y., Macmillan, $1; Munro, paper, 25 c.

Both in 1 vol., N. Y., Macmillan, $1.25.

Dougall, Lily.

Canadian novelist. Her scenes are in England and Canada, and two of her novels involve serious discussion of social subjects. Her style is clear and vigorous, and, while not sentimental, she shows strong sympathy with sinners who are the victims of adverse circumstances. **813.40.**

BEGGARS ALL. N. Y., Longmans, $1.

A sustained analysis of good and evil; the hero is a burglar.

WHAT NECESSITY KNOWS. N. Y., Longmans, $1.

The Second Adventists in the height of their popularity, fifty years ago, are described.

THE MERMAID. N. Y., Appleton, $1; paper, 50 c.

A romantic love-story of the Magdalen Islands, in the Gulf of St. Lawrence.

Douglas, Amanda Minnie. [1838- .]
New Jersey novelist. Her plots generally involving romantic mystery, are fairly ingenious combinations of well-worn materials. With nothing remarkable to tell or original to say she excites enough mild interest to last through her books. 823.80.
FOES OF HER HOUSEHOLD. Bost, Lee & S., $1.50.
SHERBURNE HOUSE. N. Y., Dodd, $1.50.

Doyle, A. Conan. [1859- .]
English novelist, historical and modern. His best books are narratives of military adventure, though perhaps the most popular describe the commission and detection of crime. He describes historical events vividly, and by selecting rather humble persons for heroes adds the interest of unknown character and fortune. In the pictures of battles he is particularly clear, skilfully avoiding technical detail, yet never meagre or indefinite. 823.89.
MICAH CLARKE. N. Y., Lovell, Coryell, $1; also 50 c.
A story of the Monmouth rising in the reign of James II. It goes with a fine swing, culminating in a splendid description of the battle of Sedgemoor. One of the best of recent historical romances.
THE WHITE COMPANY. N. Y., Burt, 75 c.; Lovell, Coryell, paper, 50 c.
A story of the adventures of free-lances fighting for fun and booty in the Middle Ages. Very vigorous and entertaining.
THE REFUGEES. N. Y., Harper, $1.75.
A story of the persecution of certain Huguenots in France and their subsequent adventures in Canada. The interest is rather broken in the middle, but once in Canada and started on a new line revives and holds to the end.
THE ADVENTURES OF SHERLOCK HOLMES. N. Y., Harper, $1.50.
MEMOIRS OF SHERLOCK HOLMES. N. Y., Harper, $1.50.
Some of the adventures of this remarkable detective are quite marvellous, and show vast resource of invention.

"Duchess, The" (*pseudonym*). *See* Hungerford, Mrs. M. (H.).

Du Maurier, George. [1834- .]
English artist and novelist. His surprising success in fiction may owe something to his reputation as an artist, but the quality of his literary work is remarkable enough to have launched an absolutely unknown author. Imaginative, with great fluency and variety of expression, keenly observant and capable of extremes in emotion, it is quite to be expected that his two good things may be succeeded by something better. 823.80.
PETER IBBETSON. N. Y., Harper, $1.50.
The animating idea is rarely imaginative. Though passing the bounds of probability it captivates the fancy and would force unconditional acceptance were it not too much elaborated. The first chapters describing family life at Passy are charming, and the subsequent tragedy most justly arrived at through character and event.
TRILBY. N. Y., Harper, $1.75.
Better when regarded as a reminiscence of the author's youth in Paris than as a novel. Trilby is really nothing more than a peg on which to hang vivacious sketches of people, places and incidents. The author's ecstatic descriptions of his heroine are not made good by her recorded deeds and words. There is nothing wholly probable about her. The style is very different from the careful, easy flow of Peter Ibbetson, being scrappy and colloquial, pointed and very lively.

Duncan, Sara Jeannette. *See* Cotes, Mrs. S. J. D.

Edgeworth, Maria. [1767-1849.]
Irish novelist and writer of tales in late years of 18th century and first half of 19th. Miss Edgeworth has been most highly esteemed for her tales for children, but her tales of Irish life and character are really her best work. Sir Walter Scott said that "the rich humor, pathetic tenderness and admirable tact of her Irish portraits first set him thinking that something might be done for his own countrymen." She took up the Absentee Landlord question, the land question, and, in fact, all the questions which permanently agitate the Irish mind. Her tales of English fashionable life show much observation and spirit in delineation. The artistic effect is injured and the utility impaired by a too obvious moral intention and conventional award of happiness to the virtuous and ruin to the foolish or vicious. 823.72.
BELINDA. N. Y., Dodd, 2 vols., $2.
A combination of disquisition on morals and delineation of fashionable life.
THE ABSENTEE. N. Y., Harper, paper, 25 c.; Munro, paper, 25 c.
CASTLE RACKRENT. [With "The Absentee," 1 vol.] N. Y., Macmillan, $1.25.
Irish tales.

Edwardes, *Mrs.* Annie.
English novelist of the light society variety. She shows considerable experience of several sides of life, but little reflection. Her novels are all readable and unimportant. 823.80.
ARCHIE LOVELL. Lond., Chatto, 3s. 6d.; N. Y., Munro, paper, 25 c.
OUGHT WE TO VISIT HER? Lond., Bentley, 6s.; N. Y., Munro, paper, 25 c.
A VAGABOND HEROINE. N. Y., Munro, paper, 25 c.

Edwards, Amelia Blandford. [1831-1892.]
English novelist. Her stories were drawn from the middle and upper classes of English society. They describe the common affairs and feelings of average mortals, and though not especially notable, are romantic, agreeable and interesting. In her later years the author's mind was given to archæology, and she won reputation as an Egyptologist. 823.80.
DEBENHAM'S VOW. N. Y., Ward & Lock, $1; Harper, paper, 50 c.
MISS CAREW. N. Y., Ward & Lock, $1; Munro, paper, 25 c.
HAND AND GLOVE. N. Y., Munro, paper, 25 c.

Eggleston, Edward. [1837- .]
A Western novelist. He describes the life of Western pioneers and early settlers, and was one of the earliest reproducers or inventors of local dialect. His characters are vigorous, frequently humorous, and, though not always interesting, have the substance of drawings from life. Of late years Mr. Eggleston has resided in New York and devoted himself to writing history. 813.42.
THE HOOSIER SCHOOLMASTER. N. Y., Orange Judd Co., $1.25.
THE GRAYSONS. N. Y., Century Co., $1.50.
THE CIRCUIT RIDER. N. Y., Scribner, $1.50.
THE FAITH DOCTOR. N. Y., Appleton, $1.50.

Eliot, George (*Mrs.* Marian (Evans) Lewes, *afterwards* Cross). [1819-1880.]
One of the great English novelists, and among the world's greatest women of letters. In variety of natu-

ral qualities and completeness of intellectual equipment Sir Walter Scott is her only equal in English prose fiction. George Eliot may be regarded as the first of the moderns. Heroes whose deeds shine before men had no attraction for her; she took no interest in the exceptional, the dazzling or the picturesque; she had apparently no belief in primitive human emotion or passion uninfluenced by thought or reason as the spring of action. She gave to fiction a new laurel and allied it with abstract philosophy, mental and moral. With the scientist's gift of analysis she combined the artist's power of creation. The vitality and completeness of her figures and their movement through her selected train of circumstances towards the logical destiny of character are the masterly expression of both the analytic and creative mind. The one principle to which she was devoutly attached was that of duty, the idea of the nobility of self-sacrifice, and the one just criticism involving her whole work is that this attachment to a splendid idea of right leaves a depressing realization of the unmitigated sorrow of living. No novelist ever exercised a profounder moral influence on contemporaries, and none has delivered so clear and strong a message for the right conduct of life. 823.88.

ADAM BEDE. N. Y., Harper, 75 c.; Lovell, Coryell, 50 c.; Munro, paper, 25 c.

FELIX HOLT, THE RADICAL. N. Y., Harper, 75 c.; Lovell, Coryell, 50 c.; Munro, paper, 25 c.

THE MILL ON THE FLOSS. N. Y., Harper, 75 c.; Lovell, Coryell, 50 c.; Munro, paper, 25 c.

SILAS MARNER. N. Y., Harper, 75 c.; Lovell, Coryell, 50 c.; Munro, paper, 25 c.

SCENES OF CLERICAL LIFE.

"Silas Marner" and "Scenes of Clerical Life," in 1 vol., N. Y., Harper, 75 c.

MIDDLEMARCH. N. Y., Harper, 2 vols., 75 c. each; Lovell, Coryell, 50 c.; Munro, paper, 25 c.

Very particular criticism would be needful to indicate the superiority of any one of these six novels of English rural and village life. Each in a way is as good as the others, and all are true to nature and a grand ideal. For mere form "Adam Bede" is the most artistic, "Middlemarch" has the widest, most comprehensive scheme, and "The Mill on the Floss" is the most touching and pathetic.

DANIEL DERONDA. N. Y., Harper, 2 vols., 75 c. each; Lovell, Coryell, 50 c.; Munro, paper, 25 c.

In the title character the author loses her grasp, and for once is sentimental and ineffective. Lengthy expositions of Jewish faith and customs retard the movement, and the Jewish characters do not involve much interest or sympathy. Gwendolin Harleth is one of her most original characterizations.

ROMOLA. N. Y., Harper, 75 c.; Lovell, Coryell, 50 c.; Munro, paper, 25 c.

The scene is in Florence under the rule of Lorenzo di Medici. The revival of taste for Greek ideals in letters and art is splendidly contrasted with the austere piety of Savonarola. The story is very fascinating and beautiful, but the character of Romola does not appear to be in harmony with her age, race and circumstances. She is a serious, conscientious, high-minded, modern English woman rather than a mediæval Florentine.

WORKS. N. Y., Scribner, 21 vols. Fiction, 17 vols.; Essays, 2 vols.; Poems, 2 vols., $26.25.

Also, N. Y., Crowell, 10 vols., $15; and 6 vols., $6.

Elliott, Sarah Barnwell.

As the daughter of Stephen Elliott, first Protestant Episcopal Bishop of Georgia, this writer, in her candid treatment of religious and social questions, has won deserved attention. 813.49.

JERRY. N. Y., Holt, $1.25.

Scenes in Southwestern and far Western States. The title character is strongly imagined and drawn with frank recognition of the unexpected variations in character developed by and exhibited through change and extremes of fortune. From the pilgrimage of the forlorn little boy towards the setting sun, through all his vicissitudes of poverty and wealth the reader is conscious of impending tragic fate, whose shadow is at times intolerably painful. With much romantic adventure and dramatic situation there is united realistic presentation of a variety of character, which together make a remarkable novel.

THE FELMERES. N. Y., Holt, $1.25.

A story depicting the conflict between rationalism and Christianity. The heroine is a young woman of great purity of character, carefully brought up without creed of any kind.

JOHN PAGET. N. Y., Holt, $1.25.

An arraignment of fashionable religion.

Fargus, Frederick John ("Hugh Conway"). [1847-1885.]

CALLED BACK. Bristol, Eng., Arrowsmith, 1s. 6d.; N. Y., Munro, paper, 25 c.

The book on which the author's reputation will probably rest. An Englishman, unknown in letters, it brought him immense notoriety. The action is very rapid, the situations are dramatic, and suspense is finely held to the end. In the few years intervening between publication of his first book and his death the author wrote several stories in the same vein, but none nearly so good. 823.89.

Farjeon, Benjamin Leopold. [1833-.]

English novelist. His numerous books include almost every variety of plot, turning on strange adventure, love and crime of almost infinite degrees of enormity. Many of his scenes are in Australia, but most of them in London. His observation of vagabonds and outcasts is wide, and his sympathy with them sometimes misplaced. In drawing eccentric and comic characters he shows ability akin to that of Dickens, by whom he was undoubtedly influenced. He has also Dickens' tendency towards melodrama and sentimentality. Fluent in composition, ingenious in construction and amusing in dialogue, any of his stories provides an hour's distraction. Among the best are: 823.89.

GRIF. Lond., Ward & D., 2s.; N. Y., Munro, paper, 25 c.

GREAT PORTER SQUARE. Lond., Ward & D., 2s.; N. Y., Harper, paper, 20 c.

JOSHUA MARVEL. N. Y., Harper, paper, 40 c.

Farrar, Frederic William. [1831-.]

DARKNESS AND DAWN. N. Y., Longmans, $2.

The time of the distinguished English clergyman's historical novel is the reign of Nero, and the place Rome. The plot turns on the persecution of the Christians; the descriptions of life and manners include all classes of Roman society. The first chapters are bewildering, but when once the drama begins it moves on smoothly, with increasing interest. 823.89.

ST. WINIFRED : OR THE WORLD OF SCHOOL. N. Y., Dutton, $1.75.

ERIC. N. Y., Dutton, $1.75.

JULIAN HOME. N. Y., Dutton, $1.75.

Three capital books for young people.

Fawcett, Edgar. [1847-.]

A New York novelist. New York society, with its worship of money, artificiality and vulgarity, is the theme of most of his work. As he represents it, it is a society gorgeous and dull. Much of his work is clever, too consciously so, but none of it is very agreeable. His form is better than his thought, and while very fussy about perfection of manners, he is little concerned about the perfection of heart or mind. **813.40.**

A GENTLEMAN OF LEISURE. Bost., Houghton, $1.

TINKLING CYMBALS. Bost., Houghton, $1.50.

A NEW YORK FAMILY. N. Y., Cassell, $1; paper, 50 c.

AN AMBITIOUS WOMAN. Bost., Houghton, $1.50; paper, 50 c.

Ferrier, Susan Edmonstone. [1782-1854.]

This Scotch woman, an admired friend of Sir Walter Scott, in her humorous and satirical novels, has portrayed middle-class life in Scotland with an insight and skill that remind the reader of Jane Austen's gifts. **823.89.**

MARRIAGE. N. Y., Routledge, 80 c.

THE INHERITANCE. N. Y., Routledge, 80 c.

DESTINY. N. Y., Routledge, 80 c.

Fielding, Henry. [1707-1754.]

English 18th century novelist. A great figure; many think the greatest in English fiction. Inspired by a desire to travesty the sentimental, analytic work of his contemporary, Richardson, his genius conquered his mischievous intention and launched him in the delineation of the life that he knew, the scenes he had shared and the people he loved, hated or despised. This life was, on the whole, not a decent one, the scenes were not finically refined, and his likes and dislikes were not distributed on the principle of admiration for austere virtue or propriety. But he never stooped to conceal or palliate, rarely to apologize. He was witty, satirical, humorous, pathetic and unimpeachably sincere. His work rests on its intrinsic sincerity, the effects wrought by romantic imagination and by picturesque rhetoric were unknown to him. As his heroes were far from patterns of civil or domestic virtue, the general respectable public of the 19th century long cherished the notion that he was profoundly immoral. The good men he drew were ignored, his detestation for hypocrisy and deceit overlooked, and not a whisper heard of his admiration for loyalty, bravery and charity. This tendency still needs correction. The strongest impressions received from a book are necessarily those to which the reader's mind is most open; it seems incredible that persons of sense and intelligence can derive from Fielding only the impression of wickedness rejoicing. **823.52.**

HISTORY OF TOM JONES, A FOUNDLING. N. Y., Lovell, Coryell, $1; Routledge, paper, 50 c.

A famous American said all that is necessary about this novel when he remarked, "this is not a book, but a man." It was not written for children or young girls, and they probably would not be paid to read it. It is one of the mileposts in the great tradition of English letters.

AMELIA. N. Y., Lovell, Coryell, $1; Routledge, paper, 25 c.

Of all the author's books the most agreeable to women and least offensive to modern taste. The intermittent remorse of Captain Booth for his backsliding shows the author more severe on sins of the flesh than in his two earlier books. "Amelia" is said, on good authority, to have been carefully drawn from Fielding's own wife. With due allowance for a facility in fainting, apparently common to ladies of her period, she is a lovely and lovable person, a type of the good women of all periods and countries.

Fletcher, Julia Constance ("George Fleming"). **813.49.**

KISMET. Bost., Roberts, $1; paper, 50 c.

A very readable novel. Most of the action is in Egypt, the actors being a party of English and American tourists. The scenes are well touched and the conversation is amusing. None of the author's later novels is as good, but all showed cleverness and some skill.

VESTIGIA. Bost., Roberts, $1.25.

Italian life. The author's most finished story.

THE HEAD OF MEDUSA. Bost., Roberts, $1.50.

MIRAGE. Bost., Roberts, $1; paper, 50 c.

Foote, *Mrs.* Mary Hallock. [1847-.]

Most of her stories are descriptive of life in Western mining towns. Her style is pleasant and careful, and her love affairs are prettily told. **813.49.**

THE LED-HORSE CLAIM: a romance of a mining camp. Bost., Houghton, $1.25; paper, 50 c.

JOHN BODEWIN'S TESTIMONY. Bost., Houghton, $1.25; paper, 50 c.

CŒUR D'ALENE. Bost., Houghton, $1.25.

IN EXILE. Bost., Houghton, $1.25.

Short stories.

Ford, Paul Leicester. [1865-.]

Best known as an editor of Americana and of bibliographies covering important periods of American history. Mr. Ford's incidental observation of municipal politics has led him to write his only work of fiction. **813.49.**

THE HONORABLE PETER STIRLING, and what people thought of him. N. Y., Holt, $1.50.

Sketches the rise and progress of a boss from the chairmanship of a primary to the dictator's throne. The story of his social experience and love-making is interwoven; part of it might have been spared. A very good novel despite faults of style.

Fothergill, Jessie. [1851-1891.]

English novelist. Her construction is rather feeble, but for single scenes and bits of character her skill is noticeable. Her manner is refined yet vigorous, and her stories have a charm both of sentiment and style. **823.89.**

THE FIRST VIOLIN. N. Y., Holt, $1; paper, 30 c.

KITH AND KIN. N. Y., Burt, 75 c.; Munro, paper, 25 c.

A MARCH IN THE RANKS. Lond., Hurst, 3s. 6d.; N. Y., Lovell, Coryell, $1; Munro, paper, 25 c.

ORIOLES' DAUGHTER. N. Y., Lovell, Coryell, $1.

Francillon, Robert Edward. [1841-.]

An English novelist whose vocation is law. His imagination sets all possibility at defiance, yet preserves interest with artistic skill. Some of his psychological studies of character betoken rare gifts of analysis. **823.89.**

FACE TO FACE. N. Y., Harper, paper, 15 c.

GOLDEN BELLS. N. Y., Harper, paper, 25 c.

Francis, M. E.(Mrs. Francis Blundell).**813.49.**

THE STORY OF DAN. Bost., Houghton, $1.25.

A touching tragedy of Irish domestic life. The form is excellent, and the extravagant note in Irish nature, whether pathetic or comic truthfully hit off.

Frederic, Harold.

A New York journalist and novelist. His stories display close study of American history, especially of the history of his own State; he uses his materials judiciously and graphically. His tone is rather sombre, and would be the better for a little more humor.
813.40.

IN THE VALLEY. N. Y., Scribner, $1.50.

A well-composed picture of Revolutionary times in the Dutch homes of the Mohawk Valley, at the Patroon's Manor House in Albany, and on the field among bullets and tomahawks. The Dutch major's love-story is well told.

SETH'S BROTHER'S WIFE. N. Y., Scribner, $1.25.

A story of to-day in rural New York.

THE LAWTON GIRL. N. Y., Scribner, $1.25; paper, 50 c.

A small manufacturing town is described, with its turmoil—political, industrial, and social.

THE COPPERHEAD. N. Y., Scribner, $1.

Portrays the prejudices of an honest mind. The period is that of the Civil War.

French, Alice ("Octave Thanet"). [1850-.]

Born in Massachusetts; early in life removed to Iowa, which has furnished her with scenes and incidents for her stories. Miss French delineates the poor and ignorant with powers of observation plainly quickened by sympathy. The dialect of her characters is amusing, and by Western readers who know, is declared to be accurately rendered.
813.40.

KNITTERS IN THE SUN. Bost., Houghton, $1.25.

Short stories of the simplest emotions and experiences of plain people.

EXPIATION. N. Y., Scribner, $1; paper, 50 c.

Deals with social conditions in Arkansas at the close of the Civil War.

WE ALL. N. Y., Appleton, $1.50.

Treats of negro superstitions, and the power of the Ku Klux Klan in Arkansas.

OTTO THE KNIGHT, and other Trans-Mississippi stories. Bost., Houghton, $1.25.

Gardner, *Mrs.* **Sarah M. H.**

QUAKER IDYLS. N. Y., Holt, 75 c.

A volume of sketches, very nicely written, showing sympathy with the subjects, humor and some ability in management of dramatic situations and heart tragedies.
813.40.

THE FORTUNES OF MARGARET WELD. Bost., Arena Pub Co., paper, 50 c.

The heroine is an artist, who demands the same moral law for men and women.

Garland, Hamlin.

MAIN-TRAVELLED ROADS: six stories of the Mississippi Valley. Chic., Stone & K., $1.25.

Written with uncompromising realism. Throughout, the point of view, as well as the literary manner, is consistently American. But this does not prevent the conclusion of the first story from showing an indifference, not American, to the question of morality.

PRAIRIE FOLKS. Chic., Schulte, $1.25; paper, 50 c.

There is no lack of local color in these sketches;

there is, in fact, but little else. The author brings out with the fidelity of a conscientious realist the cruel necessity which grinds the poor, either of the city or the country.

Gaskell, *Mrs.* **Elizabeth Cleghorn.** [1810-1865.]

English novelist of middle period of 19th century. She described the social and domestic life of her day gracefully and clearly, uniting with a lively mind, wide sympathy, humor, and tenderness for humanity. Her women, even when youth and beauty have faded, have some charm of heart, or mind, or manner which makes them especially engaging. She was noticeably free from affectation, and never sought to heighten interest by artificial surprise or climax.
823.80.

CRANFORD. N. Y., Scribner, $1; Harper, paper, 25 c.

A delightful picture of English village life when ladies went about in poke-bonnets and pattens. The delineation of genteel poverty and the shifts of refined, timorous ladies to keep up appearances, of their pleasures and pains and absorbing interest in each other's affairs, is uncommonly touching and amusing and an example of delicate literary art.

MARY BARTON. N. Y., Scribner, $1; Ward, 75 c.; Harper, paper, 20 c.

The scene is in Manchester during the very hard times preceding the enactment of free-trade laws in England. The people are mostly poor factory operatives, and the strength of Mrs. Gaskell's presentation of their hardships excited, at the time, much public sympathy. The story is natural, pathetic, and not sentimental.

NORTH AND SOUTH. N. Y., Scribner, $1.

SYLVIA'S LOVERS. N. Y., Scribner, $1.

WIVES AND DAUGHTERS (unfinished). N. Y., Scribner, $1; Harper, paper, 60 c.

Gerard, Emily D. *See* Laszowska, Mrs. Emily D. G.

Gissing, George (Robert). [1857- .]

English novelist. His stories involve by illustration the discussion of social problems. He is direct and frank, both in statement and judgment, and inclined, like many modern realists, to harp on the dreary and rather awful phases of existence. His people are solidly and particularly drawn and his story interesting.
823.80.

THE ODD WOMEN. N. Y., Macmillan, $1.

DENZIL QUARRIER. N. Y., Macmillan, $1.

EVE'S RANSOM. N. Y., Appleton, $1; paper, 50 c.

Godwin, Mary. *See* Shelley, *Mrs.* Mary G.

Godwin, William. [1756-1836.]

ADVENTURES OF CALEB WILLIAMS. Cincin., James, paper, 50 c.; N. Y., Warne, paper, 20 c.

A forerunner of the modern purpose-novel, published in 1794. The author's motive was to promulgate his (then) revolutionary notions of the perfectibility of man and of the need of legal and social reforms. He was fascinated by theories of Rousseau and by the animating ideas of the French Revolution. The story, though not feeble in drama, is interesting chiefly for its place in the history of letters.
823.70.

Goldsmith, Oliver. [1728-1774.]

THE VICAR OF WAKEFIELD. Chic., McClurg, $1; N. Y., Routledge, half cloth, 40 c.; arper, paper, 25 c.

No figure in our literature is at once so simple and

so impressive, so ideal and so human as the *Vicar*, and once the acquaintance of the Primrose family is made, they and their misfortunes become a dear and imperishable memory. The purity of style is equal to that of the conception. The idea and expression are indeed inseparable. Goldsmith's great contribution to the art of fiction was his frank rejection of conventional temporal punishment of iniquity and reward of goodness. **823.64.**

Gordon, Julien *(pseudonym)*. *See* Cruger, Mrs. Julia Grinnell.

Grant, James. [1822-1887.]
Scotch novelist of middle period of 19th century. An indefatigable writer with some military experience, he could invent a tale for every scene where British arms have won glory and develop it with ease and considerable spirit. His heroes generally belonged to famous Scotch regiments. **823.89.**

THE WHITE COCKADE. N. Y., Routledge, boards, 80 c.

FRANK HILTON, or the Queen's Own. N. Y., Routledge, boards, 80 c.

THE ROMANCE OF WAR. N. Y., Routledge, boards, 80 c.

THE KING'S OWN BORDERERS. N. Y., Routledge, boards, 80 c.

Grant, Robert. [1852-.]
A New England novelist, who sketches every-day life with a light and entertaining touch. He is a shrewd observer, and has a vein of refined sentiment. **813.49.**

AN AVERAGE MAN. Bost., Houghton, $1.25; paper, 50 c.

THE CONFESSIONS OF A FRIVOLOUS GIRL. Bost., Houghton, $1.25; paper, 50 c.

THE CARLETONS. N. Y., Bonner, $1; paper, 50 c.

MRS. HAROLD STAGG. N. Y., Bonner, paper, 50 c.

THE REFLECTIONS OF A MARRIED MAN. N. Y., Scribner, $1.

Green, Anna Katharine. *See* Rohlfs, Mrs. Anna K. G.

Greene, *Mrs.* **Sarah Pratt (McLean).** [1855-.]
New England novelist and writer of tales. Her sketches of New England seaboard people are vivid, though somewhat exaggerated. Roaming abroad, she seems to lose all faculty for characterization, and becomes rather wild and ridiculous. **813.40.**

CAPE COD FOLKS. Bost., DeWolfe, Fiske, $1.25; paper, 50 c.
A series of sketches, the author's first and best work. The fictitious characters were so easily identified with their exaggerated or caricatured models that the publishers had in consequence to pay damages in a libel suit. The author gained wide notoriety. **813.40.**

VESTY OF THE BASINS. N. Y., Harper, $1.25; paper, 50 c.
Story of the coast of Maine.

LEON PONTIFEX. Bost., DeWolfe, Fiske, $1.25.
A British clergyman called to take charge of a church in an obscure New England village is the hero.

Grey, Maxwell *(pseudonym)*. *See* Tuttiett, M. G.

Guthrie, Thomas Anstey ("F. Anstey"). [1856-.]
English writer, chiefly of farcical or fantastic stories. He assumes a ludicrous hypothesis, works it out gravely, generally with ingenuity, energy, and enjoyable humor. His method resembles that of Mr. F. R. Stockton, but he has less of artistic restraint than his American rival. **823.89.**
He sprang into reputation with

VICE VERSA. N. Y., Appleton, $1; paper, 50 c.
A tale founded on the exchange of nature between a father and his school-boy son. The first chapters are excruciatingly funny, but the idea does not bear its lengthy exposition. The author's first serious novel was

THE GIANT'S ROBE. N. Y., Appleton, $1.25; paper, 50 c.
The plot is well sustained and the strain of suspense admirably lightened by touches of farcical comedy. Among the author's later works the best is:

TOURMALIN'S TIME CHECKS. N. Y., Appleton, boards, 50 c.

Habberton, John. [1842-.]
HELEN'S BABIES. N. Y., G. W. Dillingham, paper, 25 c.; Phila., Peterson, $1.
A story about children, very amusing to older folks. It captured the public, and some of the children's sayings became household words. The author's subsequent works are much less striking. **813.49.**

BRUETON'S BAYOU. Phil., Lippincott, $1; paper, 50 c.
A Western story of original motive, full of bright conversation.

OUT AT TWINNETT'S. N. Y., J. A. Taylor & Co., paper, 50 c.
Chiefly descriptive of Wall Street and its methods.

Haggard, Henry Rider. [1856-.]
English novelist. The scene of most of his marvellous or exciting adventures is in Africa. He is ingenious, with a capital notion of the dramatic, and frequently funny. His great faults are exaggeration and a proneness to platitudinous reflection. Enthusiastic admirers compare him favorably with R. L. Stevenson, but they have not quite appreciated the depth of the latter's thought or the beauty of his style. **823.89.**

KING SOLOMON'S MINES. N. Y., Longmans, 75 c.; Harper, 20 c.
A first-rate story of wonderful adventure It introduces Allan Quatermain, a great lion-hunter and hero of several later stories.

SHE. N. Y., Longmans, 75 c.; paper, 25 c.
A very sensational and popular novel. *She*, a repulsive and impossible witch, ages old, is the mysterious cause for narration of innumerable daring exploits and adventures. A wonderful exhibition of imagination, unrestrained by reason or art.

ALLAN QUATERMAIN. N. Y., Longmans, 75 c.; paper, 25 c.

ALLAN'S WIFE. N. Y., Longmans, 75 c. paper, 25 c.

JESS. N.Y., Longmans, 75 c.; paper, 25 c.

HEART OF THE WORLD. N. Y., Longmans, $1.25.

Hale, *Rev.* Edward Everett. [1822–.]
New England writer of novels and tales. Much of his work is especially addressed to the young. He is generally animated by a spirit of patriotism and a desire to inculcate good morals, hence a little tiresome, however excellent. His style is colloquial, showing some strain to achieve wit and humor, not always successful. **813.40.**

THE MAN WITHOUT A COUNTRY. Bost., Roberts, $1.25; paper, 50 c.

UPS AND DOWNS. Bost., Roberts, $1.50.

Haliburton, Thomas Chandler ("Sam Slick"). [1797–1865.]

THE CLOCKMAKER. Bost., Houghton, $1; N. Y., Routledge, 80 c.; Warne, paper, 20 c.
In writing this book Judge Haliburton, a Nova Scotian, founded the school of humor since developed by Artemus Ward and Mark Twain. In the guise of a Yankee clock peddler the author airs Tory convictions of an extreme type, and satirizes the folly of leaning on politics for prosperity. "The Clockmaker" was written nearly sixty years ago, and its style is often hurried and careless, yet many of its chapters are as amusing as ever. Phases of provincial life long vanished are here painted by a keen observer. The occasional descriptions of nature are sympathetic and genuine. **813.30.**

THE ATTACHÉ. N. Y., Routledge, 80 c.

NATURE AND HUMAN NATURE. N. Y., Dick & F., paper, 75 c.

Hamerton, Philip Gilbert. [1834–1894.]
An English art critic, whose novels bear the mark of artistic feeling and of trained sympathy with nature. He tells a pleasant story with skill, yet story-telling is plainly but a bye-pursuit with him.

WENDERHOLME: a tale of Yorkshire and Lancashire. Bost., Roberts, $2.
Describes reverses of fortune with quiet power.

MARMORNE. Bost., Roberts, $1; paper, 50 c.
The scene is laid in Burgundy. Gives some of the best descriptions of French country life in English literature.

HARRY BLOUNT: passages in a boy's life on land and sea. Bost., Roberts, $1.25.

Hardy, Arthur Sherburne. [1847–.]
Formerly professor of mathematics at Dartmouth College, exemplifying that imagination, so far from being foreign to science, may be characteristic of it. His stories are well put together, and his style is careful, yet easy and graceful. **813.40.**

PASSE ROSE. Bost., Houghton, $1.25; paper, 50 c.
A delightful romantic tale of Charlemagne and chivalry. The career o the waif, Passe Rose, is beautifully imagined and ex ellently told.

BUT YET A WOMAN. Bost., Houghton, $1.25; paper, 50 c.
This book made the author's reputation as a novelist.

THE WIND OF DESTINY. Bost., Houghton, $1.25; paper, 50 c.

Hardy, Thomas. [1840–.]
English novelist. The region anciently known as the kingdom of Wessex, particularly the County of Dorset is his chosen field. Thoroughly acquainted with the history of the country, as well as with its modern life, he depicts the influence of new ways and new ideas, breaking up traditional customs and convulsing character but recently brought in contact with the world's movements. His design is at once free and firm, and, though the detail of description of scene and circumstance is minute and the characters involved in the action are of great variety, he manages to preserve unity and to give the impression that every part is essential to completeness of the whole. Life, as he sees it, is tragic or comic, and either way not very pleasant. Humanity under his interpretation appears far from admirable, yet he compels us for the time to accept his view. His women, especially those whom he appears really to care for, are more remarkable for violent animal instinct than for any mental or spiritual grace. On the whole, his work is strong, interesting, and disagreeable. **823.80.**

THE RETURN OF THE NATIVE. N. Y., Lovell, Coryell, 75 c. or $1; Munro, paper, 25 c.
A very powerful rural tragedy, brought about by one of the author's most vulgar and detestable, yet most artistically drawn, women.

TESS OF THE D'URBERVILLES. N. Y., Harper, $1.50.
Another impressive rural tragedy. The movement is grand, very vigorous and passionate, and many of the characters show the author at his best. The artistic effect is spoiled by his interpolated justifications of the principal character. His defence of Tess is quite superfluous and expresses great confusion of mind in regard to decent standards of behavior.

FAR FROM THE MADDING CROWD. N. Y., Harper, $1.50; Lovell, Coryell, 50 c. or $1; Munro, paper, 25 c.
A charming story of English country life. It is the book which first brought the author fame.

A PAIR OF BLUE EYES. N. Y., Lovell, Coryell, 75 c.; Munro, paper, 25 c.

THE WOODLANDERS. N. Y., Lovell, Coryell, $1; Harper, paper, 20 c.

Harland, Henry ("Sidney Luska"). [1861–.]
New York novelist. His plots are somewhat sentimental, but very well carried out. His best work is drawn from Jewish life in the city of New York. **813.40.**

AS IT WAS WRITTEN. N. Y., Cassell, $1; paper, 50 c.
A Jewish musician's story.

MRS. PEIXADA. N. Y., Cassell, $1; paper, 50 c.

THE YOKE OF THE THORAH. N. Y., Cassell, $1; paper, 50 c.

MADEMOISELLE MISS. N. Y., Lovell, Coryell, $1.
Short stories.

Harland, Marion (*pseudonym*). *See* Terhune, Mrs. M. V.

Harraden, Beatrice.

SHIPS THAT PASS IN THE NIGHT. N. Y., Putnam, $1; paper, 50 c.
The scene is in Switzerland, and the slight story is prettily told. The characters are very modern, and their shades of thought and feeling are cleverly indicated. The book is deservedly popular. **823.80.**

IN VARYING MOODS. N. Y., Putnam, $1.

Harris, Joel Chandler. [1848-.]

Southern writer of negro folk-tales and stories of Southern life. His understanding of negro character, its fun, pathos and savagery, is deep, and his presentation admirable. He manages negro dialect with apparent truth and precision. **813.40.**
His reputation was made by

UNCLE REMUS AND HIS FRIENDS. Bost., Houghton, $1.50.

The material for this volume of negro folk-lore, held together by delightful old Uncle Remus, was gathered at first-hand from plantation negroes. The "Creetur" tales and the manner of their telling are uniquely funny—an endless delight for children and their elders. This book was followed by

NIGHTS WITH UNCLE REMUS. Bost., Houghton, $1.50; paper, 50 c.

Three new-comers help Uncle Remus with his tales, each maintaining his own peculiarity of dialect and distinct personality. Quite as good as the first volume. All the author's work is good.

MINGO AND OTHER SKETCHES. Bost., Houghton, $1.25; paper, 50 c.

Harris, Mrs. Miriam (Coles). [1834-.]

A New York novelist. Very productive and popular. Her novels always appear to be made on a given receipt, varying only in the quantity of ingredients used. To a lively mind they should be conducive of profound sleep. **813.40.**

RUTLEDGE. Bost., Houghton, $1.25.

ST. PHILIP'S. Bost., Houghton, $1.25.

LOUIE'S LAST TERM AT ST. MARY'S. Bost., Houghton, $1.

Harrison, Mrs. Constance Cary (Mrs. Burton Harrison). [1835-.]

Southern novelist. She describes life in Virginia and New York; mostly the life of the rich and fashionable. Her intuition is not very keen, nor her thought very deep, but she writes smooth-flowing stories, easily read and as easily forgotten. **813.49.**

ANGLOMANIACS. N. Y., Cassell, $1; paper, 50 c.

A DAUGHTER OF THE SOUTH. N. Y., Cassell, $1.
Short stories.

SWEET BELLS OUT OF TUNE. N. Y., The Century Co., $1.25.

Harrison, Mrs. Mary (" Lucas Malet ").

English novelist. This daughter of Charles Kingsley inherits her father's imagination and literary power, but her mind is attracted to different subjects. She deals with the complications of modern life, and especially with the facility with which mortals fall into sin. She is sympathetic with the passions of human nature and free from sentimentality in developing the consequences of their indulgence. **823.80.**

THE WAGES OF SIN. Lond., Sonnenschein, 6s.; N. Y., Munro, 25 c.

A strong novel of modern English life. The principal incident is a favorite one with cheap sensational novelists, but is handled by the author with originality and truth. The movement is dramatic and the characters thoughtfully and courageously drawn. The payment exacted for sin is shown to depend on the temperament and character of the sinner.

A COUNSEL OF PERFECTION. N. Y., Appleton, $1; half boards, 75 c.; paper, 50 c.

MRS. LORIMER. N. Y., Appleton, $1; paper, 50 c.

Harte, Francis Bret. [1839-.]

Writer of Western stories; he has for many years made his home in England. The first to celebrate the " forty-niners " and other pioneers of the Pacific coast. Many have followed him, few equalled and none excelled him. With a natural gift for literary expression and form, a sympathy with vagabonds and outcasts, and much experience of rough-and-ready phases of life, he was pre-eminently fitted to make a figure in American literature. His later stories have neither the originality nor authority of the earlier, but are generally far above mediocrity. **813.49.**

THE LUCK OF ROARING CAMP. Bost., Houghton, $1.
Short stories.

MRS. SKAGGS'S HUSBANDS. Bost., Houghton, $1.25.
More short stories.

TALES OF THE ARGONAUTS. Bost., Houghton, $1.25.

A PHYLLIS OF THE SIERRAS. Bost., Houghton, $1.

A SAPPHO OF GREEN SPRINGS. Bost., Houghton, $1.25; paper, 50 c.

GABRIEL CONROY. Hartford, Conn., Am. Pub. Co., $1.

Hartley, Mrs. May (" May Laffan ").

Irish novelist. Draws a variety of Irish characters with great skill. Her stories are full of the national warmth, sorrow, and fun. **823.89.**

FLITTERS, TATTERS AND THE COUNSELLOR. N. Y., Macmillan, $1; U. S. Book Co., paper, 10 c.

ISMAY'S CHILDREN. N. Y., Macmillan, $1.

HOGAN M. P. Lond., Macmillan, 2s. 6d.; N. Y., U. S. Book Co., paper, 10 c.

Hatton, Joseph. [1839-.]

An English journalist and novelist, with a good sense of plot and a keen eye for character.

JOHN NEEDHAM'S DOUBLE. N. Y., Harper, paper, 25 c.

The story of a murder ingeniously told: the basis of a popular play.

THE GREAT WORLD. N. Y., Harper, paper, 20 c.

THE QUEEN OF BOHEMIA. Harper, paper, 15 c.

Hawkins, Anthony Hope (" Anthony Hope ").

English writer of tales. He represents the late reaction from realism in its limited sense of reproduction of ordinary people and every-day experience. He narrates a romantic adventure, of which the participants are all that is real and modern. His stories are short, of excellent literary form, and brilliant in dialogue and characterization. **823.89.**

THE PRISONER OF ZENDA. N. Y., Holt, 75 c.

An admirable story, very romantic in conception and real in presentation. The chain of impossible circumstances is perfectly linked, and the characters are so life-like and interesting that the impossibility of all is a cold afterthought. The hero, though a modern English gentleman, is as romantic and captivating as a fairy prince.

THE INDISCRETION OF THE DUCHESS. N. Y., Holt, 75 c.

THE GOD IN THE CAR. N. Y., Appleton, $1; paper, 50 c.

Speculation in railroad stocks in South Africa is the theme.

Hawthorne, Julian. [1846-.]

New England novelist and miscellaneous writer. His imagination applied to the supernatural and to strange crime shows an affinity with the weird or inexplicable similar to that of his father, Nathaniel, but immeasurably less subtle and refined. His books are interesting and vigorous, more noticeable for incident and action than for development of character or presentation of problems of conduct. 813.40.

ARCHIBALD MALMAISON. N. Y., Funk, 75c.; paper, 15 c.

A "creepy" tale with a good idea, very boldly worked out, and exciting plain horror rather than sympathy.

FORTUNE'S FOOL. Bost., Houghton, $1.50; paper, 50 c.

MRS. GAINSBOROUGH'S DIAMONDS. N. Y., Appleton, paper, 25 c.

Hawthorne, Nathaniel. [1804-1864.]

New England writer of novels and tales of middle period of 19th century. The most distinguished American novelist and the finest exponent in literature of New England Puritanism and mysticism, that is, a combination of exalted imagination and conscience. The great strength of his delineation is on the spiritual side, and the struggle between the flesh and the spirit is ever uppermost. His sense of the dramatic and picturesque was sufficient for action and situation, but he never depended on either for effect. As a writer of beautiful imaginative prose no other American is his equal and few Englishmen are his superiors. 813.33.

THE SCARLET LETTER. Bost., Houghton, $1 or 30 c.

For idea, structure and style is as nearly perfect as a novel can be. The horror of sin concealed, and the anguish of sin confessed, are depicted in most moving drama and with absolute adequacy. With this theme is woven a wonderful representation of New England life and thought in early Colonial times.

THE MARBLE FAUN. Called in England "Transformation." Bost., Houghton, $2.

The scene is in Rome and the tale reveals the very curious influence of Old World myth and atmosphere on an imagination free as air and a moral nature firmly founded on Puritan principles. It is fantastic, fascinating and romantic, but in no way so fine an expression of the author's genius as are his New England stories:

THE HOUSE OF THE SEVEN GABLES. Bost., Houghton, $1 or 30 c.

MOSSES FROM AN OLD MANSE. Bost., Houghton, $2; linen, 30 c.

TWICE-TOLD TALES. Bost., Houghton, $2; linen, 30 c.

Many historical incidents are included in these and many are weirdly imaginative. All very fine.

A WONDER-BOOK; TANGLEWOOD TALES; and GRANDFATHER'S CHAIR. Bost., Houghton, $2.

The best stories for girls and boys ever written in America. Grown folk read them with delight.

Hay, Mary Cecil. [1840-1886.]

English novelist. Her tales of domestic and social life are compounded of stock material—a love affair, a mystery frequently involving some sort of crime among the aristocracy, and an inevitable catastrophe. Her early books were rather good for character and description of scenes. 823.89

OLD MYDDLETON'S MONEY. N. Y., Lovell, Coryell, 50 c.; Munro, paper, 25 c.

THE SQUIRE'S LEGACY. N. Y., Lovell, Coryell, 50 c.; Munro, paper, 25 c.

THE ARUNDEL MOTTO. N. Y., Lovell, Coryell, 50 c.; Munro, paper, 25 c.

Hayes, Henry (*pseudonym*). *See* Kirk, Mrs. Ellen W. O.

Hearn, Lafcadio. [1850-.]

A Southerner of foreign birth whose chief distinction as a writer is in the field of travel. He has vivid imagination and unpruned luxuriance in description. His unusual opportunities for portraying out-of-the-way people give his books a refreshing picturesqueness.

YOUMA. N. Y., Harper, $1.

A tale of the negro insurrection in the West Indies.

CHITA: A Memory of Last Island. N. Y., Harper, $1.

Hector, *Mrs.* **Annie French** ("Mrs. Alexander"). [1825-.]

English novelist of social and domestic life. Her scenes and people are generally English varied by excursions to Germany and France. Drawing most of her characters from the middle and upper classes, she develops them with composure through the not too thrilling vicissitudes of a somewhat mechanical, carefully built plot. Her good people (especially women) are natural and pleasing, a little garrulous: her bad are more artificial, less suggestive of personal acquaintance 823.89.

HER DEAREST FOE. N. Y., Lovell, Coryell, 75 c.; Munro, paper, 25 c.

One of the author's first and best novels with qualities that characterize all her subsequent work. The love-story is pretty, the tangle about a lost will scrupulously made straight, the heroine a sprightly, independent, healthy English woman, and the interminable conversations neither very brilliant nor very dull. The most popular among the author's numerous subsequent works are:

THE WOOING O'T. N. Y., Lovell, Coryell, 50 c.; Munro, paper, 25 c.

WHICH SHALL IT BE? N. Y., Lovell, Coryell, 75 c.; Munro, paper, 25 c.

RALPH WILTON'S WEIRD. N. Y., Munro, paper, 25 c.

Henderson, Isaac. [1850–.]

THE PRELATE. Bost., Houghton, $1.50; paper, 50 c.

A sensational story of the American colony in Rome. The author, a New Yorker, long resident in Europe, contrives interesting situations with art.

AGATHA PAGE. Bost., Houghton, $1.50; paper, 50 c.

Another Roman tale.

Herman, Henry. *See under* Murray, David C., for novel written in collaboration—"He Fell Among Thieves."

Holmes, *Mrs.* **Mary Jane (Hawes).**

Her works are unknown to the cultured reader, but are very popular among people of limited education, experience, and opportunity to get books better worth while. They are not sensational or vicious; they are, indeed, rather prosy and dull. The secret of their long popularity has never been divulged by their readers. **813.49.**

LENA RIVERS. N. Y., G. W. Dillingham, paper, 50 c.

MILLBANK. N. Y., G. W. Dillingham, paper, 50 c.

Holmes, Oliver Wendell. [1809–1894.]

A New Englander, more distinguished as poet and essayist than as writer of fiction. At the time of his death, 1894, the last survivor of the great New England literary group born about the first of the century. All his work is distinguished for keen perception, wit, and grace of expression. **813.49.**

ELSIE VENNER. Bost., Houghton, $1.50; paper, 50 c.

A psychological study. Elsie Venner is supposed to have the blood of a rattlesnake in her veins.

THE GUARDIAN ANGEL. Bost., Houghton, $1.50; paper, 50 c.

A study in heredity.

Hope, Anthony. *See* Hawkins, Anthony H.

Howard, Blanche Willis (now Mrs. Teuffel). [1847–.]

New England novelist. She is frequently amusing, but like many of her countrywomen, always struggling "to be bright." Several of her stories have European scenes and characters, but the best are descriptive of her own country and compatriots. **813.49.**

ONE SUMMER. Bost., Houghton, $1.25.

Here the author is "bright" all through. The people who conduct the slight drama are thoroughly American. The little book created a sensation when first published, and will probably be read when the author's later works are forgotten.

GUENN. Bost., Houghton, $1.50; paper, 50 c.

The scene is laid in Brittany and the local color is very well given.

TONY THE MAID. N. Y., Harper, $1.

Very good light comedy.

THE OPEN DOOR. Bost., Houghton, $1.50; paper, 50 c.

Howe, Edgar Watson. [1854–.]

THE STORY OF A COUNTRY TOWN. Bost., Houghton, $1.25; paper, 50 c.

A strong, realistic novel. The life depicted is hard and sordid and the characters are not agreeable. It is all too painfully true ever to have been written. The first edition was set up and printed by the author and editor of a newspaper in the dreary Western town where the scene is laid. **813.49.**

MOONLIGHT BAY. Bost., Houghton, $1.50; paper, 50 c.

THE MYSTERY OF THE LOCKS. Bost., Houghton, $1.25.

Howells, William Dean. [1837–.]

Born in Ohio, resides in New York, poet, novelist, and miscellaneous writer. In his literary career he, an apostle of realism in fiction, has been most faithful to one idea, the delineation of American life, particularly that of New England, in its least exceptional aspect. To be properly understood and appreciated he must be judged by all his work and not by single volumes. It is true that, on the whole, he seems to ignore the existence of deep emotion and passion and their enormous influence on human destiny, but this apparent limitation is fairly explained by the fact that the people whom he represents are really more intelligent than emotional, more practical than passionate. A fairer criticism would refer to his comparative neglect of the finely intellectual or spiritual New Englander, but again it must be remembered that this man is not so common as he was in the generation just passing away when Mr. Howells began to write. His latest novels dwell more on the American's likeness to the rest of humanity than on his deviations from the eternal type. This is not change, but development, partly accounted for by an extended sphere of observation, and partly, perhaps, by the wider understanding and deeper sympathy which years bring to one who thinks and feels. Of his vivacity in portraiture, his humor and wit, it is unnecessary to speak; his severest critics have never questioned them. **813.43.**

{ A CHANCE ACQUAINTANCE. Bost., Houghton, $1.

{ THEIR WEDDING JOURNEY. Bost., Houghton, $1.

Charming sketches, through which the author became widely known to the public.

{ THE RISE OF SILAS LAPHAM. Bost., Houghton, $1.50; paper, 50 c.

{ A MODERN INSTANCE. Bost., Houghton, $1.50; paper, 50 c.

Taken singly, the author's strongest and hardest works. Each embodies a literal, merciless representation of a conspicuous American type, and a subtle interpretation, perfectly clear and cold, in which, while nothing is extenuated, nothing is set down in malice.

A HAZARD OF NEW FORTUNES. N. Y., Harper, 2 vols., $2; 1 vol., paper, $1.

Here the author steps into a wider world than Boston, is occupied with greater movements, and begins to note the large tragedies of life.

A TRAVELER FROM ALTRURIA. N. Y., Harper, $1.50; paper, 50 c.

A discussion of human wrongs and grievances under existing social order. The "Traveler" describes the perfection of things in Altruria. More valuable as an illustration of the tendency of the author's interests and thoughts, and for the literary treatment, than as a possible guide towards attainment of social perfection.

A FOREGONE CONCLUSION. Bost., Houghton, $1.50; paper, 50 c.

APRIL HOPES. N. Y., Harper, $1.50; paper, 75 c.

INDIAN SUMMER. Bost., Houghton, $1.50; paper, 50 c.

Hungerford, *Mrs.* **Margaret (Hamilton)** (" The Duchess ").

A contemporaneous Irish novelist. She is frivolous, sentimental, slangy, and popular. Her first novels were fresh, touched with genuine pathos, and frequently witty. Her later books are feeble repetitions. 823.80.

BEAUTY'S DAUGHTERS. Phila., Lippincott, $1; N. Y., Munro, paper, 25 c.

AIRY, FAIRY LILIAN. Phila., Lippincott, $1; N. Y., Munro, paper, 25 c.

MRS. GEOFFREY. Phila., Lippincott, $1; N. Y., Munro, paper, 25 c.

MOLLY BAWN. Phila., Lippincott, $1; N. Y., Burt, 75 c.; Munro, paper, 25 c.

PHYLLIS. Phila., Lippincott, $1; N. Y., Munro, paper, 25 c.

Hunt, Helen. *See* Jackson, Helen H.

Ingelow, Jean. [1830– .]

English poet, whose few contributions to prose fiction are worth reading. The description of scenes and events have poetic quality, and are touched with the womanly tenderness and sentiment which distinguish the author's verse. 823.89.

OFF THE SKELLIGS. Bost., Roberts, $1.

FATED TO BE FREE. Bost., Roberts, $1.
Full of pleasant descriptions of family life. The author is specially happy in describing children.

DON JOHN. Bost., Roberts, $1.
The story of the lives of two children exchanged by a wet-nurse.

JOHN JEROME. Bost., Roberts, $1.25.
John Jerome's thoughts on art, religion, and nature are full of suggestion.

MOPSA, THE FAIRY. Bost., Roberts, $1.25.

Iron, Ralph (*pseudonym*). *See* Schreiner, Olive.

Irving, Washington. [1783–1859.]

A New Yorker of early part of 19th century. His works include histories, biographies, essays, and tales. In manner and style he carried on the tradition of English prose established by the 18th century writers, and is especially comparable with the Queen Anne essayists. In his books, descriptive of Old World scenes, he appears more imitative than original. His best work is that which gives to the legends of his native land imperishable literary forms. 817.24.

KNICKERBOCKER'S HISTORY OF NEW YORK. N. Y., Putnam, 75 c. and upwards; Cassell, 2 vols., paper, 20 c.

A very entertaining combination of fact and fiction. The fun is occasionally forced and extravagant, but there is abundance of genial humor. With no great pretension to seriousness, it probably gives a very truthful account of the transplanted Dutchman's habits and manners.

THE SKETCH BOOK. N. Y., Putnam, 75 c. and upwards; Munro, paper, 25 c.

These include American, English, and Continental European tales and sketches. The best are the tales of the Hudson, such as "Rip Van Winkle" and the "Legend of Sleepy Hollow," but they are all artistic in conception, while the execution is uniformly smooth and graceful.

BRACEBRIDGE HALL. N. Y., Putnam, 75 c. and upwards.

WOLFERT'S ROOST. N. Y., Putnam, 75 c. and upwards.

TALES OF A TRAVELER. N. Y., Putnam, $1 and upwards.

Jackson, *Mrs.* **Helen Maria (Fiske)** (" H. H."). [1831–1885.]

New England novelist, poet, and writer of tales. Her stories of life, both in the Eastern and Western States, are thoughtful, interesting, and well told. She had great tenderness for suffering and misfortune in whatever shape, and her best characters illustrate the beauty of moral courage. 813.40.

SAXE HOLM'S STORIES. N. Y., Scribner, 2 vols., each $1; paper, each 50 c.
Rank high among the best short tales of American life.

RAMONA. Bost., Roberts, $1.50.
A tale of unjust treatment of Indians by the United States Government. Mrs. Jackson was well informed as to her facts. The story is sympathetic and dramatic.

HETTY'S STRANGE HISTORY. Bost., Roberts, $1.

MERCY PHILBRICK'S CHOICE. Bost., Roberts, $1.

NELLY'S SILVER MINE. Bost., Roberts, $1.50.

BETWEEN WHILES. Bost., Roberts, $1.25; paper, 50 c.

ZEPH (unfinished). Bost., Roberts, $1.25.

James, *Mrs.* **Florence Alice (Price)** (" Florence Warden ").

THE HOUSE ON THE MARSH. N. Y., Lovell, Coryell, 50 c.; Appleton, paper, 25 c.
A sensational tale. The heroine, a governess, finds herself in the house of a highwayman. 823.80.

RALPH RYDER OF BRENT. N. Y., National Book Co., $1.25; paper, 25 c.
A story of mistaken identity.

A TERRIBLE FAMILY. N. Y., International News Co., $1; paper, 50 c.

A PERFECT FOOL. N. Y., International News Co., $1; paper, 50 c.

James, George Payne Rainsford. [1801–1860.]

English novelist. For productiveness he is comparable with the elder Dumas; between 1822 and 1860 he wrote over one hundred novels, besides other works. He had a martial and romantic spirit, and pranced about through centuries, over continents, pouncing with much discrimination upon the men and events suitable for imaginative treatment. The figure of the solitary horseman pursuing his pensive way down a lonely glen is sacred to his memory. His books are exciting and tend to establish admiration for physical courage and less obvious heroic virtues. The best are : **823.89.**

RICHELIEU. N. Y., Warne, paper, 20 c.

AGINCOURT. N. Y., Warne, paper, 20 c.

DARNLEY. N. Y., Routledge, 80 c.; Warne, paper, 20 c.

HENRY OF GUISE. N. Y., Routledge, 80 c.

James, Henry. [1843-.]

Born in New York, resident in England. As a writer of short stories and novels, he is a famous representative of the analytical and psychic school. His attention is given to examination of mind and feeling rather than to action. Like Mr. Howells, with whom in years and reputation he is contemporary, he began with studies of American character, but preferred the American abroad to the American at home. The justice and subtlety of his perceptions are as indisputable as are the correctness of his literary form and the fineness of his expression. He has always had the light, swift touch and the perfection of ironical humor. But more and more he has abandoned himself to the perfecting of the word, and thus separated himself from the public. He is not human enough to attract popular regard. Nevertheless, any one who is willing to learn to admire skilled literary workmanship, to know how subtle and delicate an art that of expression is, cannot do better than study Mr. James in all his works.   **813.40.**

DAISY MILLER.
Introduces " Daisy Miller," at one time the typical American girl tourist in Europe.

AN INTERNATIONAL EPISODE.
The two preceding in 1 vol. N. Y., Harper, $3.50.

DIARY OF A MAN OF FIFTY—A BUNDLE OF LETTERS. N. Y., Harper, paper, 25 c.

THE PORTRAIT OF A LADY. Bost., Houghton, $2.

THE PRINCESS CASAMASSIMA. N. Y., Macmillan, $1.25.

THE LESSON OF THE MASTER. N. Y., Macmillan, $1.
Short stories.

THE BOSTONIANS. N. Y., Macmillan $1.

THE REVERBERATOR. N. Y., Macmillan, $1.

Jamison, *Mrs.* **Celia V.** (formerly Mrs. C. V. Hamilton).
Southern writer, born in Louisiana. **813.40.**

THE STORY OF AN ENTHUSIAST. Bost., Houghton, $1.50; paper, 50 c.

A boy with an artist nature is forced to live among humdrum English people. At seventeen he starts for Italy in search of one of Raphael's pictures. A fairly interesting study in the psychology of genius and the influence of heredity.

LADY JANE. N. Y., Century Co., $1.50.
A story of child-life; the scene is New Orleans among the poorer classes.

TOINETTE'S PHILIP. N. Y., Century Co., $1.50.
A romantic story of New Orleans life.

Janvier, Thomas Allibone. [1849-.]
Writer of tales and sketches. He is equally at home in Mexico and in New York. His incidents are well chosen and his characters fit his scenes. His style is light, smooth, and happy. **813.40.**

COLOR STUDIES. N. Y., Scribner, $1; paper, 50 c.
Stories of that part of New York formerly known as Greenwich Village. The characters are mostly disciples of art, simple and kindly and well fitted for the air of romance that hangs about their quarter.

AN AZTEC TREASURE-HOUSE. N. Y., Harper, $1 50; paper, 75 c.

THE UNCLE OF AN ANGEL. N. Y., Harper, $1.25; paper, 50 c.

Jenkin, *Mrs.* **Henrietta Caroline (Campbell).** [1808-1885.]
English novelist.

WHO BREAKS, PAYS. N. Y., Lovell, Coryell, 75 c.
A very good novel with original treatment of an old subject. The scenes are in England, France, and Italy. The character of the heroine is cleverly dissected and her personality sympathetically presented. **823.80.**

JUPITER'S DAUGHTERS. N. Y., Munro, paper, 20 c.

MADAME DE BEAUPRÉ. N. Y., Munro, paper, 20 c.

SKIRMISHING. N. Y., Munro, paper, 20 c.

WITHIN AN ACE. N. Y., Lovell, Coryell, 75 c.

COUSIN STELLA. N. Y., Lovell, Coryell, 75 c.

Jewett, Sarah Orne. [1849-.]
New England novelist and writer of tales and sketches. Many writers have attacked New England life and character with good effect, but none has given so truthful and vivid an expression, within limitations, as Miss Jewett. She is especially the interpreter of women living on lonely farms and in small villages. Their bare external life, their moral courage, their eccentric tempers and ironical humor are set forth with infinite sympathy, skill, and variety. Always free from extravagance, she has attained an ease and naturalness which are the crowning graces of literary art. All her stories are good. **813.49.**

A COUNTRY DOCTOR. Bost., Houghton, $1.25; paper, 50 c.

DEEPHAVEN. Bost. Houghton, $1.25.
Short stories.

A WHITE HERON. Bost., Houghton, $1.25.
Short stories.

A NATIVE OF WINBY. Bost., Houghton, $1.25.
Short stories.

Johnson, Samuel. [1709-1784.]

RASSELAS, PRINCE OF ABYSSINIA. Chic., McClurg, $1; N. Y., Routledge, 50 c.; Munro, paper, 25 c.

An early example of the deliberately didactic novel, and permanently valuable both for sentiment and style. The didactic novel is generally the product of a feeble mind and good effect, but " Rasselas " had the luck to be written by one who for wisdom ran Solomon pretty close, and who concerned himself more with the goodness of acts than of intentions. The fable through which the lofty yet practical moralizing on conduct is conveyed is pleasing and fanciful; the style is Johnston at his best, impressive and stately, but not ponderous. The book was first published in 1780. **823.09.**

Johnston, Richard Malcolm. [1822–.]

Southern novelist and writer of tales. His works are descriptive of life in middle Georgia in the first half of the century. There is decided monotony of type and interest but a strong sense of humor in the narration of petty social strife and the bitterness of conflicting religious opinions. The dialect talked is presumably correct (since the author writes of his own people), but is among the most grotesque corruptions of the English tongue ever committed to print. **813.40.**

OLD MARK LANGSTON. N. Y., Harper, $1.

MR. ABSALOM BILLINGSLEA and Others. N. Y., Harper, $1.25.
Short stories.

WIDOW GUTHRIE. N. Y., Appleton, $1.50.

CHRONICLES OF MR. BILL WILLIAMS. N. Y., Appleton, $1; paper, 50 c.

DUKESBOROUGH TALES. N. Y., Appleton, $1; paper, 50 c.

THE PRIMES AND THEIR NEIGHBORS. N. Y., Appleton, $1; paper, 50 c.

Keddie, Henrietta ("Sarah Tytler"). [1827–.]

Her stories of Continental and English life are of unequal quality—some very good, some the reverse. Many of her women and girls are well drawn and attractive. The composition is frequently imperfect in detail, and the movement at times flags unnecessarily. Her best novels are semi-historical. **823.89.**

CITOYENNE JACQUELINE. Lond., Chatto, 2s.

A HUGUENOT FAMILY. N. Y., Harper, $1.50.

DAYS OF YORE. N. Y., Ward & Lock, 75 c.

FRENCH JANET. Lond., Smith & Elder, boards, 2s.; N. Y., Harper, paper, 30 c.

King, *Captain* Charles. [1844–.]

New York novelist, who writes stories of military life in frontier stations. With the jingle of spurs and the blare of trumpet a sentimental love affair is interwoven, generally running through not too strange vicissitude to a happy end. His stories are readable and popular. **813.40.**

THE COLONEL'S DAUGHTER. Phila., Lippincott, $1.25.

KITTY'S CONQUEST. Phila., Lippincott, $1.

A WAR-TIME WOOING. N. Y., Harper, $1.

UNDER FIRE. Phila., Lippincott, $1.25.

King, Grace.

Southern writer of tales. Her work is local, confined to the Gulf States. Her pictures of Creole society are refined and graceful, and some of her incidents are dramatic. **813.40.**

BALCONY STORIES. N. Y., Century Co., $1.25.
This volume is beneath the author's usual standard, and represents impressionism run mad; it is spasmodic, hysterical, and artificial.

MONSIEUR MOTTE. N. Y., Armstrong, $1.25.
Short stories.

TALES OF A TIME AND PLACE. N. Y., Harper, $1.25.

Kingsley, Charles. [1819–1875.]

English clergyman and novelist of the middle period of the 19th century. Most of his novels are historical and romantic. With an enthusiasm for heroic virtue, wide cultivation and profound religious sentiment, he was well fitted to describe both physical prowess and spiritual struggles. His books combine both interests in a notable way, and have well survived forty years of existence. **823.85.**

HYPATIA. N. Y., Macmillan, $1; Crowell, 75 c.; Warne, paper, 25 c.
The scene is in Alexandria, and the movement involves the spectacle of Paganism expiring in the new birth of Christianity. Very dramatic and picturesque. Hypatia is a brilliantly imagined woman and a dignified, tragic figure.

WESTWARD, HO! N. Y., Macmillan, $1; Crowell, 75 c.; Warne, paper, 25 c.
Fine story of adventure in the reign of Queen Elizabeth. The scenes are in England, South America and on the high seas.

THE WATER BABIES. N. Y., Macmillan, $1; Lovell, Coryell, 50 c.; Munro, paper, 25 c.
An exquisite fairy tale.

HEREWARD, THE LAST OF THE ENGLISH. N. Y., Macmillan, $1; Crowell, 75 c.; Warne, paper, 25 c.

ALTON LOCKE. N. Y., Macmillan, $1; Crowell, 75 c.; Warne, paper, 25 c.

TWO YEARS AGO. N. Y., Macmillan, $1; Crowell, 75 c.; Warne, paper, 25 c.

Kingsley, Henry. [1830–1876.]

English novelist and brother of Charles Kingsley. Though the less popular of the two, his method is really the better, and his indication of complex character more subtle. He travelled much, observed many sorts of men, and drew them with less reflection of his own temperament, mind, and moral nature. **823.89.**

THE RECOLLECTIONS OF GEOFFREY HAMLYN. N. Y., Ward & Lock, $1; Munro, paper, 25 c.
A good story of Australian life, containing some of the best descriptions ever written of the colony's early days.

THE HILLYARS AND THE BURTONS. N. Y., Ward & Lock, $1; Munro, paper, 25 c.

RAVENSHOE. N. Y., Ward & Lock, $1.

AUSTIN ELLIOT. N. Y., Ward & Lock, $1.

Kipling, Rudyard. [1865–.]

A great story-teller. The only Englishman equal to the best French and American writers of short tales and sketches. Whatever he writes is life itself. For tragedy and comedy, whether illustrated in action or character, his gift is remarkable. He may be said to have introduced India to Europe and America, and especially to have immortalized "Tommy Atkins," the British soldier. He has defects of manner and expression, assurance that touches impertinence, and frankness that reaches coarseness and brutality. A modification of such offences against taste is desirable, but they do not seriously impair the essential excellence of his work. His Indian stories have been published in many volumes. **823.89.**

The best collection is entitled :

INDIAN TALES: containing PLAIN TALES FROM THE HILLS, SOLDIERS THREE, THE PHANTOM 'RICKSHAW. N. Y., Lovell, Coryell, $1.50.

MANY INVENTIONS. N. Y., Appleton, $1.50. Short stories.

THE JUNGLE BOOK. N. Y., Century Co., $1.50.

Short stories of human beings and other animals, chiefly the other animals.

THE LIGHT THAT FAILED. N. Y., Macmillan, $1.50; Lovell, Coryell, $1; paper, 50 c.

A novel with some striking episodes; not so good as the short stories.

THE NAULAHKA. N. Y., Macmillan, $1.50; paper, 50 c.

A novel written in collaboration with Walcott Balestier. The scene is in India and the subject an intrigue to secure possession of a costly necklace. Some of it is admirable, but the whole lacks unity and sustained interest.

MINE OWN PEOPLE: DINAH SHADD, and other stories. N. Y., Lovell, Coryell, $1.

Keary, Annie Maria. [1825-1879.]

An Irish novelist whose tales display refined sentiment and close observation of interesting types. **823.89.**

CASTLE DALY. Phila., Porter & Coates, $1.50.

OLDBURY. Phila., Porter & Coates, $1.50.

THE NATIONS AROUND ISRAEL. N. Y., Macmillan, $1.25.
The scene is Palestine.

A YORK AND A LANCASHIRE ROSE. N. Y., Macmillan, $1.

Kirby, William. [1817-.]

A poet and novelist of English birth, long resident in Canada. His special field is Canadian historical and legendary lore. **813.40.**

THE GOLDEN DOG: A ROMANCE OF THE DAYS OF LOUIS QUATORZE IN QUEBEC. N. Y., Lovell, Coryell, $1.

An historical romance founded on a Quebec legend of the early days of the fur trade. The story, though somewhat long drawn out, is told with dramatic realism and strong local color.

Kirk, Mrs. Ellen Warner (Olney). [1842-.]

New England writer of novels and short stories. Without much of originality her work is entertaining and popular. **813.40.**

QUEEN MONEY. Bost., Houghton, $1.25; paper, 50 c.

Treats of the dearth in New York social life of features which attract the intellect and arouse emotion.

THE STORY OF MARGARET KENT. Bost., Houghton, $1.25; paper, 50 c.

A story of violent social contrasts, brisk in movement. It excites interest, but not an elevating interest.

CIPHERS. Bost., Houghton, $1.25; paper, 50 c.

Kirkland, Joseph. [1830-1894.]

ZURY: THE MEANEST MAN IN SPRING COUNTY. Bost., Houghton, $1.50; paper, 50 c.

A story of Illinois life in the early days. Realistic in portraiture; formless and undramatic in development.

THE MCVEYS. Bost., Houghton, $1.25.

Introduces many of the characters of "Zury" under gradually improving social conditions. **813.40.**

Laffan, May. (*See* Hartley.)

Lamb, Mary [1765-1847] and **Charles** [1775-1834].

MRS. LEICESTER'S SCHOOL. N.Y., Armstrong, $1.50.

This volume, written by the great English essayist and his sister, is addressed to children, but may well be enjoyed by older people, on account both of sweetness of thought and simple beauty of expression. **823.00.**

Lang, Andrew. [1844-.]

Scotch essayist, journalist, and writer of tales. With originality he combines large worldly experience and so much knowledge of ancient and modern literature that his work expresses both observation and literary cultivation. His contributions to fiction are not important; the best are in the form of adaptations of old fairy tales. **823.80.**

THE BLUE, GREEN, RED, AND YELLOW FAIRY BOOKS. N. Y., Longmans, 4 vols., each $2.

Laszowska, Mrs. Emily D. (Gerard) von.

THE WATERS OF HERCULES. Lond., Blackwood, 3s. 6d.; N. Y., Harper, paper, 25 c.

An excellent romantic novel. The scene is on the borders of Hungary and Roumania. The descriptions of country and people, little known to the Western world, are vivid and charmingly interwoven with ancient legend. The drama is well fitted to its setting. **823.80.**

THE LAND BEYOND THE FOREST. N. Y., Harper, $1.50.
Transylvania.

Lean, Mrs. Florence (Marryat). [1837-.]

English society novelist. Her sentiment is generally false and her representation extravagant. A transient distraction is the most that can be gained from her numerous shallow and silly books. **823.89.**

HOW LIKE A WOMAN. N. Y., Lovell, Coryell, $1; paper, 50 c.

THERE IS NO DEATH. N. Y., Lovell, Coryell, $1.

Lever, Charles. [1806-1872.]

The great Irish novelist. His delineation of his own countrymen equals in vividness, though perhaps not in variety, that of the Scotch people by Scott. His best novels describe military and romantic adventure and present in succession thrilling situations, amusing scrapes and blunders. Extravagant fun, reckless daring, and high spirits characterize his prominent figures. In his later days the spirit waned, but to the last he preserved in a degree his youthful mirth and wit. **823.80.**

CHARLES O'MALLEY. N. Y., Ward & Lock, $1; Burt, paper, 25 c.

The author's most famous novel. Brave, reckless, and gallant, both in love and war, the young Irish officer is typical of his race and class. Beside him stands Micky Free, the incarnation of Irish fun, fidelity, and capacity for blundering.

HARRY LORREQUER. N. Y., Ward & Lock, $1; Burt, 75 c.; Warne, paper, 20 c.

JACK HINTON, THE GUARDSMAN. N. Y., Ward & Lock, $1; Warne, paper, 20 c.

TOM BURKE OF OURS. N. Y., Ward & Lock, $1; Burt, 75 c.; Warne, paper, 20 c.

Lewes, *Mrs.* **G. H.** *See* Eliot, George.

Linton, *Mrs.* **Eliza (Lynn).** [1822-.]

English novelist and miscellaneous writer. She depicts contemporary English social and domestic life with a discussion of conspicuous movements and tendencies, political, social, and moral. Her novels are well put together and interesting. She has expended much satire on feminine morals and follies of two generations, and stands a barrier of conservatism against the new woman sighing for new worlds. Her work would be more useful had she more humor and less prejudice. **823.80.**

SOWING THE WIND. Lond., Chatto, 3s. 6d.; N. Y., Harper, paper, 25 c.

PATRICIA KEMBALL. Phila., Lippincott, $1.50.

THE WORLD WELL LOST. Phila., Lippincott, $1.25.

THROUGH THE LONG NIGHT. Lond., Hurst, 5s.; N. Y., Harper, paper, 25 c.

THE ONE TOO MANY. Chic., Neely, $1.25.

THE NEW WOMAN. Bost., Arena Pub. Co., $1.50.

The last two treat the questions of woman's rights and livelihoods.

Loughead, *Mrs.* **Flora Haines.**

THE ABANDONED CLAIM. Bost., Houghton, $1.25.

An entertaining story of a farming enterprise in California undertaken by some children. Besides the story there is useful practical detail of the work the children had to do. **813.40.**

THE MAN WHO WAS GUILTY. Bost., Houghton, $1.25.

Lover, Samuel. [1797-1868.]

Irish poet and novelist. As funny as Lever, his contemporary and compatriot, he was not so romantic or picturesque. His deep sympathy with his own people is expressed in all his verse and prose. He had little capacity for delineating any but the comic side of character, so his books are most enjoyable taken in fragments, and not all at once. **823.80.**

The most popular are:

HANDY ANDY. N. Y., Routledge, 80 c.; paper, 25 c.

RORY O'MORE. N. Y., Routledge, 80 c.; paper, 25 c.

IRISH STORIES AND LEGENDS. N. Y., Ward & Lock, 75 c.

Luska, Sidney (*pseudonym*). *See* Harland, Henry.

Lyall, Edna (*pseudonym for* Bayly, Ada Ellen).

Irish novelist. Her books have a serious, generally religious, motive, which is cleverly and thoughtfully developed. She writes a good, though long, story, and is especially able in drawing serious, amiable people. **823.80.**

IN THE GOLDEN DAYS. N. Y., Harper, 75 c.; Appleton, paper, 50 c.

A very good novel of the reign of Charles II. Conflicts in politics and religion are cleverly described and the drama is well constructed.

DONOVAN: A MODERN ENGLISHMAN. N. Y., Burt, 75 c.; Appleton, $1; paper, 50 c.

WE TWO. N. Y., Burt, 75 c.; Appleton, $1; paper, 50 c. A sequel to "Donovan."

The story and religious argument run closely together. There is too much of both, but they have to be taken together or not at all.

WON BY WAITING. N. Y., Appleton, $1; paper, 50 c.

DOREEN: The Story of a Singer. N. Y., Longmans, $1.50.

AUTOBIOGRAPHY OF A SLANDER. N. Y., Longmans, $1.50; Appleton, paper, 25 c.

Lytton, Edward George E. L. Bulwer-Lytton. *See* Bulwer-Lytton, E. G. E. L.

McCarthy, Justin. [1830-.]

Irish historian, novelist, and political writer. All his novels are entertaining. They generally involve a political intrigue, an Irish grievance, a love affair, and pictures of London society. The people are very much alike and of an interesting sort. **823.80.**

MY ENEMY'S DAUGHTER. Lond., Chatto, 3s. 6d.; N. Y., Harper, paper, 50 c.

The leading character is said to be drawn from George Henry Lewes, the husband of George Eliot.

PAUL MASSIE. N. Y., Munro, paper, 15 c.

THE WATERDALE NEIGHBOURS. Lond., Chatto, 3s. 6d.; N. Y., Harper, paper, 35 c.

THE DICTATOR. N. Y., Harper, $1.25.

A picture of modern London.

In collaboration with Mrs. Campbell-Praed, he has written two excellent novels with political life in London for theme:

THE LADIES' GALLERY. N. Y., Appleton, 75 c.; paper, 50 c.

THE RIGHT HONOURABLE. N. Y., Appleton, 75 c.; paper, 50 c.

McClelland, Margaret Greenway.

Southern novelist. Her scenes and characters are drawn in North Carolina chiefly, and the pictures of Southern life and manners are clustered around romantic and interesting plots. She is one of the best of the Southern writers impelled to fiction by the disasters of the Civil War, and by the great social changes which it brought about. **813.40.**

OBLIVION. N. Y., Lovell, Coryell, $1.

THE PRINCESS. N. Y., Lovell, Coryell, $1.

JEAN MONTEITH. N. Y., Lovell, Coryell, $1.

MADAME SILVA. N. Y., Cassell, 75 c.; paper, 50 c.

MacDonald, George. [1824–.]

Scotch novelist. His scenes are generally in Scotland and his people of humble condition. His own religious convictions and rare personality permeate his works; he is especially successful in depicting the religious and moral side of Scotch character. He observes natural scenery closely and describes it truthfully and poetically. With many good and strong points it cannot be denied that his work is, on the whole, a trifle dull. **823.80.**

HEATHER AND SNOW. N. Y., Harper, $1.25.

Begins in Scotland, then for a time shifts to India during the mutiny. The story of a good girl's influence on men and women.

ANNALS OF A QUIET NEIGHBOURHOOD. N. Y., Harper, $1.25; paper, 50 c.

ALEC FORBES OF HOWGLEN. N. Y., Routledge, $1.50.

WILFRID CUMBERMEDE. N. Y., Routledge, $1.50.

ROBERT FALCONER. N. Y., Routledge, $1.50.

Mackay, Marion ("Marie Corelli"). [1864–.]

An English novelist dealing in the supernatural and mystical in some of her stories. Her characters are well drawn, and she enjoys great popularity, especially in England, where the Queen is said to admire her works cordially. **823.89.**

VENDETTA. N. Y., Lovell, Coryell, 50 c.
Founded on the cholera of 1884 in Naples.

WORMWOOD: A DRAMA OF PARIS. N. Y., Lovell, Coryell, paper, 50 c.

THE SOUL OF LILITH. N. Y., Lovell, Coryell, $1.25; paper, 50 c.

A ROMANCE OF TWO WORLDS. N. Y., Lovell, Coryell, $1; paper, 50 c.

THELMA: A SOCIETY NOVEL. N. Y., Burt, 75 c.; Lovell, Coryell, $1; paper, 50 c.
Scene is chiefly Norway.

Maclaren, Ian (*pseudonym*). *See* Watson, John M.

Macquoid, Mrs. Katharine S. [1835–.]

English novelist. Her stories are simple and pleasantly narrated, her women being especially attractive. In descriptions of both England and France she shows nice observation of social life and natural scenery. **823.89.**

PATTY. Lond., Macmillan, 2s.; N. Y., Harper, paper, 50 c.

AT THE RED GLOVE. N. Y., Harper, $1.50; Munro, paper, 25 c.

FISHERMAN OF AUGE. N. Y., Appleton, paper, 20 c.

APPLEDORE FARM. Lovell, Coryell, $1; paper, 50 c.

BERRIS. N. Y., Lovell, Coryell, $1; paper, 50 c.

Malet, Lucas (*pseudonym*). *See* Harrison, Mrs. Mary.

Marryat, Florence. *See* Lean, Mrs. Florence.

Matthews, Brander. [1852–.]

A New York dramatist and writer of tales and essays. An accomplished writer of short stories, his incident pathetic, humorous, or fanciful, is vividly presented, and his cleverness in indication or suggestion of character gives great vitality to very slight sketches. His scenes and figures are generally American. **813.49.**

WITH MY FRIENDS. N. Y., Longmans, $1.

IN THE VESTIBULE LIMITED. N. Y., Harper, 50 c.

VIGNETTES OF MANHATTAN. N. Y., Harper, $1.50.

A FAMILY TREE. N. Y., Longmans, $1.25; paper, 50 c.
Short stories.

THE LAST MEETING. N. Y., Scribner, $1.

Maxwell, Mrs. Mary Elizabeth Braddon. [1837–.]

English novelist, probably the best known and most productive writer of purely sensational fiction; that is, fiction not much concerned with truth of characterization, dealing with the extraordinary, the exceptional, and appealing to curiosity. She has constructive ability and much versatility in devising plots. The interest is in what people do, not what they are; they are often immoral, but the author's intention is not vicious, and the worst that may be said of her books is that the impression of life conveyed by them is generally false. **823.89.**

LADY AUDLEY'S SECRET. N. Y., Lovell, Coryell, 50 c.; Munro, paper, 25 c.

One of the author's most popular works. A well-devised narrative of improbable and purposeless crime. It is well to begin Miss Braddon with this book, because the chances are that a person of sense and taste will want no more from her.

AURORA FLOYD. N. Y., Crowell, 75 c.; Munro, paper, 25 c.

ASPHODEL. Lond., Simpkin, 2s. 6d.; N. Y., Munro, paper, 25 c.; Harper, paper, 15 c.

FENTON'S QUEST. N. Y., Munro, paper, 25 c.

ELEANOR'S VICTORY. Lond., Simpkin, 2s. 6d.

TO THE BITTER END. Lond., Simpkin, 2s. 6d.; N. Y., Munro, paper, 25 c.

THE CHRISTMAS HIRELINGS. N. Y., Harper, $1.25.

Melville, Herman. [1819–1891.]

A New Yorker who went to sea early in life and founded his romances upon what he saw and felt through years of voyaging and adventure. In powers of description and weird imagination he is among the very first writers of sea stories. **813.36.**

TYPEE: A ROMANCE OF THE SOUTH SEAS.
N. Y., Lovell, Coryell, $1.50.
    So vividly depicted are the scenes of this romance that many of its readers at first believed it to be a statement of matter of fact.

OMOO: A SEQUEL TO TYPEE. N. Y., Lovell, Coryell, $1.50.
    The scene is still in the South Seas, but the author's imagination is now detected in its flights; the illusion of the reader vanishes.

WHITE JACKET; OR, THE WORLD IN A MAN-OF-WAR. N. Y., Lovell, Coryell, $1.50.
    A truthful and entertaining picture from life.

Meredith, George. [1828-.]
    English novelist. Opinion as to whether he is the greatest or poorest of English novelists is divided and posterity shall decide. He is certainly the hardest to understand. Whether it is worth while to struggle with his obscurity and artificial eccentricity is purely a matter of taste. If one has patience and some faculty for extracting ideas from apparently senseless verbiage, he may undoubtedly be read with profit. A powerful and passionate story and original investigations of human character may with pains and perseverance be discovered in his books. 823.89.

BEAUCHAMP'S CAREER. Bost., Roberts, $1.50; N. Y., Munro, paper, 25 c.
    The story of a valiant young aristocrat turned democrat.

DIANA OF THE CROSSWAYS. Bost., Roberts, $1.50.
    The author's most artistic story. Diana is said to be drawn from Sheridan's daughter, Caroline Norton.

THE EGOIST. Bost., Roberts, $1.50; N. Y., Burt, 75 c.
    An exhaustive study of selfishness, especially masculine selfishness. The character of Vernon Whitford is said to portray Leslie Stephen.

THE ORDEAL OF RICHARD FEVEREL. Bost., Roberts, $1.50.
    The story of a motherless boy reared by his father strictly according to theory. The outcome is tragic.

RHODA FLEMING. Bost., Roberts, $1.50; N. Y., Burt, 75 c.; Munro, paper, 25 c.
    The heroine's life-work is to right the wrong done her sister.

THE TALE OF CHLOE, and other stories. N. Y., Ward & Lock, $1.50.
    Good stories; their brevity serves as a capital restraint upon the author.

LORD ORMONT AND HIS AMINTA. N. Y., Scribner, $1.50.
    A story of wrong with labored and unsuccessful attempt at justification.

Miss Toosey's Mission and Laddie. Bost., Roberts, 50 c.
    Two anonymous stories of uncommon pathetic interest by an English writer. Miss Toosey devoted her life to the heathen at her own door. Laddie is a sad story; one of the few that really does intended good.

TIP CAT. By the same author. Bost., Roberts, $1.
    Recites how a manly young fellow struggled to support his two little sisters. An amusing story with less pathos than its predecessors.

Mitford, Mary Russell. [1786-1855.]
    English dramatist and writer of tales and sketches of early part of 19th century. 823.79.

OUR VILLAGE. N. Y., Macmillan, 2 vols., $2; Harper, paper, 25 c.
    In these sketches of rural life and scenery in Berkshire, Miss Mitford appears as a forerunner of the modern chroniclers of local character and scenery. The sketches are the fruit of observation rather than imagination, are graceful, mildly humorous, and thoroughly readable.

Mulock, D. M. See Craik, Mrs. D. M. M.

Murfree, Mary Noailles ("Charles Egbert Craddock"). [1850-.]
    Southern writer of novels and tales about the Tennessee mountains. Her short stories rank with Bret Harte's best, being vivid in incident, vigorous and distinct in characterization, splendidly picturesque. The mountaineers' dialect is not overdone, and, instead of disfiguring, completes their portraits. Her novels are weak in construction, and are principally valuable for detachable episodes and characters. 813.49.

IN THE TENNESSEE MOUNTAINS. Bost., Houghton, $1.25.
    Collection of tales, every one of which is a delightful addition to fiction.

THE PROPHET OF THE GREAT SMOKY MOUNTAINS. Bost., Houghton, $1.25.

WHERE THE BATTLE WAS FOUGHT. Bost., Houghton, $1.25.

THE DESPOT OF BROOMSEDGE COVE. Bost., Houghton, $1.25.

Murray, David Christie. [1847-.]
    English novelist and journalist. His novels are clever and the characters are all shown busy with the actual affairs of life and not abandoned to carrying on a romantic mystery, the plot, so-called, being frequently very commonplace. An excellent delineator of cosmopolitan life. 823.89.

THE WAY OF THE WORLD. Lond., Chatto, 3s. 6d.; N. Y., Harper, paper, 20 c.
    A clever novel, in which society journalism and journalists are satirized.

TIME'S REVENGES. N. Y., Harper, $1.25.

IN DIREST PERIL. N. Y., Harper, $1.25.

HE FELL AMONG THIEVES. N. Y., Macmillan, $1.25; Munro, paper, 25 c.
    In collaboration with Henry Herman.

Needell, *Mrs.* **John Hodder.**
    English novelist. Her stories are interesting and naturally developed. She is particularly clever in depicting those domestic tragedies which ensue from contact of uncongenial temperaments or trivial misunderstandings. 823.89.

LUCIA, HUGH AND ANOTHER. N. Y., Appleton, $1; paper, 50 c.

STEPHEN ELLICOTT'S DAUGHTER. N. Y., Appleton, $1; paper, 50 c.

PASSING THE LOVE OF WOMEN. N. Y., Appleton, $1; paper, 50 c.

THE VENGEANCE OF JAMES VANSITTART. N. Y., Appleton, $1; paper, 50 c.

Nicholls, *Mrs.* **Charlotte (B.).** *See* Brontë, Charlotte.

Norris, William Edward. [1847-.]

English novelist. His books have a large plan, thoughtfully worked out, and, in the catastrophe, generally illustrating the logic of character and circumstance without reference to poetic justice. His manner is especially easy and deliberate, and he talks about life like an accomplished philosopher in a satirical, but not unkindly, strain. He is decidedly one of the best and most agreeable of living writers of fiction. **823.80.**

MATRIMONY. Lond., Smith & Elder, 2s. 6d.; N. Y., Munro, paper, 25 c.

Probably the author's best work. The question of matrimony is discussed by illustration on various sides. The several groups are brought within the central interest, and yet move serenely in their own orbits. The style is noticeably finished and clever.

NO NEW THING. Lond., Smith & Elder, 3s. 6d.; N. Y., Munro, paper, 25 c.

HEAPS OF MONEY. N. Y., Lovell, Coryell, 75 c.; Munro, paper, 25 c.

MADEMOISELLE DE MERSAC. Lond., Smith & Elder, 2s. 6d.

THE COUNTESS RADNA. N. Y., Lovell, Coryell, $1; paper, 50 c.

HIS GRACE. N. Y., Lovell, Coryell, $1; paper, 50 c.

Oliphant, Laurence. [1829-1888.]

English novelist and general writer. As diplomatist, traveller, and man of letters, one of the remarkable Englishmen of his century. With a love of physical adventure, enjoying high social position, of sensitive spirituality, his life was uncommonly full of varied and interesting experience. In his later years he became a devoted spiritualist and wrote, as he believed, under spiritual influence two books of very mystical and incomprehensible Buddhistic philosophy. **823.89.**

His tendency to mysticism is shown in the novel:

ALTIORA PETO. Lond., W. Blackwood, 3s. 6d.; N. Y., Harper, paper, 25 c.

His earlier fiction has the impress of wide worldly experience and observation; it is entertaining and satirical, though less significant than when it first appeared:

PICCADILLY. Lond., W. Blackwood, 3s. 6.; N. Y., Harper, paper, 25 c.

TENDER RECOLLECTIONS OF IRENE MACGILLICUDDY. N. Y., Harper, paper, 15 c.

An amusing skit satirizing the exchange of American millions for foreign titles.

Oliphant, *Mrs.* **Margaret Oliphant (Wilson).** [1828-.]

Scotch novelist and miscellaneous writer. An indefatigable worker for nearly fifty years, her novels comprise a wide variety of English and Scotch domestic and social life. Many of her books are excellent, the story flowing on smoothly and the characters distinctly defined. Though she takes no pleasure in elaborating baseness and wickedness, she recognizes their existence and influence on destiny. Her works express a refined, broad, and sympathetic nature, and a sincere admiration for virtue struggling with adverse circumstances. **823.80.**

The Chronicles of Carlingford include

SALEM CHAPEL. N. Y., Munro, paper, 25 c.

The Same, with THE DOCTOR'S FAMILY. Lond., Blackwood, 3s. 6d.

THE PERPETUAL CURATE. N. Y., Munro, paper, 25 c.

The Same, with THE RECTOR. Lond., Blackwood, 3s. 6d.

MISS MARJORIBANKS. N. Y., Harper, paper, 50 c.

PHOEBE, JUNIOR. N. Y., Harper, paper, 35 c.

In these the author is at her best. The movement of the drama is slow but not tedious, and the characters are presented de iberately but without prolixity. The style is easy, adequate, and unaffected.

AGNES. N. Y., Harper, paper, 50 c.

JOHN. N. Y., Munro, paper, 25 c.

THE LAIRD OF NORLAW. Phila., Lippincott, $1.50.

WHITE LADIES. N. Y., Munro, paper, 25 c.

WHO WAS LOST AND IS FOUND. N. Y., Harper, $1.50.

CUCKOO IN THE NEST. N. Y., Lovell, Coryell, $1; paper, 50 c.

THE HEIR PRESUMPTIVE AND THE HEIR APPARENT. N. Y., Munro, paper, 25 c.

Orford, Horace Walpole, 4th Earl of. *See* Walpole, Horace.

Ouida. *See* De la Ramé.

Page, Thomas Nelson. [1853-.]

Southern writer of short stories. His tales collectively make an epic of the Civil War, narrating, under various names and in divers places, the adventures of the youthful Southerner who went forth seeking glory and victory and met defeat and death. Many of his tales are told in negro dialect, which is only occasionally incomprehensible. **813.49.**

ELSKET, and other stories. N. Y., Scribner, $1.

The other stories are of the Southern States and much better than the Norwegian Elsket's.

IN OLD VIRGINIA. N. Y., Scribner, $1.25.

ON NEWFOUND RIVER. N. Y., Scribner, $1.50.

MARSE CHAN. N. Y., Scribner, $1.50.

Parker, Gilbert. [1861-.]

Canadian writer of novels and tales. His presentation is vivid and modern, quite above any sentimental desire to conceal defect or palliate offensiveness. Therefore, though not always agreeable, he is generally striking. **813.40.**

PIERRE AND HIS PEOPLE. Chic., Stone & Kimball, $1.25.

Tales of Hudson Bay and the Canadian Northwest. Pierre is a detestable person well drawn. The incidents are natural in the region; scene and people are clearly represented.

THE TRAIL OF THE SWORD. N. Y., Appleton, $1; paper, 50 c.

An historical novel. The time is early in the 18th century and the scene in Canada. Admiral Phipps's disastrous attempt to capture Quebec is among the incidents. The plot is romantic and runs along very well, entailing numerous heroic exploits and exciting adventures.

MRS. FALCHION. N. Y., Home Pub. Co., $1; paper, 50 c.

THE TRANSLATION OF A SAVAGE. N. Y., Appleton, 75 c.

THE TRESPASSER. N. Y., Appleton, $1; paper, 50 c.

Parr, Mrs. Louisa (Taylor).

English novelist, historical and modern. She writes agreeably and sympathetically of interesting people, whether in the upper or lower classes. Many of her characters are seen struggling with moral temptations, and the desirability of self conquest is kept in view. 3.80.

ROBIN. N. Y., Munro, paper, 25 c.

LOYALTY GEORGE. N. Y., Munro, paper, 25 c.
A tale of Devonshire in the early part of the century; excellent for drama and character.

Payn, James. [1830-.]

English novelist and journalist. His novels with dramatic, but not very original plots, emphasizing the sunny and shady sides of English society, emphasizing most strongly the latter. The worldling's point of view is uppermost, but there is due appreciation of those who do right and live cleanly. Having written long, he do s not always write well; his earlier books are much bet er than his later. 823 89.

LOST SIR MASSINGBERD. Lond., Chatto, 3s. 6d.

A BEGGAR ON HORSEBACK. N. Y., Harper, 35 c.

LESS BLACK THAN WE'RE PAINTED. Lond., Chatto, 3s. 6d.; N. Y., Harper, paper, 35 c.

AT HER MERCY. Lond., Chatto, 2s.; N. Y., Harper, paper, 30 c.

FALLEN FORTUNES. Lond., Chatto, 2s.; N. Y., Appleton, 75 c.

WHAT HE COST HER. Lond., Chatto, 2s.; N. Y., Harper, paper, 40 c.

Peard, Frances Mary. [1835-.]

English novelist. Her chronicles of English life are fairly amusing, naturally and pleasantly written. 823.80.

MADEMOISELLE. Lond., Innes, 2s. 6d.
A very good story of the Franco-Prussian War, with descriptions of Paris during the siege.

AN INTERLOPER. N. Y., Harper, $1.25.
A story of life in France.

THE COUNTRY COUSIN. N. Y., Harper, paper, 40 c.

THE BARONESS. N. Y., Harper, paper, 50 c.

Pendleton, Louis.

IN THE WIRE GRASS. N. Y., Appleton, 75 c.; paper, 50 c.
A story of Southwestern life. With an interesting romance are combined very good descriptions of local scenes and manners. 813.40.

SONS OF HAM. Bost., Roberts, $1.
Written to show that the "color line" in society must remain.

KING TOM AND THE RUNAWAYS. N. Y., Appleton, $1.50.

THE WEDDING GARMENT: a Tale of the Life to Come. Bost., Roberts, $1.

Perry, Nora. [1841-.]

New England novelist. Her tales are neither very true to nature, nor very imaginative, but fairly descriptive of several kinds of sentimental young girls for whom they are written, and with whom they are popular. 813.40.

A FLOCK OF GIRLS. Bost., Houghton, $1.50.

A ROSEBUD GARDEN OF GIRLS. Bost., Little, Brown, $1.50.

Phelps, Elizabeth Stuart. See Ward, Mrs. E. S. P.

Poe, Edgar Allan. [1811-1849.]

Southern poet and writer of imaginative tales in middle period of 19th century. Splendidly and rather morbidly imaginative, he is unrivalled in his sphere by any American writer. He had a genius for form and emotionally impressive language. His best short tales excite intense horror, as much by the manner of narration as by the conception. The perfect expression of his genius and art is found in: 813.30.

TALES. N. Y., Ward & Lock, 75 c.

Pool, Maria Louise.

ROWENY IN BOSTON. N. Y., Harper, $1.25.
An amusing, rather satirical story about a young woman from the country who went to Boston to study art. Some very well observed types of rather foolish people are sketched. 813.40.

MRS. KEATS BRADFORD. N. Y., Harper, $1.25.
Sequel to "Roweny in Boston."

THE TWO SALOMES. N. Y., Harper, $1.25.
A strange story of a New England girl with two distinct natures, good and evil. According to her surroundings these natures by turns assert themselves.

OUT OF STEP. N. Y., Harper, $1.25.
Sequel to "The Two Salomes."

Porter, Jane. [1776-1850.]

THE SCOTTISH CHIEFS. N. Y., Appleton, $2.50; Ward & Lock, 75 c.; Warne, paper, 20 c.
Written in the early part of the 19th century, Miss Porter's so-called historical romances were more romantic than historical. In this novel the heroism of Sir William Wallace is the theme—pitched in a superlatively heroic key. Though the conception of character is purely imaginative and the style stilted, the narrative is conducted with spirit; the motive to inspire in the young admiration for the brave and the free is well sustained. 823.75.

THADDEUS OF WARSAW. Phila., Porter & Coates, 75 c.; N. Y., Warne, paper, 20 c.
The story of a teacher of languages, a Polish refugee.

Praed. Mrs. R. M. (Campbell). See under McCarthy, J., for novels written in collaboration.

Pyle, Howard. [1853-.]

Delaware artist and writer of tales. His stories of

romantic adventure are picturesque with plenty of exciting situation. **813.49.**

WITHIN THE CAPES. N. Y., Scribner, $1; paper, 50 c.

A MODERN ALADDIN. N. Y., Harper, $1.25.

THE ROSE OF PARADISE. N. Y., Harper, $1.25; paper, 50 c.

"Q" (*pseudonym*). See Couch, Arthur T. Q.

Radcliffe, *Mrs.* **Anne (Ward).** [1764-1823.]

English novelist of last period of 18th century. The most distinguished writer of prose fiction representing the great romantic reaction from the realistic school of her century. She founded a school which ripened and then rotted in the modern sensational novel. **823.60.**

THE MYSTERIES OF UDOLPHO. N. Y., Routledge, $1.25.

The best of the author's works and typical of all. Intensely serious and appealing to the passion of fear, both of physical peril and unknown supernatural dangers. The literary principle involved is of sustained mystery and suspense. The scene is in Paris towards the end of the 17th century; the general theme the woes of a matchless maiden brought about by the machinations of an unspeakable villain. Great use is made of gloomy scenery and awe-inspiring weather. The sliding panel, subterranean passage, and hideous family secret, remain with us to attest Mrs. Radcliffe's power of invention.

THE ROMANCE OF THE FOREST. N. Y., Routledge, $1.25.

Raymond, Walter (" Tom Cobbleigh ").

English writer of stories with local rural interest. He can be both serious and entertaining.

GENTLEMAN UPCOTT'S DAUGHTER. N. Y., Cassell, 50 c.

A story of the yeomanry and landed gentry of Somersetshire.

LOVE AND QUIET LIFE: Somerset Idylls. N. Y., Dodd, $1.25.

A story of the time immediately preceding the Oxford Tractarian movement. Religious prejudices and the local customs of Somersetshire are worked into the tale.

TRYPHENA IN LOVE. N. Y., Macmillan, 75 c.

The hero is a deformed boy to whom love revealed artistic talent, and who learned, by cultivating his mind, to forget his bodily misfortunes. A prose love idyl told with finish.

Reade, Charles. [1814-1884.]

English novelist of middle period of 19th century. He had always a good story to tell and frequently a public wrong to rage about. His action was swift, his detail profuse but necessary for accurate structure. He was hard, imperious, superficial, a little vulgar, but always vigorous and entertaining. He so detested the phrases that he adopted a rough, brusque style which frequently annoys but never bores. None of his books is dull and all are worth reading. **823.85.**

THE CLOISTER AND THE HEARTH. N. Y., Harper, 75 c.

A very good romantic, historical novel. By many critics considered the author's best book, it is an exception in thought, treatment, and style. The period immediately precedes the Reformation. Gerard, the hero, is supposed to be the father of Erasmus, the Reformer.

PEG WOFFINGTON, CHRISTIE JOHNSTONE, and other stories. N. Y., Harper, 75 c.

"Peg Woffington" is an excellent story of a versatile actress. The character is still a favorite on the stage.

IT IS NEVER TOO LATE TO MEND. N. Y., Harper, 75 c.

A famous novel including a severe criticism of English prison discipline, and adventures in quest of Australian gold.

VERY HARD CASH. N. Y., Harper, 75 c.

FOUL PLAY. (With Dion Boucicault.) N. Y., Harper, 75 c.; Munro, paper, 25 c.

GRIFFITH GAUNT. N. Y., Harper, 75 c.; Munro, 25 c.

PUT YOURSELF IN HIS PLACE. N. Y., Harper, 75 c.

A novel of uncommon interest dealing with tradeunionism.

LOVE ME LITTLE, LOVE ME LONG. N. Y., Harper, 75 c.

WORKS. Bost., DeWolfe, 16 vols., $12 and $24; N. Y., Harper, 7 vols., $7; 14 vols., $10 and $25.

Reid, Christian (*pseudonym*). See Tiernan, Mrs. Frances E. (Fisher).

Rice, James. *See under* Besant, W.

Richardson, Samuel. [1689-1761.]

English 18th century novelist. His only predecessor in the art of sentimental analysis was the Elizabethan, Sir Philip Sidney, whose " Arcadia " Richardson perhaps never read. His novels, written as letters, describe women in love, their mental agonies and joys, with all the innumerable intermediate stages thereof. They are wonderful performances but inexpressibly tedious. The sentiment is everything, the action nothing. The author's declared intention was to promote the love and practice of virtue. But on examination his idea of virtue appears restricted, a matter of form rather than of essence, and the results ascribed to its observance or neglect are quite remote from actual experience. He was worshipped by contemporary ladies of " sensibility "; his books had a marked influence both on English and French fiction. **823.61.**

CLARISSA HARLOWE. Abridged by Mrs. Ward. N. Y., Routledge, $1. Condensed by C. H. Jones. N. Y., Holt, $1; paper, 35 c.

A novel of middle-class life. Considered the author's best work. It has been translated into many languages.

PAMELA. Abridged by Mrs. Ward. N. Y., Routledge, $1.

Richardson's first novel. The story of a servant girl. Written to turn young people from the pomp and parade of romance-writing which prevailed at the time.

SIR CHARLES GRANDISON. Abridged by Mrs. Ward. N. Y., Routledge, $1.

A novel of high life. Richardson had been criticised for his heroes, and in this novel he tried to create a perfect man.

Ritchie, *Mrs.* **Anne Isabella (Thackeray).** [1838-.]

English novelist and miscellaneous writer. Her literary gift is much smaller than was that of her father, but, as far as it goes, of nice quality. Her work is not brilliant yet smooth and graceful, her stories are remembered less vividly than the delicate, pleasant manner of their telling. **823.80.**

MISS ANGEL. Lond., Smith & Elder, 6s.
A very interesting historical tale, founded on the romantic life of the artist, Angelica Kauffman.

THE VILLAGE ON THE CLIFF. Lond., Smith & Elder, 6s.
Tells of the siege of Paris and of the Commune.

OLD KENSINGTON. Lond., Smith & Elder, 6s.; N. Y., Harper, paper, 60 c.

DA CAPO. N. Y., Harper, paper, 20 c.

THE STORY OF ELIZABETH; TWO HOURS; FROM AN ISLAND. Lond., Smith & Elder, 6s

Rives, Amélie. *See* Chanler, Mrs. A. R.

Robinson, Frederick William. [1830-.]
English novelist. His plots include many varieties of crime, and the stock lost heirs, family secrets, and the like. The mysteries are well kept up, are generally not improbable, and move dramatically. The best characters and scenes are drawn from the lower middle class of London and the very poor; all his books are readable. **823.89.**

THE COURTING OF MARY SMITH. N. Y., Harper, paper, 20 c.
The story of the wooing of a girl of nineteen by an illiterate Lancashire cotton-spinner of fifty-five. Written with refreshing common sense.

POOR HUMANITY. Lond., Hutchinson, 2s. 6d.; N. Y., Harper, paper, 50 c.

SLAVES OF THE RING. Lond., Hutchinson, 2s. 6d.

STERN NECESSITY. N. Y., Harper, paper, 40 c.

SECOND COUSIN SARAH. N. Y., Harper, paper, 50 c,

CHRISTIE'S FAITH. N. Y., Harper, $1.75.

Roche, Regina Maria. [1765-1845.]

THE CHILDREN OF THE ABBEY. N. Y., Routledge, $1; Warne, paper, 20 c.
Written by an Englishwoman and first published in 1796. Rather a famous example of the end of the 18th century romantic school founded by Mrs. Radcliffe. Extremely sentimental, mysterious, and improbable, but with interest well sustained and much sympathy, at high pressure, with virtue in distress. **823.79.**

Roe, Edward Payson. [1838-1888.]
New York novelist. It is said that he wished to wean Americans from their morbid interest in the corrupt British aristocracy as shown by their appetite for fiction devoted to that class, so he wrote tales supposed to represent the doings of virtuous republicans. This was a good and patriotic motive and so far successful that he became our most popular novelist. It cannot, however, be said that his popularity is complimentary to the literary taste of America. His books are so unnatural, so false to character and fact, so full of cant and bad English, that they offer a melancholy illustration of a cure that is worse than the disease. **813.40.**

BARRIERS BURNED AWAY. N. Y., Dodd, 40 c. and $1.50.

THE OPENING OF A CHESTNUT BURR. N. Y., Dodd, 40 c. and $1.50; paper, 50 c.

AN ORIGINAL BELLE. N. Y., Dodd, $1.50; paper, 25 c.

Rohlfs, Anna Katharine (Green). [1846-.]
New York novelist. She revels in elaborate mystery and crime, and shows decided ingenuity. She scorns probability both in plot and character, and, to persons of reason, her books are tiresome and nonsensical. From her popularity it would appear that reason is scarce and that what is most desired by many novel-readers is mental distraction pure and simple. **813.40.**

THE LEAVENWORTH CASE. N. Y., Putnam, $1; paper, 50 c.
Her best story.

A STRANGE DISAPPEARANCE. N. Y., Putnam, $1; paper, 50 c.

THE MILL MYSTERY. N. Y., Putnam, $1; paper, 50 c.

A MATTER OF MILLIONS. N. Y., Bonner, $1.50; paper, 50 c.

Russell, William Clark. [1844-.]
English novelist. His sea tales combine romantic imagination and actual experience. They are well told and abound in thrilling adventures. He has or late years repeated himself again and again. **823 80.**

THE WRECK OF THE GROSVENOR. N. Y., Burt, 75 c.; Lovell, Coryell, $1 25; paper, 50 c.
A capital story, probably the author's best.

LIST, YE LANDSMEN! N. Y., Cassell, $1.
Every chapter has a sensation of its own.

MYSTERY OF THE OCEAN STAR. N. Y., Appleton, 75c.; paper, 50 c.

THE EMIGRANT SHIP. N. Y., Cassell, $1.

THE ROMANCE OF A TRANSPORT. N. Y., Cassell, $1.

Rutherford, Mark. *See* White, W. Hale.

Sartoris, Mrs. Adelaide Kemble. [1814-1879.]

A WEEK IN A FRENCH COUNTRY HOUSE. Lond., Smith & Elder, 8s. 6d.; N. Y., Munro, paper, 20 c.
A charming story of which the title is descriptive, written with rare grace and fine sentiment. **823.80.**

Schreiner, Olive ("Ralph Iron"). [1863-.]
A South African author, the daughter of a Lutheran clergyman at Cape Town. **823.80.**

THE STORY OF AN AFRICAN FARM. N. Y., Lovell, Coryell, 50 c.; Munro, paper, 25 c.
The scene is ugly and dreary and the thought pessimistic; nevertheless the book appeals strongly both to intelligence and imagination. It is the expression of a mind grappling the deepest problems of life, and arriving at conclusions interesting but wrong, drawn not from wide observation but from a morbid inner consciousness.

DREAM LIFE AND REAL LIFE. Bost., Roberts, 60 c.

Three short stories. The first, a painful little tragedy of South Africa; the other two illustrating the magnanimity of two women.

DREAMS. Bost., Roberts, 60 c.

Scott, Michael. [1789-1835.]

A Scotchman who dwelt for some time in Jamaica and who diversified his life as a man of business by many voyages. He knew the sea in all its phases as have very few writers of sea stories. 823.79.

TOM CRINGLE'S LOG. N. Y., Routledge, 80 c.; Warne, paper, 20 c.

A West Indian tale of the sea: a classic.

THE CRUISE OF THE MIDGE. N. Y., Routledge, 80 c.; Warne, paper, 20 c.

Scott, Sir Walter. [1771-1832.]

Scotch novelist. Chief among writers of prose fiction in English, and, if greatness may be measured by the amount of happiness given to humanity, one of the greatest and best of men. For nearly seventy years his novels have delighted millions of people of every civilized country and his popularity does not wane. To the young he is especially charming, and if it is well to implant in children admiration for the noblest virtues, courage physical and moral, truth, loyalty and purity of life, his books are the very best that can be given to them. He wrote with 18th century realism and romanticism, and, by a remarkable balance of qualities, gave the combination unity and poetry. In greatness of heart, sympathy, and versatility, he is own brother to Shakespeare. His novels are all historical, but some only in the sense of depicting bygone social life and manners. In characterization he laid stress on essential, eternal human qualities, and thus his people are antiquated only in unimportant matters of speech and manners. 823.73.

WAVERLEY. N. Y., Macmillan, 40 c. and $1.25; paper, 25 c.

Turns on the rising of the Clans for Prince Charlie in 1745, their victories, and defeat at Culloden.

GUY MANNERING. N. Y., Macmillan, 40 c. and $1.25; paper, 25 c.

Scotland is the scene. Smugglers, gypsies, and other social outlaws fill the canvass. Here appears "Meg Merrilies."

THE ANTIQUARY. N. Y., Macmillan, 40 c. and $1.25; paper, 25 c.

Depicts life in a little Scottish fishing village at the close of the 18th century.

ROB ROY. N. Y., Macmillan, 40 c. and $1.25; paper, 25 c.

Portrays with evident sympathy the career of the Robin Hood of Scotland.

OLD MORTALITY. N. Y., Macmillan, 40 c. and $1.25; paper, 25 c.

A picture gallery of the Covenanters.

HEART OF MIDLOTHIAN. N. Y., Macmillan, 40 c. and $1.25; paper, 25 c.

Tells the affecting story of Jeanie and Effie Deans.

THE BRIDE OF LAMMERMOOR. N. Y., Macmillan, 40 c. and $1.25; paper, 25 c.

A tragic and fateful story in Scott's most elevated key. Relieved by touches of truest humor.

IVANHOE. Macmillan, 40 c. and $1.25; paper, 25 c.

Time of Richard I. of England. Normans and Saxons are shown in conflict.

KENILWORTH. N. Y., Macmillan, 40 c. and $1.25; paper, 25 c.

Time of Elizabeth. The ill-starred Lord Leicester moves through the scene.

QUENTIN DURWARD. N. Y., Macmillan, 40 c. and $1.25; paper, 25 c.

France in the time of Louis XI; his power, cunning, and superstition are vividly presented.

FORTUNES OF NIGEL. N. Y., Macmillan, 40 c. and $1.25; paper, 25 c.

London in the reign of James I.

THE TALISMAN. N. Y., Macmillan, 40 c. and $1.25; paper, 25 c.

Pa'estine in the days of Richard I. of England.

THE WAVERLEY NOVELS, all Scott's fiction. N. Y., Appleton, 6 vols., $6, $10, $15; Harper, 24 vols., $30, $48, $72; Macmillan, 25 vols., $10, $15, $20, $30; paper, $6.25; also in 12 vols., $17.50.

Seawell, Molly Elliot.

Southern novelist and historical writer. She describes life in the Southern States pleasantly and with evident knowledge of place and character. 813.40.

THROCKMORTON. N. Y., Appleton, $1; paper, 50 c.

Scene, a lowland Virginia neighborhood; time, immediately after the Civil War.

MAID MARIAN. N. Y., Appleton, $1; paper, 50 c.

Short stories.

THE BERKELEYS AND THEIR NEIGHBORS. N. Y., Appleton, $1; paper, 50 c.

Virginia families. Some of the members finally drift to Washington.

CHILDREN OF DESTINY. N. Y., Appleton, $1; paper, 50 c.

A picture of luxurious living in the South fifty years ago.

Sergeant, Adeline.

English novelist. She relies a little too much on plot, yet generally manages to construct a pretty good one. Her scenes are in divers countries, and her characters, not too deeply sounded, are interesting and agreeable. 823.89.

BEYOND RECALL. N. Y., Munro, paper, 25 c.

A very good novel about English people in Egypt. The pictures of social life are graphic, including both natives and foreigners.

CHRISTINE. N. Y., Tait, $1; paper, 50 c.

The scene is Egypt. The people move in English military circles.

THE SURRENDER OF MARGARET BELLARMINE. N. Y., International News Co., $1.25; paper, 50 c.

A story of religious doubts and the return of an intellectual woman to orthodox faith.

NAME AND FAME. N. Y., Munro, paper, 25 c.

Written in collaboration with A. S. Ewing Lester. The original hero is said to be drawn from George Henry Lewes, husband of George Eliot.

Shaw, Flora L.

HECTOR. Bost., Roberts, $1; N. Y., Macmillan, paper, 35 c.
　The story of an English orphan living in France, told by his Cousin Zélie. The narrative is simple and natural and the description of scene delicate and clear. **823.80.**

CASTLE BLAIR. Bost., Roberts, $1.
　The scene is in Ireland. Wild and riotous young people are subdued by a young girl in a delightful way.

COLONEL CHESWICK'S CAMPAIGN. Bost., Roberts, $1.25.

A SEA CHANGE. Bost., Roberts, $1; N. Y., Munro, paper, 20 c.

Shelley, *Mrs.* Mary Godwin. [1798-1851.]

FRANKENSTEIN. N. Y., Routledge, 40 c.; paper, 25 c.
　In 1816 the poets Byron and Shelley and Mrs. Shelley were living in Switzerland, and, inspired by German myths, all three wrote divers tales of horror. Of these Mrs. Shelley's "Frankenstein" was the most successful. Frankenstein creates a being formed like a man, a giant of strength, a demon of evil. The impossibility of many incidents is often evident, but the whole is powerfully imagined and excites prolonged, genuine terror. **823.79.**

Shorthouse, John Henry. [1834-.]
　English novelist, historical and modern. He discusses questions of faith and has a strong tendency towards an æsthetic mysticism. In style and thought he is always a touch above common mortals. **823.80.**

JOHN INGLESANT. N. Y., Macmillan, $1.
　The author's best and best-known book—one of the most striking novels in the English language. The scene is in the reign of Charles I., and the differences of religious opinion in the Roman Catholic Church are cleverly set forth. The romance is interesting and the historical painting vivid.

SIR PERCIVAL. N. Y., Macmillan, $1; Munro, paper, 25 c.

THE COUNTESS EVE. N. Y., Macmillan, $1; Harper, paper, 25 c.

BLANCHE LADY FALAISE. N. Y., Macmillan, $1.

A TEACHER OF THE VIOLIN. N. Y., Macmillan, $1.
　Short stories.

Slick, Sam (*pseudonym*). *See* Haliburton, T. C.

Smith, Francis Hopkinson. [1838-.]
　Southern civil engineer, artist, and writer of tales. His stories are brilliant, amusing, and artistic. **813 49.**

COLONEL CARTER OF CARTERSVILLE. Bost., Houghton, $1.25.
　The Colonel is a very vivid presentation, and, allowing for a little dramatic exaggeration, typical of his time and Southern latitude.

A DAY AT LAGUERRE'S, AND OTHER DAYS. Bost., Houghton, $1.25.
　Nine admirable short impressions of scenes and men in Mexico and other places.

Southworth, *Mrs.* Emma Dorothy Eliza (Nevitte). [1818-.]
　She has perpetrated about fifty novels, devoted chiefly to the narration of various crimes and the contrasting of hideous villains with patterns of virtue. Her distortion of truth and fact is wonderful, and her sentimental appalling. Nevertheless, her books continue to be devoured by a reading public which would doubtless be wiser and more sensible if it had never learned how to read. **813.40.**
　Among her most popular and worthless stories are:

NEAREST AND DEAREST. N. Y., Bonner, $1.

A LEAP IN THE DARK. N. Y., Bonner, $1; paper, 50 c.

THE MISSING BRIDE. N. Y., Ivers, paper, 25 c.

THE LOST HEIRESS. N. Y., Ivers, paper, 25 c.

Spofford, *Mrs.* Harriet Elizabeth (Prescott). [1835-.]
　New England novelist. Her plots are very good, but her characters are generally improbable, and she revels in depicting material luxury. Excepting in some short stories she quite fails to create an illusion of probability, much less of reality. **813.40.**

HESTER STANLEY AT ST. MARK'S. Bost., Roberts, $1.25.
　A probable school-girl's story, fairly natural.

A SCARLET POPPY. N. Y., Harper, $1.25.
　Short stories.

THE MARQUIS OF CARABAS. Bost., Roberts, $1.

Stannard, *Mrs.* Henrietta Eliza Vaughan (Palmer) ("John Strange Winter"). [1856-.]
　English writer of tales of military life. Her heroes are seen in peace, not in war, and are good-natured and muscular, not specially intelligent. **823.80.**
　Her best story is

BOOTLE'S BABY. N. Y., Munro, paper, 25 c.
　Touches natural emotions rather deftly.

ARMY TALES. N. Y., Lovell, Coryell, $1.
　This includes "Bootle's Baby."

THE EXPERIENCES OF A LADY HELP. N. Y., Lovell, Coryell, $1; paper, 50 c.
　A tale of a governess's life, related with much vivacity.

HOUP LA! N. Y., Harper, 25 c.

Steel, *Mrs.* Flora Annie.
　Anglo-Indian writer of novels and tales. Her pictures of native life are very varied, effective, and sincere. Her novels are interesting with dramatic situations, but defective in construction. **823 80.**

THE FLOWER OF FORGIVENESS. N. Y., Macmillan, $1.
　Short stories.

MISS STEWART'S LEGACY. N. Y., Macmillan, $1; paper, 50 c.

THE POTTER'S THUMB. N. Y., Harper, $1.50.

Stephenson, Eliza (Tabor).
　An English writer whose tales have, as a rule, appeared anonymously. She describes, with insight, the uneventful lives of secluded people.

EGLANTINE. N. Y., Harper, paper, 40 c.

THE LAST OF HER LINE. N. Y., Harper, paper, 15 c.

META'S FAITH. N. Y., Harper, paper, 35 c.

Stevenson, Robert Louis (Balfour). [1850-1894.]

Scotch novelist, historical and modern. He combined with extraordinary skill romantic adventure and psychical analysis. In most of his work the interests of direct sustained narrative and of the conflict between good and evil are indissolubly linked together. His style is imaginative, elevated, and discreetly restrained. It has the personal charm, impressiveness, and distinction which give classic dignity. Considering the progress toward perfection discernible in his works, had he lived longer, he would probably have ranked with the very greatest writers of fiction. Love plays but a subordinate part in his romances, and he has drawn the portraits of very few women. 823.89.

KIDNAPPED. N. Y., Scribner, $1.50; (with "Treasure Island" and "Dr. Jekyll," Harper, paper, 20 c.); and sequel, DAVID BALFOUR, N. Y., Scribner, $1.50.

The action is chiefly in Scotland shortly after the rising in support of Prince Charlie in 1745. The stories are told by David Balfour, a Lowlander and a Whig, through whose mouth the author manages very adroitly to excite sympathy with the Stuarts and their Highland followers. No better stories at once romantic and real were ever written.

TREASURE ISLAND. Bost., Roberts, $1; paper, 50 c.; with "Kidnapped" and "Dr. Jekyll," Harper, paper, 20 c.

THE MASTER OF BALLANTRAE. N. Y., Scribner, $1.50; paper, 50 c.

STRANGE CASE OF DR. JEKYLL AND MR. HYDE. N. Y., Scribner, $1; paper 25 c.

NEW ARABIAN NIGHTS. N. Y., Scribner, $1; paper, 50 c.

Short stories of the highest merit.

Several of Mr. Stevenson's later books were written in collaboration with his stepson, Mr. Lloyd Osbourne, and narrate adventures in the South Seas. These are neither as interesting nor artistic as the stories by Mr. Stevenson alone:

The WRECKER. N. Y., Scribner, $1.50.

The opening chapters, descriptive of artists' life in Paris, are interesting for their own sake, but do not prepare the reader for the wild adventures, commercial and romantic, which follow. The climax of the story is brutal, but absolutely demanded to cut the complicated knot of circumstance.

THE EBB TIDE. Chic., Stone & Kimball, $1.25.

Illustrates Mr. Stevenson's dominating motives, narration of adventure, and interpretation of character subjected to extraordinary temptations. There are chapters written in Mr. Stevenson's very best manner.

Stockton, Francis Richard. [1834-.]

A Philadelphian. His stories, even when they narrate incidents of actual life, are tinged with the fanciful and grotesque. His strength is in pure invention of an impossible situation, which he proceeds with great gravity and delightful humor to make appear probable. He is pre-eminently original and amusing in short stories, while his deliberately planned novels are feeble and uninteresting. 813.40.

RUDDER GRANGE. N. Y., Scribner, $1.25; paper, 60 c.

THE CASTING AWAY OF MRS. LECKS AND MRS. ALESHINE; and its sequel, THE DUSANTES. N. Y., Century Co., $1.

THE LADY OR THE TIGER, and other stories. N. Y., Scribner, $1.25; paper, 50 c.

THE CHRISTMAS WRECK, and other stories. N. Y., Scribner, $1.25; paper, 50 c.

THE BEE-MAN OF ORN. N. Y., Scribner, $1.25.
Short stories.

THE ADVENTURES OF CAPTAIN HORN. N. Y., Scribner, $1.50.

Stowe, Mrs. Harriet Elizabeth (Beecher). [1812-.]

New England novelist. She observed character keenly and with much humor. Her stories and sketches of New England life, forty or fifty years ago, appear to be perfectly true and preserve pictures of customs and types of mind that have passed away. 813.37.

Her reputation was made by and will probably rest upon

UNCLE TOM'S CABIN. Bost., Houghton, 50 c. and $1; paper, 25 c. and 50 c.

This is one of the most famous of "timely" books. It was not half true, it was written with passion and prejudice and it accomplished what all the cool, judicial statements in the world would have failed in. To this day there are probably people who derive from Mrs. Stowe's highly imaginative presentation their only notions of slavery days in the South. It is impossible to separate the fictitious case from the actual, but since the passionate antagonisms of that time have been long dead and the fiction still survives, it is fair to assume that the book has vital qualities all its own.

OLD TOWN FOLKS. Bost., Houghton, $1.50.
SAM LAWSON'S FIRESIDE STORIES. Bost., Houghton, $1.50.
Excellent sketches of primitive Yankee life.

THE MINISTER'S WOOING. Bost., Houghton, $1.50; paper, 50 c.

MY WIFE AND I. Bost., Houghton, $1.50.

WE AND OUR NEIGHBORS. Sequel to "My Wife and I." Bost., Houghton, $1.50.

Stuart, Mrs. Ruth McEnnery.

Southern writer of short tales. The scenes and characters are Southern, the negro figuring prominently. The tales are clearly conceived and effective. 813.40.

THE GOLDEN WEDDING. N.Y., Harper, $1.50.
Short stories.

CARLOTTA'S INTENDED. N.Y., Harper, $1.50.
Short stories.

THE STORY OF BABETTE. N. Y., Harper, $1.50.
New Orleans life, with description of the Mardi Gras festivities.

Sturgis, Julian Russell. [1848-.]

English barrister and novelist. His stories are generally of English life in English scenes. He is particularly clever in drawing young men starting in life with fine ambitions and finding their way to success or failure, according to strength or weakness of character. 813.49.

AFTER TWENTY YEARS. N. Y., Longmans, $1.
Short stories of English life.

JOHN MAIDMENT. N. Y., Appleton, 75 c.; paper, 50 c.

DICK'S WANDERINGS. N. Y., Appleton, 75 c.; paper, 50 c.

JOHN-A-DREAMS. N. Y., Appleton, paper, 25 c.

AN ACCOMPLISHED GENTLEMAN. N. Y., Appleton, 60 c.; paper, 25 c.

Sullivan, James W. [1848–.]

A Pennsylvanian living in New York; journalist and trades-union leader. A lengthy sojourn in Switzerland has made him an untiring advocate of Swiss political methods for America. His short stories are his best literary work; they are singularly terse and convincing. For the most part they describe phases of cosmopolitan life in New York, and give a painful echo to the stress of its hardships. **813.49.**

TENEMENT TALES OF NEW YORK. N. Y., Holt, 75 c.
This little book is a series of miniatures painted in abodes of poverty. Touches of fun and mischief lighten up the prevailing sadness.

Swift, Jonathan. [1667–1745.]

GULLIVER'S TRAVELS. N. Y., Crowell, 75 c.; Routledge, $1; paper, 25 c. Edited and adapted for use in schools by Thos. Parry. N. Y., Longmans, 30 c.
The irony of destiny in the case of Swift is in nothing more conspicuous than in the spectacle of his savage political and social satire surviving, far into its second century, as an entertaining extravagance much enjoyed by children. Assuming absurdities, Swift proceeds to make them real by his own perfect gravity, and by the minuteness of detail which gives verisimilitude to the central enormity. **823.5.**

Tautphœus, Jemima (Montgomery) *Baroness.* [1807–1893.]

English novelist of middle period of 19th century. Her books are made up of pictures of English social life and romantic adventure in Germany. They are long, very proper, sentimental, and still popular. **823.89.**

QUITS. Phila., Lippincott, $1.50; N. Y., Westermann, (Tauchnitz), 2 vols., paper, 50 c. each.
Life in southern Germany. A travelling Englishman is the hero.

INITIALS. N. Y., Scribner, $1.50; Westermann, (Tauchnitz), 2 vols., paper, 50 c. each.
Student life in Munich.

AT ODDS. Phila., Lippincott, $1.50; N. Y., Westermann, (Tauchnitz), 2 vols., paper, 50 c. each.
The scene is the Tyrol. The German nobility is well characterized.

Taylor, Bayard. [1825–1878.]

Pennsylvanian poet, writer of fiction and travels. His novels are the least significant of his literary productions, yet they are interesting, suggestive, and abound in fine ideas and good descriptions of American scenery. **813.30.**

HANNAH THURSTON. N. Y., Putnam, $1.50; paper, 50 c.
Written just when the woman with large ideas about humanity and "rights" made her first appearance. The title character is interesting but goes to pieces in a commonplace way at the end.

JOSEPH AND HIS FRIENDS. N. Y., Putnam, $1.50.
A story of Pennsylvania.

JOHN GODFREY'S FORTUNES. N. Y., Putnam, $1.50.
A Pennsylvania country boy enters New York literary circles.

STORY OF KENNETT. N. Y., Putnam, $1.50.
A story of country life in a Pennsylvania town at the end of the last century.

Terhune, *Mrs.* **Mary Virginia (Hawes)** ("Marion Harland"). [1830–.]

Southern novelist and writer on household economy. Her stories are romantic and sentimental, chiefly concerned with joys and sorrows of young people in love and full of good intention. Her tales bring in a good deal of her thought as to the training of girls and the ordering of households. **813.19.**

HIS GREAT SELF. Phila., Lippincott, $1.25.
Scene, Virginia, a century and a half ago.

THE HIDDEN PATH. N. Y., G. W. Dillingham, $1.50.

ALONE. N. Y., G. W. Dillingham, $1.50.

MIRIAM. N. Y., G. W. Dillingham, $1.50.

Thackeray, Anne. *See* Ritchie, Anne T.

Thackeray, William Makepeace. [1811–1863.]

English novelist of middle period of 19th century. The legitimate successor of Henry Fielding, in his books realism presents a different aspect reflecting the changed spirit and taste of his time and his own high-bred personality. His satire is as keen as Fielding's, yet more delicate; his imagination freer, and his criticism of life ennobled by a permanent regard for ideal beauty in conduct. Like Fielding, he deals broadly with life, and his views express wisdom, beauty, and truth. Though his constructive ability has been questioned, a close examination shows great skill in grouping a large number and variety of characters, and a just distinction between dramatic and theatrical effect. His style is uniformly fine and frequently magnificent. Almost without reference to the matter, the manner interests the intelligence, charms the imagination, and touches the emotions. In characterization he failed to make his good women interesting, but there is no historical evidence to show that good English women of his day were not a trifle namby-pamby.

THE HISTORY OF HENRY ESMOND. Phila., Lippincott, $1.25; N. Y., Harper, paper, 20 c.
By many critics considered Thackeray's best novel. The plot is more sustained and interest more concentrated than in the others. The story is founded on the connection of a noble English family with the fallen fortunes of the Stuarts. The pictures of life in the Queen Anne period are unsurpassed for vividness and charm. The style illustrates the finest possibilities of imaginative prose. Beatrix Esmond is perhaps the most brilliant and fascinating woman in English fiction. The fortunes of the Esmonds are continued in

THE VIRGINIANS. Phila., Lippincott, $1.25; N. Y., Munro, paper, 2 vols., each 25 c.
Like most sequels to famous novels this is inferior,

nevertheless, it is unmistakably the work of a master. Most of the action takes place in Virginia. The story is told in the language of the time—that of Addison and Steele.

VANITY FAIR. Phila., Lippincott, $1.25; N. Y., Munro, paper, 25 c.

Thackeray's first novel. The most remorseless in truthful development of character and in social satire. Extraordinary power in portraiture and reflection are obvious in every page. Becky Sharp will stand for all time as the type of a woman of brains without heart. Amelia Sedley of a woman of heart without brains.

THE NEWCOMES. Phila., Lippincott, $1.25; N. Y., Harper, paper, 90 c.; Munro, paper, 25 c.

A novel of English life in the early part of the 19th century. Never did an author create a nobler gentleman than Colonel Newcome.

THE HISTORY OF PENDENNIS. Phila., Lippincott, $1.25; N. Y., Harper, paper, 75 c.; Munro, 2 vols., 25 c. each.

A very great novel, largely autobiographical. It portrays the mishaps in love and otherwise of a young man with decided streaks of selfishness and folly in him. His friend, George Warrington, noble and true, is one of Thackeray's finest creations. He is manly, kind, and unfortunate. Mr. and Miss Costigan figure inimitably in the story.

WORKS, including the foregoing with "The Adventures of Philip" and "Lovel, the Widower." N. Y., Harper, 6 vols., $7.50; Bost., Houghton, 6 vols., $7.50.

COMPLETE WORKS. Bost., Houghton, 22 vols., $33 and upwards. This edition includes 2 vols. not hitherto collected in any other edition. Lippincott, Phila., publishes editions of Thackeray in great variety, from $13.50 upwards.

Thanet, Octave (*pseudonym*). *See* French, Alice.

Tiernan, Mrs. Frances C. ("Christian Reid").

Southern novelist. She is not attached to any locality, but places a group of commonplace people in America or Europe, involves some of them in love affairs, and permits the rest to look on. Her ideals are conventional and correct in morals. **813.40**.

BONNY KATE. N. Y., Appleton, $1.25; paper, 75 c.

HEARTS AND HANDS. N. Y., Appleton, paper, 75 c.

VALERIE AYLMER. N. Y., Appleton, $1.25; paper, 75 c.

MISS CHURCHILL. N. Y., Appleton, $1.50; paper, 50 c.

Tincker, Mary Agnes. [1833–.]

Novelist of New England birth, long resident in Italy. Her plots are romantic and not very fresh, but the interest is fairly well kept up, and, in all the characters, original points are made. The scenes are in America and Europe. Her convictions as a Roman Catholic give distinct color to her work. **813.40**

SAN SALVADOR. Bost., Houghton, $1.25.

San Salvador is a Utopian community, where a young Venetian girl finds peace and rest.

THE HOUSE OF YORKE. N. Y., Catholic Pub. Soc., $1.50.

BY THE TIBER. Bost., Roberts, $1.50.

SIGNOR MONALDINI'S NIECE. Bost., Roberts, $1.

Tourgee, Albion Winegar. [1838–.]

The best part of his novels is the way he sets forth his purpose, which is to describe the social condition of the South in the Reconstruction period, subsequent to the Civil War. By many men of different political faiths his observations are pronounced correct and his opinions judicious. **813.40.**

His best-known books are:

A FOOL'S ERRAND and THE INVISIBLE EMPIRE. N. Y., Fords, $1.50.

The experience of a Federal officer who went South after the war and lived there fifteen years. A picture of the "carpet bagger" period vividly painted; the Ku Klux Klan is incidentally described.

BRICKS WITHOUT STRAW. N. Y., Fords, $1.50; paper, 50 c.

A political novel of the South, treating broadly various social conditions resulting from slavery.

BUTTON'S INN. Bost., Roberts, $1.25.

Describes Mormonism as it was.

PACTOLUS PRIME. N. Y., Cassell, $1.

Hero a bootblack in a hotel in Washington. Senators, doctors, lawyers, and judges are his customers, and he discusses with them aspects of the negro question.

Townsend, Virginia Frances. [1836–.]

New England novelist and writer of tales. Occasionally her sketches of American character are pointed and original, but her stories, on the whole, are commonplace and not true to nature. **813.40**.

THE HOLLANDS. Bost., Lee & S., $1.

THE MILLS OF TUXBURY. Bost., Lee & S., $1.

LENOX DARE. Bost., Lee & S., $1.50.

BUT A PHILISTINE. Bost., Lee & S., $1.50.

Trollope, Anthony. [1815–1882.]

English novelist of middle period of 19th century. His people belong to the upper middle-class and aristocracy. Whether clergymen, politicians, hunting squires, positive autocratic dames, or amiable, rather colorless damsels, they have the stamp of life itself. His distinguished merit was in showing the whole every-day life of his people and their interdependence. His defect a lack of sentiment, a tendency to linger on the practical and to extol the idea of getting on in life—doing well for oneself. Still (as in the beautiful character of the Warden) he shows himself appreciative of spirituality and self-sacrifice. His manner is singularly downright; his style without grace. He had a mania for telling everything, which is, at times, tedious, and to some minds, intolerable, yet his work will probably stand as most faithful photography of the society in which he moved. The volumes known as the Barchester series thoroughly represent the author at his best. The scenes are in a cathedral town and the country round about. The clergy (bishops, archdeacons, rectors, and curates) are conspicuous and admirably drawn. The scheme includes the life and interests of a county. There is a thread of connection, but each volume is a complete story: **823.87.**

THE WARDEN. N. Y., Dodd, $1.25; Westermann, (Tauchnitz), paper, 50 c.

BARCHESTER TOWERS. N. Y., Dodd, 2 vols., $1.25 each; Westermann, (Tauchnitz), 2 vols., paper, 50 c. each.

"The Warden" and "Barchester Towers," together, N. Y., Harper, paper, 60 c.

DOCTOR THORNE. N. Y., Dodd, 2 vols., $1.25 each; Harper, paper, 50 c.

FRAMLEY PARSONAGE. N. Y., Dodd, 2 vols., $1.25 each; Westermann, (Tauchnitz), 2 vols., paper, 50 c. each.

THE SMALL HOUSE AT ALLINGTON. N. Y., Dodd, 3 vols., $1.25 each; Westermann, (Tauchnitz), 3 vols., paper, 50 c. each.

LAST CHRONICLES OF BARSET. N. Y., Dodd, 3 vols., $1.25 each; Westermann, (Tauchnitz), 3 vols., paper, 50 c. each.

Among his other works are:

RALPH THE HEIR. N. Y., Ward & Lock, $1.

HARRY HEATHCOTE. N.Y., Ward & Lock, $1.

ORLEY FARM. N. Y., Ward & Lock, $1.

CAN YOU FORGIVE HER? N. Y., Ward & Lock, $1.

Tuttiett, M. G. ("Maxwell Grey").

English novelist. She throws the strongest interest into development of character and motive rather than event. Her plots are somewhat romantic and her descriptions of English scenery are distinct and pleasant. Many of her rustics are very amusing. **813.80.**

THE SILENCE OF DEAN MAITLAND. N. Y., Appleton, 75 c.; paper, 50 c.; Burt, paper, 25 c.

The study of the burden of sin borne in secret by a Christian conscience is clever and careful. It is written with insight, knowledge, and passion, and is on the whole a powerful novel, reminiscent of "The Scarlet Letter."

THE REPROACH OF ANNESLEY. N. Y., Appleton, 75 c.; paper, 50 c.; Burt, paper, 25 c.

IN THE HEART OF THE STORM. N. Y., Appleton, 75 c.; paper, 50 c.

THE LAST SENTENCE. N. Y., Lovell, Coryell, $1.50; paper, 50 c.

Twain, Mark (*pseudonym*). See Clemens, S. L.

Tytler, Sarah (*pseudonym*). See Keddie, Miss Henrietta.

Walford, *Mrs.* **Lucy Bethia (Colquhoun).** [1845–.]

Scotch novelist. Her stories turn on slight complications of social life, and, though of uneven merit, have all a light touch, a cheerful spirit, and a very natural transition from gayety to gravity. **823.80.**

THE BABY'S GRANDMOTHER. N. Y., Longmans, $1; Munro, paper, 25 c.

MR. SMITH. N. Y., Longmans, $1; paper, 25 c.

TROUBLESOME DAUGHTERS. N.Y., Longmans, $1; Munro, paper, 25 c.

THE MISCHIEF OF MONICA. N. Y., Longmans, $1; Munro, paper, 2 vols., each 25 c.

THE ONE GOOD GUEST. N. Y., Longmans, $1; paper, 50 c.

Wallace, Lewis. [1827–.]

Western writer of romances. In his two well-known books he has chosen Oriental scenes and historical events. He has dramatic imagination, and is lavish in details of scenes and pageantry. His books are extremely long, the construction is intricate, and the grammar imperfect. He is immensely popular. **813.40.**

BEN HUR: a Tale of the Christ. N. Y., Harper, $1.50.

The title explains itself.

THE PRINCE OF INDIA; OR, WHY CONSTANTINOPLE FELL. N. Y., Harper, 2 vols., $1.25 each.

The hero takes the character of the Wandering Jew. Gives a florid picture of the Byzantine Empire in the fifteenth century.

THE FAIR GOD. Bost., Houghton, $1.50.

The author's best constructed novel. Tells the story of ancient Mexico and describes the religious rites of the Aztecs.

Walpole, Horace. [1717–1797.]

THE CASTLE OF OTRANTO. N. Y., Cassell, 25 c.; paper, 10 c.

This fantastic story, published in 1764 by the famous Englishman of fashion and of letters, was a protest against what he called "the cold common sense of the present age." He made use of a great deal of material intended to excite shudders in his readers, but lacked the power to touch emotion. Thirty years later Mrs. Radcliffe really did what he tried to do, and founded the school of fiction given over to terrors and creepy mysteries. **823.00.**

Walworth, *Mrs.* **Jeannette Ritchie (Hadermann).** [1837–.]

Pennsylvanian novelist. Some of her descriptions of Southern life about the time of the Civil War are interesting. She discusses public questions rather emotionally, and her manner is a little stagey. **813.49.**

NEW MAN AT ROSSMERE. N. Y., Cassell, 75 c.; paper, 50 c.

WITHOUT BLEMISH. N. Y., Cassell, 75 c.; paper, 50 c.

THE BAR SINISTER. N. Y., Cassell, 75 c.; paper, 50 c.

Ward, *Mrs.* **Elizabeth Stuart Phelps.** [1844–.]

New England novelist and writer of tales. Most of her scenes are in New England, and, though external life is well observed, her strength is greatest in analysis of difficulties mental and spiritual. The problem of immortality has engaged her attention deeply, and her ideas about a future life are original, frequently abounding in unconscious humor. Her style is on the whole vigorous and clear, but she occasionally drops into ponderous obscurity. **813.40.**

THE GATES AJAR. Bost., Houghton, $1.50.

Published about a quarter of a century ago, attracted much attention because of the rejection of the orthodox, theological idea of Heaven, and substitution of an existence in which the interests and occupations of this life are continued. The idea was crude, but, at the time, novel, and was presented with considerable skill.

{ BEYOND THE GATES. Bost., Houghton, $1.25.
{ THE GATES BETWEEN. Bost., Houghton, $1.25.

The same idea, much developed and expanded.

THE SILENT PARTNER. Bost., Houghton, $1.50.

A story of factory life in New England. Ahead of the fashion for discussion of social problems in fiction, it shows original thought and observation. The devices for lightening the burdens of the poor are rather sentimental than practical.

THE STORY OF AVIS. Bost., Houghton, $1.50; paper, 50 c.

An American girl goes to Italy to study art. She marries. The conflict between artistic ambitions and a New England conscience is set forth with skill. The author's most carefully written novel.

DOCTOR ZAY. Bost., Houghton, $1.25; paper, 50 c.

The story of a woman physician in an obscure New England village.

HEDGED IN. Bost., Houghton, $1.50.

Ward, *Mrs.* Mary Augusta (Mrs. T. Humphry Ward). [1851-.]

The most famous English writer of the modern "purpose-novel," that is the novel which discusses and may propagate new ideas in politics, religion, or social reform. Her books are thoughtful and well-informed, but not artistic. She is a much better preacher than story-teller. She has been compared with George Eliot for creative power and scholarship. Such comparison is injudicious. She has not created but reflected popular ideals; her scholarship is not shown, as was George Eliot's, by the talk appropriately ascribed to certain characters, but by generalization and reference to authors and names of books. Nevertheless, she is a clever and serious student of complex modern society, and all her work commands respect. **823.89.**

ROBERT ELSMERE. N. Y., Macmillan, $1; Munro, paper, 2 vols., each 25 c.

The question of formal versus ethical religion.

THE HISTORY OF DAVID GRIEVE. N. Y., Macmillan, $1.

A study in self-education and in freeing the life from conventional restraints. David Grieve is an unselfish man of unhappy domestic experiences.

MARCELLA. N. Y., Macmillan, $1; paper, 50 c.

Develops socialism versus vested rights and aristocratic privilege. The heroine begins as a Radical, and, by plain lessons of experience, comes to the temperance of reform. Mrs. Ward's best story.

Warden, Florence (*pseudonym*). *See* James, Mrs. Florence Alice.

Ware, William. [1797-1852.]

A clergyman. He had poetic imagination and deep religious feeling. His books depict the Roman Empire as it sank to its ruin; an observant traveller and faithful scholar, he manages to put much truth into his fiction. **813.39.**

ZENOBIA, OR THE FALL OF PALMYRA. N. Y., Warne, $1.25; Burt, 75 c.

Describes Palmyra under Roman rule at the beginning of the third century, with Christianity and paganism confronting each other.

JULIAN; OR SCENES IN JUDEA. N. Y., Warne, $1.25; Munro, paper, 25 c.

The hero is a Roman of Hebrew blood. The Emperor Julian is introduced and characterized.

AURELIAN; OR ROME IN THE THIRD CENTURY. N. Y., Warne, $1.25; Munro, paper, 25 c.

Warner, Susan ("Wetherell, Elizabeth"). [1819-1885.]

Novelist of the middle period of 19th century. Her books are exceedingly pious, and formal piety is usually rewarded at the expense of essential virtue. They are tremendously prosy and garrulous, but even at a time when professed piety is considered less important than moral rectitude, continue to be read. **813.39.**

THE WIDE, WIDE WORLD. Phila., Lippincott, 75 c.; paper, 50 c.

QUEECHY. N. Y., Ward, Lock, 75 c.; Phila., Lippincott, $1; paper, 50 c.

Watson, John Maclaren ("Ian Maclaren"). [1845-.]

BESIDE THE BONNIE BRIER BUSH. N. Y., Dodd, $1.25.

Short stories of Scottish country life, somewhat in Mr. Barrie's manner. The sketch of the country doctor is a masterpiece. The author, a Liverpool clergyman of Scottish birth, has so much talent for pathos that occasionally his pathos is beyond nature. His style is usually swift and direct, without the waste of a syllable. **823.89.**

Wetherell, Elizabeth. *See* Susan Warner.

Weyman, Stanley J. [1855-.]

English novelist. Like Anthony Hope, he represents the modern reaction from dry realism. His novels are historical, romantic, and entertaining. **823.89.**

THE HOUSE OF THE WOLF. N. Y., Longmans, $1.25.

The scene is in France in the reign of Charles IX. The massacre of St. Bartholomew is included in the drama.

A GENTLEMAN OF FRANCE. N. Y., Longmans, $1.25.

The time is during the reign of Henry III. and Henry IV. (of Navarre).

UNDER THE RED ROBE. N. Y., Longmans, $1.25.

During the administration of Cardinal Richelieu (Louis XIII.). The adventures of Gil de Bérault are admirably narrated.

MY LADY ROTHA. N. Y., Longmans, $1.25.

White, William Hale ("Mark Rutherford").

AUTOBIOGRAPHY OF MARK RUTHERFORD; and MARK RUTHERFORD'S DELIVERANCE. Separately, Lond., Unwin, 3s. 6d. each. Together, N. Y., Scribner, $2.25.

Sets forth the perplexities, domestic and religious, of a sensitive and thoughtful man destitute of gumption. If these chapters are not autobiography they certainly read as if they were. Seldom are the springs of motive, the griefs of a weak will, bared with so true a touch. The incidental account of life in the early part of the century among the English lower middle class is skilful and depressing. **823.80.**

THE REVOLUTION IN TANNER'S LANE. N. Y., Putnam, $1.25.

Tanner's Lane is a small, dissenting chapel in England; its story involves the political and religious ferment of the early decades of the 19th century. Unconventional characters of French blood reappear on a canvas largely taken up with the affairs of a sleepy village. As in his preceding books, the author's reflections are of searching quality, expressed with utmost directness.

CATHARINE FURZE. N. Y., Macmillan, $1.

Whitney, Mrs. Adeline Dutton (Train). [1824–.]

New England novelist. Most of her stories describe domestic life in New England; they are popular among young girls. Sometimes her manner is strained and affected, but she is generally sincere and simple. The complications and situations of her stories are natural and interesting. 813.40.

FAITH GARTNEY'S GIRLHOOD. Bost., Houghton, $1.25.

THE GAYWORTHYS. Bost., Houghton, $1.25.

LESLIE GOLDTHWAITE. Bost., Houghton, $1.25.

Wiggin, Kate Douglas (*Mrs.* Riggs).

A Californian whose tales, chiefly for the young, are both humorous and pathetic. She tells her stories prettily, and wherever she can, argues for children's rights. 813.40.

THE STORY OF PATSY. Bost., Houghton, 60 c.

The hero is a deformed little boy. Life in the slums is described with humor.

TIMOTHY'S QUEST. Bost., Houghton, $1.

A little girl is rescued from a baby-farm. The quest is for her mother.

A SUMMER IN A CAÑON: A CALIFORNIA STORY. Bost., Houghton, $1.25.

Sundry amusing folk meet in vacation time.

A CATHEDRAL COURTSHIP AND PENELOPE'S ENGLISH EXPERIENCES. Bost., Houghton, $1.

A thread of romance runs through descriptions of a tour among the celebrated cathedrals of England.

THE BIRD'S CHRISTMAS CAROL. Bost., Houghton, 50 c.

An entertaining story for parents as well as for children.

POLLY OLIVER'S PROBLEM. Bost., Houghton, $1.

Wilkins, Mary Eleanor.

New England writer of novels and tales. Her reputation rests on sketches of New England country people. These are, in most respects, admirable, but with just a touch of exaggeration throughout. She has not attained the perfection of Miss Jewett, whose work in the same field is at once more natural and artistic. 813.40.

A HUMBLE ROMANCE. N. Y., Harper, $1.25.

Short stories.

A NEW ENGLAND NUN. N. Y., Harper, $1.25.

Short stories.

PEMBROKE. N. Y., Harper, $1 50.

A fine story based on the conflict of two strong wills.

GILES COREY, YEOMAN: A PLAY. N. Y., Harper, 50c.

A play founded on the persecution of the Salem witches in 1692.

THE POT OF GOLD. Bost., Lothrop, $1.50.

Short stories.

Wilson, *Mrs.* **Augusta Jane Evans.** [1838–.]

Southern novelist, remarkable chiefly for her habit of pouring out quotations from and references to ancient Asiatic literature. Her men are generally alluringly wicked and rich in the beginning, and angels (still rich), and sometimes in the earthly form of clergymen, at the end. The girls, by contrast, are often poor, and always virtuous. Both classes are monuments of learning; they dispense erudition free of charge with reckless prodigality. In mind, manners, and feelings they are incalculably remote from any known specimens of the race. The author was once very popular, but with the new wisdom of a new generation she has (or ought to have) lapsed into obscurity. 813.40.

BEULAH. N. Y., G. W. Dillingham, $1.75.

ST. ELMO. N. Y., G. W. Dillingham, $2.

VASHTI. N. Y., G. W. Dillingham, $2.

INFELICE. N. Y., G. W. Dillingham, $2.

Winter, John Strange. *See* Stannard, Mrs. Henrietta E. V.

Winthrop, Theodore. [1828–1861.]

New England novelist. His literary career was scarcely begun when he entered the Northern Army in the Civil War, and was killed in one of the earliest battles. His work was almost all posthumous, and though immature, shows imagination of a very high order. 813.40.

CECIL DREEME. N.Y., Lovell, Coryell, $1.25.

The scene is in New York City and describes particularly the vicinity of Washington Square. One of the principal characters is said to have been drawn from a man at the time well known in society and letters. The story is imaginative and the struggle of conflicting passions depicted with uncommon power. A biographical note by George W. Curtis appears in this volume.

JOHN BRENT. N. Y., Lovell, Coryell, $1.25.

The scene is the Western plains. It has not the local truth of later Western tales, but is vigorous both in description and characterization.

EDWIN BROTHERTOFT. N. Y., Lovell, Coryell, $1.25.

THE CANOE AND THE SADDLE. N. Y., Lovell, Coryell, $1.25.

Adventures among Northwestern rivers and forests.

Wood, *Mrs.* **Ellen (Price).** [1814–1887.]

English novelist of middle period of 19th century. She depended on plot, which she constructed accurately and with a good sense of theatrical situation and climax. Her material was chiefly secret marriages and skeletons in closets. There is generally little perceptible motive beyond the unravelling of mystery, but the tendency is not immoral, and the work is much better than most of its class. 823.70.

Her most famous work is widely read for its sensational interest.

EAST LYNNE. Phila., Porter & Coates, 75 c.; N. Y., Burt, paper, 25 c.

Still holds its place on the melodramatic stage.

DANESBURY HOUSE. With introduction by Frances E. Willard and Lady Somerset.

N. Y., Revell, $1; Rand, paper, 50 c.
Written to popularize the total abstinence movement. A very good story, the purpose being adroitly served by indirection.

THE CHANNINGS. N. Y., Westermann, (Tauchnitz), 2 vols., paper, $1.

ROLAND YORKE. N. Y., Westermann, (Tauchnitz), 2 vols., paper, $1.

Woods, Katharine Pearson. [1853-.]

A native of West Virginia, a teacher by profession. Local conflicts between labor and capital have impelled her to faith in Christian socialism as the sole remedy for industrial war. Her novels are written to expound this faith; they have the strength which comes of conviction, and, apart from their preaching, are graphic and interesting. 813.40.

METZEROTT, SHOEMAKER. N. Y., Crowell, $1.50; paper, 50 c.
The scene is amid a German-American population of every variety of creed and no creed. A Christian socialist is the hero.

FROM DUSK TO DAWN. N. Y, Appleton, $1.25.
The hero is a young clergyman in a poor parish. He exerts uncommon influence over men and women disposed to groan under the burdens of reform.

A WEB OF GOLD. N. Y., Crowell, $1.25.
The labor problem is discussed once more, and the Italian society of the Mafia is introduced.

Woods, *Mrs.* Margaret L.

A VILLAGE TRAGEDY. Lond., Bentley, 3s. 6d.; N. Y., Westermann, (Tauchnitz), paper, 50 c.; Munro, paper, 25 c.
A good example of the modern realistic tale, narrating distressing facts with pain increasing to a most dismal catastrophe. It is technically good art (except for the introduction of a superfluous and most hideous idiot), but it is baneful art—only temporarily intensifying the consciousness of sorrow without suggestion for its relief. 823.80.

ESTHER VANHOMRIGH. N. Y., Hovenden Co., $1; paper, 50 c.
Founded on the love-story of Dean Swift; endeavors to explain his seeming inconsistencies as due to his passion for power. Swift's literary friends, Steele, Addison, Pope, and Bolingbroke, come upon the scene.

THE VAGABONDS. N. Y., Macmillan, $1.50.
Depicts a travelling circus in England. There is some good character-drawing, but the book is not equal to its predecessors.

Woolson, Constance Fenimore. [1848-1894.]

New England novelist, grandniece to James Fenimore Cooper. No American woman has written so much uniformly good fiction as Miss Woolson. Her novels combine romanticism and realism, and include innumerable vivid sketches of a great variety of her countrymen and women, besides charming descriptions of life and natural scenery from Michigan to Florida. Always refined, natural, sympathetic, generally seeing clearly the probability of character, and rarely lapsing into sentimentality in development, any of her books may give pleasure to the critical as well as to those who read stories for entertainment solely. 813.40.

ANNE. N. Y., Harper, $1.25.
The heroine goes forth into the world and maintains her brothers and sisters. A capital story.

FOR THE MAJOR. N. Y., Harper, $1.
A woman marries a man very much her junior. Her efforts to keep young are touchingly told.

JUPITER LIGHTS. N. Y., Harper, $1.25.
A story of the all-pardoning love of two good women.

EAST ANGELS. N. Y., Harper, $1.25.
Florida before and during the Civil War. Full of realistic Southern portraits.

HORACE CHASE. N. Y., Harper, $1.25.
Asheville, N. C., and St. Augustine, Fla., as they were twenty years ago, are the background of the story. Incidentally the work wrought by Northern energy is described.

RODMAN, THE KEEPER. N. Y., Harper, $1.
Southern sketches.

Yates, Edmund Hodgson. [1831-1894.]

English novelist. His stories move smoothly and show, in characterization and comment, the observation and reflection of the clever, sensible man of the world. They are entertaining and often sharply satirical. 823.80.

BLACK SHEEP. N. Y., Routledge, 80 c.

NOBODY'S FORTUNE. N. Y., Routledge, 80 c.

A SILENT WITNESS. N. Y., Routledge, 80 c.

Yonge, Charlotte M. [1823-.]

English novelist. Her books are historical and modern, particularly addressed to young people. They are cheerful and healthy in spirit and fluent in style. She is deservedly popular. 823.70.

THE HEIR OF REDCLYFFE. N. Y., Macmillan, $1; Burt, 75 c.; paper, 25 c.

THE DAISY CHAIN. N. Y., Macmillan, $1.

THE ARMOURER'S PRENTICES. N. Y., Macmillan, $1; Munro, paper, 25 c.

DOVE IN THE EAGLE'S NEST. N. Y., Macmillan, $1; Lovell, Coryell, 50 c.

Zangwill, Israel. [1864-.]

English novelist and miscellaneous writer. His descriptions of Jewish life and character are striking and vigorous. His other work is less significant; it is all more clever than agreeable or refined. 823.80.

THE CHILDREN OF THE GHETTO. N. Y., Macmillan, $1.50.
Stories of Jewish life.

THE KING OF SCHNORRERS. N. Y., Macmillan, $1.50.

THE MASTER. N. Y., Harper, $1.75.
Story of a young Canadian who goes to Europe to study painting. Discusses art with intelligence.

BIOGRAPHY.

CHOSEN BY THE ASSISTANT LIBRARIANS NEW YORK FREE CIRCULATING LIBRARY.

New York, June, 1895.

> BIOGRAPHY, especially the biography of the great and good, who have risen by their own exertions from poverty and obscurity to eminence and usefulness, is an inspiring and ennobling study. Its direct tendency is to reproduce the excellence it records.—HORACE MANN.

See also under LITERATURE *for additional biographies of authors.*

Adams, John *and* **Abigail.**
FAMILIAR LETTERS OF JOHN ADAMS, and his wife, Abigail Adams, during the Revolution. With a memoir of Mrs. Adams. Edited by Charles Francis Adams. Bost., Houghton, $2.
A faithful portrayal of a New England wife; an illustration of the part such a wife plays in the life of her husband.... This volume is one of the most valuable documents of our revolutionary history.—*Nation.* 923.2.

Addison, *Rev.* **Daniel D.**
LIFE, LETTERS, AND DIARY OF LUCY LARCOM. Bost., Houghton, $1.25.
Mr. Addison has done his work well and made a most agreeable and interesting book.... A chapter covers the period of which Miss Larcom wrote so pleasantly in "A New England Girlhood." The sensible reader will at once possess himself of that, if it is not already known to him. (Included in this list, see Larcom.) 928.1.

Alcott, Louisa M. *See* Cheney, E. D.

Andersen, Hans Christian.
STORY OF MY LIFE. Bost., Houghton, $1.
The history of my life will say to the world what it says to me: "There is a loving God who directs all things to the best."—*Author.* 839.8.

Appleton's ENCYCLOPÆDIA OF AMERICAN BIOGRAPHY. N. Y., Appleton, 1888, 6 vols., $30.
Much the best work for American names. Well illustrated. 027.3

Austen, Jane. *See* Smith, Goldwin.

Birrell, Augustine.
LIFE OF CHARLOTTE BRONTË. (Great Writers series.) N. Y., Scribner, $1; A. Lovell, 40 c.
Avoiding the amiable prolixity of Mrs. Gaskell, and the dogmatism of Mr. Reid, Charlotte Brontë's former biographers, Mr. Birrell gives us a small book which thoroughly covers the field, fresh in style and perspicacious.—*Critic.* 823.81.

Blind, Mathilde.
MADAME ROLAND. (Famous Women series.) Bost., Roberts, $1.
The author writes graphically, and describes scenes in the French Revolution with great picturesqueness.—*Boston Evening Transcript.* 920.

Bolton, Sarah Knowles.
FAMOUS TYPES OF WOMANHOOD. N. Y., Crowell, $1.50.
Contents: Queen Louise of Prussia; Madame Recamier; Susanna Wesley; Harriet Martineau; Jenny Lind; Dorothea Lynde Dix; Ann, Sarah, and Emily Judson; Amelia Blanford Edwards.
Each portrait presents a distinct phase of womanly influence; each has its lesson of faith, endurance, and love for others.—*Literary World.* 920.7.

LIVES OF GIRLS WHO BECAME FAMOUS. N. Y., Crowell, $1.50.
Contents: Harriet Beecher Stowe; Helen Hunt Jackson; Lucretia Mott; Mary A. Livermore; Margaret Fuller Ossoli; Maria Mitchell; Louisa M. Alcott; Mary Lyon; Harriet G. Hosmer; Madame de Staël; Rosa Bonheur; Elizabeth Barrett Browning; George Eliot; Elizabeth Fry; Elizabeth Thompson Butler; Florence Nightingale; Lady Brassey; Baroness Burdett-Coutts; Jean Ingelow.
Mrs. Bolton's books, though without originality of treatment or style, are yet valuable as presenting much information in clear and concise form.—*Critic.* 920.7.

Boswell, James.
LIFE OF SAMUEL JOHNSON. N. Y., Crowell, $1.25.
The best biography in the English language. An edition with notes of the highest interest by George Birkbeck Hill. N. Y., Harper, 6 vols., $10.
See under Johnson for Essays on Boswell's Life of Johnson. 824.63.

Brandes, G.
EMINENT AUTHORS OF THE NINETEENTH CENTURY. Translated by R. B. Anderson. N. Y., Crowell, $2.
These literary portraits represent their author's best work, and Brandes at his best is the peer of any living critic.—*Nation.* 830.8.

Bridgman, Laura D. *See* Lamson, Mary S.

Brontë, Charlotte. *See* Birrell, A.

Brooks, Elbridge Streeter.
HISTORIC BOYS: Their Endeavors, Their Achievements, and Their Times. N. Y., Putnam, $2.
Contents: Marcus of Rome; Brian of Munster; Olaf of Norway; William of Normandy; Baldwin of Jerusalem; Frederick of Hohenstauffen; Harry of Monmouth; Giovanni of Florence; Ixtlil of Tezcuco; Louis of Bourbon; Charles of Sweden; Van Rensselaer of Rensselaerwyck.
The author has selected the careers of a dozen young fellows of different lands and epochs, and these stories of boy life, in the stirring days of old, have been based upon historic facts and prepared with a due regard to historic and chronologic accuracy. 920.

HISTORIC GIRLS WHO HAVE INFLUENCED THE HISTORY OF THEIR TIMES. N. Y., Putnam, $2.
Contents: Zenobia of Palmyra; Helena of Britain; Pulcheria of Constantinople; Clotilde of Burgundy;

Woo of Hwang-Ho; Edith of Scotland ; Jacqueline of Holland ; Catarina of Venice ; Theresa of Avila ; Elizabeth of Tudor ; Christina of Sweden ; Ma-ta-oka of Pow-ha-tan.

Interesting to younger as well as older girls.—*Literary World.* 020.7.

Cabot, James Elliot.

MEMOIR OF RALPH WALDO EMERSON. Bost., Houghton, 2 vols., $3.50.

Mr. Cabot has done a difficult task with singular skill and success. The chief regret with which one lays down the book is that he has not given us more.—*Nation.* 812.

Cassell's NEW BIOGRAPHICAL DICTIONARY. N. Y., Cassell, 1893, $2.50.

A compact work of reference ; fullest in British names.

Cheney, Ednah D.

LOUISA MAY ALCOTT ; Her Life, Letters, and Journals. Bost., Roberts, $1.50.

It is an unstudied, almost fragmentary memoir which Mrs. Cheney has edited with wise reserve and good taste. . . . The book is at once a reproach to the self-indulgent and a warning to young writers.—*Atlantic.* 02E.1.

Clay, Henry. *See* Schurz, C.

Cobbe, Frances Power, LIFE OF. By herself. Bost., Houghton, 2 vols., $4.

Miss Cobbe's life has been a useful, interesting, and important one, and she has told her story of it better, on the whole than any other biographer could do it.—*Nation.*

Gives a picture of the position of woman in the world to-day as contrasted with seventy years ago. 020.

Coffin, Charles Carleton.

LINCOLN. N. Y., Harper, $3.

A sketch rather than a biography ; the author carefully refrains from attempts at characterization. Mr. Coffin knew Lincoln personally, visited the scenes of his early life, and had many interviews with those who knew Lincoln in early days. The strong points of this book are its readableness, its happy selection of matter likely to be of general interest, its numerous illustrations of places connected with Lincoln's early career, and its portraits of leading men during war times.—*Literary World.* 023.1.

Columbus. *See* Irving, W.; Seelye, Eliz. E.; Winsor, J.

Cone, Helen Gray, *and* **Gilder, Jeannette L.**

PEN PORTRAITS OF LITERARY WOMEN, by themselves and others. N. Y., Cassell, 2 vols., $3.

The choice of personages is excellent. It ranges from Miss Burney to Miss Brontë, and from Mme. Sand to Mme. Ossoli (Margaret Fuller), and includes a remarkable variety of characters both unfamiliar and familiar to the present generation.—*Nation.*

Margaret Fuller is unfairly treated ; a quotation regarding her from Hawthorne is given without justification or palliation.—*Literary World.* 020.7.

Cross, J. W.

LIFE AND LETTERS OF GEORGE ELIOT. N.Y., Harper, 3 vols., $2.25; Crowell, 1 vol., $1.

Mr Cross has done his work with tact and delicacy. The letters singularly fail to reveal the great powers which George Eliot possessed as a novelist.—*London Spectator.* 825.14.

Cushman, Charlotte. *See* Stebbins, Emma.

Dante. *See* Ward, May Alden.

Darwin, Francis.

CHARLES DARWIN'S LIFE. N. Y., Appleton, $1.50.

Retains as far as possible the personal parts of the two large volumes (" Life and Letters of Charles Darwin "), omitting many of the more purely scientific letters, or giving but short citations from them. There is but little abridgment of the account of writing " The Origin of Species."—*Literary World.* 92.251.

See next entry.

LIFE AND LETTERS OF CHARLES DARWIN. With an autobiographical chapter. N. Y., Appleton, 2 vols., $4.50.

The book is at once a biography, an autobiography, and the history of a great idea. . . . The man and his work are so presented as never to be dissociated.—*London Spectator.* 02.251.

See preceding entry.

Dictionary OF [ENGLISH] NATIONAL BIOGRAPHY. Edited by Sidney Lee. Early vols. edited by Leslie Stephen. N. Y., Macmillan, $3.75 per vol.

In course of publication (latest), vol. xlii. to June 1895, ends with Owen. 024.2.

A monumental work. Much the fullest and best.

Dole, Nathan Haskell.

SCORE OF FAMOUS COMPOSERS. N. Y., Crowell, $1.50.

Contents: Giovanni Pierluigi da Palestrina ; Henry Purcell ; Johann Sebastian Bach ; George Frederick Handel ; Christoph Willibald Gluck ; Franz Joseph Haydn ; Wolfgang Amadeus Mozart ; Ludwig Van Beethoven ; Gioachino Rossini ; Carl Maria von Weber ; Schubert ; Louis Spohr ; Meyerbeer ; Mendelssohn ; Schumann ; Frederic François Chopin ; Mikhail Ivanovitch Glinka ; Hector Berlioz ; Franz Liszt ; Richard Wagner.

Brief and sketchy.

Useful as an elementary text-book in biography for those beginning their acquaintance with the lives of great composers.—*Critic.* 027.8.

Dora, Sister. *See* Lonsdale, Margaret.

Douglass, Frederick.

LIFE AND TIMES. By himself. Bost., De Wolfe, $2.50.

Describes his early life as a slave, his escape to freedom, and his life career. 023.6.

Duffy, Bella.

MADAME DE STAEL. (Famous Women series.) Bost., Roberts, $1.

Written with discrimination and insight, with clear appreciation of Madame de Stael's influence on the politics and literature of her time.—*Critic.* 844.

Edgeworth, Maria. *See* Hare, A. J. C.

Eliot, George. *See* Cross, J. W.

Emerson, R. W., LIFE OF. *See* Cabot, J. E.

Emerson, Ralph Waldo.

REPRESENTATIVE MEN. Bost., Houghton, $1.

Discerning characterizations of Plato, Swedenborg, Montaigne, Shakespeare, Napoleon, and Goethe 814.30.

Fawcett, Millicent Garrett.

SOME EMINENT WOMEN. N. Y., Macmillan, 75 c.

Brief sketches of twenty-two English women and of two American abolitionists—Prudence Crandall and Lucretia Mott. 020.7.

Fields, James Thomas.

YESTERDAYS WITH AUTHORS. Bost., Houghton, $2.

The reminiscences of a famous publisher, recalling eminent men of letters. 820.0.

Franklin, Benjamin.

AUTOBIOGRAPHY. Edited, with notes, by John Bigelow. N. Y., Putnam, $1. Without notes, N. Y., Cassell, 25 c.; paper, 10 c.

Franklin's fame as a writer chiefly rests on this autobiography.

See Morse, J. T., Jr., for biography. 023.2.

Froude, James A.

CÆSAR: a Sketch. N. Y., Harper, 60 c.; Scribner, $1.50.

In addition to its value as biography, this is a study of the conversion of the Roman republic into a military empire. 87.

Fuller, Margaret. *See* Howe, Julia Ward, for notes on three biographies.

Gilchrist, Anne.

MARY LAMB. (Famous Women series.) Bost., Roberts, $1.

The character of Mary Lamb is one which has always drawn readers out of all proportions to the fulness of their knowledge, and many will be grateful to Mrs. Gilchrist for bringing together into a simple, unrestrained narrative all that is to be learned of Charles Lamb's sister.—*Atlantic.* 025.161.

Gilder, Jeannette L. *See* Cone, Helen Gray.

Goethe, Caroline Elizabeth.

CORRESPONDENCE WITH GOETHE, WIELAND, AND OTHERS. Translated by Alfred S. Gibbs. N. Y., Dodd, $2.

Gives a picture of Goethe's mother as a most amusing, racy, and delightful woman. We obtain of Goethe more familiar and life-like glimpses than have come to us in any other way.—*Nation.* 928.3.

Goethe. *See* Grimm, H.

Greely, Adolphus W.

EXPLORERS AND TRAVELLERS. (Men of Achievement series.) N. Y., Scribner, $2.

Contents: Louis Joliet; Peter le Moyne; Jonathan Carver; Captain Robert Gray; Captain Meriwether Lewis and Lieut. William Clark; Zebulon Montgomery Pike; Charles Wilkes; John Charles Frémont; Elisha Kent Kane; Isaac Israel Hayes; Charles Francis Hall; George Washington De Long; Paul Belloni Du Chaillu; Stanley Africanus and the Congo Free State.

The scope of this volume is necessarily confined to explorations of great importance or peculiar interest and when made by men of American birth who are no longer living. Two exceptions have been made; Du Chaillu and Stanley, Americans by adoption—otherwise African exploration would have been unrepresented. 020.

Grimm, Hermann.

LIFE AND TIMES OF GOETHE. Translated by Sarah Holland Adams. Bost., Little, $2.50.

Gives a more natural and human delineation of Goethe than any other biography. Notwithstanding prolixity and eulogy the best single work on Goethe up to this time (1881) for old and young.—*Nation.* 028.3.

Hare, A. J. C.

LIFE AND LETTERS OF MARIA EDGEWORTH. Bost., Houghton, 2 vols., $4.

The letters of one so clear-sighted and sagacious are valuable not only from the light they throw on an honest, generous, high-minded character, but as a record of her times and of many prominent figures in them.—*New York Sun.* 825.3.

Hawthorne, Julian.

NATHANIEL HAWTHORNE AND HIS WIFE. Bost., Houghton, 2 vols., $5.

So instinct with a tender respect and unquestioning love, so full of a frank, boyish spirit of the loyalty that has never contemplated the King doing wrong, that the critic is constrained to take his point of view and accept this biography, not as a critical and complete life, but as a friendly confidence.—*Nation.* 812.31.

Henry, Patrick. *See* Tyler, Moses C.

Herndon, William H., *and* Weik, Jesse W.

ABRAHAM LINCOLN. New and revised edition, with an introduction by Horace White. N. Y., Appleton, 2 vols., $3.

Mr. Herndon was a friend of Lincoln's, and his law-partner for twenty years. This book will doubtless remain the most trustworthy source of information concerning Lincoln in the period prior to his election to the presidency.... Facts here are not selected with art to compose a predetermined picture; but we feel that an honest chronicler, who thoroughly knew his subject, has collated nearly everything authentic which can be known of Lincoln before his great elevation.—*Nation.* 023.1.

Howe, Julia Ward.

MARGARET FULLER. (Famous Women series.) Bost., Roberts, $1.

An admirable study of a great woman; gives emphasis to culture as the keynote to Margaret Fuller's career.

Margaret Fuller's first biographers were James Freeman Clarke, Ralph Waldo Emerson, and William Henry Channing, [Bost., Roberts, 1852, $1.50.] Their book lays stress on Margaret Fuller's transcendentalism.

Thos. W. Higginson's "Margaret Fuller Ossoli" [Bost., Houghton, 1884, $1.25], which contains a list of her writings, deems philanthropy to have been her chief idea and mission. 928.1.

Irving, Washington.

LIFE AND VOYAGES OF CHRISTOPHER COLUMBUS; to which are added those of his companions. N. Y., Putnam, 3 vols., $3; abridged, 1 vol., $1.50.

Perhaps the best biography in the language; infused with generous and elevating sentiment. It needs, however, to be revised in the light of researches since Irving's day.—*Critic.* 023.0.

Jefferson, Joseph.

AUTOBIOGRAPHY. N. Y., Century Co., $4.

Reveals Mr. Jefferson as a true and whole-souled man, patient and cheerful in adversity, and unspoiled by the harder trial of prosperity. This book proves his faithfulness to the stern demand of great and high art.—*Literary World.* 027.

Johnson, Samuel.

CHIEF LIVES OF THE POETS: those of Milton, Dryden, Swift, Addison, Pope, and Gray.

which deserve the charge ... century and a half, is as sparkling and amusing as ever.—*London Spectator.* 824.

Morse, J. T., jr.

ABRAHAM LINCOLN. American Statesmen series. Bost., Houghton, 2 vols., $2.50.

Should have given us a much fuller account of Lincoln's life before the Civil War ... all Lincoln's gifts... made prior to the coming... to the community... it holds this... ere although the author is himself... While Mr. Morse cautions his readers ... against the aptness of Lincoln's wit and Hay, yet he is constantly siding with him and is of divinity in a lesser degree.—*Nation.* 923.1.

BENJAMIN FRANKLIN. American Statesmen series. Bost., Houghton $1.25.

Though largely a political piece of work, this volume has some good chapters. Its chapter on the Hutchinson letters is an adequate and satisfactory. The hostile influences under which Franklin as a diplomatist had to contend are made clear. On the subject of the Treaty of Peace with England in 1783 Mr. Morse has availed himself of new and important materials recently brought to light.—*Nation.* 923.2.

Napoleon.

Among the most important of the systematic works that have appeared there are the letters and dispatches of Napoleon to Joseph, 10 vols., by the Government of France; Lanfrey's History of Napoleon I, N. Y., Macmillan, 4 vols. $4.; Taine's Modern Regime N. Y. Holt, vols. I. and II. $2.50 each; Seeley's Short History of Napoleon, Bost., Roberts, $1.50; Ropes's The First Napoleon. Bost., Houghton, $0. Among memoirs of contemporary writers of note, written by personal observers, are those by Madame Junot, Duchess d'Abrantes N. Y., Appleton, 2 vols., $3.; Rémusat, N. Y., Appleton; Talleyrand, Meneval, Marbot, Pasquier, Meneval, de Meneval, Gourgaud de Bourrienne, N. Y., Crowell, 4 vols., $4.; Las Casas, O'Meara, N. Y., Sampson, 2 vols., $2.50; Marmont, Massena, Savary, Ségur, Miot de Melito, President CHARLES KING, Appleton's *Cyclopedia.*

The memoirs of Compte Barras, Member of the Directorate during the last years of the obscure Lieutenant and his imperial highness Emperor, are being published by Harper, No I. Vol. II brings the history of Napoleon down to 1794. Vol. III and IV are (June, 1895) still to appear. $3.75 per vol.

Nicolay, John G., and Hay, John.

ABRAHAM LINCOLN, a History. N. Y., Century Co., 10 vols. $30.

The writers were private secretaries to President Lincoln. They describe his private life and public career in terms of eulogy. They present the causes of the Civil War and the inside history of the war with facsimiles of important documents. Interesting and informing throughout. 923.1.

Plutarch's Lives.

"Among the most delightful sketches ever written. As an ultimate and positive authority they cannot be accepted. But they are to be perused, to charm, and to instruct. They take the reader into the heroic air of Roman and Grecian times."—*A. H. Axson.*

There are many editions of Plutarch, English and American, the largest being in 5 and 6 vols. The so-called Dryden translation made by others, however, as revised and edited by Clough, is excellent, Bost., Little, $5.; other translations are the Langhorne's N. Y. Routledge $1.25; Stewart and Long's Bohn's Library N. Y. Macmillan, 4 vols. $5. The most accurate and brief edition for boys and girls is edited with an introduction by John S. White, N. Y. Putnam $1.75 or $2.50. 888.6.

Poe, Edgar A. *See* Woodberry, G. E.

Roland, Madame. *See* Blind, Mathilde.

Schurz, Carl.

LIFE OF HENRY CLAY. American Statesmen series. Bost., Houghton 2 vols. $2.50.

In reality a political history of the United States based upon the life of Henry Clay. We do not know of any book of like compass so well suited to give young Americans a knowledge of their country during those stirring years at once accurate, graphic, and pervaded by a strong moral sense.—*Nation.* 923.2.

Scott, Sir Walter.

FAMILIAR LETTERS. Edited by David Douglas. Bost., Houghton, 2 vols., $6.

JOURNAL 1825-1832. N. Y., Harper, 2 vols. $2.50.

These letters and this journal deepen the reader's love and respect for the man who penned them. 923.73.

LIFE OF. *See* Lockhart, J. G.

Scudder, Horace E.

GEORGE WASHINGTON. AN HISTORICAL BIOGRAPHY. Riverside Library for Young People. Bost., Houghton, 75 c.

Can be heartily commended.—*Nation.*

Equally delightful to girls and boys. 923.1.

Seelye, Elizabeth Eggleston.

THE STORY OF COLUMBUS. Edited by Edward Eggleston. N. Y., Appleton, $1.75.

One of the most attractive and reliable of the shorter volumes about Columbus.—*Literary World.* 923.9.

THE STORY OF WASHINGTON. Edited by Edward Eggleston. N. Y., Appleton, $1.75.

Intended to furnish young readers especially with a vivid and correct impression of Washington. Author has paid much attention to the details of his private life. The result is that he stands before us a more genial and human figure than he has usually been depicted.—*Literary World.* 923.1.

Sevigné, de, Madame. *See* Thackeray, Anne.

Siddons, Mrs. *See* Kennard, Nina H.

Smith, Goldwin.

LIFE OF JANE AUSTEN. (Great Writers series). N. Y., Scribner, $1; A. Lovell, 40 c.

The first and best chapter contains an excellent sketch of Jane Austen's life; the other chapters analyze her novels with delicate taste and fine critical parity.—*Athenæum.* $23.74.

Somerville, Mary (Fairfax) Greig.

PERSONAL RECOLLECTIONS FROM EARLY LIFE TO OLD AGE. With selections from her correspondence by her daughter, Martha Somerville. Bost., Roberts. $2.50.

The complete impression on the reader's mind of an admirable and lovable character, the feeling it gives him as of having been in the company of a superior woman, lend to these reminiscences a veritable personal charm.—*Nature.* 920.

Staël, de, Madame. *See* Duffy, Bella.

Stebbins, Emma.

CHARLOTTE CUSHMAN. Her Letters and Memories of Her Life. Bost., Houghton, 2 vols., $2.50.

Despite a diffuse style and a decidedly uncritical spirit, this book is entertaining, and from its perusal one rises with both kindlier views of his fellow-men and with a more earnest heart for duty and trial—*Harper's Monthly.* 020.

Stephens, Alexander H. *See* Johnston, R. M.

Stowe, Charles E.

LIFE OF HARRIET BEECHER STOWE. Bost., Houghton, $3.50.

Mrs. Stowe is allowed to tell her own story, in letters and well-selected extracts from her journals, with only such thread of connection in narrative and incident as is necessary or fit.—*Literary World.* 020.

Thackeray, Anne (Mrs. Richmond Ritchie).

LIFE AND LETTERS OF MADAME DE SÉVIGNÉ. Phila., Lippincott, $1.

An entertaining life, enlivened with copious extracts from letters, forming a graphic and interesting picture of the times.—*Nation.* 020.

Trevelyan, George Otto.

LIFE AND LETTERS OF LORD MACAULAY. N. Y., Harper, 2 vols., $5; or 1 vol., $1.75.

One of the best biographies in the language.—*Leslie Stephen.* 020.

Tyler, Moses Coit.

PATRICK HENRY. (American Statesmen series.) Bost., Houghton, $1.25.

One of the best and most readable of American biographies. May be fairly said to reconstruct the life of Patrick Henry, and to vindicate his memory from the unappreciative and injurious estimate which has been placed upon it.—*Nation.* 020.

Victoria, Queen. *See* Wilson, G. Robert.

Ward, May Alden.

DANTE: A SKETCH OF HIS LIFE AND WORKS. Bost., Roberts, $1.25.

A good introduction to the study of Dante.

Washington, George. *See* Lodge, H. C.; Scudder, H. E.; Seelye, Eliz. E.

WRITINGS OF. Including diaries and correspondence. Edited by Worthington C. Ford. N. Y., Putnam, 14 vols., $70.

"The father of his country" is to be found entire in these volumes, which cannot be read without increased admiration for Washington, and without a sense of obligation to his latest editor.—*Nation.* 320.8.

Washington, Mary *and* **Martha.** *See* Benson, J. Lossing.

Willard, Frances E.

GLIMPSES OF FIFTY YEARS: the autobiography of an American woman. Chic., Woman's Temperance Pub. Assoc., $2.75.

Very far from being put together with any skill, or with any feeling for literary effect. . . . But the intrinsic interest of the story is very great.—*Nation.* 020.

Wilson, Robert.

LIFE AND TIMES OF QUEEN VICTORIA. With many illustrations and portraits. N. Y., Cassell, 2 vols., $4 each.

A work of as much historical as biographical interest. 042.08.

Winsor, Justin.

CHRISTOPHER COLUMBUS, and How he Received and Imparted the Spirit of Discovery. Bost., Houghton, $4.

John Fiske, in the preface to his "Discovery of America," declares that Mr. Winsor is wrong in portraying Columbus as a "feeble, mean-spirited driveller." . . . Nevertheless, on the whole, Mr. Winsor's book is the best as yet written on its theme.—*Nation.*

Mr. Winsor has made an invaluable contribution to the critical literature of the discovery of America. . . . But he has succeeded in demonstrating afresh that a lack of historic imagination and a deficiency in primal human sympathy cannot be made good by the most elaborate erudition. With all his faults as an investigator of the sources of history, Washington Irving had this imagination and this sympathy in no small degree. . . . No one who lacks them can show us the great man of any time as he was.—*Literary World.* 923.0.

Woman of the Century: 1470 biographical sketches, accompanied by portraits of leading American women. Edited by Frances E. Willard and Mary A. Livermore. Buffalo, N. Y., C. Wells Moulton, $10. 927.3.

Woodberry, George E.

EDGAR ALLAN POE. (American Men of Letters series.) Bost., Houghton, $1.25.

Perhaps final as a biography; faulty in criticism of Poe as a writer. As Stedman has said: "Poe's place is rather with Doré than with the masters of art."—*Nation.* 028.

SERIES.

Important series of biographies are the following:

AMERICAN MEN OF LETTERS, edited by Charles Dudley Warner. Bost., Houghton, $1.25 per vol.

AMERICAN RELIGIOUS LEADERS. Bost., Houghton, $1.25 per vol.

AMERICAN STATESMEN, edited by John T. Morse, Jr. Bost., Houghton, $1.25 per vol.

FAMOUS WOMEN. Bost., Roberts, $1 per vol.

GREAT COMMANDERS, edited by Gen. James Grant Wilson. N. Y., Appleton, $1.50 per vol.

GREAT WRITERS, edited by Prof. Eric S. Robertson, with complete bibliography to each volume by J. P. Anderson. N. Y., Scribner, $1 per vol.; A. Lovell & Co., 40 c. per vol.

HEROES OF THE NATIONS, edited by Evelyn Abbott. N. Y., Putnam, $1.50 per vol.

MEN OF ACHIEVEMENT. N. Y., Scribner, $2 per vol.

HISTORY.

A SELECTION FROM ITS LITERATURE,

ANNOTATED BY

REUBEN GOLD THWAITES,
Secretary of the State Historical Society of Wisconsin.

"Let us not think that there can be any real progress made which is not based on a sound knowledge of the living institutions and the active wants of mankind."—FREDERIC HARRISON, in "The Meaning of History."

Madison, Wis., June, 1895.

UNIVERSAL HISTORY.

Fisher, George Park.

OUTLINES OF UNIVERSAL HISTORY. N. Y., Am. Book Co., 1885. 674 p., D. $2.40.

Compact in style, and excellent in arrangement, with many maps and tables. Useful for general reference, and for serious students who purpose taking up history in course, and desire in advance a bird's-eye view. **000.**

THE UNITED STATES.

Period of Discovery.

Fiske, John.

DISCOVERY OF AMERICA. Bost., Houghton, 1892. 2 vols., 516, 631 p., D. $4.

Fiske performs the useful and honorable office of marshalling the facts deduced by the best and latest monographists, and presenting them to the reading public in a coherent form. He has a keen sense of historical perspective and proportion, takes a large, philosophic view of his subject, and has a charming literary style. The study of American history has been popularized by his books; thousands, heretofore indifferent to it, have first been led by the works of Fiske to see that we have a national history which is highly picturesque and deserves our closest attention. This work is one of the best from his hand, and is important as laying a solid foundation for the study of American history. The introductory chapter is the most satisfactory popular presentation of the characteristics, customs, and antecedents of the Indians, which we have in print. **073.1.**

Short General Histories.

Epochs of American History. (1) THE COLONIES, 1492-1750, by Reuben G. Thwaites, 301 p. (2) FORMATION OF THE UNION, 1750-1829, by Albert B. Hart, 278 p. (3) DIVISION AND REUNION, 1829-1889, by Woodrow Wilson, 326 p. N. Y., Longmans, 1891-93, $1.25 each.

The aim of the series is to study causes rather than events—the development of the American nation out of scattered and inharmonious colonies; the throwing off English control, the growth out of narrow political conditions; the struggle against foreign domination, and the extension of popular government. Marginal analyses, working bibliographies, well-executed maps, and indices, have been provided. The series is designed both for general reading and class work. **073.**

Eggleston, Edward.

HOUSEHOLD HISTORY OF THE UNITED STATES AND ITS PEOPLE. For Young Americans, N. Y., Appleton, 1888. xvi + 395 p., O. $2.50.

Its literary merits, its prodigality of maps and illustrations, ensure for this book a high and permanent place among popular histories.—*Literary World.*

Contains 75 maps and 300 illustrations. The principal features are contained in the author's School History, also published in 1888 (N. Y., Am. Book Co., $1.05). **073.**

Fiske, John.

HISTORY OF THE UNITED STATES. Bost., Houghton, 1894. 474 p., D. $1.

Designed as a school-book, but useful as an elementary handbook for general reading. Clear, concise, and popular in style, like all Fiske's works. The maps and illustrations are excellent. An attempt is made, by a different hand, to give a selected bibliography of each State; but it is defective and misleading, in that it chiefly mentions out-of-print books, many of them long since discredited, and recognizes but few modern works that have been published by rival houses. **073.**

Smith, Goldwin.

THE UNITED STATES: AN OUTLINE OF POLITICAL HISTORY, 1492-1871. N. Y., Macmillan, 1893. 312 p., D. $2.

A literary masterpiece, as readable as a novel, remarkable for its compression without dryness, and its brilliancy without any rhetorical effort or display. What American could, with so broad a grasp, and so perfect a style for those who, in Edward Fitzgerald's phrase, "like to sail before the wind over the surface of an even-flowing eloquence," have rehearsed our political history from Columbus to Grant in 300 duodecimo pages of open type?—*Nation.*

Chiefly interesting, nevertheless, as the view of an Englishman long resident in Canada. Excuses the Tory attitude in the Revolution. Has a tide-water conception of the spread of the American people, ignoring the great influence of the West in the building of the American nation. **073.**

Thomas, Allen C.

HISTORY OF THE UNITED STATES. Bost., Heath, 1894. 532 p., D. $1.12.

An interesting compendium, useful for ready reference as well as general reading. Illustrations, maps, tables, topical analyses, foot notes, a bibliography, and a good index, are helpful features. **073.**

Under the Constitution.

Bryce, James.

THE AMERICAN COMMONWEALTH. New edition, revised and enlarged; with new chapters on the Tammany Ring in New York City; the Home of the Nation; The South Since the War; Present and Future of the Negro. N. Y., Macmillan, 1895, 2 vols., $4.

A study of the political and social institutions of the United States by one of the most distinguished of English publicists.

"There are few things for which a civilized people have more cause to be thankful than for an impartial but kindly estimate of their institutions and their character by a thoroughly competent judge. . . . All who have a patriotic and intelligent interest in the country will welcome Professor Bryce's book as one of the most weighty and important contributions ever offered us in the study of the gravest questions of public and social concern. . . . Prof. Bryce divides his work into four principal parts; first, the framework and constitutional machinery of the nation; second, the same of the several States; third, the methods by which this machinery is worked, including party organizations and the men who 'run' them; fourth, the ulterior forces which move the whole and give it direction. This last includes (as subdivisions) public opinion, the influence of religion and of various social institutions. Illustrations of the good and bad working of methods and of forces are introduced; and the whole is supplemented by estimates of the worth of what has been here developed, with some forecast of the future. . . . No earnest and intelligent American can afford to remain ignorant of this work. His education will be incomplete as a preparation for his duties as a citizen if he does not take advantage of the helps to a sound judgment and a noble purpose which are here given."—*Nation.* **342.730.**

McMaster, John Bach.

HISTORY OF THE PEOPLE OF THE UNITED STATES, FROM THE REVOLUTION TO THE CIVIL WAR. To be completed in 6 vols., O. (Vol. IV. issued in 1895.) N. Y., Appleton, $2.50 per vol.

It is our only systematic attempt to obtain a faithful picture of the social conditions of the American people at successive stages of their continued development; and though such successive photographs cannot be expected to be so successful as in the case of the horse in motion, the success in this case is certainly beyond any of our past criterions.—*Nation.*

The earlier volumes are better than the later. He has in the main skilfully handled a great mass of original material, but his perspective is often faulty, and he is too free in vituperation Vol. IV. carries the reader to the admission of Missouri (1821). **973.**

Schouler, James.

HISTORY OF THE UNITED STATES UNDER THE CONSTITUTION. N. Y., Dodd, Mead & Co., 1890. 5 vols., O. $11.25.

Though very far from perfection, in many respects the most real history of the United States yet produced for the period which it covers. It is marked by constant and complete recourse to original sources, a competence for accuracy, and a willingness for fair judgment, a judicious observance of proport on, and a very sound historical sense to unite and vivify the whole.—*Nation.* **073.**

Special Periods.

Campbell, Douglas.

THE PURITAN IN HOLLAND, ENGLAND, AND AMERICA. 3d ed. revised. N. Y., Harper, 1893. 2 vols., O. $5.

The author attacks the old-time theory that American institutions are chiefly traceable to English example, and gives much credit to Dutch influence.

Our Northern States were settled by Puritans—Scotch, Irish, Dutch, Welsh, English—who in their political procedure departed widely from the precedents set them in the British monarchy. Many of the founders, religious teachers, military leaders and constitution-makers of New England had been long residents of Holland. There they had enjoyed peace, prosperity, and often citizenship itself, in a country where the ancient spirit of Teutonic freedom was most vital. The common lands and common schools, the written ballots, municipalities, religious tolerance, a federal union of states, the play of national and local government, the supremacy of the judiciary—in short, most of the precedents of things usually supposed to be of American initiation were in vogue . . . While other scholars have said this in general terms, Mr Campbell, with scholarly diligence and with the acumen of a metropolitan lawyer, has sought out facts and authorities in minute detail, and has massed them with convincing force.—*Critic.* **074.**

Fiske, John.

THE AMERICAN REVOLUTION. Bost., Houghton, 1891. 2 vols., 344, 305 p., D. $4.

As the plan of the book contemplates nothing more than a general history of the Revolutionary War, the author premises that he has not even undertaken to mention all the events of that period, but only those which are of prime significance The reader, therefore, must not turn to these volumes in hopes of finding new facts. . . . Mr. Fiske puts us on our guard against such a presumption; but he may turn to them with full assurance of faith for a fresh rehearsal of the old facts, which no time can stale, and for new views of those old facts, according to the larger framework of ideas in which they can now be set by the master of a captivating style, an expert in historical philosophy.—*Nation.*
073.3.

THE CRITICAL PERIOD OF AMERICAN HISTORY, 1783–1789. Bost., Houghton, 1888. 368 p., D. $2.

The "critical period" is that between the close of the Revolution and the adoption of the Federal Constitution. It is shown how near the new nation came to disaster amid a storm of sectional jealousies, and how arduous were the labors of the fathers of the Constitution oefore their work was accepted by the people, and the union of the States assured. **739.3.**

Johnson, Rossiter.

SHORT HISTORY OF THE WAR OF SECESSION Bost., Houghton, 1888. 552 p., O. $2.50.

The best one-volume history of the War of 1861–65. Interesting and accurate . . . except so far as later monographic publications have brought new light to bear on details. The maps frequently inserted in the text are helpful. **973.7.**

Parkman, Francis.

JESUITS IN NORTH AMERICA IN THE 17TH CENTURY. Bost., Little, Brown & Co., 1867. 463 p., O. $1.50.

Parkman ranks with the best historical writers in the English language. His theme, the struggle for the mastery of this continent, between the national giants of the seventeenth and eighteenth centuries, is at first thought not a popular one, but no one who has once read a volume of Parkman can readily stop short of the entire twelve; for to rare honesty, persistence, and clear-headedness as an investigator, he added a charming literary style which, without the faintest touch of false color or undue proportion, lends to his story all the fascination of romance.

The "Jesuits" is probably the best volume with which to commence, or it may be separately read with profit. The story it tells is one of the most romantic and thrilling in human history. The introductory chapter, on the Indian tribes, is a truthful picture of savage life and manners. The books of Parkman's series in their historical o der, are: "Pioneers of France in the Old World," "The Jesuits in North America," "La Salle and the Discovery of the Great West," "The Old Regime in Canada," "Count Frontenac and New France under Louis XIV.," "A Half-Century of Conflict" (2 vols.), "Montcalm and Wolfe" (2 vols.), and "The Conspiracy of Pontiac" (2 vols.). [Bost., Little, all $1.50 per vol.] "Montcalm and Wolfe" is the best existing account of the French and Indian War, and should not be neglected by any student of American history.

"The Oregon Trail" (Bost, Little, $1.50), an independent book, written before the above series, is a graphic portrayal of the author's life among trans-Missouri tribes before the advent of railways, and in interest ranks with Irving's "Captain Bonneville's Adventures" (N. Y., Putnam, 75 c.), and "Astoria" (N. Y., Putnam, $1; paper, 60 c.). The boy who has read these charming and truthful narratives of life on the plains, by Irving and Parkman, will be forever cured of a taste for nickel and dime libraries of Western adventure. **017.**

Roosevelt, Theodore.

THE WINNING OF THE WEST. N. Y., Putnam, 1889–94. 3 vols., 352, 427, 339 p., O. $2.50 each.

Parkman incidentally gives us the story of the region between the Alleghany Mountains and the Mississippi River, up to the close of the Pontiac conspiracy (1763). Roosevelt in these three volumes tells in vigorous, picturesque style, of the West specifically, from the downfall of New France to the year 1706; a fourth volume, yet to be written, will doubtless carry the story forward to the admission of Ohio (1800), the first Northwestern commonwealth. A general knowledge of Western history is essential to a full understanding of American history in general Too little attention has been paid to the West by our historians, most of whom appear to think that all of the United States that is worth considering lies east of the Alleghanies; this common neglect of many of the mainsprings of national development has resulted in the presentation of a distorted picture. American history will have soon to be rewritten from a larger appreciation of Western conditions; and for this work of the future, Roosevelt wi l be one of the leading authorities. Meanwhile, the general reader shou'd supplement the ordinary histories of the United States with special histories, such as "The Winning of the West."

Hinsdale's "Old Northwest" (Bost, Silver, Burdett, $2.50) may profitably be used in deta led study of the triangular region between the Ohio River, the Great Lakes, and the Mississippi River. **074.3.**

History.

Walker, Francis A.

THE MAKING OF THE NATION, 1783-1817. N. Y., Scribner, 1895. (American History series.) 314 p., D. $1.25.

A careful, at times thrilling, story of this important period of national growth. President Walker's contention is, that during this period the new constitution was under trial, and that we emerged from the second war with England for the first time a nation. In pure English, he freshly relates the circumstances which led to the constitutional convention, the story of its formation and adoption, the practical difficulties in statesmanship which beset the path of the first President, the early settlement of vexed constitutional questions, and incidents relative to the admission of new States, the Louisiana Purchase, and the diplomatic quarrels with England and France, the whole closing with an admirable summary of the War of 1812-15.

Other books already published in this series are: Prof. G. P. Fisher's "The Colonial Era," and Prof. W. M. Sloane's "The French War and the Revolution"; a fourth, in 2 vols., by Prof. J. W. Burgess, is to cover the sixty years following 1817. ($1.25 per vol.) 037.

A General Study.

Shaler, Nathaniel Southgate, *Editor.*

THE UNITED STATES OF AMERICA: a Study of the American Commonwealth, Its Natural Resources, People, Industries, Manufactures, Commerce, and Its Work in Literature, Science, Education, and Self-Government. N. Y., Appleton, 1894. 2 vols., large O. $10.

A work by several writers, many of them of prominence in their several specialties, but largely by the editor himself. It has great value in supplementing the direct reading or study of history. The following chapter headings indicate its scope:

Vol. 1: I.—The continent, and the reasons for its fitness to be the home of a great people; II.—Natural conditions of the East and South; III.—What nature has done for the West; IV.—The North American Indians; V.—The Mississippi Valley; VI.—The Pacific coast; VII.—The farmer's opportunities; VIII.—Minerals and mining; IX.—The forests and lumber industry; X.—The maritime industries of America; XI.—Our military resources.

Vol 2: I.—Productive industry; II.—Transportation. III.—Typical American inventions; IV.—The place of corporate action in our civilization; V.—Our cities; VI.—Education in the United States; VII.—Science in America; VIII.—Literature, art, and architecture; IX.—The physical state of the American people; X.—Political organization of the United States; XI.—How we are governed; XII.—Industry and finance; XIII.—Public hygiene in the United States; XIV.—The place of the individual in American society; XV.—The summing up of the story.

Prof. Shaler has set himself the delightful task of telling the story of the marriage of wild nature with a new and vigorous race of men; and of the giant progeny which came of it, physical, industrial, mental, political. . . . Students of special departments may not always agree with the conclusions here reached, and the standpoint of those treating allied subjects may not be identically the same, but the book is not a controversial one. It is a picture and not a discussion. As a picture it is greatly stimulating, even inspiring, and must be regarded as a remarkable success.—*Nation.* 017.3.

Notes.

The literature of American history is so extensive, and much of it so excellent, that any selection is but arbitrary and open to criticism. Many of the works here mentioned have elaborate bibliographies, which will suffice for readers who desire to pursue the period or topic treated.

George Bancroft's "History of the United States" (author's rev. ed., 6 vols., Appleton, 1884-85, $15) is a stately work, but lacks proportion, is discursive sometimes inaccurate, and not in touch with existing methods of historical study. It may, however through its analytical table of contents, often be used with profit upon special topics.

Richard Hildreth's "History of the United States" (new ed., 6 vols., N. Y., Harper, $12), was written as long ago as 1850. It is comparable with Bancroft's work, is in the main accurate and fair, but dull in style. Most students will find the second half the more profitable.

Hubert Howe Bancroft's stupendous compilation, (37 large octavo volumes, San Francisco, History Co., $4.50 each), upon Central America, Mexico, and the country acquired by the United States from Mexico, should not be overlooked. The work is too detailed for general reading, but may be freely turned to as a cyclopaedia of facts regarding the Pacific States and the Southwest.

The volumes in the several series published by Houghton, "American Statesmen," "American Commonwealths," and "American Men of Letters" ($1.25 per vol.), should not be neglected. A few of the "Story of the States" series (Host., Lothrop, $1.50 per vol.) may also be profitably used. For a popular illustrated history, Higginson's " Larger History of the United States" (N. Y., Harper, $3.50) is recommended. Young people who wish their history sugar-coated will find Coffin's series to their liking—" Boys of '76," " Story of Liberty," " Building the Nation," " Drumbeat of the Nation," " Marching to Victory," " Redeeming the Republic," and " Freedom Triumphant " (N. Y., Harper, $3 each), and " Daughters of the Revolution," also by Coffin (Host., Houghton, $1.50). In a more serious vein, though still popular, are Drake's excellent handbooks: " The Making of New England," " The Making of Virginia and the Middle Colonies," " The Making of the Ohio Valley States," and " The Making of the Great West" (N. Y., Scribner, $1.50 each). Johnston's " United States " (N. Y., Scribner, $1) gives a rapid view of the economic and political features of our history; and in this connection Ely's " Labor Movement in America" (N. Y., Crowell, $1.50) is valuable. Lucy Larcom's " New England Girlhood " (Host., Houghton, 75 c.), an inspiring book for girls, gives an interesting picture of industrial conditions half a century ago.

For ready reference, the student should be familiar with Lossing's " Popular Cyclopaedia of U. S. History" (N. Y., Harper, $10), Jameson's " Dictionary of U. S. History" (Bost., Puritan Pub. Co., $2.75), and Appleton's " Cyclopaedia of American Biography," and Winsor's " Narrative and Critical History of America " (Host., Houghton, 8 vols., $44) is a well of information, that may always be profitably drawn from.

Under Biography are titles of books which may pleasantly and usefully supplement the reading of American history; see Adams, Clay, Douglass. Franklin, Henry, Lee, Lincoln, Madison, and Washington.

The American Historical Association (Dr. Herbert B. Adams, Johns Hopkins Univ., Baltimore, secretary) meets annually, during the Christmas holidays, at Washington. Applicants for membership must be approved by the executive council. The annual membership fee is $3. The Association Papers are annually-published volumes made up of important monographic contributions to American history. Several State and local historical societies have achieved marked success in their respective fields, and have with more or less regularity published notable volumes of " Collections" and " Transactions"—chief among these being the California, Chicago, Kansas, Massachusetts, Michigan, Minnesota, Montana, New York, Pennsylvania, Rhode Island, Southern (Richmond, Va.), Virginia, and Wisconsin societies, Prince Society (Boston), and Gorges Society (Portland, Me.).

"The American Historical Register," of Philadelphia, is the organ of the "patriotic-hereditary societies of the United States." Steps have been taken for the inauguration, in October, 1895, of "The American Historical Review," which is to be conducted on a high plane as a worthy representative of this branch of American literature; six leading universities are represented in the editorial board; Prof. J. F. Jameson, Brown University, Providence, R. I., is to be managing editor; subscription, $3 per annum. N. Y., Macmillan & Co. Some of the historical societies publish magazines of varying merit, devoted to their respective sections—most worthy of mention being those of the Iowa, Maine, Pennsylvania, and Virginia State societies, Dedham (Mass.), New England Historic-Genealogical Society, and New York Genealogical and Biographical Society.

CANADA.

Bourinot, John George.

MANUAL OF THE CONSTITUTIONAL HISTORY

OF CANADA. Montreal, Dawson, 1888, 238 p., D. $1.25.

A well-executed, reliable book, covering the field from the earliest periodto the year of publication. The struggle with the mother country for self-government is the chief theme. 342.071.

Kingsford, William.

HISTORY OF CANADA FROM THE EARLIEST TIMES TO 1841. Toronto, Rowsell & Hutchinson. To be completed in 9 vols. Vol. VII., coming down to 1807, was published in 1894; Vol. VIII. will appear Oct., 1895; Vol. IX. Oct., 1896. $3 per vol.

Based upon original documents and carefully sifted testimony; a trustworthy and thoroughly interesting work. The Canadian reader or student who has time for more than a one-volume history of his country should certainly be familiar with this work. The American reader will find it contains informing sidelights on the relations of Louisiana and Canada, the causes of the Revolution, and much else of importance to him. 071.

Machar, Agnes M.

STORIES OF NEW FRANCE. Bost., Lothrop, 1890, 313 p., D. $1.50.

A collection of historic tales illustrating the French *régime*, " the heroic age of Canada." Well calculated to interest young people in the story of the Dominion. 071.

Macmullen, John M.

HISTORY OF CANADA. Brockville, Ont., Macmullen, & Co., 1892, 2 vols., $5.

A useful work brought down to 1892. 071.

Miles, H. H.

HISTORY OF CANADA UNDER FRENCH RÉGIME —1553-1763. Montreal, Dawson, 1872, 521 p., D. $2.

Neither original nor brilliant, but readable, accurate, and fair. The best one-volume work on the most picturesque period of Canadian history. 071.

Smith, Goldwin.

CANADA AND THE CANADIAN QUESTION. N. Y., Macmillan; Toronto, Hunter, Rose & Co., 1891. 325 p., D. $2.

The result of twenty years' observation and study by one of the first historians of the time. He presents a candid and frequently severe criticism of Canadian political history. Argues against the policy which attaches Canada to the British Empire, and favors political, or at least commercial union with the United States. For an opposite view, see G. R. Parkin's " The Great Dominion " (N. Y., Macmillan, 1895, $1.75). 071.

Withrow, William H.

POPULAR HISTORY OF THE DOMINION OF CANADA. Revised edition. Toronto, Wm. Briggs, 1893, 692 p., O. $3.

The best one-volume general history. The author is a Methodist clergyman, and often unfair to French Catholics and Tory Episcopalians and Presbyterians; it seems difficult for Canadian historians to free themselves of religious or political bias. The literary style is lifeless; nevertheless, it is a useful book. The several provinces, and Newfoundland, are included in the treatment, which brings down the story to 1893. 071.

Note.

Of course Parkman's works, previously enumerated, hold the first rank for the period of French *régime*. The English period is dull, except during the War of 1812-15, a brilliant episode not yet impartially treated, for the materials are just becoming available.

ELSEWHERE IN AMERICA.

SPANISH AMERICA.

Winsor's " Narrative and Critical History of America" (Bost., Houghton, 8 vols., $44) contains much material. Mackenzie's " America : A History " (N. Y., Harper) gives the best brief, all-around historical account of Spanish America. Hale's "Story of Mexico" (Story of the Nations series, N. Y, Putnam, $1.50) is the most convenient handbook concerning that country. Prescott's " Conquest of Mexico " (Phila., Lippincot t, $1.50) and "Conquest of Peru" (Phila., Lippincott, $1) are charming works, viewed as literature, but they must be read with caution, for modern archæological investigation has quite exploded the fanciful notions of the early historians concerning the stage of Aztec and Peruvian civilization. The opening chapter of Fiske's " Discovery of North America " (Bost., Houghton, 2 vols., $4) will set the reader right, if studied in connection with Prescott.

WEST INDIES, AND OTHER COLONIES.

Excellent handbooks—historical, economic, and descriptive—are those of the series " Foreign Countries and British Colonies" (Lond., Samps n Low, 3s. 6d. each), which includes Eaton's " West Indies " and Markham s "Peru." Other useful books are Cotton and Payne's "Colonies and Dependencies" (English Citizen series, N. Y., Macmillan, $1), Payne's " History of European Colonies" (Lond , Macmillan, 4s. 6d., Freeman's Historical series), and Lucas's " Historical Geography of European Colonies " (Vol. I. Mediterranean and Eastern Colonies, excluding India, $1.25 ; Vol. II. The West Indian Colonies, $1.90; Vol. III. West Africa, $2: N. Y., Macmillan). Froude's " English in the West Indies " (N. Y., Scribner, $1.75) is noteworthy ; but the reader should consult its antidote, Thomas's " Froudacity " (Phila., Gebbie, $1.25).

THE UNITED KINGDOM.

Freeman, Edward A.

OLD ENGLISH HISTORY FOR CHILDREN. New edition. N. Y., Macmillan, $1.50.

From the landing of Cæsar to the coronation of William the Conqueror. Written for the historian's own children. Delightful for children of a larger growth. Simple, clear, and accurate.

Gardiner, Samuel Rawson.

STUDENT'S HISTORY OF ENGLAND. FROM THE EARLIEST TIMES TO 1885. Illus. In 3 vols., $1.20 each (sold separately), or in 1 vol., $3. N. Y., Longmans.

If we do not greatly mistake, this history of England will supplant all others used as text-books in schools and colleges. The name of the author . . . would prepossess any one in its favor, and a perusal of its pages only accentuates the feeling that here at last we have an accurate, succinct, and entertaining book, fit for schools as well as for the general reader. . . . The illustrations, a notable feature . . . are not the old-fashioned and hackneyed ones to be found in most so-called illustrated histories . . . they are illustrative of the text, and afford an excellent study in the manners of the times.—*Critic.*

The *Nation* says: " Among the living historical writers of England, Mr. Gardiner stands now admittedly the first. But while possessing the capacity for clear narration, and an absolute command of his subject, he often fails in imagination and in dramatic power. . . . Combined with deficiency in the appreciation of violent feeling, there is patent, at any rate in Mr. Gardiner's later writings, a minor fault which mars the effect of his narrative, and even, it may be suspected, occasionally vitiates his judgment. He looks at the events which he is studying rather in piecemeal than as a whole. There is a real danger of his becoming rather a chronicler than an historian." Mr Gardiner's other works, all of which have attracted marked attention, are: " History of England from the Accession of James I. to the Outbreak of the Civil War, 1603 42 " (10 vols., $20); " History of the Great Civil War, 1642-49" (4 vols., $8); " The first two Stuarts and the Puritan Revolution, 1603 60 " ; Epochs of Modern History series, $1); " The Thirty Years' War, 1618-48 " (Epochs of Modern History series, $1; " History of the Commonwealth and the Protectorate, 1649-60, Vol. I., $7. All published by Longmans N Y. 042.

Greeu, John Richard.

SHORT HISTORY OF THE ENGLISH PEOPLE. N. Y., Harper, 1889, 872 p., O. $1.20.

A shelf of pictures, graphic if ever a history was, full of the life and lore of the inextinguishable people (so neglected by previous historians), breathing of cities and towns and hedgerows and the multitudinous movement of trade and commerce, and making itself vivid in every line with traits and characteristics taken directly from the landscape, literature, customs, and eloquence of popular England.—*Critic.*

A richly illustrated large octavo edition in four volumes ($5 each) has been issued by Harper (1893–95). It deserves the attention of the student, because of its wealth of portraits and reproductions of contemporary art. **042**

Hallam, Henry.

THE CONSTITUTIONAL HISTORY OF ENGLAND FROM THE ACCESSION OF HENRY VII. TO THE DEATH OF GEORGE III. N. Y., Armstrong, 1885, 3 vols., O. $4.50.

Later writers have thrown so much new light upon the topics treated by Hallam that much of his work now seems antiquated. Nevertheless, it still holds its own, as a general view, and will always be admired for its impartial tone and the rare erudition of the author. (See MAY.) **342.429**

Higginson, Thomas W., *and* Channing, Edward.

ENGLISH HISTORY FOR AMERICANS. N. Y., Longmans, $1.20.

A text-book of merit, with maps, chronological tables, and bibliography. Mainly devoted to the events most influential on the history and institutions of the United States. **042**

Lecky, William E. H.

HISTORY OF ENGLAND IN THE EIGHTEENTH CENTURY. N. Y., Appleton, 1894, 7 vols., $7. Together with History of Ireland in the Eighteenth Century, Library edition. N. Y., Appleton, 8 vols., $20.

The author seeks "to disengage from the great mass of facts those which relate to the permanent forces of the nation, or which indicate some of the more enduring features of national life." To this end, he avoids the chronological treatment of events, minute records of court and camp, and discusses those larger affairs of England which have influenced political progress, religious development, the manners and thought of the people.

C. K. Adams says: "The most interesting portions to most readers will probably be chap. iii. of Vol I., on the general condition of the people, and the last chapter in Vol. II., on the religious revival and the growth of Methodism." **042.07**

HISTORY OF IRELAND IN THE EIGHTEENTH CENTURY. N. Y., Appleton, 5 vols., $5. Together with History of England in the Eighteenth Century, Library edition. N. Y., Appleton, 8 vols., $20.

By far the best consecutive history of Ireland during the two centuries from the Tudor conquest . . . till the Union.—*Nation.* **041.57**

McCarthy, Justin.

SHORT HISTORY OF OUR OWN TIMES. N. Y., Harper, 1880, 448 p., D. $1.50.

The work next mentioned, condensed. **042.08**

HISTORY OF OUR OWN TIMES, FROM THE ACCESSION OF QUEEN VICTORIA TO THE BERLIN CONGRESS. N. Y., Harper, 1880, 2 vols., 559, 686 p., D. $2.50.

In an interesting, journalistic style, by a Member of Parliament famous in the cause of Irish Home Rule.

The Same. The unabridged text, with an introduction and supplementary chapters, bringing the work down to March, 1894, with new index, and additions to the survey of the literature of the reign of Queen Victoria, by G. Mercer Adam. N. Y., Lovell, Coryell, 1895, 2 vols., $3. **942.08**

THE EPOCH OF REFORM, 1830–50. N. Y., Longmans, $1.

Treats of the important changes in the English political system, from the introduction of Lord Grey's reform bill to the death of Sir Robert Peel—"that marvellous period of political activity." The author has an incisive style, and presents striking pictures of the leading statesmen of that time on both sides of the party fence. He truly says: "No period of equal length in English history encloses a greater number of remarkable figures than the statesmen, orators, and politicians from Lord Grey, Lord John Russell, and O'Connell, to Sir Robert Peel, Lord Palmerston, and Mr. Cobden." **042.08**

Mackintosh, John.

THE STORY OF SCOTLAND. N. Y., Putnam, 1890, 336 p., D. (Story of the Nations series), $1.50.

From the earliest times to the present century. Not as attractively written as some others of this series, but a convenient compendium. **041**

May, Thomas Erskine.

CONSTITUTIONAL HISTORY OF ENGLAND. N. Y., Armstrong, 2 vols., $2.50.

Takes up the subject very nearly where Hallam left off (see HALLAM), that is, commencing with the accession of George III., and carrying the story down to 1870. May's literary style is more entertaining than Hallam's, and the work is one of distinct historical value. **342.420**

Strickland, Agnes.

LIVES OF THE QUEENS OF ENGLAND. With portraits, autographs, and vignettes. N. Y., Macmillan, 8 vols., $16. Un-illustrated, 6 vols., $9. Abridged, 1 vol., $1.75.

A work of very great interest, largely historical. Written from a standpoint which attracts girls and women. **023.1**

Notes.

The following histories may be used for reference, where fuller information is desired for topical work: Green's "History of the English People" (N. Y., Harper, 4 vols., $10), Guizot's "History of England" (N. Y., Lovell, Coryell, 4 vols., $3), Knight's "Popular History of England" (N. Y., Lovell, Coryell, 9 vols., $6.75), Freeman's "History of the Norman Conquest of England" (N. Y., Macmillan, 6 vols., $27), Freeman's "Growth of the English Constitution" (N. Y., Macmillan, $1.75), Traill's "Social England" (now appearing, by various writers, Lond., Cassell, 15s. per vol.), Molesworth's "History of England," from 1810 to 1874 (N. Y., Scribner, 3 vols., $7.20), Morley's "First Sketch of English Literature" (N. Y., Cassell, $2), and Burton's "History of Scotland" (N. Y., Scribner, 9 vols., $25), Longmans (N. Y.) edition of the helpful "Epochs of English History" series, complete in one volume ($1.50), is also recommended for detailed study.

Hume's "History of England" (N. Y., Harper, 6 vols., $3) covers the period from the invasion of Julius Cæsar to the Revolution in 1688. For over a century it has been regarded as a classic; but although elegant in style, and delightfully clear, it abounds in mistakes and is not the product of original research, and is no longer cited as an authority. Macaulay's "History" (cheapest editions, N. Y., Harper, 5 vols., paper, $1; cloth, $1.25; Longmans, 2 vols., $2) commences with the accession of James II., and although covering but seventeen years, will, because of its superb style, doubtless always remain in the first rank of historical literature; modern students have proved it sometimes faulty in its facts, and the author's strong political bias as a Whig caused him to be at times grossly unfair. Froude's work (N. Y., Scribner, 12 vols., $18) treats only of the period from the fall of Wolsey to the death of Elizabeth; it is skilfully written, spirited in style, and highly popular, but Froude is constantly taking sides and sacrificing truth to rhetorical effect.

Montgomery's "Leading Facts of English History" (Bost., Ginn, $1 12) is a useful and attractive handbook, which the student would do well to own. Acland and Ransome's "Handbook in Outline of the Political History of England" (N. Y., Longmans, $2) is valuable for chronologies and summaries, and ready reference. "The Dictionary of English History," by Low and Pulling (N. Y., Cassell, $6), will, as its name indicates, be of daily service to the student.

Allen's "Reader's Guide to English History" (Bost., Ginn, 25 c.) gives not only selected lists of histories, but genealogical tables, and lists of novels, poems, and dramas illustrating the life and manners of the several periods. This manual should be owned by students wishing to engage in detailed study.

EUROPEAN CONTINENT.

General.

Duruy, Victor.

HISTORY OF MODERN TIMES. Translated by E. A. Grosvenor. N. Y., Holt, 1894, 540 p., D $1.60.

Covers the general history of European states from the close of the Middle Ages to "the commencement of contemporaneous history"—that is, from the fall of Constantinople (1453) to the French Revolution. A valuable compendium, by one of the foremost French historians of our day; but the style is dry, making it difficult of perusal by the reader who desires entertainment as well as information. **040.5.**

Emerton, Ephraim.

INTRODUCTION TO THE STUDY OF THE MIDDLE AGES. (A.D. 375–814.) Bost., Ginn, 1888, 268 p., D. $1.12.

"One of the best, if not indeed the very best short history of the Middle Ages which has been published in any language.... The author has, it seems to us, done himself especial credit in his clear description of the Christian Church.... The style is almost too familiar; for, though written especially for younger students, we are quite certain that the book will attract many older readers."—*Critic.* **040.1.**

MEDIÆVAL EUROPE. Bost., Ginn, 1894, 607 p., D. $1.50.

Covering the period from the death of Charlemagne (814) to the close of the fourteenth century. Quite as interesting as the "Introduction," but addressed to students more advanced. An admirable manual, and authoritative; with bibliographical introduction, maps, and plans. **040.1.**

Fyffe, C. A.

HISTORY OF MODERN EUROPE. N. Y., Holt, 1886–90, 3 vols., 540, 513, 572 p., O. $6.

The most important work in English on general European history from the outbreak of the French Revolution (1792) to the Congress of Berlin (1878). Readable and reliable. **040.**

Keary, C. F.

THE DAWN OF HISTORY: AN INTRODUCTION TO PRE-HISTORIC STUDY. New edition. N. Y., Scribner, 1889, 367 p., D. $1.25.

The author's purpose is to present "An account of the ascertainable doings and thoughts on the part of the people who have gone to make up the historic races of the world—to leave the reader, so to say, at the door of history." As a study of the early growth in culture of the primeval nations of the earth, this work is important in laying the foundation to a broad course of historical study. Although profound in treatment, the style is clear and readable, and many errors in the earlier edition have been corrected in this. The appendix of "Notes and authorities" is useful as a guide to more detailed study. **572.**

Michaud, Joseph F.

HISTORY OF THE CRUSADES. N. Y., A. C. Armstrong & Son, 3 vols., $3.75.

Although stress is laid on the part played by France in the Crusades, the history is told with fairness. The first is the most interesting volume. **040.4.**

Myers, P. V. N.

OUTLINES OF MEDIÆVAL AND MODERN HISTORY. Bost., Ginn, 1886, 740 p., D. $1.50.

Commencing with the fall of Rome (476), the story of the ages is brought down to our own day. Unlike most "outlines," the book is readable. There are several good maps, and analyses for collegiate work. **040**

Myers, P. V. N., *and* Allen, W. F.

ANCIENT HISTORY FOR COLLEGES AND HIGH SCHOOLS. Part I. (Myers), EASTERN NATIONS AND GREECE, 369 p.; Part II. (Allen), SHORT HISTORY OF THE ROMAN PEOPLE, 370 p., D. Bost., Ginn, 1890–94, $1.50.

The first part is a revision of the major portion of Myers's excellent "Outlines of Ancient History"; the second part is a new work, remarkable for breadth of grasp and skilful condensation. A helpful feature of Allen's work is its reference to historical novels and popular works for collateral reading. **037.**

Seebohm, Frederic.

THE ERA OF THE PROTESTANT REVOLUTION. N. Y., Longmans, 1877 (Epochs of Modern History), 236 p., S. $1.

Limited to the events of the sixteenth century. A convenient manual for the general reader. A more elaborate treatment for special study will be found in Hausser's "Period of the Reformation" (N. Y., Am. Tract Soc., $2). **040.7.**

Greece and Rome.

Blümner, H.

HOME LIFE OF THE ANCIENT GREEKS. Translated by Alice Zimmern. Illus. N. Y., Cassell, 1893, $2.

Contents include: Costume, Education, Marriage and women, Daily life within and without the house, Music and Dancing, Worship, Festivals the Theatre, War, Agriculture, Trade and Handicrafts, Slavery. Charming pictures of the most artistic and intellectual race known to history. **938.**

Fowler, W. Warde.

THE CITY-STATE OF THE GREEKS AND ROMANS. N. Y., Macmillan, 1893, 332 p., D. $1.

The author outlines the history of the form of state which was in vogue among the Greeks and Romans until it was absorbed in the Roman empire, and shows to what extent modern civilization has adopted ancient political ideas. Valuable as an introduction to the study of ancient history. **930.**

Froude, James A.

CÆSAR: A SKETCH. N. Y., Harper 1882, 436 p., D. 60 c.

A careful study of "the conversion of the Roman republic into a military empire." Froude, though didactic, is always readable, and the student will from this book obtain a good outline picture of Roman life and conditions at the time of Cæsar. **87.**

Gibbon, Edward.

HISTORY OF THE DECLINE AND FALL OF THE ROMAN EMPIRE. With notes by Dean Milman, M. Guizot, and A. W. Smith. N. Y., Harper, 6 vols., $12. With notes by Dean Milman and M. Guizot. N. Y., Harper, 6 vols., $3.

The same, Abridged. N. Y., Harper, 1 vol., $1.25.

> Probably still entitled to be esteemed as the greatest historical work ever written. The period embraced extends from the middle of the second century of our era to the fall of Constantinople, in 1453.... Two objections have often been urged, with reason, against this work; its style has an unbending stateliness; and Gibbon had a strong bias against Christianity.—C. K. ADAMS.
>
> Dr. Smith's notes add so much to the value of the work that the first of the three editions here named is decidedly the best. **037.00.**

Kingsley, Charles.

THE ROMAN AND THE TEUTON. N. Y., Macmillan, 1864, 340 p., O. $1.25.

> "These lectures throw no light upon any of the difficult and disputed points in the history of the Middle Ages. But this fact does not detract from their value. They were intended not as a history, but rather as a commentary on the significance and influence of historical events. They are to be judged, therefore, simply as the speculations of a remarkably ingenious and interesting mind; and as such, they form, for the general reader, one of the most stimulating volumes ever written on this somewhat dreary period."—C. K. ADAMS. **040.**

Mahaffy, J. P.

OLD GREEK LIFE. (History Primers series.) N. Y., Am. Book Co., 101 p., T. 35 c.

> A convenient and interesting handbook. The other volumes of the Primer series may also be cordially recommended to those desiring a brief elementary survey of the field treated, before entering upon closer study. **038.**

Oman, C. W. C.

A HISTORY OF GREECE. N. Y., Longmans, 1894, 560 p., S. $1.50.

> Covers the story of Greece from the earliest times to the death of Alexander the Great, in clear, orderly fashion. An admirable handbook in many ways, with abundant maps and plans. **038.**

Preston, Harriet W., *and* Dodge, Louise.

THE PRIVATE LIFE OF THE ROMANS. Bost., Leach, 1894 (Students' Series of Latin Classics), 107 p., D. $1.25.

> An elementary handbook for young readers. **037.**

France.

Carlyle, Thomas.

HISTORY OF THE FRENCH REVOLUTION. N. Y., Harper, 2 vols., D. $2.50; Crowell, 1 vol., $1.25.

> A remarkable collection of vividly drawn portraits, and philosophical dissertations thereon. One of the most striking of Carlyle's works; intensely characteristic of his peculiar genius, it is not a history in the generally accepted sense. The reader should be well acquainted with the subject before taking up this book. **044.04.**

Duruy, Victor.

HISTORY OF FRANCE. Translated by J. F. Jameson. N. Y., Crowell, 1889, 706 p., D. $2.

> The study of French history is of prime importance, for the story of France is the story of Europe. From the earliest times her interests have been more or less intimately linked with those of her continental neighbors. There is a growing tendency among teachers to instruct in general European history, through the medium of French history. Hence the citation in the present list of so many works in this field. Duruy's is the best one-volume history; eminently useful to students, but lacks color, and repels the general reader. This edition is without the illustrations, which are so valuable a feature of the original, but is abundantly supplied with maps. Montgomery's "Leading Facts of French History" (Bost.,

(Ginn, $1.12), and Creighton's elementary "First History of France" (N. Y., Longmans, $1.25), are useful. The best of the large histories of France is Guizot's (Bost., Estes, 8 vols., $10). **044.**

Gardiner, Bertha Meriton.

THE FRENCH REVOLUTION, 1789-95. N. Y., Longmans, 1889 (Epochs of Modern History), 262 p., S. $1.

> A thoroughly reliable handbook. **044.04.**

Lacombe, Paul.

THE GROWTH OF A PEOPLE. Translated by L. A. Stimson. N. Y., Holt, 1883, 224 p., S. 80 c.

> A charmingly written elementary view of French history, from the earliest times, chiefly tracing the growth of the evils which the Revolution eradicated, and showing how necessary was that upheaval to the perfect development of the nation. **044.**

Germany.

Bryce, James.

THE HOLY ROMAN EMPIRE. N. Y., Macmillan, 1866, 465 p., D. $1.

> Invaluable to the student who desires thoroughly to study the foundations of German history. **043.**

Carlyle, Thomas.

HISTORY OF FREDERICK THE SECOND, CALLED FREDERICK THE GREAT. N. Y., Lovell, Coryell, 4 vols., $4.50.

> "The book is founded on the most exhaustive study and the most careful observation. The author even visited the more important of Frederick's battle-fields, and had surveys made in the interests of absolute accuracy. Every scrap of German writing that would throw light on the reign appears to have been examined and weighed. The result is one of the most remarkable books in the English language, and one which, all things considered, is unquestionably the best history of Frederick the Great in any language."—C. K. ADAMS.
>
> Books II. and III., Vol. I., give a succinct history of Prussia from 928 down to the birth of Frederick (1712). **023.143.**

Henderson, E. F.

HISTORY OF GERMANY IN THE MIDDLE AGES. N. Y., Macmillan, $2.60.

> The best work for this period in English. The same author is preparing works covering the Time of the Reformation and the Thirty Years' War, and Modern Times.
>
> See also S. Baring-Gould's "Story of Germany" (Story of the Nations series), N. Y., Putnam, $1.50; this author's "History of Germany" (N. Y., Dodd, $1.50) is fuller, and designed for advanced students. Sime's "History of Germany" (in Freeman's "Historical Course for Schools," N. Y., Holt, 80 c.) is brief, and in many ways excellent, but dry reading. **043.**

Holland.

Motley, John Lothrop.

RISE OF THE DUTCH REPUBLIC. N. Y., Harper, Library edition, sold only in sets, 3 vols., $6; Original edition, 3 vols., sold separately, $3.50 each.

> In clearness of diction, strength of characterization, and dramatic power, Motley has few equals among historical writers; but while his manner charms, and noble impulses are quickened by his sturdy love of freedom, the critical reader feels that often the author's statement is not judicial and that there must be another side to the shield.
>
> "The work, after an historical introduction of ninety-two pages, is devoted to that turbulent age from the abdication of Charles V., in 1555, to the assassination of William of Orange, in 1584. Much of this period, therefore, is the same as that treated by Prescott in his

"History of Philip II."; but the point of view is essentially different. While the one is looking from Spain, the other is looking from Holland. Throughout the history, William of Orange is Motley's idol and his client. In his behalf he has certainly made a magnificent plea; but it is a plea, not a decision."—C. K. ADAMS. **949.203.**

HISTORY OF THE UNITED NETHERLANDS; FROM THE DEATH OF WILLIAM THE SILENT TO THE TWELVE YEARS' TRUCE—1609. N. Y., Harper, Library edition, 4 vols., sold only in sets, $8; Original edition, 4 vols., sold separately, $3.50 each.

"There have been few more important years in all modern history than those during which was matured the great Spanish project of conquering England and the Netherlands, and bringing them again under Catholic rule. The intimate connection of the kingdom of England and the republic of Holland at the time when the fate of Protestantism rested with them alone, made the history of the two commonwealths, in many respects, nearly identical. It is this period and this struggle, as well as the interior government of the Netherlands, that Motley has portrayed in the work before us."—C. K. ADAMS.

Has the same characteristics as the "Rise of the Dutch Republic"—a glowing style, but a partisan presentation. **949.203.**

Italy.

Symonds, John Addington.

A SHORT HISTORY OF THE RENAISSANCE IN ITALY. N. Y., Holt, 1894, 335 p., D, $1.75.

This is a condensation, by Alfred Pearson, of Symonds's large work, in 5 vols., "The Renaissance in Italy" (N. Y., Holt, $14), which ranks as perhaps the best on that subject, although too ponderous for any save special students. Mrs. Symonds certifies in the Preface that the essence of her husband's work "has been reproduced without any important omission." **945.05.**

Scandinavia.

Otté, E. C.

SCANDINAVIAN HISTORY. N. Y., Macmillan, 1874, 399 p., S. $1.25.

The best general history, in our language, of all the Scandinavian countries—Denmark, Norway, and Sweden. The style is smooth and the interest well sustained. Maps and genealogical tables materially assist the reader.

Also to be recommended are Boyesen's "Story of Norway" (Story of the Nations series, N. Y., Putnam, $1.50), which will be found interesting and spirited; and Keary's "Norway and the Norwegians" (N. Y., Scribner, $1.50), equally interesting and more descriptive than Boyesen's work. Scandinavia has indirectly played a large part in European history, and her story should be more generally understood. **948.**

METHODS OF HISTORICAL STUDY.

Adams, Herbert B.

METHODS OF HISTORICAL STUDY. Balt., Johns Hopkins Press, 1884, 137 p., O. 50 c.

Chiefly devoted to an account of methods in vogue at Johns Hopkins University, with glimpses of methods of a few other representative colleges in the United States and Europe. Full of practical suggestions to teachers of history and advanced students. **007.**

Freeman, Edward A.

METHODS OF HISTORICAL STUDY. N. Y., Macmillan, 1886, 335 p., O. $2.50.

Originally delivered as lectures at Oxford. The relations of history to other studies are considered, its peculiar difficulties pointed out, and discussions entered into concerning the nature of historical evidence, original and subsidiary authorities, and the importance of geography and travel upon historical study. There are brief estimates of ancient, mediæval, and modern historians—altogether, an important book for the student who seeks to make this his peculiar field. **907.**

Harrison, Frederic.

THE MEANING OF HISTORY, AND OTHER HISTORICAL PIECES. N. Y., Macmillan, 1895, 482 p., O. $2.25.

An inspiring book, well calculated "to stimulate the systematic study of general history." The third chapter, "Some Great Books of History," seeks to aid the reader in the choice of books, and has practical value bibliographically. A good work for the serious student to dip into at various points. **907.**

Hinsdale, B. A.

HOW TO STUDY AND TEACH HISTORY, WITH PARTICULAR REFERENCE TO THE HISTORY OF THE U. S. N. Y., Appleton (International Education series), 1894, 23+346 p., D. $1.50.

The author is professor of the science and art of teaching in the University of Michigan. Elementary and secondary teachers, whom he has had mainly in mind, will find much in this book to interest and stimulate, even although they are familiar with recent thought upon this subject. This work should prove of great value to scholars in normal and high schools, and to college students. Prof. Hinsdale begins with an examination of the nature of history, interweaves theories of writing and teaching it, and concludes with a practical example of proper methods, drawn from the history of the United States.—*Nation.* **907.**

GENERAL NOTES.

Historical Dictionaries.

Larned's "History for Ready Reference" (Springfield, Mass., C. A. Nichols & Co., 1895, 5 vols, $5 per vol), gives, on the dictionary plan, skilfully condensed excerpts from the leading authorities on each topic. A rich storehouse of information, invaluable to teacher, student, and casual reader.

Brewer's "The Historic Note-Book" (Phila., Lippincott, $3.50) is a standard dictionary of universal history, containing many curious data elsewhere difficult of access.

On somewhat different lines is Heilprin's "Historical Reference Book" (N. Y., Appleton, $3), valuable for chronological tables and geographical notes.

Bibliographies.

Advanced students may consult with profit Adams's "Manual of Historical Literature" (N. Y., Harper, 1889, $2.50), the largest and best historical bibliography.

The student should own Allen's "History Topics" (Heath, 25 c.), which gives lists of best histories, with brief comments thereon, of various epochs and countries; also, lists of novels, poems, and plays, to be read in connection with historical studies.

For historical and descriptive fiction, consult also Griswold's Lists of American, International, Romantic, and British Novels (Cambridge, Mass, 1891).

Series.

We can in the main recommend The Story of the Nations (N. Y., Putnam, $1.50 each), particularly in addition to those already cited, the volumes on Egypt, Phœnicia, Chaldæa, Assyria, Persia, Alexander's Empire, The Crusades, Switzerland, Russia, Holland, Spain and The Jews. This series "dwells particularly upon the dramatic phases of historical events, and concerns itself but slightly with the growth of institutions and sociological phenomena"—serious limitations these, resulting often in painful lack of proportion.

The Heroes of the Nations (N. Y., Putnam, $1.50 each) is a series open to the same objections, but the volumes are convenient and generally readable. The most useful in a line of study are those on Nelson, Gustavus Adolphus, Pericles, Theodoric, Sir Philip Sidney, Cæsar, Cicero, and Henry of Navarre.

It is difficult to select from the Epochs series (N. Y. Longmans, $1 per vol.); of "Epochs of Ancient History," the two volumes on the Roman Empire are the most interesting; of "Epochs of Modern History," the only ones dealing with general European history, which have not herein been mentioned, are the "Thirty Years' War" and "Frederick the Great."

TRAVEL AND EXPLORATION.

CHOSEN BY ADELAIDE R. HASSE,
Office of Superintendent of Documents, Washington, D. C.

Washington, D. C., July, 1895.

"Home-keeping youth have ever homely wits."
—SHAKESPEARE: *Two Gentlemen of Verona.*

Africa. *See* Stanley, H. M., and Vincent, Frank.

Alaska. *See* Finck, H. T.; Scidmore, Miss E. R.

Amicis, D', E.

HOLLAND AND ITS PEOPLE. Translated by Caroline Tilton. Illus. N. Y., Putnam, 1880, $2.25.
By an Italian traveller of rare powers of sympathetic observation. **014.02.**

SPAIN AND THE SPANIARDS. Translated by W. W. Cady. Illus. N. Y., Putnam, 1881, $2.
The most interesting and informing book on modern Spain. **014.**

Appleton's

CANADIAN GUIDE-BOOK. Maps and illus. N. Y., Appleton, 1895, $1.50.
Prof. C. G. D. Roberts describes Eastern Canada; supplementary chapters take the tourist through Western Canada, through Manitoba and the Territories to British Columbia. **917.1.**

GENERAL GUIDE TO THE UNITED STATES AND CANADA. Maps and illus. N. Y. Appleton, 1895. In 1 vol., complete, $2.50. New England and Middle States and Canada, $1.25; Southern and Western States, $1.25.
The best guide in small compass. **917.3.**

GUIDE TO MEXICO. Including chapter on Guatemala, and English-Spanish vocabulary. By A. R. Conkling. N. Y., Appleton, 1889, $1.50. **917.2.**

Arctic Regions. *See* Greely, Lieut.; Nansen, F.; Nordenskiold, A. E.; Peary, Mrs. J. D.

Argentina. *See* Child, T.

Bacon, Alice M.

JAPANESE GIRLS AND WOMEN. Bost., Houghton, 1891, $1.25.
Education; marriage and divorce; motherhood; court life; women in the palace and hut, and as laborers and servants in country and city. The first clear, full, and trustworthy presentation of women in Japan.—*Literary World.*

A JAPANESE INTERIOR. Bost., Houghton, 1893, $1.25.
The Japanese home faithfully sketched from a woman's point of view. **015.2.**

Baedeker's GUIDE-BOOKS TO THE UNITED STATES, CANADA, AND COUNTRIES OF EUROPE, ASIA, AND AFRICA. Various prices. Traveller's Manual of Conversation in English, German, French, and Italian, 90 c.; Conversation Dictionary in same languages, 90 c. N. Y., Scribner.

Ball, J. Dyer.

THINGS CHINESE. N. Y., Scribner, 1893, $3.
Modelled on Prof. B. H. Chamberlain's "Things Japanese." Author is an English civil service officer. For the general reader, the intending tourist who needs a guide through the literature of China, this handy work of reference is without a peer.—*Nation.* **015.1.**

Bates, H. Walter.

THE NATURALIST ON THE RIVER AMAZONS: a Record of Adventures, Habits of Animals, Sketches of Brazilian and Indian Life. Bost., Roberts, 1874, $2.50.

The Same : WITH A MEMOIR OF THE AUTHOR BY E. CLODD. N. Y., Appleton, 1893, $5.
Lapse of time since the material was gathered has not impaired the value of this book, but rather, as a record of facts, for purposes of comparison, and in view of the changes that have occurred in the region traversed, its importance has increased, while it has lost none of its interest and freshness as a narrative of personal adventures on the borders of civilization as they were in the Amazon forests forty years ago. Bates had an ability to see things in their actual relations, and a breadth of view that are rare. [He first observed and explained Protective Mimicry.] He had the spirit of the true naturalist, one of the few deserving the name as compared with the many who collect, dissect, or toy with nature otherwise ; who are not naturalists, but only manipulators. . . . With so many elements of value and permanence, the work is one that cannot be superseded ; it is worthy a place in any library.—*Nation.* **018.1.**

Benjamin, S. G. W.

PERSIA AND THE PERSIANS. Bost., Houghton, 1886, $3.
Careful in observation, effective in description, with the quality of positive interest.—*Critic.* **935.5.**

Bisland, Elizabeth.

THE ART OF TRAVEL, a chapter (Vol. I., p. 371) in the Woman's Book. N. Y., Scribner, 1894, 2 vols., $7.50.
The same work gives (Vol. II., p. 319) a full list of guide-books, works of travel, tables of distances, of health resorts, of foreign money, and so on.

Borrow, George.

THE BIBLE IN SPAIN. N. Y., Scribner, $1 ; Ward, Lock, 75 c.
An interesting record of travel in Spain in 1841, by an accomplished linguist. **014.0.**

Brandes, G.

IMPRESSIONS OF RUSSIA. Translated from the Danish by S. C. Eastman. N. Y., Crowell, 1889, $1.25.
By far the most important book on Russia that has been published for some years. The author (one of the foremost authors of Europe) is no novice in travel. He understands how to compare, how to discriminate, and how to judge what he has seen and read.—*Nation.* **014.7.**

Brassey, Anne (Alnutt), Lady.

AROUND THE WORLD IN THE YACHT "SUNBEAM." N. Y., Holt, 1891, $2.
The "Sunbeam" sailed from Cowes, England, July 6, 1876, having on board the entire Brassey family, con-

Travel and Exploration.

sisting of the well-known M. P., the author, and their four children. The volume is one of the most popular of circumnavigation accounts.—*Nation.* 910.4.

Brazil. See Bates, H. W.

Canada. See Appleton's Canadian Guide-Book; Appleton's General Guide to the United States and Canada; Parkin, G. R.; Parkman, F.

Chamberlain, Basil Hall.

THINGS JAPANESE. N. Y., Scribner, 1890, $3.50.

A valuable and comprehensive work. Treats old and new Japan. The author's qualifications are ample; he is a thorough master of Japanese, has long resided in the country. With kindness, and with critical powers of a high order, he calls things by their right names and speaks his mind freely.—*Nation.* 915.2.

Child, Theodore.

SPANISH-AMERICAN REPUBLICS. N. Y., Harper, 1891, $3.50.

The Argentine Confederacy, Chili, Peru, Uruguay, and Paraguay in 1890-91. General conclusions unfavorable to Spanish-American populations. Describes condition of country after war with Chili.—*Critic.* 918.

Chili. See Child, T.

China. See Ball, J. Dyer; Smith, A. T.

Corea. See Griffis, W. E.

Cotes, *Mrs.* **Everard** (Sarah Jeanette Duncan).

A SOCIAL DEPARTURE. N. Y., Appleton, $1.75; paper, 75 c.

Tells how two women went around the world by themselves. Full of keen observation, fun and wit. 910.

Custer, *Mrs.* **Elizabeth B.**

BOOTS AND SADDLES; OR, LIFE IN DAKOTA WITH GEN. CUSTER. N. Y., Harper, 1885, $1.50.

A book breezy with open air and cheery with horse and hound. Mrs. Custer has written a most vivid account of army life, and many of her experiences must be repeating themselves to the devoted wives now on the military frontier.—*Nation.* 970.5.

Dana, Richard H.

TWO YEARS BEFORE THE MAST. New ed. Bost., Houghton, $1.

A classic. Narrates with the utmost charm the author's voyage from Boston in 1835-7, round Cape Horn to the western shores of North America. In "Twenty-four Years After," his closing chapter, Mr. Dana describes the wonderful changes wrought in California between 1835 and 1859. 910.4.

Darwin, Charles.

JOURNAL OF RESEARCHES DURING THE VOYAGE ROUND THE WORLD OF H. M. S. "BEAGLE." New illustrated edition, with maps and 100 views. N. Y., Appleton, 1890, $5.

CHEAP ED., without new illustrations. $2.

The greatest book of travels yet produced, and one of the most charming. Time has done little to invalidate its observations. Forever interesting as the unrecognized herald of the doctrine of evolution.—*Nation.* 508.3.

Dufferin and Ava, Marchioness of.

OUR VICE-REGAL LIFE IN INDIA: Selections from my Journal, 1884-88. 2 vols. N. Y., Scribner, 1889, $2.50.

The distinct value of the book is in the detailed description of the vice-regal round, ceremonial and practical, of native customs and costumes, contrasts of life, Indian and English. A truthful, unpretentious account, without moral, religious, or political bias.—*Nation.* 915.4.

Duncan, Sarah Jeanette (*pseudonym*). See Cotes, Mrs. Everard.

Edwards, Amelia Blandford.

A THOUSAND MILES UP THE NILE. Illus. N. Y., Routledge, 1891, $2.50.

It would be difficult for one who wished to spend a winter on the Nile intelligently and profitably to find a more excellent companion and guide than this book. The parts relating to the ancient history of the country, and the interpretation of inscriptions, have been revised and corrected so as to conform to the latest conclusions of Egyptologists.—*Nation.* 916.2.

Egypt. See Edwards, Amelia B.

England. See Hawthorne, N.; Smith, Goldwin; Winter, W.

English MANUAL OF CONVERSATION, AND DICTIONARY FOR TRAVELERS. See Baedeker, and Murray.

Finck, Henry Theophilus.

PACIFIC COAST SCENIC TOUR. N. Y., Scribner, 1890, $2.50.

A continuous journey northward from the Mexican border to Sitka; of the Canadian Pacific route eastward to Lake Superior; of Yellowstone Park to the Colorado Canyon. In point of readableness and interest the narrative leaves nothing to be desired.—*Nation.* 917.3.

French MANUAL OF CONVERSATION, AND DICTIONARY FOR TRAVELERS. See Baedeker, and Murray.

German MANUAL OF CONVERSATION, AND DICTIONARY FOR TRAVELERS. See Baedeker, and Murray.

Germany. See Mahaffy and Rogers; Millet, F. D.

Greece. See Mahaffy.

Greely, *Lieut.* **A. W.**

THREE YEARS OF ARCTIC SERVICE: An Account of the Lady Franklin Bay Expedition of 1881-84, and the Attainment of the Farthest North. N. Y., Scribner, 1886, 2 vols., $10; 1 vol., $5.

The style of the narrative is excellent, easy and unpretentious. . . . The discussion of the causes which led to the misfortunes of the party is brief, and, in all essentials, is in harmony with the views generally entertained by Arctic experts who know the facts.—*Nation.* 910.8.

Griffis, W. E.

COREA, THE HERMIT NATION. 3d ed., revised and enlarged, with new chapter on Corea in 1888. N. Y., Scribner, 1888, $2.50.

An admirable account of an interesting people. 951.9.

Hapgood, Isabel F.

RUSSIAN RAMBLES. Bost., Houghton, 1895, $1.50.

Miss Hapgood not only is familiar with the language and ways of the people she describes, she is also capable of feeling with them, of judging by other than a narrow American standard, and of sympathizing with much that was strange to her as it is to her readers.—*Nation.* 914.7

Hare, A. J. C.

FLORENCE. N. Y., Routledge, 1884. $1.

Mr. Hare is the author of several books on Italy and its cities, which serve to supplement guide-books in the happiest way. His pages are richly freighted with historical allusion, with all the informal details of art and poetry that serve to add charm and interest to a leisurely tour. 045.5.

STUDIES IN RUSSIA. Illus. N. Y., Routledge, 1885, $2.

Contains many citations from the best literature descriptive of Russia. A capital handbook for the tourist. 014.7.

VENICE. N. Y., Routledge, 1884, $1.

A little encyclopedia of information about each palace, or picture, or famous spot; very little of the information is given by Mr. Hare himself, the book consisting almost entirely of extracts from the best literature; makes the most valuable kind of guide-book one may have.—*Critic*. 045.3.

Hawthorne, Nathaniel.

OUR OLD HOME. Bost., Houghton, 1892, $1.

English sketches during Hawthorne's sojourn in England, 1853-1857, as American consul at Liverpool. The incidental criticism is candid. 014.2.

Hearn, Lafcadio.

GLIMPSES OF UNFAMILIAR JAPAN. Bost., Houghton, 1894, 2 vols., $4.

These volumes mark a distinct point of progress in our acquaintance, through books, with the Japanese. . . . Here, too, are descriptions of travel, wonderful accounts of famous temples and neighborhoods, charming stories of personal experience; . . . but beyond and above these things, Mr. Hearn has succeeded in photographing, as it were, the Japanese soul.—*Nation*. 015.2.

TWO YEARS IN THE FRENCH WEST INDIES. N. Y., Harper, 1890, $2.

Brilliant. Mainly on Island of Martinique. Descriptive portion largely interwoven with legends, poems, music, and folk-lore.—*Nation*. 017.208.

Higginson, Thomas W.

YOUNG FOLKS' BOOK OF AMERICAN EXPLORERS. Illus. N. Y., Longmans, $1.20.

Contents: Legends of the Northmen; Columbus and his companions; Cabot and Verazzano; Cabeza De Vaca; the French in Canada; De Soto; the French in Florida; Sir Humphrey Gilbert; lost colonies of Virginia; unsuccessful New England settlements; Capt. John Smith; Champlain on the warpath; Hudson and the New Netherlands; Pilgrims at Plymouth; Massachusetts Bay Colony.

Brief sketches of high interest. 010.

Holland. *See* Amicis, D', E.

Hudson, C. H.

IDLE DAYS IN PATAGONIA. N. Y., Appleton, 1893, $4.

Although this volume has not the absorbing interest for the naturalist of the author's work on La Plata, it is yet full of suggestive observations and reflections, and gives one a very vivid picture of both animate and inanimate nature in one of the least-known portions of the Southern Hemisphere.—Alfred Russel Wallace, in *Nature*. 018.

THE NATURALIST IN LA PLATA. N. Y., Appleton, 1892, $4.

Written by a native to whom the various tribes of beasts, birds, and insects of his country have been familiar from childhood, and who for twenty years has observed carefully and recorded accurately everything of interest in the life-history of the various species with which he has become acquainted. . . . Never have I derived so much pleasure and instruction from a book on the habits and instincts of animals. It will long continue a storehouse of facts and observations of the highest value to the philosophical naturalist, while to the general reader it is the most interesting and delightful modern book on natural history.—Alfred Russel Wallace, in *Nature*. 018.

India. *See* Dufferin.

Italian MANUAL OF CONVERSATION AND DICTIONARY FOR TRAVELERS. *See* Baedeker.

Italy. *See* Hare, A. J. C.; Florence, and Venice.

Japan. *See* Bacon, Alice M.; Chamberlain, B. H.; Hearn, L.; Tracy, A.

Kinglake, Alexander.

EOTHEN; OR, TRACES OF TRAVEL BROUGHT HOME FROM THE EAST. N. Y., Putnam, $1.

The journey was made about 1835. Rather a delightful record of personal impressions than of outward facts.—*Leslie Stephen*. 015.6.

Knox, Thomas W.

HOW TO TRAVEL. N. Y., Putnam, 1888, 75 c.

Hints, advice, and suggestions to travellers by land and sea. The outcome of more than twenty years' world-wide travel. A chapter, by a lady, gives excellent advice to ladies. 010.2.

Lippincott's GAZETTEER OF THE WORLD. Phila., Lippincott, 1893, $12. 910.3.

Loomis, L. C.

INDEX GUIDE TO TRAVEL AND ART-STUDY IN EUROPE. N. Y., Scribner, 1892, $3.

Part I. Scenery, Arts, History, Legend and Myth Part II. Catalogue of the noted works of art in the principal galleries of Central Europe. Part III. Routes, embracing the principal through lines of travel.

The value of the Guide is incontestable.—*Nation*. 014.

Mahaffy, J. P.

RAMBLES AND STUDIES IN GREECE. N. Y., Macmillan, 1878, $3.

By a famous professor of Greek. Includes chapters on Mycenæ, and on Greek music and painting. The "rambles" are delightful. To the "studies" scholars demur. 013.38.

Mahaffy, J. P., *and* **Rogers, J. E.**

SKETCHES OF A TOUR THROUGH HOLLAND AND GERMANY. N. Y., Macmillan, 1888, $2.

Shows a clear insight into the peculiar social conditions of Holland. The chapters devoted to Germany are chiefly interesting because they describe a part of the country rarely visited, viz., the Baltic provinces and some old cities in the interior.—*Nation*. 014.

Martin, *Mrs.* **Annie.**

HOME LIFE ON AN OSTRICH FARM. N. Y., Appleton, 1892. $1.25.

A perfect book of its kind. A description of a South African home by a writer of keen observing powers and great love of Nature. Her pictures are admirable, especially those of her dumb companions.—*Nation*. 010.8.

Meriwether, Lee.

A TRAMP TRIP; HOW TO SEE EUROPE ON FIFTY CENTS A DAY. N. Y., Harper, 1887, $1.25.

A book quite out of the range of and above the ordinary volumes of travel. It gives a fair, comprehensive idea of the hard labor and miserable poverty of the European masses.—*Nation*. 014.

Mexico. *See* Appleton's guide to.

Millet, Francis Davis.

THE DANUBE FROM THE BLACK FOREST TO THE BLACK SEA. N. Y., Harper, 1892, $2.50.

Journey made by three friends in 1892—one an artist, Alfred Parsons; one an author, Poultney Bigelow; and one an artist and author, F. D. Millet. Spirited and unhackneyed. **914.**

Murray's ENGLISH HANDBOOKS AND FOREIGN HANDBOOKS. Various prices. Travel Talk, $1.40. Handbook Dictionary, English, French, and German, $2.40. N. Y., Scribner.

Nansen, Fridtjof.

ESKIMO LIFE. Translated by Wm. Archer. Illus. N. Y., Longmans, 1893, $2.50.

A description of Arctic life by a man of science. **919.**

Nordenskiold, A. E., *Baron.*

VOYAGE OF THE VEGA. N. Y., Macmillan, 1886, $1.75.

Gives an account of the first circumnavigation of Europe and Asia, in 1878-9. Sketches previous Arctic voyages, with details of their scientific results. The work is a mine of unusual richness for the student of science, while so written as to be both intelligible and delightful to the ordinary reader.—*Nation.* **910.4.**

Oliphant, Laurence.

HAIFA; OR, LIFE IN MODERN PALESTINE. Edited, with introduction, by Chas. A. Dana. N. Y., Harper, 1886, $1.75.

The chief interest of the letters is their portrayal of the social and political conditions during 1882-85. **915.69.**

Palestine. *See* Oliphant, L.; Thomson, W. M.

Paraguay. *See* Child, T.

Parkin, George R.

THE GREAT DOMINION: STUDIES OF CANADA. Maps. N. Y., Macmillan, 1895, $1.75.

A most readable survey of the Canadian provinces and territories, their resources, trade relations, and political tendencies. Of much value and interest to the traveller in Canada. The author is a staunch upholder of British connection, and regards Canada as of great and increasing importance to the remainder of the British Empire. For an opposite view see Goldwin Smith's "Canada and the Canadian Question" (N. Y., Macmillan, $2). **917.1.**

Parkman, Francis.

HISTORIC HANDBOOK OF THE NORTHERN TOUR; Lakes George and Champlain, Niagara, Montreal, Quebec. Bost., Little, Brown & Co., 1885, $1.50.

Author is the famous historian. **073.2.**

Patagonia. *See* Hudson, C. H.

Peary, *Mrs.* **Josephine D.**

MY ARCTIC JOURNAL: A Year (1891-92) Among Ice-Fields and Eskimos. Illus. N. Y., Contemporary Pub. Co., 1893, $2.

Includes a narrative by Robert E. Peary of his journey across Greenland. Not as scientifically exact as Nansen's "Eskimo Life," but less gloomy.—*Literary World.* **919.8.**

Persia. *See* Benjamin, S. G. W.

Peru. *See* Child, T.

Ralph, Julian.

OUR GREAT WEST. N. Y., Harper, 1893, $2.50.

Sketches, by a practised observer and journalist, of Chicago, the Dakotas, Montana, Washington, Colorado, Wyoming, Utah, and San Francisco. Interesting, informing, sympathetic. **917.3.**

Russia. *See* Brandes, G.; Hapgood, Isabel F.; Hare, A. J. C., "Studies in Russia"; Wallace, D. M.

Satchel Guide: for the Vacation Tourist in Europe. Bost., Houghton, 1894, $1.50.

The essentials for the traveller are here. **914.**

Scidmore, *Miss* **Elizabeth Ruhamah.**

ALASKA; ITS SOUTHERN COAST AND THE SITKAN ARCHIPELAGO. Map and illus. Bost., Lothrop, 1885, $1.50; paper, 50 c.

Accurate. Good account of mining industry in Southeastern Alaska. Graphic description of the scenery of the archipelago, and thoughtful presentation of some historical facts.—*Nation.* **917.08.**

Smith, A. T.

CHINESE CHARACTERISTICS. N. Y., F. H. Revell Co., 1894, $2.

Twenty-two years' residence among the people, with command of their language, has enabled Mr. Smith to see the Chinese as they are. While pitilessly telling the truth, there is nothing of the cynic about him. On the contrary, every page shows the author's kindness of heart and willingness to set forth the facts both in the light and the shade.—*Nation.* **915.1.**

Smith, Goldwin.

A TRIP TO ENGLAND. N. Y., Macmillan, 1892, 75 c.

A few of the subjects touched upon are: Historical Britain; the Celts; Roman England; Saxon England; England in the Middle Ages; the cathedrals; the monasteries; old city walls; Elizabethan manor houses; the age of the Stuarts; the universities; the great public schools; the royal palaces; English climate; London society; suburban life. Written in a key of elevated sentiment by a man who sees much of beauty passing with the old order. **914.2.**

Spain. *See* Amicis, D', E.; Borrow, George.

Spanish VOCABULARY. *See* Appleton's guide to Mexico.

Stanley, Henry M.

IN DARKEST AFRICA. N. Y., Scribner, 1890, 2 vols., $7.50.

The first volume carries us to Lake Albert Nyanza, on whose shores the lost Emin Pasha was found; the second volume carries us to Zanzibar. It is all a wonderful panorama of scenery incomparable, of humanity unmatched, of effort prodigious, of incident as true as truest history.—*Literary World.* **916.**

Thomson, W. M., *D.D.*

THE LAND AND THE BOOK; OR, BIBLICAL ILLUSTRATIONS DRAWN FROM THE MANNERS AND CUSTOMS, THE SCENES AND SCENERY, OF THE HOLY LAND. 3 vols. Vol. I., Southern Palestine and Jerusalem. Vol. II., Central Palestine and Phœnicia. Vol. III., Lebanon, Damascus and Beyond Jordan. N. Y., Harper, 1885, $7.50.

Dr. Thomson combines in an eminent degree a lively sense for the striking and picturesque in Nature, with great familiarity with the Bible. His work is fresh, quickening to feeling and fancy, and redolent of simplicity and the fragrance of the field.—*Nation.* **915.60.**

Tracy, Albert ("Albert Leffingwell").

RAMBLES THROUGH JAPAN WITHOUT A GUIDE. N. Y., Baker & Taylor, 1894. $1.50.

As a traveller's impressions and as a diary of small compass, it is the most realistic, the most entertaining, the most trustworthy book of the sort we have seen.—*Nation*. 015.2.

Trollope, *Mrs.* **Frances E. (Milton).**

DOMESTIC MANNERS OF THE AMERICANS. N. Y., Dodd, Mead & Co., 1894, 2 vols., $3.50.

This sixty-year-old classic ought to be read with the greatest avidity, for it is history in its most taking form. Mrs. Trollope's reflections have still a salutary lesson for us—her book enables us to learn something about the development of American manners and character in our dark ages.—*Nation*. 017.3.

United States. *See* Appleton's general guide; Finck, H. T.; Ralph, Julian; Warner, C. D.

Uruguay. *See* Child, T.

Vincent, Frank.

ACTUAL AFRICA; OR, THE COMING CONTINENT. N. Y., Appleton, 1895, $5.

A comprehensive and most informing book on Africa, especially as a continent of vast resources undeveloped. Author is a traveller of world-wide experience. 910.

AROUND AND ABOUT SOUTH AMERICA. N. Y., Appleton, 1890, $5.

A narrative of twenty months' circumnavigation of South America, every page of which not only gives evidence of personal experience, but abounds with minute pictures of scenery, architecture, human groups and figures—all the varied life of a fascinating continent.—*Literary World*. 018.

Wallace, Donald MacKenzie.

RUSSIA. N. Y., Holt, 1877, $2.

Author lived in Russia six years; learned its language and travelled widely, studying the most characteristic classes of the population. He gives a thorough account of the government, and of the religious and social life of the people; especially full and clear in explaining the Mir, or Russian village community.—*Nation*. 014.7.

Warner, Chas. Dudley.

STUDIES IN THE SOUTH AND WEST, WITH COMMENTS ON CANADA. N. Y., Harper, 1889, $1.75.

A book which will inform Eastern and Northern people . . . how small a section of the United States they belong to; it will enable them to think rightly of the tendencies of thought and life which make the Great West.—*Literary World*. 017.3.

Winter, William.

GRAY DAYS AND GOLD IN ENGLAND AND SCOTLAND. N. Y., Macmillan, 1892, 75 c.

A record of sentimental journeyings in muse-haunted regions of England and Scotland, 1888–90.—*Literary World*. 014.

SHAKESPEARE'S ENGLAND. Illus. N. Y., Macmillan, 1891, 75 c.

"Relates largely to Warwickshire, and depicts not so much the England of fact as the England created and hallowed by the spirit of poetry of which Shakespeare is the soul." 014.

LITERATURE.

A SELECTION OF THE BEST ENGLISH AND AMERICAN AUTHORS IN THE DEPARTMENTS OF POETRY AND BELLES-LETTRES; WITH BRIEF NOTES ON THE ACCEPTED EDITIONS,

BY G. MERCER ADAM,
Author of "A Precis of English History," etc.

LITERATURE consists of all the books—and they are not so many—where moral truth and human passion are touched with a certain largeness, sanity, and attraction of form. My notion of the literary student is of one who through books explores the strange voyages of man's moral reason, the impulses of the human heart, the chances and changes that have overtaken human ideals of virtue and happiness, of conduct and manners, and the shifting fortunes of great conceptions of truth and virtue. Poets, dramatists, humorists, satirists, masters of fiction, the great preachers, the character-writers, the maxim-writers, the great political orators—they are all literature in so far as they teach us to know man and to know human nature. This is what makes literature, rightly sifted and selected and rightly studied, not the mere elegant trifling that it is so often and so erroneously supposed to be, but a proper instrument for a systematic training of the imagination and the sympathies, and of a genial and varied moral sensibility.—JOHN MORLEY: *On the Study of Literature.*

Anthologies.

Coates, Henry T., *Editor.*
FIRESIDE ENCYCLOPÆDIA OF POETRY. 28th edition. Phila., Porter & Coates, $5.
An excellent collection, representing four hundred and fifty poets, English and American. With portraits and fac-similes of their handwriting. **808.**

Dana, Charles A., *Editor.*
HOUSEHOLD BOOK OF POETRY. New and enlarged edition, with engravings. N. Y., Appleton, $5.
An essentially household anthology of English and American song, compiled with sympathy, judgment, and taste. The poems are grouped topically. **808.**

Lighthall, William D., *Editor.*
CANADIAN POEMS AND LAYS. Selections from Native Verse, reflecting the Seasons, Legends, and Life of the Dominion. (Canterbury Poets series.) London. Walter Scott, 1s.; N. Y., A. Lovell, 40 c.
A characteristic anthology of Canadian song, selected with taste and good judgment. The volume embraces the popular work of Sangster, Reade, Heavysege, Murray, Martin, and Kirby, among the earlier bards, and of Roberts, Lampman, Scott, McLennan, Thomson, Campbell, and others of a later era. The poems treat of the many picturesque phases of Canadian scenery, sports, and other outdoor life, with the expression of native poetic thought in history and legend. **808.**

Mackay, Charles, *Editor.*
A THOUSAND AND ONE GEMS OF POETRY. N. Y., Routledge, $1.50.
A good collection for handy and popular use, uniform with the same editor's "A Thousand and One Gems of Prose," N. Y., Routledge, $1.50. **808.**

Sladen, Douglas B. W., *Editor.*
AUSTRALIAN BALLADS AND RHYMES. (Canterbury Poets series.) London, Walter Scott, 1s.; N. Y., A. Lovell, 40 c.
The promising first-fruits in song of a group of young Australian nations. Well-selected examples are given of the representative verse, including Bush songs, of native writers, Adam Lindsay Gordon, Henry Kendall, the editor, and others.

Ward, T. Humphry, *Editor.*
THE ENGLISH POETS. Vol. I., Chaucer to Donne; Vol II., Ben Jonson to Dryden; Vol. III., Addison to Blake; Vol. IV., Wordsworth to Tennyson and Rossetti. Students' edition. N. Y., Macmillan, 4 vols., $4.
An invaluable collection, with prefatory critical notices by scholars and writers, and a general introduction by Matthew Arnold. **821.08**

Selections, chiefly Prose.

Craik, Henry, *Editor.*
ENGLISH PROSE SELECTIONS. Students' edition. N. Y., Macmillan, 5 vols., $1.10 per vol.
A useful working cyclopædia of English prose, with critical introductions by various writers, and general introductions to each period—from the 14th to the 19th century—by the editor. Vol. V. in preparation June, 1895. **820.8.**

Pancoast, Henry S.
REPRESENTATIVE ENGLISH LITERATURE. N. Y., Holt, $1.75.
An excellent compend, illustrative, expository, and critical. Good selections. **820.8.**

Stedman, Edmund Clarence, *and* **Hutchinson, Miss E. M.**
LIBRARY OF AMERICAN LITERATURE. N. Y., Wm. Evarts Benjamin, 11 vols., $30 and upwards.
A comprehensive work, compiled with judgment and taste, by the well-known poet and critic, Mr. Stedman, assisted by Miss Hutchinson. Over 1200 American authors are represented by selections from their best prose and verse, the whole forming a treasure-house of national literary reference. Well illustrated with portraits and other engravings. **810.6.**

Histories and Criticism.

Brooke, Stopford A.
PRIMER OF ENGLISH LITERATURE. N. Y., Am. Book Co., 35 c.
The most compact and useful introduction. **820.7.**

Hawthorne, Julian, *and* **Lemmon, Leonard.**
AMERICAN LITERATURE: a Text-Book for Schools and Colleges. Bost., Heath, $1.25.
Critical and stimulating, with a good body of selections.

Oliphant, *Mrs.* **M. O. W.**
VICTORIAN AGE OF ENGLISH LITERATURE. Students' edition. N. Y., Lovell, Coryell, 2 vols. in 1, $2.
An appreciative and intelligent survey of the literature of the era, with a critical analysis and exposition of the characters and writings of over 500 eminent English authors, from the founding of the great Quarterlies to the literary and journalistic activities of to-day **820.7.**

Literature.

Richardson, Charles F.

AMERICAN LITERATURE, 1607-1885. N. Y., Putnam, 2 vols. in 1, $3.50.

Contents: (1) The Development of American Thought; (2) American Poetry and Fiction.

An interesting compendium, giving a good, though hardly a critical, survey of the field. Diffuse in style. **810.0.**

Taine, Hippolyte A.

HISTORY OF ENGLISH LITERATURE. Translated by H. Van Laun. N. Y., Holt, 2 vols., Library edition, $5; Students' edition, 2 vols. in 1, $1.20.

A standard work by an acute and, on the whole, well-informed French critic. **820.0.**

Tyler, M. Coit.

HISTORY OF AMERICAN LITERATURE, 1607-1705. N. Y., Putnam, 2 vols. in 1, $3.

A thorough and exhaustive chronicle of American literary annals, down to the Revolution. **810.0.**

The Bible.

Cook, Albert S.

THE BIBLE AND ENGLISH PROSE STYLE. Bost., Heath, 55 c.

Displays the Bible as a superb model of literary style. Gives extracts from the English version of 1611. **220.**

Individual Authors.

Addison, Joseph. [1672-1719.]

English essayist, and associate with Sir Richard Steele in the production of *The Spectator*, *The Tatler*, and *The Guardian*, publications at the time of a new order, in which literature, politics, and morals were treated in an original and graceful style. Addison's literary career began in 1704 with *The Campaign;* he met with instantaneous success as a writer of pure idiomatic English, of unfailing genial philosophy, and withal exceeding happy as an observer of life and manners. His prose style was deemed by Johnson so admirable as to call forth the well-known eulogy: "Whoever wishes to attain an English style, familiar but not coarse, and elegant but not ostentatious, must give his days and nights to the study of Addison." To his charming and felicitous essays, the happiest of which is that on "Sir Roger de Coverley," Addison solely owes his fame. For delicate humor, coupled with sound common-sense, he has hardly a rival. Literature owes him a debt for being the first to bring Milton's writings to the knowledge of the reading world. **824.52.**

COMPLETE WORKS. With Notes by Bishop Hurd (Bohn). N. Y., Macmillan, 6 vols., $6.

Contains besides the *Spectator*, *Tatler*, and *Guardian* essays, his plays, poems, and letters.

ESSAYS. Chosen and edited by J. R. Green (the historian). N. Y., Macmillan, $1.

{ SIR ROGER DE COVERLEY.
SELECTIONS FROM THE *Spectator*.
CATO : A TRAGEDY.

With Notes for school use in English Classic series. N. Y., Maynard, paper, 12 c. each.

Aldrich, Thomas Bailey. [1836-.]

New England poet and novelist. His verse is artistic, graceful in thought, and delicate in workmanship. Many of his lyrics and sonnets are almost faultless in their art, and give him perhaps the chief place among living American poets. His poetical writings include "The Ballad of Baby Bell, and Other Poems," "Mercedes, a Drama," and "Later Lyrics," and : **811.4.**

POEMS. Household edition. Bost., Houghton, $1.50.

A characteristic and comprehensive collection.

THE SISTERS' TRAGEDY, with Other Poems, Lyrical and Dramatic. Bost., Houghton, $1.25.

CLOTH OF GOLD, and Other Poems. Bost., Houghton, $1.50.

FLOWER AND THORN. Bost., Houghton, $1.25.

LYRICS AND SONNETS. Bost., Houghton, $1.

Arnold, Matthew. [1822-1888.]

Poet and critic, an acute and independent thinker, an accomplished scholar, a master of English prose. As became a son of Thomas Arnold, the famous master of Rugby, he was essentially a religious man, yet he early broke away from traditional theology as a stern critic of English Christianity. Here his most characteristic book is "Literature and Dogma." In "Culture and Anarchy" he bears down upon Philistinism, upon the vulgar notion that puts the means of living above life. To this theme throughout his works he returns again and again. In the realm of poetry Arnold has genuine dramatic insight and a deep idealism, joined to fine sensibilities and a rare distinction of art and manner. He is the greatest of European elegiac poets, and the melancholy of his verse is often relieved by many passages of calm and even buoyant beauty.

PASSAGES FROM THE PROSE WRITINGS. N. Y., Macmillan, $1. **824.85.**

LITERATURE AND DOGMA. N. Y., Macmillan, $1.50.

CULTURE AND ANARCHY, and FRIENDSHIP'S GARLAND. N. Y., Macmillan, $1.50.

COMPLETE PROSE WORKS. N. Y., Macmillan, 9 vols., $13.50.

POETICAL WORKS. N. Y., Macmillan, 3 vols., $5; Globe edition, 1 vol., $1.75. **821.8.**

Bacon, Francis, *Lord.* [1561-1626.]

Philosopher, statesman, and man of letters, whom Izaak Walton called "the great secretary of nature and all learning." To Bacon, the literature of philosophy is indebted for the impulse he gave to scientific inquiry by his powerful and eloquent exposition of its methods in his "Novum Organum" and "Advancement of Learning," while literature in general owes acknowledgment to him for his popularization of the essay. While his scientific treatises created a revolution in the domain of philosophy, and, as Macaulay says, produced a vast influence on the opinions of mankind, it is "in the essays alone that the mind of Bacon is brought into immediate contact with the minds of ordinary readers." The essays are the observations and deductions of a great intellect occupied with the problem of human life, and actuated by the desire to disseminate prudential counsels in their direction and guidance. Their wisdom, their pithiness of style, are unapproached in English literature. **824.3.**

ESSAYS ; OR, COUNSELS, CIVIL AND MORAL. N. Y., Lovell, Coryell, 75 c.

Includes, besides the Essays, the Apothegms, Elegant Sentences, and the series of mythological fables, entitled "The Wisdom of the Ancients."

ESSAYS, with annotations by Archbishop Whately. Bost., Lee & S., $1.50; N. Y., Longmans, $3.50.

The annotations are often as good as the essays.

NOVUM ORGANUM, and ADVANCEMENT OF LEARNING. (Bohn.) N. Y., Macmillan, $1.50.

Browning, Elizabeth Barrett. [1809-1861.]

The greatest English poetess, a woman of rare culture, delicate sensibilities, and fine emotions. As an artist her main fault is over-fluency. Her longest work, "Aurora Leigh," first published in 1856, is a novel in blank verse, into which, as the author tells us, "her highest convictions upon life and art have entered." Besides a large body of miscellaneous verse, characterized by much grace of style and delicacy of feeling, Mrs. Browning wrote "Casa Guidi Windows," which deals mainly with the Italian aspirations for liberty and unity—themes that engrossed the minds of both herself and her husband; and "Sonnets from the Portuguese," a series of the finest love poetry in the language—the outpourings of a woman's richest thought and tenderest feeling. At an early age she published a fine translation of the "Prometheus Bound," of Æschylus, and, in her later years, "Poems Before Congress." In "Elizabeth Barrett Browning," an essay (Bost., Houghton, 40 c. or 75 c.), Edmund Clarence Stedman gives a thoughtful characterization of the poet; the volume also contains Mrs. Browning's "Lady Geraldine's Courtship," and favorite poems from Robert Browning; the essay appears as a chapter in Mr. Stedman's "Victorian Poets." 821.82.

POEMS AND LETTERS. N. Y., Lovell, Coryell, 7 vols., $5.

POETICAL WORKS. N. Y., Crowell, 75 cents and upwards.

Browning, Robert. [1812-1889.]

Most eminent of psychological poets, and great contemporary writer of dramatic idyls and monologues. If too metaphysical to be popular, Browning is not the less worthy of the poetical student's attention for the profound thought that underlies his often rugged and sometimes obscure verse. His greatest achievement is "The Ring and the Book," a series of poetized versions of a tragedy which took place at Rome at the close of the 17th century. His other writings include "Strafford," an historical tragedy; "Sordello," a psychological narrative; "Paracelsus," a drama delineating the history of a soul aiming to reach perfection but thwarted in its pursuit; "Fifine at the Fair," dramas on Greek subjects; and a story of Brittany—"Red-Cotton Night-Cap Country." His more popular and generally appreciated writings are, however, to be found in his minor poems and lyrics, which include such graphic pictures of human character and passion as "Evelyn Hope," "In a Year," and "Home Thoughts from Abroad"; and some fine historical poems, such as the battle of La Hogue, in "Hervé Riel," and "How They Brought the Good News from Ghent to Aix." 821.83.

COMPLETE WORKS. N. Y., Macmillan, 9 vols., $20; Bost., Houghton, 7 vols., $11.25.

SELECTIONS FROM THE POETICAL WORKS. N. Y., Macmillan, 2 vols., $2.50.

SELECTIONS. N. Y., Crowell, 75 cents and upwards.

A meritorious volume.

DRAMATIC IDYLS. (1st and 2d series.) N. Y., Macmillan, $1.50.

BROWNING PRIMER. By Esther P. Defries, with Introduction by Dr. F. J. Furnival. N. Y., Macmillan, 40 c.

A useful introduction with sympathetic criticism.

BROWNING : CHIEF POET OF THE AGE. By William G. Kingsland. Bost., Poet-Lore Co., $1.25.

Biographical and critical, admirably suited to the student beginning to explore Browning, and who may next take up the books by Mrs. Orr, Prof. Corson, or Mr. Cooke.

INTRODUCTION TO BROWNING. By Hiram Corson, LL.D. Bost., Heath, $1.50.

Intelligent and acute criticism, dealing with Browning's dramatic art and supplying the arguments of his poems. Omits explanation of the poet's many puzzling allusions.

HANDBOOK TO ROBERT BROWNING'S WRITINGS. By Mrs. Sutherland Orr. N. Y., Macmillan, $1.75.

An approved Browning Manual and key to the poet's writings. It had his general supervision.

GUIDE-BOOK TO THE POETIC AND DRAMATIC WORKS OF ROBERT BROWNING. By George Willis Cooke. Bost., Houghton, $2.

Furnishes notes and introductions to all the poems. The *Nation* says: "It may fairly be called a compendious Browning library in itself." Written after Mrs. Orr's book, and with fuller information.

BROWNING CYCLOPÆDIA. By Dr. Edward Berdoe. N. Y., Macmillan, $3.50.

Comprehensive and trustworthy.

Bryant, William Cullen. [1794-1878.]

One of the earliest of eminent native poets. His verse, unfortunately meagre in volume, maintains the distinction which it from the first won, for its fine contemplative character and rare moral beauty. Bryant drew not a little of his inspiration from Wordsworth, and, like the greatest of the Lake Poets, he was profoundly responsive to the influences and the beauty of Nature. But Bryant had a voice and characteristics of his own, which are expressive of the New rather than of the Old World. "Thanatopsis," written at the age of nineteen, remains the high-water mark of his poetic genius. It is a woodland meditation on death. Of merit almost as high are his "Hymn of the City," "Forest Hymn," "June," "The Antiquity of Freedom," "To the Fringed Gentian," and "To a Water-Fowl." For many years of Bryant's busy life he was Editor-in-Chief of the New York *Evening Post*. In his declining years he found solace in translating the "Iliad" and "Odyssey" into English blank verse. 811.33.

POETICAL WORKS, PROSE WRITINGS, LIFE, AND CORRESPONDENCE. Edited by Parke Godwin. With portraits. N. Y., Appleton, 6 vols., $18.

An authoritative edition, edited by the poet's son-in-law. It includes his Essays, Tales, Travels, Addresses, and Orations.

POETICAL WORKS. N. Y., Appleton, Household edition, $1.50; Cabinet edition, $1.

HOMER'S ILIAD and ODYSSEY. Translated. Bost., Houghton, $2.50 each.

Especially strong in the descriptive passages.

W. C. BRYANT. By John Bigelow. (American Men of Letters series.) Bost., Houghton, $1.25.

A sympathetic and adequate biography.

Burns, Robert. [1759-1796.]

Scotland's greatest poet, and one of the sweetest writers of lyrics and songs in the language. A man of passionate sympathy with his fellow-men, he has interpreted for us, as no other has, the thought, feeling, and manners, as well as the life, of the Scottish peasant. With an intense love of Nature, and an eye to see the tender and humorous side of life, and to reveal it in good fellowship, often to his moral harm, Burns appeals to all humanity, or to those at least who care to master his homely Lowland Scotch. A certain coarseness in places disfigures his work, as certain failings marred his life. But with all his defects he was a man, and no mincing sentimentalist, and has left behind him a great treasury of melodious, touching, and true-hearted song. **821.07.**

POEMS, SONGS, AND LETTERS. Edited by Alexander Smith. N. Y., Macmillan, $1.75.

The Complete Works, in compact form, with Memoir, sympathetically edited.

POEMS. Edited by G. A. Aitken. (Aldine Poets.) N. Y., Macmillan, 3 vols., $2.25.

A handy, readable edition, in good type.

ROBERT BURNS. By Principal J. C. Shairp. (English Men of Letters series.) N. Y., Harper, 75 c.

A very satisfactory life of the poet and critical estimate of his genius.

Byron [Lord], George Gordon Noel. [1788-1824.]

One of the greatest and most prolific of England's poets, as he is the most misanthropic and defiant of the conventionalities of her moral, religious, and social life. His independent, restless, masterful spirit breathes through writings characterized by passionate energy, intense subjectivity highly tinged with scepticism, and a romantic picturesqueness, expressed in a remarkable flow of melodious and nervous language. A large portion of his verse deals with Oriental tales, many of them drawn from the scenery, history, and legends of Greece, into whose cause, while that country was throwing off the yoke of the Turk, the poet ardently threw himself, at the cost of an early and much regretted death. Greece, it has been said, made Byron a poet; to his travels we owe the two works by which he is best known, "Don Juan" and "Childe Harold's Pilgrimage." In the former we have a poetic medley of description and narration, reciting the roaming adventures of a youth, around whom the poet has hung "his wealth of wit, humor, satire, pathos, and descriptive beauty." "Childe Harold," which first brought Byron fame, is a poem of extraordinary power, full of the energy of scorn and the passion of despair. Its misanthropy, the genuineness of which is questioned, is relieved by the grand strain of passion that characterizes the verse, and by a force of superb diction that carries the reader irresistibly through canto after canto of metrical eloquence. **821.76.**

POETICAL WORKS. N. Y., Routledge, 3 vols., $4.50; in 1 vol., 80c. and $1.50.

CHILDE HAROLD'S PILGRIMAGE. N. Y., Routledge, 40 c.

POETRY. Chosen and arranged by Matthew Arnold. N. Y., Macmillan, $1.

Preserving verse only of the highest quality.

LORD BYRON. By Prof. John Nichol. (English Men of Letters series.) N. Y., Harper, 75 c.

A competent and sympathetic biography, which, however, does not spare the weaknesses of the poet.

Carlyle, Thomas. [1795-1881.]

Biographer, historian, and essayist, a writer who, in spite of his vehement cynicism and the verbal eccentricities of his style, exercised a profound influence on the thought of his age. His gifts were many both as a thinker and as a writer. He had fervid imagination, forceful powers of description, a marvellous gift of depicting character, and, to use Jeffrey's phrase, "a dreadful earnestness." His historical works are elsewhere touched upon; here we have only to do with his miscellaneous writings. These include, besides a large body of critical essays, translations, and contributions to reviews, a "Life of John Sterling," poet and critic; lectures on "Heroes and Hero-Worship," in which Carlyle expresses his passionate regard for the heroic in history and for the commanding hero, right or wrong; his "Sartor Resartus" (the tailor remade), professedly a review of a German treatise on dress, but really a vent for its author's own speculations and "inward agonies"; and "Past and Present," a vehement arraignment of political and religious ideas prevailing fifty years ago in England, with a trenchant indictment of quacks, charlatans, and the gospel of Mammon, which the Sage held was destroying reverence for all that was best in the past.

For informing characterization see Minto's "Manual of English Prose Literature" (Bost., Ginn, $1.10). **824.82.**

COMPLETE WORKS. N. Y., Lovell, Coryell, 10 vols., $12.

PAST AND PRESENT. N. Y., Lovell, Coryell, 75 c.

HEROES AND HERO-WORSHIP. N. Y., Lovell, Coryell, 75 c.

ESSAYS. N. Y. Routledge, $1.50; Ward, Lock, 75 c.

Comprising "Heroes and Hero-Worship," "Sartor Resartus," "Past and Present."

LIVES OF SCHILLER AND JOHN STERLING. N. Y., Routledge, $1.50.

Admirable biographies, full of insight and knowledge, in Carlyle's earlier and saner literary style.

THOMAS CARLYLE. By Richard Garnett. (Great Writers series.) N. Y., Scribner, $1; A. Lovell, 40 c.

Chaucer, Geoffrey. [1340-1400.]

Chaucer, "the true forerunner and prototype of Shakespeare," has given us his best work in "The Canterbury Tales." Here he shows his knowledge and love of men and women as they are, the sagacity and wit that make him worthy of almost the highest place in English letters. "The Tales" are somewhat difficult to read without the aid of a glossary, since they were written when our mother tongue was just emerging from its early rude and little organized form. Despite its many obsolete words and unfamiliar idioms, it is a delightful poem, breathing the very air of chivalry. "The Tales" did much to fix a standard for the language as well as to give impulse to English poetry. They are supposed to be told by a party of pilgrims, of diverse ranks and callings, on the way to the shrine of St. Thomas à Becket at Canterbury. Chaucer's other work includes "The Legend of Good Women," "Troilus and Cressida," and a humorous poem, "The Parliament, or Assembly, of Foules" (Fowls). For a scholarly and charming estimate of Chaucer, see Lowell's "My Study Windows." **821.17.**

THE OXFORD CHAUCER. Edited from numerous MSS. by Prof. W. W. Skeat. N. Y., Macmillan, 6 vols., $24.

A definitive edition, amply annotated by a great English scholar, enriched with various readings and elaborate introductions. Portrait and fac-similes.

THE STUDENTS' CHAUCER. Edited by Prof. W. W. Skeat. N. Y., Macmillan, $1.75.

A most serviceable and compact edition, reduced from the above monumental work.

THE CANTERBURY TALES. Edited by John Saunders. N. Y., Macmillan, $1.60.

A useful introduction to Chaucer, whose text the editor in part modernizes.

STUDIES IN CHAUCER. By Prof. T. R. Lounsbury. N. Y., Harper, 3 vols., $9.

By an accomplished American scholar, learned in Chaucer's era and his work. It deals with the poet's life, historical and legendary, with the genuine and spurious writings, and, critically, with his text, his genius, and his learning.

THE PARLIAMENT OF FOULES. Edited by Prof. Lounsbury. Bost., Ginn, 50 c.

A revised text, with literary and grammatical introduction, notes, and glossary.

THE PROLOGUE, KNIGHTES TALE, NONNE PREESTE'S TALE. Edited by Prof. Skeat. N. Y., Macmillan, 70 c.

An excellent edition, annotated for schools. A fuller selection of "The Canterbury Tales," by the same editor, is also issued (N. Y., Macmillan, $1.10).

COMPLETE POETICAL WORKS. Edited by Thomas Tyrwhitt. N. Y., Routledge, $3.

A good library edition, with an essay on Chaucer's language and versification, life, notes, and a glossary.

CANTERBURY TALES. Edited by Thomas Tyrwhitt. N. Y., Routledge, $1.40.

A good and handy text, with glossary, notes, and introduction.

CHAUCER FOR CHILDREN. By Mrs. H. R. Haweis. N. Y., Scribner, $1.25.

CHAUCER FOR SCHOOLS. By Mrs. H. R. Haweis. N. Y., Scribner, $1.

Excellent popularizations, after the manner of "Lamb's Tales from Shakespeare."

CHAUCER. By Prof. A. W. Ward. (English Men of Letters series.) N. Y., Harper, 75 c.

A biography of high merit.

Coleridge, Samuel Taylor. [1772–1834.]

Poet, miscellaneous writer, and great converser, whose genius, at the best desultory and vagrant, was unhappily enslaved by the opium-habit. Having imbibed the democratic ideas of the era of the French Revolution, Coleridge formed the project to found, with his friend Southey, and other revolutionary youth of the period, a "Pantisocracy" on the banks of the Susquehanna, but emigration was balked by lack of funds, and the scheme of a communistic society, like many other of Coleridge's projects, came to nothing. A man of fine intellect, varied knowledge, great powers of reflection, and rare critical taste, with the true lyrical gift, he left comparatively little behind him. His verse, which like much of his prose, is that of a dreamer, has a haunting beauty, a poetic grace and imaginative fervor, which show what literature has lost by his mental infirmity. Besides his poems, his chief prose works are his "Aids to Reflection," "The Friend," "Table Talk," "Biographia Literaria," and a volume of "Lectures on Shakespeare."

POETICAL WORKS. Edited by J. Dykes Campbell. N. Y., Macmillan, $1.75.
821.72.

TABLE TALK, THE ANCIENT MARINER, and CHRISTABEL. Edited by Prof. H. Morley. N. Y., Routledge, 50 c. **824.7.**

Cowper, William. [1731–1800.]

If the poet's life was as placid as his own "Sleepy Ouse," his recluse existence was favorable to meditation. It is the gentle round of his domestic life, with the clicking of the knitting-needles and the hissing of the tea-urn, that interests us. His verse is mainly of a religious and didactic character, deeply tinged with melancholy. It was of value in breaking English poetry away from the artificial versification of Pope and his imitators, and bringing it back to truth and nature. **821.65.**

COMPLETE WORKS. Edited by Robert Southey. (Bohn.) N. Y., Macmillan, 8 vols., $8.

The Standard Edition, with an interesting memoir, and the poet's correspondence. Besides the poems, it includes the Homer translations, undeservedly thrown in the shade by the rhymed couplets of Pope.

POETICAL WORKS. Edited by Rev. Wm. Benham. N. Y., Macmillan, $1.75.

By far the best single-volume edition. Edited with useful notes and a good memoir.

POEMS. Edited by John Bruce. (Aldine Poets series.) N. Y., Macmillan, 3 vols., $2.25.

A handy, approved edition, in good type.

SELECTIONS FROM THE POEMS. Edited by Mrs. Oliphant. N. Y., Macmillan, $1.

COWPER'S LETTERS. Selected and edited by Rev. W. Benham. N. Y., Macmillan, $1.

COWPER. By Goldwin Smith. (English Men of Letters series.) N. Y., Harper, 75 c.

The man, the poet, his work, and his age, portrayed by a scholarly hand.

Curtis, George William. [1824–1892.]

Essayist, journalist, publicist, and man of letters. At an early age Curtis attained celebrity as the writer of a series of prose-poems of travel, in which humor, pathos, and graceful sentiment happily blend with the polished talk of a thoughtful and highly cultured mind. The series embraces "Lotus-Eating," "Nile Notes of a Howadji," and "The Howadji in Syria," which abound in picturesque descriptions and vividly written incidents of travel in the East. These were followed by "The Potiphar Papers," in which humor and satire are delightfully interwoven. His "Prue and I" belongs to fiction and is elsewhere dealt with.

The last four decades of Curtis's life were devoted to journalistic and magazine work in connection with *Harper's Magazine* and *Harper's Weekly*. In the former of these he conducted the "Easy Chair," an editorial department to which he contributed a great store of essays, disquisitions, and talks, in which his cultured mind and large experience of men and the world found rich and entertaining expression, lit up at times by refined humor and warmed by the contagion of cheerful philosophy. Selected volumes of these talks are published under the title of "The Easy Chair." **814.37.**

LOTUS-EATING. N. Y., Harper, $1.50.

NILE NOTES OF A HOWADJI. N. Y., Harper, $1.50.

THE HOWADJI IN SYRIA. N. Y., Harper, $1.50.

THE POTIPHAR PAPERS. N. Y., Harper, $1.50.

THE EASY CHAIR. First, Second, and Third Series. N. Y., Harper, $1 each.

LITERARY AND SOCIAL ESSAYS. N. Y., Harper, $2.50.

GEORGE WILLIAM CURTIS. By Edward Cary. (American Men of Letters series.) Bost., Houghton, $1.25.

A biography of uncommon merit.

GEORGE WILLIAM CURTIS. By John White Chadwick. N. Y., Harper, 50 c.

A brief, cordial sketch and characterization by a warm personal friend.

De Quincey, Thomas. [1785–1859.]

Essayist and philosophic writer, who, like Coleridge, and with the same fell results, was a victim to opium. How far these writers owed their inspiration to the insidious drug is never likely to be known; but curious mental parallels are to be traced in the two men, aside from the question of their learning and scholarship. Both were dreamers and seers, eloquent talkers, and gifted with marvellous analytic and introspective faculty. It has unfortunately to be added that both came short in their literary careers of the achievement promised in their remarkable powers. De Quincey is a voluminous writer on a great variety of subjects, chiefly, however, in the departments of metaphysics and speculative philosophy. His disquisitions also cover biography, criticism, and political economy, including many translations from the German. To the general reader he is, however, best known by his autobiographic sketches, including the "Confessions of an English Opium-Eater" and "Suspiria de Profundis." De Quincey is well characterized in Minto's "Manual of English Prose Literature" (Bost., Ginn, $1.50).
824.81.

CONFESSIONS OF AN OPIUM-EATER. N. Y., Lovell, Coryell, 75 c.

Includes the disquisitions on "Murder as a Fine Art," "The English Mail Coach," and "The Revolt of the Tartars."

BEAUTIES FROM THE WRITINGS OF THOMAS DE QUINCEY, with biographical sketch and portrait. Bost., Houghton, $1.50.

WORKS. Bost., Houghton, 6 vols., $10; 12 vols., $12.

WORKS, enlarged. Edited by Prof. David Masson. N. Y., Macmillan, 14 vols., $17.50.

Dryden, John. [1631–1701.]

Poet and dramatist; laureate from 1670 to 1688. Chiefly known as a translator of Virgil's "Æneid," and as author of "Absalom and Achitophel," a poem marked by vigorous sallies of satire and fancy, while the versification is at once smooth-flowing and forceful. The more notable of Dryden's other poems are his "Ode for St. Cecilia's Day," sometimes called "Alexander's Feast," and the "Hind and the Panther," a poetical defence, in the form of a fable, of the Roman Catholic Church, to which the poet had become a convert, against the Church of England. Lowell, in "Among My Books," says of Dryden: "He was hardly a great poet in the narrowest definition. But he was a strong thinker, who sometimes carried common-sense to a height where it catches the light of a diviner air, and warmed reason till it had well-nigh the illuminating property of intuition."
821.48.

POEMS. (Old Poets' Edition.) N. Y., Routledge, $3.

An excellent library edition, including the translation of the "Æneid."

POEMS. N. Y., Routledge, $1.40.

A good popular edition.

THE SATIRES. Edited by J. Churton Collins. N. Y., Macmillan, 40 c.

For school use, with memoir, introduction, and notes.

ALEXANDER'S FEAST, and MAC FLECKNOE. N. Y., Maynard, paper, 12 c.

The great Ode, and a scathing satire on Thomas Shadwell, the dramatist, whose
"Prose and verse was own'd without dispute
Through all the realms of Nonsense absolute."

ESSAY OF DRAMATIC POESY. Edited by Thomas Arnold. N. Y., Macmillan, 90 c.

An annotated edition, exemplifying Dryden's magnificent prose. The theme has never been more ably treated.

JOHN DRYDEN. By G. Saintsbury. (English Men of Letters series.) N. Y., Harper, 75 c.

Evinces much knowledge of the poet and his times.

Eliot, George (Marian Evans Lewes). [1819–1880.]

We have here to do with George Eliot only as poet and essayist. In neither of these capacities—need we say?—does she attain the rank she has reached as the greatest imaginative prose-writer of her sex. If we except the exquisite outburst, "O may I join the choir invisible!"—which, as has been well pointed out, is "an attempt to glorify the aspiration to an immortality of mortal influence"—there is little of her verse likely to live apart from her immortal novels. It has delicate, and, occasionally, rich workmanship, and a certain dramatic interest; but it is for these things, and not as poetry, that we are constrained to admire it. The *Nation* has said: "George Eliot often shows her deficiency of poetic imagination in making use of the raw material of science long before it has become familiar enough to put on a form of flesh and blood." Her chief pieces are "The Spanish Gypsy," a romantic drama in blank verse; "The Legend of Jubal," a poem dealing with the colony of Cain, its primitive occupations and arts; "Armigart," a drama of the stage; and a number of minor poems. More interesting, though perhaps too didactic and radical, are her miscellaneous essays.

THE LEGEND OF JUBAL, THE SPANISH GYPSY, AND OTHER POEMS. N. Y., Crowell, 75 c. and upwards. **821.8.**

ESSAYS. N. Y., Harper, 75 c.; paper, 20 c.; Funk & Wagnalls, $1; paper, 25 c. **824.8.**

Emerson, Ralph Waldo. [1803–1882.]

Emerson, as has been well said, "stands as one of the few great original forces in literature." Of the New England Transcendentalists he was the acknowledged chief. Though the philosophy underlying his writings is somewhat vague and the style rhapsodical, his essays hold a high place in the literature of power. Of these the first and second series are best. All abound in pithy passages, displaying profound insight, sure-footed common-sense, and unfailing optimism. Lowell has remarked of him as a lecturer in "My Study Windows": "He is full of that power of strangely-subtle association whose indirect approaches startle the mind into almost painful attention, of those flashes of mutual understanding between speaker and hearer that are gone ere one can say it lightens." His verse, though that of a recluse, has the same inspiring ethical philosophy and elevated tone that give distinction to the essays; always unprofessional, it is often over-weighted with thought, and, at times, faulty in its art. In "The Problem," "Each and All," "The Snowstorm," "Seashore," "Days," and "Threnody," he is beyond criticism. For an acute and sympathetic estimate of Emerson, see Stedman's "Poets of America" (Bost., Houghton, $2.25).
814.36.

COMPLETE WORKS. Riverside Edition. Bost., Houghton, 12 vols., $21.

A worthy Library edition, including besides the Poems and both series of the Essays, the Addresses, Lectures, and the longer Prose Works, English Traits, Representative Men, Conduct of Life, Society and Solitude, etc.

COMPLETE WORKS. Little Classic Edition. Bost., Houghton, 12 vols., $15.

In arrangement and contents the same as the above, but without index.

ESSAYS. First and Second Series. Bost., Houghton, $1; paper, 50 c.

POEMS. Bost., Houghton, $1.25, $1.50, and upwards.

With portrait.

REPRESENTATIVE MEN, NATURE, LECTURES AND ADDRESSES. Bost., Houghton, $1.

EMERSON AND CARLYLE'S CORRESPONDENCE. Bost., Houghton, 2 vols., $3.

Prof. C. E. Norton's edition of the Letters, written between the years 1834 and 1872.

MEMOIR OF EMERSON. By J. E. Cabot. Bost., Houghton, 2 vols., $3.50.

EMERSON, R. W. By Oliver Wendell Holmes. Bost., Houghton, $1.25.

Gilder, Richard Watson. [1844–.]

Poet, journalist, and man of letters. Since 1881 Mr. Gilder has been editor of *The Century Magazine*.

His first volume of collected poems, "The New Day," appeared in 1875, and attracted attention for its modern verve and spirit. This has been followed by four other volumes (the whole also published as one volume), which show Mr. Gilder to possess many of the higher qualities of song, with a refinement of expression and a daintiness of touch that harmonize well with his command of the resources of emotion.
811.4.

THE NEW DAY. N. Y., Century Co., 75 c.; paper, 35 c.

THE CELESTIAL PASSION. N. Y., Century Co., 75 c.; paper, 35 c.

LYRICS, AND OTHER POEMS. N. Y., Century Co., $1; paper, 50 c.

THE GREAT REMEMBRANCE, AND OTHER POEMS. N. Y., Century Co., $1.

TWO WORLDS, AND OTHER POEMS. N. Y., Century Co., 75 c.

FIVE BOOKS OF SONG. N. Y., Century Co., 1894, $1.50.

A complete collection.

Goldsmith, Oliver. [1728–1774.]

Poet, and "booksellers' hack"; but, as Thackeray aptly terms him, "the most beloved of English writers." Of the latter, who of them has written with more tender feeling, or with purer or more artless grace? As are his writings, so is the man. He is a paragon of good-nature; luckless, indeed, but, with all his faults, genuine, true, simple-hearted, and humane. "He raised money and squandered it, by every artifice of acquisition and folly of expense," says Dr. Johnson; "but let not his frailties be remembered: he was a very great man!" Goldsmith was a fertile as well as a charming writer; but his fame rests mainly on his novel, "The Vicar of Wakefield" (elsewhere referred to), and on his poems, "The Traveller" and "The Deserted Village." One of the best of his comedies, "She Stoops to Conquer," still holds its place on the stage.
823.04.

WORKS. Edited by Peter Cunningham. N. Y., Harper, 4 vols., $8.

An approved Library Edition, embracing, besides the Poetical Works, Comedies, and "Vicar of Wakefield," "The Citizen of the World," "The Bee," Essays, Life, Letters, and Miscellaneous Writings.

MISCELLANEOUS WORKS. Edited by Professor Masson. N. Y., Macmillan, $1.75.

An excellent and well-edited students' edition, including the poems and chief prose works.

THE TRAVELLER and the DESERTED VILLAGE. N. Y., Maynard, paper, each 12 c.

Good school texts, with notes, and a brief life.
821.04.

LIFE OF GOLDSMITH. By William Black. (English Men of Letters series.) N. Y., Harper, 75 c.

Inferior to the more copious Lives by Forster and Washington Irving; but judiciously presenting, in brief compass, the familiar facts and incidents, as well as the genial characteristics of the poet.

Harte, Francis Bret. [1839–.]

Poet, journalist, and writer of prose tales and sketches, with a marked California coloring. His early years, spent in mining and journalistic life on the Pacific coast, gave him the opportunity, of which he has taken full advantage, to study Western manners and reproduce them, with a vivid and intense realism, in his poems and prose sketches. His poems, many of which are in dialect, have an original and delectable humor, united to genuine dramatic power. The best known of them, and those which won fame for him abroad, are "Jim," "Dow's Flat," "Dickens in Camp," "The Society upon the Stanislaus," and "The Heathen Chinee." 811.4.

POEMS. Bost., Houghton, Household edition, $1.50; Cabinet edition, $1.

EAST AND WEST POEMS. Bost., Houghton, $1.50.

Hayne, Paul Hamilton. [1830-1886.]

A tuneful Southern poet, with a high martial strain, in which he honors the lost Confederate cause. Hayne was a native of Charleston, S. C., and a graduate of the University of South Carolina. He was for a time editor of the Charleston *Literary Gazette*, but found leisure in his journalistic work to pay ardent court to the Muses. His first collection of poems appeared in 1855; and was favorably received especially by those who sympathized with the culture characteristic of the South. 811.42.

POEMS. Bost., Lothrop, $3.

LEGENDS AND LYRICS. Phila., Lippincott, $1.50.

Herbert, George. [1593-1633.]

Divine and poet; one of the early English writers of religious verse. He was the friend of Lord Bacon, the intimate of the poet Donne, and the famed Izaak Walton wrote his life. He was brother to the celebrated Lord Herbert, of Cherbury, historian of the times of Henry VIII., and himself received preferment in the English Church at the hands of Charles I. Herbert's poetical works are chiefly of a sacred and devotional character, with a curious admixture of profound insight, odd conceits, homely shrewdness, and sly humor, set forth with the true lyrical gift. In "Man" he shows a surprising fore-feeling of modern scientific discovery—is not every true poet seer as well as singer? Herbert was one of the favorites of Emerson, whose verse has much the same jeweled quaintness. 821.38.

POEMS. With Prefatory Notice by Ernest Rhys. Lond., Walter Scott, 1s.; N. Y., A. Lovell & Co., 40 c.

Comprises, besides "The Temple," a number of other justly admired minor poems, "Man," "Sunday," and "The Pulley," attuned to a fervent devotional spirit. Izaak Walton's Life of the poet is added.

Holmes, Oliver Wendell. [1809-1894.]

Physician, poet, and prose-writer, familiarly known as "The Autocrat"—the title of his chief work, a series of discursive papers, "The Autocrat of the Breakfast-Table." Here we have the wise and witty talk of a mature mind, splendidly equipped. Holmes belongs to the "old school poets"—to the gay band of punning rhymsters, Saxe, Hood, and Praed, with such variations of theme as attach to his professional and academic life in the cultured circles of New England. His verse, as in "The Last Leaf," "The Chambered Nautilus," "The Living Temple," expresses his bright, joyous, youthful nature: its graceful strains represent many moods—the jocund, the serious, the brilliant, and the familiar. His stronger and sturdier muse is seen in his later pieces, in patriotic themes, fraternal greetings, academic odes—poems for occasions. Holmes' personality, with its sprightly humor and genial optimism, is equally exhibited in his prose-work, especially in the earlier volumes. Hardly anything could be more delightful than the several issues of the "Breakfast Table" series.

THE BREAKFAST-TABLE SERIES. Bost. Houghton, 4 vols., $1.50 per vol. 817.32.

POEMS. Bost., Houghton (Household Edition), $1.50. 814.

ONE HUNDRED DAYS IN EUROPE. Bost., Houghton, $1.50. 817.32.

COMPLETE POETICAL AND PROSE WORKS. Bost., Houghton, 13 vols., $1.50 per vol. and upwards. 817.32.

Hood, Thomas. [1798-1845.]

Poet and humorist, best known by his pathetic "Bridge of Sighs," and the immortal "Song of the Shirt." Though a brooding melancholy overshadows even his gayest and most ludicrous verse, it has freshness, originality, and power. He had a wonderful gift of rhyming, and, in an unexcelled degree, saw the ludicrous side of things. Not a few of his poems were called forth by the deep human interests of his time, and touch the heart to-day as closely as when first they saw the light. With capacity for great poetry, his needs kept him for the most part busy in turning out whimsicalities for the *Comic Annual*, *Hood's Magazine*, and *Punch*. There are few satires in the language as severe as his "Ode to Rae Wilson. Esquire." 827.72.

POETICAL WORKS. Illustrated. N. Y., Routledge, $1.50.

COMIC POEMS. SERIOUS POEMS. N. Y., Routledge, 40 c. each.

Handy Pocket Editions.

CHOICE WORKS IN PROSE AND VERSE. Illustrated. N. Y., Scribner, $2.75.

Includes the cream of the *Comic Annuals*, with Life and Portrait.

Hutton, Richard Holt. [1826- .]

English journalist, essayist, and critic; editor of the *London Spectator*. He is the author of the monograph on Sir Walter Scott in the "English Men of Letters Series," a delightful and discriminating piece of criticism. His collected writings embrace some five volumes of essays and criticisms, from the point of view of a cultured orthodox writer, on theological and literary subjects. They are well-informed, sane, and assured in their matter and style; and, while conservative on matters of belief, are tolerant and sympathetic. In matters of literary criticism, Mr. Hutton has the right to be authoritative. 824.8.

MODERN GUIDES OF ENGLISH THOUGHT. N. Y., Macmillan, $1.50.

Contains essays on Carlyle, F. D. Maurice, George Eliot, John Henry Newman, and Matthew Arnold.

THEOLOGICAL AND LITERARY ESSAYS. N. Y., Macmillan, 2 vols., $1.50 each.

CRITICISMS ON CONTEMPORARY THOUGHT AND THINKERS. N. Y., Macmillan, 2 vols., $1.50 each.

Selections from *The Spectator*.

Ingelow, Jean. [1820- .]

One of the considerable band of gentle minstrels

who have enriched English verse within the century with many earnest, thoughtful, and tender strains. Besides her poetry, which is characterized by sincerity, imagination, and deep feeling, she has published three or four works of pleasant fiction. Several volumes of verse have come from her pen, the best known of which is her "Songs of Seven," which includes the quaint but musical old-time ballad, "The High Tide on the Coast of Lincolnshire," and many lyrics of idyllic beauty. **821.8**.

POETICAL WORKS. N. Y., Crowell, 75 c. and upwards.

Includes selections from the "Songs of Seven," and other later verse of much sweetness and pathos.

Irving, Washington. [1783-1859.]

Irving is among the first of American Men of Letters; "the Goldsmith of our age," Thackeray called him. As an author, he is distinguished by refined feeling, delicacy of sentiment, and a charming ease and simplicity. His style was fashioned on the best model —that of Addison, Goldsmith, and Lamb—and though at times ornate and over-fanciful, it is always clear, limpid, and flowing. His reputation abroad was first won by his "Sketch Book," which Sir Walter Scott was instrumental in publishing; it was "the first link in the bond of literary sympathy between the Old World and the New." His other writings embrace the "Salmagundi" and the "Crayon" Papers, "Tales of a Traveller," "Knickerbocker's History of New York," "The Conquest of Granada," and "The Alhambra," with Lives of Columbus, Goldsmith, and Washington. Irving's own life has been written by his relative, Pierre M. Irving, and by C. Dudley Warner, the latter appearing in the "American Men of Letters Series" (Bost., Houghton, $1.25). **817.24**.

COMPLETE WORKS. Spuyten-Duyvil Edition. N. Y., Putnam, 12 vols., $15.

A compact reissue, without the Life and Letters, in good type.

COMPLETE WORKS. Hudson Edition. N. Y., Putnam, 27 vols., $1.50 per vol.; sold separately.

A good Library Edition, including the Life and Letters.

POPULAR WORKS. Sleepy Hollow Edition. N. Y., Putnam, 6 vols., 75 c. each.

Embraces The Alhambra, Bracebridge Hall, Knickerbocker's History, Crayon Miscellany, The Sketch Book, Wolfert's Roost, and other Papers.

OLIVER GOLDSMITH. A Biography. N. Y., Putnam, $1.50.

A genially written and most entertaining Life.

LIFE OF GEORGE WASHINGTON. N. Y., Putnam, $1.50.

A classic in American literature, written with sustained patriotic fervor.

WASHINGTON AND HIS COUNTRY. Abridged from Irving, with a Continuation of the History to the End of the Civil War. By John Fiske. Bost., Ginn, $1; boards, 75 c.

An adaptation for schools and the general reader, giving the cardinal events in the native history so as "to illustrate, in view of what went before and what came after, the significance of Washington's career."

LIFE OF COLUMBUS. See Biography.

Jackson, Helen Fiske Hunt ("H. H."). [1831-1885.]

One of the many daughters of American song, who, by force of earnest feeling and sympathetic culture, have done excellent work, both in prose and verse. Her poems, which are mostly in a single key, "lack," says Mr. Stedman, "the variety of mood which betokens an inborn and always dominant poetic faculty." She has, however, a cultivated mind, considerable fancy and imaginative insight, and an experience of the world, which, with tender feeling, enables her to touch the lyre deftly and move the heart. She has written some delightful books of travel, many charming stories, and one or two books of home talk for young folk. Her arraignment of the United States Government, in "A Century of Dishonor," for its inconsiderate treatment of Indians, created a sensation on its appearing, and did good. **811.4**.

VERSES. Bost., Roberts, $1.

SONNETS AND LYRICS. Bost., Roberts, $1.

COMPLETE POEMS. Bost., Roberts, $1.50 and upwards.

Keats, John. [1796-1821.]

The most gifted and promising of English poets who have died young. He had in a remarkable degree the Greek sense of the beautiful, though lacking the moral stamina to make his worship of it divine. In the lyrical quality of his verse he is unsurpassed, one might almost say unapproached, by any other writer; and, as Matthew Arnold remarks, "no one else in English poetry, save Shakespeare, has in expression quite the fascinating felicity of Keats, his perfection of loveliness." When we consider the moral defects—what Wordsworth termed "the pretty Paganisms"—of his writings, we must allow for his youth and the compelling force of his luxuriant imagination. But much is condoned by the almost perfect art of his best work, which includes the unfinished but noble epic, "Hyperion"; the poem, "Endymion," which Shelley pronounced "full of some of the highest and the finest gleams of poetry"; "The Eve of St. Agnes," one of the most perfect of the poet's works; and the narrative poem, "Lamia," with its luxurious and haunting beauty. For a brief biographical sketch and critical estimate, see Lowell's "Among My Books." **821.78**.

POETICAL WORKS. N. Y., Macmillan, $1.

SELECTIONS FROM THE POEMS. N. Y., Routledge, 40 c.

LETTERS TO HIS FAMILY AND FRIENDS. N. Y., Macmillan, $1.50.

KEATS. By Sidney Colvin. (English Men of Letters series.) N. Y., Harper, 75 c.

KEATS. By W. M. Rossetti. (Great Writers series.) Scribner, $1; Lovell, 40 c.

Kipling, Rudyard. [1864-.]

An Anglo-Indian novelist and poet of high achievement and promise. The swing of Kipling's verse, its dramatic realism, its *abandon*, together with the felicity of his words and phrases, and the vigor of his interpretative power, have given him a unique place among present day poets. Besides the freshness and spontaneity of his genius, he has fire and dash, fertile imagination, and a wonderful power of setting forth a scene or a character. His verse has the true ballad "go" and movement, now rising into tragedy and anon dropping into audacious deviltry, and fun.

821.6.

BALLADS AND BARRACK-ROOM BALLADS. New edition with additional poems. N. Y., Macmillan, 1895, $1.25.

Lamb, Charles. [1775-1834.]

Poet and essayist, and one of the masters of English humor, in its most droll, yet delicate and refined form. His audience must always be a select one, the cultivated few, who can appreciate the whims and fancies of a scholarly recluse, and are in sympathy with his thoughtful moods, his playful conceits or tender pathos. His style is Addisonian in its ease and purity, though from the early Elizabethans, for whom Lamb had a great liking, it derived a vein of the dramatic. His poetry is too scant for notice here. He is best known as an essayist, and in that field, "Elia," in his happiest moods, is the most charming companion.
824.75.

WORKS. (Bohn.) N. Y., Macmillan, $3.
Contains the excellent memoir by Sir T. Noon Talfourd.

ESSAYS OF ELIA. N. Y., Lovell, Coryell, 75 c.
Contains, also, the later essays.

TALES FROM SHAKESPEARE. By Charles and Mary Lamb. N. Y., Lovell, Coryell, 75 c.
One of the best introductions to the great dramatist, especially for young readers.

Landor, Walter Savage. [1775-1864.]

Poet, essayist, and miscellaneous writer. He belongs to the patrician order in letters, for he wrote for "the fit few," in moods as fitful as his errant, sybaritic, dilettante taste moved him. Curiously enough, he was a radical in politics, and, like Byron, was a passionate enemy of tyranny and oppression. Yet his genius recoiled from the new democracy; in manner as well as in letters he was an aristocrat ; though a man of our modern world, a devotee of ancient culture and saturated with its spirit. His poetry is chiefly dramatic, with high lyrical quality of the classic order, easy and elegant in its flow. He wrote blank verse with an almost Miltonic distinction, and his prose has the highest of qualities—those conferred by the profound thinker, who is at the same time a cultured artist. Landor is best known by his varied series of "Imaginary Conversations of Literary Men and Statesmen," and by his "Pericles and Aspasia"—the latter esteemed by Stedman "the purest creation of sustained art in English prose."

IMAGINARY CONVERSATIONS. N. Y., Macmillan, 6 vols., $7.50.
The work on which Landor's fame chiefly rests. It is a treasury, almost Shakespearian in its wealth and pithiness, of the most elevated maxims of practical wisdom. 824.8.

SELECTIONS FROM THE WRITINGS. N. Y., Macmillan, $1.

POEMS, DIALOGUES IN VERSE, AND EPIGRAMS. N. Y., Macmillan, 2 vols., $3. 821.0.

PERICLES AND ASPASIA. N. Y., Macmillan, 2 vols., $3.75.
The most characteristic of Landor's writings, "full of the sweetest and truest expressions of sensibility."
824.8.

COMPLETE WORKS. N. Y., Macmillan, 10 vols., $1.25 per vol.

LANDOR. (English Men of Letters series.) By Sidney Colvin. N. Y., Harper, 75 c.
A book the reading of which will do much to popularize this great and much neglected writer.

Lanier, Sidney. [1842-1881.]

Southern poet, critic, and musician. A new but short-lived voice, of high promise, arose in the South with Lanier. The poetical qualities are well marked in his verse, but, as in "The Marshes of Glynn," he vainly sought to express in words the ideas for which music alone is adequate. Like Hayne, he, too, espoused the Confederate cause in the war. A volume of his select verse has been edited for schools by a professor in the University of Texas; but the best and fullest collection is that edited, with an admirable memoir, by Dr. W. Hayes Ward. Lanier had an intimate acquaintance with the structure of English poetry, and published a clever analysis of it in his "Science of English Verse." He also wrote a work of merit on "The English Novel and the Principle of its Development" (N. Y., Scribner, $2). 811.4.

POEMS. Edited by his wife, with a Memorial by W. H. Ward. N. Y., Scribner, $2.

SELECT POEMS. Edited, with introduction and notes, by Prof. M. Callaway, Jr. N. Y., Scribner, $1.

THE SCIENCE OF ENGLISH VERSE. N. Y., Scribner, $2.

Longfellow, Henry Wadsworth. [1807-1882.]

Deservedly the most popular among American poets, with a deep hold, too, on the affections of English readers. A man of wide and varied culture and high literary attainments, he had the artist's as well as the poet's instinct for melody and form. His work impresses the memory by its gracefulness, felicity, and vivid beauty, although he has no profound or original message to deliver. In an especial degree, Longfellow possessed the faculty of winning hearts by his human sympathies, earnest moral nature, and power of touching the emotions. His genius, it has been said, is more European than American ; but native characteristics are well developed in such song-themes as "Evangeline," "Hiawatha," "The Courtship of Miles Standish," "The New England Tragedies," and the poetical narratives entitled "The Tales of a Wayside Inn." Perhaps the popular mind is most attracted by the poet's shorter meditative verse, of which "The Psalm of Life" and "The Day is Done" are examples. He has added to his laurels by his translation of Dante. Stedman, in "Poets of America," gives an excellent study of Longfellow.
811.34.

COMPLETE POETICAL WORKS. Bost., Houghton, Handy Volume edition, 5 vols., $6.25; New Cambridge edition, 1 vol., $2.

POEMS. (Without the dramatic works and tragedies.) Bost., Houghton, Cabinet edition, $1.

DANTE. Translation of the "Divina Commedia" : with various readings and notes. Bost., Houghton, $2.50.

LIFE. By Samuel Longfellow. Bost., Houghton, 3 vols., $6.
The authoritative biography.

LIFE. By Prof. Eric S. Robertson. (Great Writers series.) N. Y., Scribner, $1; A. Lovell, 40 c.
An appreciative and sympathetic monograph.

Lowell, James Russell. [1819-1891.]

Lowell was not only a versatile and distinguished man of letters, but a great citizen, who at home and abroad made his voice and his pen most effective in the service of his country. In nearly all he wrote he stands for right and justice, and this sharpened his wit, instead of dulling it, as happens with all artists but the best. "The Biglow Papers," the dialect for which he mastered during a rustication, are as soundly patriotic as humorous. In his "Commemoration Ode," delivered at Harvard at the close of the Civil War, he rises to the full height of his genius as an American first and always. He was in thorough sympathy with the new knowledge of his time, as readers of his fine sonnet, " I grieve not that ripe knowledge takes away," are well aware. In another and equally elevated strain is "Extreme Unction." In "The Cathedral," a poem, in the main excellent, he shows his chief defects—an inability to restrain his love of the comic, to keep a story free from intrusive and whimsical episodes. His "Fable for Critics," admirable in many of its characterizations, is not always fair, as notably in his treatment of Margaret Fuller. His prose, which includes "Fireside Travels," "Among My Books," and "My Study Windows," contains the most brilliant, witty, and withal learned criticism thus far written in America. In "My Study Windows" is the famous essay, "On a certain condescension in foreigners." For discerning and sympathetic criticism of Lowell see Stedman's "Poets of America." **811.37.**

WORKS. Bost., Houghton, 12 vols., $17.50.

Includes the Poems, the Old English Dramatists, the Political Essays, the Literary and Political Addresses, and the Latest Literary Essays and other Papers.

WORKS. Popular edition. Bost., Houghton, 6 vols., $10.50.

The Poetical Works, the Political Essays, "Fireside Travels," "Among My Books," and "My Study Windows."

POEMS. Bost., Houghton, Household edition, $1.50; Cabinet edition, $1.

Macaulay, Thomas Babington. [1800-1859.]

The most pictorial prose-writer in English literature. His power of graphic narration has enabled him to enrich the literature of history and biography with scenes and studies that become an imperishable possession to his reader. The characteristics of his style are strength and clearness. His fondness for antithetical writing often overcomes his sense of justice, and leads him, partisan fashion, to laud one man by defaming another. This is notably the case in both his history and his essays. But despite these defects, Macaulay is a very great and inspiring writer. For an excellent characterization of him see Minto's "Manual of English Prose Literature" (Bost., Ginn, $1.50). **824.83.**

CRITICAL AND HISTORICAL ESSAYS. N. Y., Longmans, $1.75.

A serviceable Student's Edition, with the author's latest revisions. The essays are fascinating as well as instructive reading, displaying vast and varied knowledge, and enriched with apt, if profuse, illustration.

ESSAYS AND POEMS. N. Y., Routledge, $1.40.

Includes those admirable specimens of "rhymed rhetoric," the "Lays of Ancient Rome."

LAYS OF ANCIENT ROME. N. Y., Routledge, 40 c.

Contains also "Ivry" and "The Armada."

LIFE AND LETTERS. Edited by G. O. Trevelyan. N. Y., Harper, $1.75.

Next to Boswell's "Johnson," the best biography in literature.

LORD MACAULAY. By J. C. Morison. (English Men of Letters series.) N. Y., Harper, 75 c.

An excellent monograph.

Miller, Cincinnatus Hiner ("Joaquin Miller"). [1842-.]

Poet and journalist, best known by his "Songs of the Sierras." A native of Indiana, Miller, when a lad, accompanied his father to Oregon, thence found his way to the mines of California, where his muse responded to the inspirations and characteristics of the time and place. Afterwards he led an expedition against hostile Indians in Oregon, and for a time became a District Judge. Miller has many of the true qualities of the poet; he has imagination, invention, poetic fire, and, at times, a thrilling descriptive faculty, especially when under the inspiration of nature in the Far West. **811.45.**

SONGS OF THE SIERRAS, and SONGS OF THE SUN LANDS. Chic., Morrill, Higgins & Co., 1892, $1.50.

SONGS OF SUMMER LANDS. Chic., Morrill, Higgins & Co., 1892, $1.50. (These publishers have failed; the present publishers of the foregoing volumes are unknown. June, 1895. Editors' note.)

MEMORIE AND RIME. N. Y., Funk & Wagnalls, 75 c.; paper, 15 c.

Stories, poems, sketches, and leaves from the author's journal.

Milton, John. [1608-1674.]

Milton united the intellectual culture of the Elizabethan with the moral grandeur of the Puritan. In his masques, odes, and epics we see the three successive states or qualities of his mind—the blithe, the pensive, and the austere. To the first two belong the poems written before his fortieth year—"L'Allegro" (the cheerful man), "Il Penseroso" (the meditative man), the masques "Arcades," and "Comus," the sonnet on Shakespeare, and the sublime ode, "On the Morning of Christ's Nativity"; to the latter belong the noble epics, "Paradise Lost" and "Paradise Regained," and the fine dramatic poem, "Samson Agonistes," written in poverty and blindness after the Restoration. Between these periods lie the years of fierce polemical controversy, in which Milton wrote, in Latin or in English, his political pamphlets and religious treatises. In sublimity and moral grandeur Milton stands higher as a poet than Shakespeare; and greater than the poet is the man. Students are commended to read Macaulay's masterly essay on Milton in his "Historical and Critical Essays" (N. Y., Longmans, $1.75). **821.47.**

ENGLISH PROSE WRITINGS. Edited by Henry Morley. N. Y., Routledge, $1.

Contains the famous "Areopagitica"; a speech for the Liberty of Unlicensed Printing; the greatest piece of prose in the language; the essay on the Doctrine and Discipline of Divorce; a Letter on Education, and treatises on Church Discipline, on Prelacy, on the Civil Power in Ecclesiastical Causes, on the Tenure of Kings and Magistrates, and on the Commonwealth.

PROSE AND POETICAL WORKS. Edited by

John Mitford. N. Y., Macmillan, 7 vols., $7.

Standard Edition of the poet's writings, issued in the Bohn Library.

COMPLETE POETICAL WORKS. Edited by Prof. David Masson. N. Y., Macmillan, 3 vols., $5; in 1 vol., $1.75.

POEMS. Edited, with notes, by R. C. Browne. N. Y., Macmillan, 2 vols., $1.75.

A scholarly annotated edition for school and college use.

LIFE OF JOHN MILTON. By Prof. David Masson. N. Y., Macmillan, 6 vols. and Index, $38.

A monument of learning which, however, attempted too much in presenting so discursive a history of the times.

MILTON. By Mark Pattison. (English Men of Letters series.) N. Y., Harper, 75 c.

A singularly able monograph, invaluable to students of Milton and his times.

Moore, Thomas. [1779-1852.]

Poet and song-writer, best known by his "Irish Melodies," and an Oriental tale, in flowery verse, "Lalla Rookh." His poetry, despite its cloying sweetness and amatory tinge, has a liquid ease and lyrical grace, much heightened—in the case of the National airs and Irish Melodies—by the music to which the words are wedded. Though Moore's facility of production was great, not much beyond his songs survives in popularity. Even these are already beginning to pall upon the public taste, which now prefers less artificiality and effeminate ornament. Besides the verse already noted, Moore wrote "The Epicurean," a prose romance, and Lives of Sheridan and Byron. The latter is of value, like his own Memoirs, for its contemporary interest. 821.75.

POETICAL WORKS. N. Y., Routledge, $1.50.

A very full edition, with Life.

IRISH MELODIES and SONGS. LALLA ROOKH. N. Y., Routledge, 60c. each.

Morley, John. [1838-.]

Essayist, *littérateur*, and statesman. His literary labors include the editing of the "English Men of Letters Series" (N. Y., Harper), a library of biographical and critical monographs on the great lights of English literature; he has written memoirs of Diderot and the French Encyclopædists, including Voltaire and Rousseau; an historical study of Edmund Burke; a memoir of Richard Cobden, the apostle of Free Trade; a work On Compromise; a monograph on Walpole; besides a number of essays collected under the general title of "Critical Miscellanies." In addition to all this, he has, for a number of years, been an active politician, and a hard-working member of the late Gladstone and Rosebery Governments. He is a man of virile intellect, independent and radical thought, and rare powers as a writer. 824.8.

COLLECTED WORKS. N. Y., Macmillan, 11 vols., $1.50 per vol.

This edition includes, with his "Studies in Literature," the works above mentioned.

WALPOLE. (Twelve English Statesmen series.) N. Y., Macmillan, 75 c.

EDMUND BURKE. (English Men of Letters series.) N. Y., Harper, 75 c.

A fine analysis and critical study of the great political thinker, his times and his work.

Morris, William. [1834-]

Poet, decorative artist, and Socialist leader. Mr. Morris's literary career began in 1858, with the appearance of "The Defence of Guenevere," a collection of pre-Raphaelite poems; followed, nine years later, by a volume of narrative verse, "The Life and Death of Jason"; and, in 1868, by his great work, "The Earthly Paradise"—a collection of classical and mediæval tales, of legendary and romantic character, in much the same setting as the classic tales of Boccaccio or Chaucer. Later have come from the poet's pen, "a morality," entitled "Love is Enough"; translations into English verse of the "Æneid" of Virgil, and the "Odyssey" of Homer; with a series of translations of the Icelandic Sagas, happily and skilfully rendered, perhaps the finest work of his poetical genius —"The Story of Sigurd the Volsung," and "The Fall of the Niblungs." Mr. Morris has great narrative charm and poetic powers of a high order. His chief fault is diffuseness of style. 821.85.

THE EARTHLY PARADISE. N.Y., Scribner, $3; Bost., Roberts, 3 vols., $4.50.

DEFENCE OF GUENEVERE. N. Y., Scribner, $3.20; Bost., Roberts, $2.

LIFE AND DEATH OF JASON. N. Y., Scribner, $3.20; Bost., Roberts, $1.50.

LOVE IS ENOUGH. N. Y., Scribner, $3; Bost., Roberts, $1.25, or $2.

SIGURD THE VOLSUNG. N. Y., Scribner, $2.40. With THE FALL OF THE NIBLUNGS. Bost., Roberts, $2.50.

ODYSSEY OF HOMER. N. Y., Scribner, $2.60.

ÆNEIDS OF VIRGIL. N. Y., Scribner, $5.60; Bost., Roberts, $2.50.

POEMS BY THE WAY. N. Y., Scribner, $2.40; Bost., Roberts, $1.25.

Pater, Walter Horatio. [1839-1894.]

A writer of high culture, whose disquisitions on art and literature have secured for him an eminent position among modern English critics. His subtle and searching insight, added to the exquisite charm of his literary style, has given new attractions to art, as well as a new delight to Greek studies and the Greek spirit. Perhaps his best known work is "Marius, the Epicurean: His Sensations and Ideas"—being the mental history of a youth perplexed with the problem of life. The four stories told in "Imaginary Portraits" have also high and distinctive merit. 824.8.

THE RENAISSANCE: Studies in Art and Poetry. N. Y., Macmillan, $2.

APPRECIATIONS: with an Essay on Style. N. Y., Macmillan, $1.75.

IMAGINARY PORTRAITS. N. Y., Macmillan, $1.50.

MARIUS, THE EPICUREAN. N. Y., Macmillan, $2.25.

The four preceding vols. together, $6.

GREEK STUDIES. N. Y., Macmillan, $1.75.

PLATO AND PLATONISM. N. Y., Macmillan, $1.75.

Poe, Edgar Allan. [1809-1849.]

Poet, journalist, and writer of weird stories. Poe's

moral weaknesses and irregular life have sadly detracted from the honors which should have been the award of his great intellectual powers and high literary gifts. His erratic career is reflected in his works, which gave point, in its day, to Lowell's familiar doggerel gibe:

"There comes Poe with his raven, like Barnaby Rudge,
Three-fifths of him genius, and two-fifths sheer fudge."

Poe, nevertheless, stands for much in American letters, despite his vagabond life, his utter lack of moral sense, and the vicissitudes which addiction to drink brought upon him. He possessed a marvellous, though at times fantastic, imagination and a phenomenal command of the resources, in prose and verse, of literary construction. Though he was an unexcelled artist in words, his workmanship is curiously uneven; in one place it is polished and melodious, in another unfiled and jolting. His themes are marked by like diversity: on one page sweet and human; on the next eerie and ghoulish. **811.32.**

WORKS. Edited by John H. Ingram. N. Y., Macmillan, 4 vols., $5.

COMPLETE WORKS. Edited by E. C. Stedman and G. E. Woodberry. Chic., Stone & Kimball, to be completed in 10 vols., $1.50 each. Vol. V. issued June, 1895.

A newly collected and definitive edition with memoir by Prof. Woodberry, literary introduction and notes by Mr. Stedman, including a complete variorum of the poems.

POETICAL WORKS. N. Y., Crowell, 75 c. and upwards.

TALES. N. Y., Ward, Lock, 75 c.

LIFE. By George E. Woodberry. (American Men of Letters series.) Bost., Houghton, $1.25.

Pope, Alexander. [1688-1740.]

In much is the follower of Dryden; his verse is of value chiefly as a reflex of the moral and social condition of his age. It represents its artificiality, its polish, and its wit. The heroic couplet is his favorite vehicle of expression, and in its satiric as well as frolicsome use Pope brought it to perfection. His most serious undertaking was his verse paraphrases of the "Iliad" and "Odyssey," which have made Homer best known to English readers. His chief poems are "The Dunciad," a bitter satire, in which Pope vindicates literature from the dullards and dunces of his time that usurped its livery; the mock-heroic poem, "The Rape of the Lock"; and the "Essay on Man," a didactic poem on the origin of evil, exemplifying his characteristic "careless thinking, carefully versified." To these three poems, Pope, in the main, owes his fame. Lowell in "My Study Windows" offers a judicious appreciation of the poet. **821.53.**

COMPLETE WORKS. Edited by J. W. Croker, Rev. W. Elwin, and W. J. Courthope. N. Y., Scribner, 10 vols., $42.

An elaborate and scholarly edition, including many original pieces and letters here first published.

POETICAL WORKS, with TRANSLATION of the "Iliad" and "Odyssey," and Life by R. Carruthers. Bohn Library. N. Y., Macmillan, 5 vols., $1.50 each.

An approved edition, and a good text. The Homer volumes are embellished with Flaxman's celebrated outline designs.

POETICAL WORKS. Edited by Prof. A. W. Ward. N. Y., Macmillan, $1.75.

POPE'S HOMER'S ILIAD AND ODYSSEY. N. Y., Routledge, $1.40.

ESSAY ON MAN. With introduction and notes, by Mark Pattison. N. Y., Macmillan, 40 c.
SATIRES AND EPISTLES. With introduction and notes, by Mark Pattison, N. Y., Macmillan, 50 c. **827.55.**

Excellent annotated editions for school use by a scholarly editor.

ALEXANDER POPE. By Leslie Stephen. (English Men of Letters series.) N. Y., Harper, 75 c.

An admirable monograph, by a great critic.

Procter, Adelaide A. [1825-1864.]

Daughter of the dramatic song-writer, Bryan Waller Procter, "Barry Cornwall." Miss Procter ranks above Mrs. Hemans, but below both Mrs. Browning and Christina G. Rossetti. Her poems have not a few of the characteristics of Mrs. Browning's muse, with a reminder here and there of Miss Mulock; but she has a note of her own, though without striking originality. A thoughtful seriousness, softened by tender feeling, pervades her writings, with the sweet grace and melody of a cultured, devout woman. "It is like telling one's beads, or reading a prayer-book," says Mr. Stedman, "to turn over her pages—so beautiful, so pure and unselfish a spirit of faith, hope, and charity pervades and hallows them." "The Lost Chord," with Sir Arthur Sullivan's fine musical setting, will keep her memory green for many a long year. Nearly as popular are "A Woman's Question" and "O Doubting Heart!" **821.8.**

LEGENDS AND LYRICS. N. Y., Crowell, 75 c. and upwards.

POETICAL WORKS. Bost., Houghton, $1.

Read, Thomas Buchanan. [1822-1872.]

Poet and artist. A Pennsylvanian. "He had," says Tuckerman, "an innate sense of beauty and the irrepressible temper of genius; a great command of language, a vivid fancy, and a musical ear." He had taste and feeling, and at times—as in his familiar "Sheridan's Ride"—rare vigor and dash of utterance. His strength, however, lies in his simple lyrics and idyls of pastoral life, which are marked by fine sensibility and imagination. His best poem is "The Closing Scene," an elegy. **811.35.**

POETICAL WORKS. Phila., Lippincott, 3 vols., $5.25; Library edition, 1 vol., $3.

These editions include "The New Pastoral" and the "House by the Sea."

THE WAGONER OF THE ALLEGHANIES, AND OTHER POEMS. Phila., Lippincott, $1.50.

Riley, James Whitcomb. [1852-.]

Known familiarly as the "Hoosier" poet. His poetry is of the rural and domestic order; it includes character studies, poems in dialect, humorous, pathetic, and sentimental, in an old-fashioned way. He distinctly leads the choir of the younger American poets who sing to the plain people. "The Old Man and Jim" is perhaps the most touching poem inspired by the Civil War. **811.4**

OLD-FASHIONED ROSES. Indianapolis, Bowen-Merrill, $1.75.
Selections from Mr. Riley's various volumes of verse.

NEIGHBORLY POEMS ON FRIENDSHIP AND FARM LIFE. Indianapolis, Bowen-Merrill, $1.25.
Earlier writings, chiefly in dialect, originally issued under the pseudonym of Benjamin F. Johnson, of Boon.

ARMAZINDY. Indianapolis, Bowen-Merrill, $1.25.
Hoosier harvest airs, child rhymes, and humorous and serious poems.

AFTERWHILES. Indianapolis, Bowen-Merrill, $1.25.

POEMS HERE AT HOME. N. Y., Century Co., $1.50.
Contains "The Old Man and Jim."

Rossetti, Christina G. [1830-1894.]
Another of those sweet feminine voices, like Mrs. Browning, Adelaide Procter, and Jean Ingelow, that have enriched English song in the Victorian era. "Of women poets," says Mr. Stedman, "Miss Rossetti still finds none beside her on the heights of spiritual vision." She has some of the mystic qualities and much of the genius of her greater brother; in her songs, hymns, and lyrics she has a woman's soulfulness, insight, and grace of touch. Her prose-writings have, in the main, a serious cast. The English editions of her verse bear the titles of "The Goblin Market" and "The Prince's Progress, and Other Poems." The latter volume is known in America as "A Pageant, and Other Poems." 821.8.

POEMS. Complete edition. Bost., Roberts, $2.

Rossetti, Dante Gabriel. [1828-1882.]
Painter and poet, or rather more poet than painter, since he believed himself "to have mastered the means of embodying poetical conceptions in the verbal and rhythmical vehicle more thoroughly than in form and design, perhaps more thoroughly than in color." Rossetti belongs to what Robert Buchanan, on moral as well as on literary grounds, termed the "fleshly school of poetry," marked by sensuousness and ultra-romanticism. His work includes sonnets, lyrics, ballads and translations, the latter being chiefly from Dante, of whom Rossetti was a devout worshipper, and whose influence is seen upon his artistic as well as his literary work. Perhaps the best known, as it is the most characteristic of Rossetti's poems, is "The Blessed Damozel," a singular and highly artistic production, which marks the high level of his poetic faculty. "Sister Helen," which is of the ballad type, with a refrain, is a poem of equal merit in another key. It tells a tale of relentless vengeance on the part of a wronged woman, and might for its dramatic quality be placed on a plane with the tragic stories of classical literature. Rossetti is, however, most worthily known by his sonnets, of which he wrote many that deserve to rank with the best of our century. 821.84.

POETICAL WORKS. Edited by W. M. Rossetti. N. Y., Scribner, $2.40; Bost., Roberts, $2.
An excellent edition, with preface and notes by the poet's brother.

COLLECTED WORKS. Edited by W. M. Rossetti. N. Y., Scribner, 2 vols., $7.20.

POEMS. N. Y., Crowell, 75 c. or $1.
A handy one-volume collection.

LIFE OF ROSSETTI. By Joseph Knight. (Great Writers series.) N. Y., Scribner, $1; A. Lovell, 40 c.
Sympathetic and well informed.

Ruskin, John. [1819- .]
Poet, critic, and eloquent prose-writer on the true and beautiful in Nature and Art. Mr. Ruskin first won fame by the publication of his "Modern Painters," a plea for the superiority in art of the modern over the ancient masters of landscape painting, and a defence, in especial, of the methods and work of Turner and the art principles of the Pre-Raphaelite School. This work was followed by "Stones of Venice" and "Seven Lamps of Architecture"; afterwards he delivered his eloquent and inspiring lay sermons on the mystical union between Nature and Art, Beauty and Utility, and their reflex, in the reverential homage for the beautiful and the worthy, in the mind and character of the race. In this latter service he has produced a great body of fine and thoughtful work, which is as instructive as its meaning is profound. Here, as elsewhere in his writings, the Ruskinian doctrines come strongly out, colored always by an amiable egotism and enforced by a more or less arrogant dogmatism. But his works, despite inconsistency and eccentricity, have deservedly become classic, no less from the wealth and impressiveness of the thought than from the eloquence and splendor of the diction. Mr. Waldstein says: "Whoever has read the works of Ruskin will thereafter approach nature with a new faculty of appreciation, will have his attention directed to what he before passed by with indifference, and will discover what was before hidden." See also ART for a note on Ruskin. 824.86.

The authorized and best edition of Ruskin's works is the " Brantwood," published by Maynard, Merrill & Co., N. Y.

MODERN PAINTERS. N. Y., Maynard, Merrill & Co., 6 vols., Illus., $48; Merrill & Baker, 5 vols., $3.50, $7.50, and upwards; Lovell, Coryell, 5 vols., $3.50, $6.25, or $7.50.

STONES OF VENICE. N. Y., Maynard, Merrill & Co., 3 vols., Illus., $36; Merrill & Baker, 3 vols., $2, $4.50, and upwards; Lovell, Coryell, $2, $3.75, or $4.50.

SEVEN LAMPS OF ARCHITECTURE. N. Y., Maynard, Merrill & Co., $2.75; Merrill & Baker, 50 c., $1, and upwards; Lovell, Coryell, 75 c., or $1.50.

CROWN OF WILD OLIVE, and SESAME AND LILIES. N. Y., Lovell, Coryell, 75 c. Separately, N. Y., Maynard, Merrill & Co., $1.50; Merrill & Baker, 50 c., $1, and upwards each.
The favorite writings of the great art critic; the former being lectures on "Work, Traffic, and War," impressively and didactically treated; the latter dealing symbolically with books and women, under the sub-titles "Of Kings' Treasuries" and "Of Queens' Gardens."

QUEEN OF THE AIR. N. Y., Maynard, Merrill & Co., $1.50; Merrill & Baker, 50 c., $1, and upwards.
Discussing Greek myths of Cloud and Storm.

ETHICS OF THE DUST. N. Y., Maynard,

Merrill & Co., $1.50; Merrill & Baker, 50 c., $1, and upwards.
One of the happiest and most inspiring books ever addressed to Little Housewives.

THE WORK OF JOHN RUSKIN: Its Influence Upon Modern Thought and Life. By Charles Waldstein. N. Y., Harper, 1894, $1.
A thoughtful characterization and criticism by an archeologist of mark. Points out how Ruskin's attitude as a moral preacher limits his right understanding of art. Gives hearty praise to his eloquence and enthusiasm.

Scott, Sir Walter. [1771-1832.]
Has, in an especial degree, the fervid patriotism characteristic of his countrymen. Beyond all the writers of North Britain—Burns alone excepted—it is Scott who has given the "Land of the Heather" its enduring fame. His literary career began by bringing out a collection of the "Minstrelsy of the Scottish Border." His enthusiasm for ballad poetry, his chivalrous spirit, and his varied antiquarian lore, coupled with a rich fancy and wonderful power of narration, account for his success first as a poet, and afterwards—when the poetic vein had worked itself out—as a novelist. It is as a poet we have here to do with him. In poetry, his lyrical gifts and powers of animated narration have given him not a pre-eminent, but still a high place. His finest productions are "Marmion; a Tale of Flodden Field," "The Lady of the Lake," and the "Lay of the Last Minstrel." Scott's style—which is far from a careful one—is easy, rapid, and graphic. His poetic fame is, however, overshadowed by the success he attained as a writer of prose fiction. **821.74.**

POETICAL WORKS. Edited with Memoir by W. B. Scott. N. Y., Routledge, $1.50.
Complete, including the dramatic works.

THE LADY OF THE LAKE. THE LAY OF THE LAST MINSTREL. MARMION. With Notes by W. J. Rolfe. Bost., Houghton, 75 c. each.
Excellent separate texts for school use, with Notes and Introductions.

SIR WALTER SCOTT. By Richard Holt Hutton. (English Men of Letters series.) N. Y., Harper, 75 c.
A monograph, both biographical and critical. For the Life of Scott, by J. G. Lockhart, his son-in-law, see BIOGRAPHY.

Shakespeare, William. [1564-1616.]
Indisputably the first of the world's dramatists and poets. His creative power, mastery of the resources of language, his many-sided intellect and soaring gifts of imagination, make him unapproachable. Vast is the bibliography connected with Shakespeare; here it is possible only to note a few of the standard contemporary editions, critical works, and more notable commentaries. The beginner does well who takes up one of these works of criticism, for there is dross as well as gold in Shakespeare, and to understand his meaning many terms and allusions need to be explained.
822.33.

A PRIMER OF SHAKESPEARE. By Prof. E. Dowden. N. Y., Am. Book Co., 35 c.
Invaluable as an introduction to the Poet and his works.

A SHAKESPEARIAN GRAMMAR. By Rev. E. A. Abbott. N. Y., Macmillan, $1.50.
Excellent to the student as a philological and grammatical text-book.

CRAIK'S ENGLISH OF SHAKESPEARE. Edited by W. J. Rolfe. Bost., Ginn, $1.
A useful exposition of the Poet's language and style, illustrated in a philological commentary on the play of Julius Cæsar.

MIND AND ART OF SHAKESPEARE. By Prof. E. Dowden. N. Y., Harper, $1.75.
A critical study of the highest value, illuminating the poet's work in every phase, while tracing with a firm hand the growth and development of his genius.

COMMENTARIES. By G. G. Gervinus. From the German. N. Y., Scribner, $5.25.
Acute, sympathetic, and thorough. Nowhere else is there so full and intelligent a study of the separate plays, or better interpretation of the poet's meaning.

INTRODUCTION TO SHAKESPEARE. By Prof. Hiram Corson. Bost., Heath, $1.50.
Presents the Poet in his attitude towards things, rather than as a textual study.

SHAKESPEARIAN CONCORDANCE. By John Bartlett. N. Y., Macmillan, $14.
A monumental work, giving the passage in which each word occurs.

SHAKESPEARE CONCORDANCE. By Charles and Mary Cowden Clarke. N. Y., Scribner, $7.50.

CONCORDANCE TO THE PLAYS. By W. Davenport Adams. N. Y., Routledge, $1.50.

THE VARIORUM SHAKESPEARE. Edited by H. Howard Furness. Phila., Lippincott, to be completed in 25 vols., $4 each.
Ten volumes are now ready: Romeo and Juliet, Macbeth, King Lear, Othello, Merchant of Venice, As You Like it, Tempest, Midsummer Night's Dream, each 1 vol., Hamlet 2 vols.

THE HARVARD SHAKESPEARE. Edited by H. N. Hudson, LL.D. Bost., Ginn, 20 vols., $25; or 10 vols., $20.
Suited to the student and the general reader. It is conveniently supplied with two sets of notes—one set, at foot of page, explaining the text; the other, at the end of each play, dealing with textual comment and criticism.

EXPURGATED SHAKESPEARE. By the same editor. Bost., Ginn, 23 vols., 50c.; paper, 35 c. each.
The Plays only, designed for school use and family reading.

COMPLETE WORKS. Edited by Howard Staunton. N. Y., Routledge, 3 vols., $18.
With illustrations by Sir John Gilbert. A fine library edition.
An edition of the same, without illustrations, N. Y., Routledge, 6 vols., $10.

COMPLETE WORKS. Knight's edition, N. Y., Routledge, 3 vols., $3.75.
In large type, with illustrations.

HANDY VOLUME EDITION OF COMPLETE WORKS. N. Y., Routledge, 13 vols., $7.50.

THE TEMPLE EDITION. (Dent, London.) N. Y., Macmillan, 40 vols., 45 c. each.
A dainty pocket or boudoir edition, of which half of the issue has appeared. It is edited, with prefaces, notes, and a glossary, by Israel Gollancz, M.A.

THE LEOPOLD SHAKESPEARE. N. Y., Cassell, $1.50.
Complete Works from the text of Prof. Delius, with "Edward III." and "The Two Noble Kinsmen," and introduction by F. J. Furnivall. Illustrated.

UNIVERSAL EDITION. N. Y., Warne, $1.
A handy edition, in good type.

SHAKESPEARE FOR THE YOUNG. By S. Brandram. Phila., Lippincott, $1.75.
Duly selected and expurgated.

THE GIRLHOOD OF SHAKESPEARE'S HEROINES: a series of fifteen tales. By Mary Cowden Clarke. Illustrated. N. Y., Scribner, $3.
A delightful picture gallery by a woman whose life has been devoted to the study of Shakespeare.

SOME OF SHAKESPEARE'S FEMALE CHARACTERS. By Helena Faucit (Lady Martin). Illustrated. N. Y., Scribner, $3.
An informing aid to the student of Shakespeare's heroines.

TALES FROM SHAKESPEARE. By Charles and Mary Lamb. N. Y., Lovell, Coryell, 75 c.
An entertaining introduction to Shakespeare's Plays, giving plot and argument.

Shelley, Percy Bysshe. [1792-1822.]

Keats' contemporary and peer in genius, though, unlike Keats, of revolutionary principles. Like Keats, he died young, though not before Shelley laid on his friend's bier the immortelle of "Adonais," an elegy which worthily ranks with Milton's "Lycidas." Shelley's chief poetical works embrace "Queen Mab"; "The Cenci," a tragedy full of passion and power; the rich but hardly sane poem, "The Revolt of Islam"; and "Prometheus Unbound," a lyrical drama of entrancing beauty. In most of these poems Shelley declares himself "a scion of infidelity," and is thoroughly repellent. Happily we have in his lyrics, odes, and briefer poems something to which we can turn with gladness unrestrained. Hardly is there anything finer in literature than the poet's odes "To a Skylark" and "To the West Wind," or anything sweeter than the rapturous passion of "The Cloud." 821.77.

POETICAL WORKS. Edited by Prof. Dowden. N. Y., Macmillan, $1.75.

POETICAL WORKS. Edited by W. M. Rossetti. N. Y., Crowell, 75 c. and upwards.

POETICAL WORKS. Edited by W. B. Scott. N. Y., Routledge. $1.50.

POEMS. Selected and edited by Stopford A. Brooke. N. Y., Macmillan, $1.

Smith, Goldwin. [1823-.]

We deal here with this eminent author, not as an historian, but as a thoughtful essayist, an acute critic, and a brilliant *littérateur*. He is one of the great prose-writers of the century, a man of wide knowledge, high culture, and an almost matchless power of terse and luminous expression. Not less notable is the high moral quality of his work. He is an independent thinker; and though his convictions are not always those of his reader, he is invariably instructive and stimulating. 824.8.

ESSAYS ON QUESTIONS OF THE DAY, Political and Social. N. Y., Macmillan, $2.25.
A collection of weighty chapters on topics of the time, on which the author holds decided, if controverted, opinions—Church Disestablishment, the Irish Question, the Jewish Question, the Woman Question, Prohibition, Social and Industrial Revolution.

Spenser, Edmund. [1552-1599.]

Elizabethan laureate, who chiefly owes his fame to his great allegorical epic, "The Faerie Queene." In its moral beauty, and in the musical flow of the poem, it takes rank with the very noblest English verse, despite the tediousness of its allegory. The motive is to describe the warfare of twelve knights against all forms of evil, which in the poet's pages become real personages, and contend with the knights who represent the chief virtues. Among his other productions are "The Shepherd's Calendar," a tender pastoral poem, dedicated to the poet's patron, Sir Philip Sidney; "Prothalamion," "a spousal verse"; the "Hymn in Honour of Beauty"; some fine sonnets; and the magnificent nuptial ode, "Epithalamion," in which Spenser celebrates, with chaste but rather cloying ardor, his own marriage. For an illuminating study of the poet, see Lowell's "Among My Books." 821.31.

THE FAERIE QUEENE. N. Y., Routledge, $1.40.

THE FAERIE QUEENE. Edited by R. Morris. N. Y., Macmillan, $1 75.
Another serviceable edition, including the Minor Poems, and Memoir by J. W. Hales.

POETICAL WORKS. N. Y., Routledge, $3.
An accepted edition of the complete works, edited by Rev. H. J. Todd, with notes from various commentators, life and glossary.

POETICAL WORKS. Edited by J. Payne Collier. N. Y., Macmillan, 5 vols., $3.75.
A choice Library edition, in handy form, in good type.

TALES FROM SPENSER, from THE FAERIE QUEENE. By Sophia M. Maclehose. N. Y., Macmillan, 50 c., or $1.25.
An admirable series.

SPENSER FOR CHILDREN. By M. H. Towry. N. Y., Scribner, $1.25.
Delightful renderings of the Poet's stories, such as "Una and the Lion," the "Red Cross Knight and the Dragon," and others.

SPENSER. By Dean Church. (English Men of Letters series.) N. Y., Harper, 75 c.
An admirable and sympathetic monograph, with critical estimate.

Stedman, Edmund Clarence. [1833-.]

American poet, critic, and man of letters. Mr. Stedman began life as a journalist, and for a time acted as a war correspondent. He afterwards forsook journalism for finance; in recent years he has devoted himself to literature. Besides writing verse of distinction, he has engaged in the work of literary criticism, of which his "Victorian Poets" and " Poets of America " are eminent examples. He has recently, with the assistance of Miss Ellen M. Hutchinson, passed through the press a great treasury of American literature, in eleven octavo volumes. Mr. Stedman is a highly competent, sane, and discerning critic, bringing to his tasks rare and scholarly acquirements, and judgment matured in the successful practice of creative art. Remarkable, also, is his catholicity of taste and judgment. In 1891 he inaugurated the Turnbull Lectureship on Poetry at the Johns Hopkins University, by a series of lectures on the nature and elements of poetry, which were repeated in the following year before the University of Columbia. 811.43.

{ POETS OF AMERICA. Bost., Houghton, $2.25.
  VICTORIAN POETS. Revised, with supplementary chapter. Bost., Houghton, $2.25.
Invaluable as a literary exposition of modern poetry, English and American. It would be difficult to point to a better or more useful body of criticism.

NATURE AND ELEMENTS OF POETRY. Bost., Houghton, $1.50.

ELIZABETH BARRETT BROWNING: an essay. With "Lady Geraldine's Courtship" and " Favorite Poems from Robert Browning." Bost., Houghton, 40 c., or 75 c.

LIBRARY OF AMERICAN LITERATURE. N. Y., Wm. Evarts Benjamin, 11 vols., $30 and upwards.

POEMS. Bost., Houghton, $1.50.

Stephen, Leslie. [1832-.]

Man of letters, and first of modern English critics. He succeeded Thackeray, whose daughter he married, in the editorship of the *Cornhill Magazine*, but resigned this to become editor, and now a valued contributor, to that great English literary enterprise, the "Dictionary of National Biography." Mr. Leslie Stephen's articles on English literary men in this dictionary are of the highest critical value, being distinguished by acute insight, great erudition, and a charming and sympathetic style. To the "English Men of Letters" series he has contributed three admirable monographs, those on Alexander Pope, Samuel Johnson, and Dean Swift. His other works embrace a "History of English Thought in the 18th Century"; a work on "The Science of Ethics"; an interesting "Life of Prof. Henry Fawcett"; and a series of literary studies, biographical and critical, under the title of "Hours in a Library." **824.8.**

HOURS IN A LIBRARY. N. Y., Putnam, 3 vols., $4.50.
Contents in part: De Foe, Richardson, Pope, Scott, Hawthorne, Balzac, Johnson, Disraeli, Massinger, Wordsworth, Landor, Macaulay, Charlotte Brontë, Shelley, Gray, Sterne, Coleridge.

JONATHAN SWIFT. SAMUEL JOHNSON. ALEXANDER POPE. (English Men of Letters series.) N. Y., Harper, 75 c. each.
Appreciative and critical studies of a high order, dealing with the age as well as with the work of each subject.

Stoddard, Richard Henry. [1825-.]

Poet and man of letters, at present literary editor of the New York *Mail and Express*. An industrious worker in varied paths of literature, an accomplished editor in biography and criticism—notably in the "Sans-Souci" and "Bric à-Brac" series—author of several volumes of collected poems. He is a graceful poet, many of his lyrical pieces having much of "the tenderness and delicacy of expression that charm us in Herrick, Tennyson, and the German Heine." He has a fine ear for melody, and his style is marked by purity and grace. His volumes of verse range over a period of forty years, the best known being "Songs of Summer," "The Book of the East," and "The King's Bell." As representative poems, may be named his "Hymn to the Sea," "The Country Life," "The Dead Master," and "The Fisher and Charon." **811.41.**

POETICAL WRITINGS. With portrait. N. Y., Scribner, $4.

THE LION'S CUB, AND OTHER VERSE. N. Y., Scribner, $1.25.

UNDER THE EVENING LAMP. N. Y., Scribner, $1.25.
Sympathetic studies of Burns and his contemporaries, of Edward Fitzgerald, of Lord Houghton, and other minor poets.

Swinburne, Algernon Charles. [1837-.]

The greatest living English poet. In his early sensuous but mellifluous verse he forfeited the recognition which his eminent abilities and fine lyrical gifts ought to have won for him. In spite of this, and of his later outbursts of Republicanism and sympathy with regicides, Swinburne's place is among the immortals of song. Few writers of verse have had a finer ear than he for melody and poetic form, or a more thorough mastery over the technicalities of metrical composition. His first successful poem was "Atalanta in Calydon," a splendid classical tragedy, flawless in form and spirit. Following this came the successive tragedies which constitute a trilogy—"Chastelard," "Bothwell," and "Mary Queen of Scots." These, with his "Songs Before Sunrise" and "Songs of the Spring Tides," comprise the bulk of Swinburne's verse. His writings include also a number of fine critical prose essays. **821.86.**

POETICAL WORKS. Selected, with introduction, by R. H. Stoddard. N. Y., Crowell, 75 c. and upwards.
Contains Atalanta in Calydon, Erechtheus, Chastelard, Bothwell, and Mary Stuart.

SONGS BEFORE SUNRISE. Lond., Chatto, 10s. 6d.

SONGS OF THE SPRINGTIDES. Lond., Chatto, 6s.

CENTURY OF ROUNDELS. Lond., Chatto, 8s.

ESSAYS AND STUDIES. Lond., Chatto, 12s.

Taylor, Bayard. [1825-1878.]

Poet, essayist, traveller, and diplomat. A versatile, accomplished, and industrious author. Bayard Taylor touched American thought on many sides, and made excellent though not great contributions to American letters. Beginning life as a journalist, he early manifested a passion for travel, the literature of which he has enriched by his "Views Afoot" and "By-Ways of Europe," as well as by his "Poems of the Orient" and "Poems of Home and Travel." His glowing, though strong, literary style makes these works attractive, apart from the incidents they describe. As an accomplished German scholar, he has left behind him one of the best English translations of Goethe's "Faust," together with an excellent series of "Studies in German Literature." His poetry, which is largely dramatic, is marked by fine ideality, manifest truth, and genuine feeling. **811.46.**

POETICAL WORKS. Bost., Houghton, $1.50.

DRAMATIC WORKS. Bost., Houghton, $1.50.

PRINCE DEUKALION. A Lyrical Drama. Bost., Houghton, $3.

LIFE AND LETTERS. Edited by his widow and H. E. Scudder. Bost., Houghton, 2 vols., $4.

Tennyson, Alfred, *Lord.* [1809-1892.]

Greatest of the Victorian poets and consummate artist in verse. He lacked the dramatic faculty, and had but slender gifts of invention and creation. But among Idyllic poets he stands pre-eminent; his "Idylls of the King" give a great legend its noblest setting. Never has literature had such a master of lyrical verse; while in stateliness and rhythm his blank verse attains almost Miltonic heights. A like comparison might be made with Milton, in that magnificent burst of elegiac song, "In Memoriam," written, like "Lycidas," to assuage a poet's grief on the loss of a friend. Tennyson's writings worthily represent his age, and manifest many of the highest qualities of the thought and art of his time. In "The Two Voices," "The Talking Oak," and in much else of his work, we see how profoundly new knowledge illuminates world-old problems, though it cannot solve them. Not less distinctively the products of the time are the story of "The Princess," the metrical romance of "Maud," and the wealth of his other descriptive, narrative, and lyrical verse. **821.81.**

COMPLETE POETICAL WORKS. Cabinet edition. N. Y., Macmillan, 10 vols., $1.50 each, or together, $12.50; 1 vol., $1.75; Bost., Houghton, 6 vols., $6; 1 vol., $1.50.

LYRICAL POEMS. Edited by F. T. Palgrave. N. Y., Macmillan, $1.75.

IDYLLS OF THE KING. N. Y., Macmillan, $1.25.

IN MEMORIAM. N. Y., Macmillan, $1.25.

THE PRINCESS, and MAUD. N. Y., Macmillan, $1.50.

THE POETRY OF TENNYSON. By Henry Van Dyke, D.D. N. Y., Scribner, $2.
Written in an excellent spirit, the treatment displaying intelligence and sympathetic insight, marred, however, by occasional eccentricity in judgment.

STUDY OF THE WORKS OF TENNYSON. By A. C. Tainsh. N. Y., Macmillan, $1.75.
A scholarly and sympathetic analysis, much esteemed by Tennysonians.

TENNYSON: HIS ART IN RELATION TO MODERN LIFE. By Stopford A. Brooke. N. Y., Putnam, $2.
The work of a cultured, highly informed writer, author of the well-known "Primer of English Literature," treating of the Poet in relation to his age and the spirit of the time.

STUDY, WITH CRITICAL AND EXPLANATORY NOTES, OF LORD TENNYSON'S POEM "THE PRINCESS." By Samuel E. Dawson. Montreal, Dawson Brothers, 1884, $1.
"The Princess" contains Tennyson's solution of the position of woman in society. Prefixed to this "Study" is a long and very interesting letter from Lord Tennyson to the author, in which the poet gives an insight into his modes of literary composition, and criticises the "Study" in one or two points, while giving it his general approval.

Thackeray, William Makepeace. [1811–1863.]
English literature knows no healthier or saner writer than the chivalrous and large-hearted Thackeray. A true humorist, who could see the droll things in life, he had a passionate dislike of the ignoble, the false, and the mean. His novels do not come within our purview; but if he had never written a work of fiction, his lectures and miscellaneous writings would have made him famous. **824.8.**

THE ENGLISH HUMORISTS OF THE EIGHTEENTH CENTURY; the FOUR GEORGES; and the ROUNDABOUT PAPERS. N. Y., Harper, $1.25.
The "Humorists" is a delightful volume of genial, but acute, criticism, dealing with Fielding, Swift, Sterne, Smollett, Steele, Addison, and other of the 18th century writers. The sketches are models of good writing, with sympathetic insight and humor. The "Four Georges," which is notable for its scathing attack on the fourth of the royal name, gives a brilliant picture of English life and manners in the early Hanoverian period. The "Roundabout Papers" are on all manner of light and grave subjects, dashed off in an easy, pleasant mood, with the utmost geniality and charity.

BALLADS. Illustrated. Bost., Houghton, $1.50.
Humorous, satirical, and sentimental, in imitation of the Odes of Horace and the Lyrics of Béranger.

THE ROSE AND THE RING. Illustrated. N. Y., Putnam, $1.25.
The history of Prince Giglio and Prince Bulbo—"a Fireside Pantomime for Great and Small Children," as the author himself sets forth.

THE PARIS SKETCH BOOK. N. Y., Routledge, 40 c.
Sketches and stories.

For complete sets of his works see FICTION.

W. M. THACKERAY. By Anthony Trollope. (English Men of Letters series.) N. Y., Harper, 75 c.
A very inadequate memoir.

W. M. THACKERAY. By H. T. Merivale and F. T. Marzials. (Great Writers series.) N. Y., Scribner, $1.
A better memoir, though unsatisfactory.

Whittier, John Greenleaf. [1807–1892.]
The poet of the cheery and homely side of human nature; a representative New Englander. His lyrical qualities, the soundness of his sentiment, and the fervor of his anti-slavery muse, endear him to the more serious type of readers. Not the least of his merits are his Quakerly purity of thought and devout feeling. His range of subjects is comparatively limited, as well as unexciting; but he has rare powers of felicitous and melodious expression. His "Snow Bound," "Prayer-Seeker," "Maud Muller," and "Barbara Frietchie," are favorite poems wherever the English language is spoken. **811.30.**

POETICAL AND PROSE WORKS. Bost., Houghton, 7 vols., $10.50.
With Notes by the author, and Portraits. The edition can be had in two separate divisions—the Poems in 4 vols., the Prose in 3 vols., at $1.50 per vol. The latter embrace the Tales and Sketches, Historical and Slavery Subjects, Margaret Smith's Journal, the Old Portraits, and Modern Sketches, etc.

POEMS. Bost., Houghton, Cabinet edition, $1; Household edition, $1.50.
A new and much enlarged collection, in convenient form.

LIFE AND LETTERS. By S. T. Pickard. Bost., Houghton, 2 vols., $4.
An authoritative, full, and sympathetic biography, with selections from the poet's correspondence.

Wordsworth, William. [1770–1850.]
Poet of reflection and contemplation, writer of sonnets, lyrics, odes, philosophical poems, and other subjective verse. Matthew Arnold esteems Wordsworth "one of the chief glories of English poetry," and places him next to Shakespeare and Milton. He frankly admits, however, that his high poetic achievement is much detracted from by a considerable volume of inferior and encumbering verse. His best work is to be found in his shorter pieces, in which he "pipes a simple song for thinking hearts." A high philosophy underlies much of his work; but its chief distinction is the poet's intense love of Nature, sympathy with human feelings and emotions, high sense of duty, and idealizing power of imagination. Added to this is a pervading elevation of tone and exquisite simplicity and beauty of language. His chief works are "The Excursion" and "The Prelude," lengthy philosophical poems in blank verse, the latter chiefly autobiographical; Lyrical Ballads, Sonnets, "Yarrow Revisited," and a romantic narrative poem, "The White Doe of Rylstone. His fame rests, however, on his shorter pieces—such as "Lucy Gray," "Peter Bell," "Laodamia," and the "Ode to Duty" and "Intimations of Immortality." For criticism, see Hutton's and Arnold's Essays, Shairp's "Aspects of Poetry" and "Poetic Interpretation of Nature," and Lowell's "Among My Books." **821.71.**

POETICAL WORKS. Edited, with memoir, by Prof. Edward Dowden. N. Y., Macmillan, 7 vols., $5.25.

COMPLETE POETICAL WORKS. With introduction by John Morley. N. Y., Macmillan, $1 75.

SELECT POEMS. Chosen and edited, with preface, by Matthew Arnold. N. Y., Macmillan, $1.
The pure gold of the poet, with Matthew Arnold's admirable estimate of Wordsworth's genius, and a critical valuation of his best work.

THE PRELUDE, $1.25. PREFACES AND ESSAYS IN POETRY, 50 c. SELECTIONS FROM THE POEMS, $1.25. Edited by A. J. George. Bost., Heath.
Valuable as school texts, with excellent notes, by a scholarly Wordsworthian. Useful, also, to reading circles, and to the general student of literature

WILLIAM WORDSWORTH. By F. W. H. Myers. (English Men of Letters series.) N. Y., Harper, 75 c.
By the best exponent of the Wordsworthian philosophy.

Stephen, Leslie. [1832-.]
Man of letters, and first of modern English critics. He succeeded Thackeray, whose daughter he married, in the editorship of the *Cornhill Magazine*, but resigned this to become editor, and now a valued contributor, to that great English literary enterprise, the "Dictionary of National Biography." Mr. Leslie Stephen's articles on English literary men in this dictionary are of the highest critical value, being distinguished by acute insight, great erudition, and a charming and sympathetic style. To the "English Men of Letters" series he has contributed three admirable monographs, those on Alexander Pope, Samuel Johnson, and Dean Swift. His other works embrace a "History of English Thought in the 18th Century"; a work on "The Science of Ethics"; an interesting "Life of Prof. Henry Fawcett"; and a series of literary studies, biographical and critical, under the title of "Hours in a Library." **824.8.**

HOURS IN A LIBRARY. N. Y., Putnam, 3 vols., $4.50.
Contents in part: De Foe, Richardson, Pope, Scott, Hawthorne, Balzac, Johnson, Disraeli, Massinger, Wordsworth, Landor, Macaulay, Charlotte Brontë, Shelley, Gray, Sterne, Coleridge.

JONATHAN SWIFT. SAMUEL JOHNSON. ALEXANDER POPE. (English Men of Letters series.) N. Y., Harper, 75 c. each.
Appreciative and critical studies of a high order, dealing with the age as well as with the work of each subject.

Stoddard, Richard Henry. [1825-.]
Poet and man of letters, at present literary editor of the New York *Mail and Express*. An industrious worker in varied paths of literature, an accomplished editor in biography and criticism—notably in the "Sans-Souci" and "Bric à-Brac" series—author of several volumes of collected poems. He is a graceful poet, many of his lyrical pieces having much of "the tenderness and delicacy of expression that charm us in Herrick, Tennyson, and the German Heine." He has a fine ear for melody, and his style is marked by purity and grace. His volumes of verse range over a period of forty years, the best known being "Songs of Summer," "The Book of the East," and "The King's Bell." As representative poems, may be named his "Hymn to the Sea," "The Country Life," "The Dead Master," and "The Fisher and Charon." **811.41.**

POETICAL WRITINGS. With portrait. N. Y., Scribner, $4.

THE LION'S CUB, AND OTHER VERSE. N. Y., Scribner, $1.25.

UNDER THE EVENING LAMP. N. Y., Scribner, $1.25.
Sympathetic studies of Burns and his contemporaries, of Edward Fitzgerald, of Lord Houghton, and other minor poets.

Swinburne, Algernon Charles. [1837-.]
The greatest living English poet. In his early sensuous but mellifluous verse he forfeited the recognition which his eminent abilities and fine lyrical gifts ought to have won for him. In spite of this, and of his later outbursts of Republicanism and sympathy with regicides, Swinburne's place is among the immortals of song. Few writers of verse have had a finer ear than he for melody and poetic form, or a more thorough mastery over the technicalities of metrical composition. His first successful poem was "Atalanta in Calydon," a splendid classical tragedy, flawless in form and spirit. Following this came the successive tragedies which constitute a trilogy—"Chastelard," "Bothwell," and "Mary Queen of Scots." These, with his "Songs Before Sunrise" and "Songs of the Spring Tides," comprise the bulk of Swinburne's verse. His writings include also a number of fine critical prose essays. **821.86.**

POETICAL WORKS. Selected, with introduction, by R. H. Stoddard. N. Y., Crowell, 75 c. and upwards.
Contains Atalanta in Calydon, Erechtheus, Chastelard, Bothwell, and Mary Stuart.

SONGS BEFORE SUNRISE. Lond., Chatto, 10s. 6d.

SONGS OF THE SPRINGTIDES. Lond., Chatto, 6s.

CENTURY OF ROUNDELS. Lond., Chatto, 8s.

ESSAYS AND STUDIES. Lond., Chatto, 12s.

Taylor, Bayard. [1825-1878.]
Poet, essayist, traveller, and diplomat. A versatile, accomplished, and industrious author. Bayard Taylor touched American thought on many sides, and made excellent though not great contributions to American letters. Beginning life as a journalist, he early manifested a passion for travel, the literature of which he has enriched by his "Views Afoot" and "By-Ways of Europe," as well as by his "Poems of the Orient" and "Poems of Home and Travel." His glowing, though strong, literary style makes these works attractive, apart from the incidents they describe. As an accomplished German scholar, he has left behind him one of the best English translations of Goethe's "Faust," together with an excellent series of "Studies in German Literature." His poetry, which is largely dramatic, is marked by fine ideality, manifest truth, and genuine feeling. **811.46.**

POETICAL WORKS. Bost., Houghton, $1.50.

DRAMATIC WORKS. Bost., Houghton, $1.50.

PRINCE DEUKALION. A Lyrical Drama. Bost., Houghton, $3.

LIFE AND LETTERS. Edited by his widow and H. E. Scudder. Bost., Houghton, 2 vols., $4.

Tennyson, Alfred, *Lord.* [1809-1892.]
Greatest of the Victorian poets and consummate artist in verse. He lacked the dramatic faculty, and had but slender gifts of invention and creation. But among Idyllic poets he stands pre-eminent; his "Idylls of the King" give a great legend its noblest setting. Never has literature had such a master of lyrical verse; while in stateliness and rhythm his blank verse attains almost Miltonic heights. A like comparison might be made with Milton, in that magnificent burst of elegiac song, "In Memoriam," written, like "Lycidas," to assuage a poet's grief on the loss of a friend. Tennyson's writings worthily represent his age, and manifest many of the highest qualities of the thought and art of his time. In "The Two Voices," "The Talking Oak," and in much else of his work, we see how profoundly new knowledge illuminates world-old problems, though it cannot solve them. Not less distinctively the products of the time are the story of "The Princess," the metrical romance of "Maud," and the wealth of his other descriptive, narrative, and lyrical verse. **821.81.**

COMPLETE POETICAL WORKS. Cabinet edition. N. Y., Macmillan, 10 vols., $1.50 each, or together, $12.50; 1 vol., $1.75; Bost., Houghton, 6 vols., $6; 1 vol., $1.50.

LYRICAL POEMS. Edited by F. T. Palgrave. N. Y., Macmillan, $1.75.

IDYLLS OF THE KING. N. Y., Macmillan, $1.25.

IN MEMORIAM. N. Y., Macmillan, $1.25.

THE PRINCESS, and MAUD. N. Y., Macmillan, $1.50.

THE POETRY OF TENNYSON. By Henry Van Dyke, D.D. N. Y., Scribner, $2.
Written in an excellent spirit, the treatment displaying intelligence and sympathetic insight, marred, however, by occasional eccentricity in judgment.

STUDY OF THE WORKS OF TENNYSON. By A. C. Tainsh. N. Y., Macmillan, $1.75.
A scholarly and sympathetic analysis, much esteemed by Tennysonians.

TENNYSON: HIS ART IN RELATION TO MODERN LIFE. By Stopford A. Brooke. N. Y., Putnam, $2.
The work of a cultured, highly informed writer, author of the well-known "Primer of English Literature," treating of the Poet in relation to his age and the spirit of the time.

STUDY, WITH CRITICAL AND EXPLANATORY NOTES, OF LORD TENNYSON'S POEM "THE PRINCESS." By Samuel E. Dawson. Montreal, Dawson Brothers, 1884, $1.
"The Princess" contains Tennyson's solution of the position of woman in society. Prefixed to this "Study" is a long and very interesting letter from Lord Tennyson to the author, in which the poet gives an insight into his modes of literary composition, and criticises the "Study" in one or two points, while giving it his general approval.

Thackeray, William Makepeace. [1811–1863.]

English literature knows no healthier or saner writer than the chivalrous and large-hearted Thackeray. A true humorist, who could see the droll things in life, he had a passionate dislike of the ignoble, the false, and the mean. His novels do not come within our purview; but if he had never written a work of fiction, his lectures and miscellaneous writings would have made him famous. 824.8.

THE ENGLISH HUMORISTS OF THE EIGHTEENTH CENTURY; the FOUR GEORGES; and the ROUNDABOUT PAPERS. N. Y., Harper, $1.25.
The "Humorists" is a delightful volume of genial, but acute, criticism, dealing with Fielding, Swift, Sterne, Smollett, Steele, Addison, and other of the 18th century writers. The sketches are models of good writing, with sympathetic insight and humor. The "Four Georges," which is notable for its scathing attack on the fourth of the royal name, gives a brilliant picture of English life and manners in the early Hanoverian period. The "Roundabout Papers" are on all manner of light and grave subjects, dashed off in an easy, pleasant mood, with the utmost geniality and charity.

BALLADS. Illustrated. Bost., Houghton, $1.50.
Humorous, satirical, and sentimental, in imitation of the Odes of Horace and the Lyrics of Béranger.

THE ROSE AND THE RING. Illustrated. N. Y., Putnam, $1.25.
The history of Prince Giglio and Prince Bulbo— "a Fireside Pantomime for Great and Small Children," as the author himself sets forth.

THE PARIS SKETCH BOOK. N. Y., Routledge, 40 c.
Sketches and stories.

For complete sets of his works see FICTION.

W. M. THACKERAY. By Anthony Trollope. (English Men of Letters series.) N. Y., Harper, 75 c.
A very inadequate memoir.

W. M. THACKERAY. By H. T. Merivale and F. T. Marzials. (Great Writers series.) N. Y., Scribner, $1.
A better memoir, though unsatisfactory.

Whittier, John Greenleaf. [1807–1892.]

The poet of the cheery and homely side of human nature; a representative New Englander. His lyrical qualities, the soundness of his sentiment, and the fervor of his anti-slavery muse, endear him to the more serious type of readers. Not the least of his merits are his Quakerly purity of thought and devout feeling. His range of subjects is comparatively limited, as well as unexciting; but he has rare powers of felicitous and melodious expression. His "Snow Bound," "Prayer-Seeker," "Maud Muller," and "Barbara Frietchie," are favorite poems wherever the English language is spoken. 811.30.

POETICAL AND PROSE WORKS. Bost., Houghton, 7 vols., $10.50.
With Notes by the author, and Portraits. The edition can be had in two separate divisions—the Poems in 4 vols., the Prose in 3 vols., at $1.50 per vol. The latter embrace the Tales and Sketches, Historical and Slavery Subjects, Margaret Smith's Journal, the Old Portraits, and Modern Sketches, etc.

POEMS. Bost., Houghton, Cabinet edition, $1; Household edition, $1.50.
A new and much enlarged collection, in convenient form.

LIFE AND LETTERS. By S. T. Pickard. Bost., Houghton, 2 vols., $4.
An authoritative, full, and sympathetic biography, with selections from the poet's correspondence.

Wordsworth, William. [1770–1850.]

Poet of reflection and contemplation, writer of sonnets, lyrics, odes, philosophical poems, and other subjective verse. Matthew Arnold esteems Wordsworth "one of the chief glories of English poetry," and places him next to Shakespeare and Milton. He frankly admits, however, that his high poetic achievement is much detracted from by a considerable volume of inferior and encumbering verse. His best work is to be found in his shorter pieces, in which he "pipes a simple song for thinking hearts." A high philosophy underlies much of his work; but its chief distinction is the poet's intense love of Nature, sympathy with human feelings and emotions, high sense of duty, and idealizing power of imagination. Added to this is a pervading elevation of tone and exquisite simplicity and beauty of language. His chief works are "The Excursion" and "The Prelude," lengthy philosophical poems in blank verse, the latter chiefly autobiographical; Lyrical Ballads, Sonnets, "Yarrow Revisited," and a romantic narrative poem, "The White Doe of Rylstone. His fame rests, however, on his shorter pieces—such as "Lucy Gray," "Peter Bell," "Laodamia," and the "Ode to Duty" and "Intimations of Immortality." For criticism, see Hutton's and Arnold's Essays, Shairp's "Aspects of Poetry" and "Poetic Interpretation of Nature," and Lowell's "Among My Books." 821.71.

POETICAL WORKS. Edited, with memoir, by Prof. Edward Dowden. N. Y., Macmillan, 7 vols., $5.25.

COMPLETE POETICAL WORKS. With introduction by John Morley. N. Y., Macmillan, $1.75.

SELECT POEMS. Chosen and edited, with preface, by Matthew Arnold. N. Y., Macmillan, $1.
The pure gold of the poet, with Matthew Arnold's admirable estimate of Wordsworth's genius, and a critical valuation of his best work.

THE PRELUDE, $1.25. PREFACES AND ESSAYS IN POETRY, 50 c. SELECTIONS FROM THE POEMS, $1.25. Edited by A. J. George. Bost., Heath.
Valuable as school texts, with excellent notes, by a scholarly Wordsworthian. Useful, also, to reading circles, and to the general student of literature.

WILLIAM WORDSWORTH. By F. W. H. Myers. (English Men of Letters series.) N. Y., Harper, 75 c.
By the best exponent of the Wordsworthian philosophy.

FINE ART.

A SELECTION FROM ITS LITERATURE BY
RUSSELL STURGIS, A.M., Ph.D.,
Fellow of the American Institute of Architects.

New York, June, 1895.

PREFATORY NOTE.

The Fine Arts are those which are concerned with beauty, expression, and the power of giving intelligent and exalted pleasure through the senses. The term is often used for those fine arts only which appeal to the eye; it is in this sense that it is used in these notes.

These fine arts are called *plastic*, or concerned with moulding and shaping; and *graphic*, or concerned with drawing.

The plastic arts we call in general *sculpture*, the graphic arts we call *painting*, which term, however, must be stretched to include drawing with many different materials, engraving, and especially engraving made for printing upon paper or other material, and also decoration in mosaic and other kinds of inlay. These last, it will be noticed, are merely applications to permanent materials and in a peculiar way, as by cutting and shaping, of the general principle of drawing on flat surfaces.

The Decorative Arts are the same fine arts applied and put to use in making necessary things beautiful. The chief of decorative arts is Architecture, in which building is made attractive and interesting by giving to it good form and good color, and sometimes by adding sculpture or painting, or both, to the building. Other decorative arts are Keramics, Glasswork which includes Enamelling, Metal Work of many kinds, Lacquering and other varnish work, Leather-Work including Book-Binding, and a multitude of arts in which these different ways of ornamenting are used to help one another.

It must be understood, before one can go very far in the enjoyment of fine and decorative art, that it is generally the object of art itself, and its own value as a work of art, that the artist is interested in. When a person makes a drawing to explain something that he has seen, or when a cut is put into a botany book to explain a flower's shape and make, that drawing or cut will not often be at all valuable as a work of art. In like manner, fine art which has a narrative or explanatory purpose is seldom very exalted art, and decorative art of course has no such purpose. Illustration, as in books and weekly papers, is the best instance there is of fine art which has story-telling or incident for its chief object. Indeed it is well to use the word "illustration" at once and generally for such art. Thus in a book of history a picture of Washington bidding farewell to his officers is *illustration* in so far as an attempt is made to tell the story and to get the costume right and the interior of the room right; it is pure fine art in so far as the light and shade and color and the grace and force of the composition are concerned. Then there are freedom and truth of gesture, naturalness of grouping, the probability of the attitudes and action of the personages, all of which partake of both illustration and fine art, and connect the two. In a general way, however, it is true that artists care most about the form and color and composition, and the resulting beauty, originality and interest in the picture or the bas-relief. The student of art should of course try to see art as artists see it; otherwise such student will remain in the dark as to what each individual work of art means.

NOTE ON TRANSLATIONS.

As the best books on fine art are generally in French or in German, it is well to say that the translations of such books into English are generally very badly done. It seems to be thought that any one who can read a foreign language with a dictionary is fit to translate a technical book. An effort should be made by librarians to have the worst errors noted.

PART I.

BOOKS ON FINE ART IN A GENERAL SENSE: BOOKS ON ALL OR MANY OF THE FINE ARTS ASSOCIATED TOGETHER: ARCHÆOLOGY, GLOSSARIES AND DICTIONARIES.

PRELIMINARY NOTE: ARCHÆOLOGY.

Much of the best writing on fine art is to be found in treatises on archæology. It is limited to certain branches; thus, a large part of Greek Archæology is confined to sculpture and painted vases. Within the narrow limits chosen by the writer the writing is apt to be very exact in meaning; and the appreciations of the relative value of ancient works of art and the classification as to dates and schools are often very just.

PRELIMINARY NOTE: GLOSSARIES AND DICTIONARIES.

Glossaries of technical terms are always very incomplete, and generally poor in that no attempt has been made to give the exact force of the noun or adjective as it would be used in a sentence written by an artist or workman who was also an accurate writer. Some glossaries are named below. As most libraries have good English dictionaries, it may be said here that the Century Dictionary contains by far the fullest vocabulary of terms used in Architecture and in the Decorative Arts of all kinds, including Heraldry and Costume, that has ever been brought together; and, also, most of the important terms used in painting, sculpture, engraving, etc. The definitions, moreover, were prepared with peculiar care. The "International" Webster Dictionary of 1890 is as careful in this respect as the Century, but only a quarter as large and as full.

Babelon, Ernest.

ARCHÉOLOGIE ORIENTALE. [Bibliothèque de l'enseignement des beaux arts. (Hereafter abbreviated as B.E.B.A.)]. Translated and enl. by B. T. A. Evetts as MANUAL OF ORIENTAL ANTIQUITIES. N. Y., Putnam, 1889, $3.

A good book by a recognized authority. By Oriental Antiquities are meant those of Babylonia, Assyria, Chaldæa, Ancient Persia and other Asiatic countries of remote antiquity. Remains of architecture and sculpture, engraved gems, metal-work, etc., are briefly but intelligently treated. 913.3.

Brownell, William C.

FRENCH ART. N. Y., Scribner, 1892, $1.25.

Although devoted to the criticism of recent French fine art, the general principles which govern all fine art are so clearly expressed, so strongly and consistently urged that this book in itself may do much to explain what a work of art is in the mind of its creator, and also how his fellow-artists look at it. There is no better criticism to be found. It is a book of the highest class. 709.44.

FRENCH TRAITS. N. Y., Scribner, 1889, $1.50.

See the chapter "The Art Instinct" and see what is said in note next foregoing of a work by the same author. 812.

Chesneau, Ernest.

L'ÉDUCATION DE L'ARTISTE. Transl. by Clara Bell as EDUCATION OF THE ARTIST. N. Y., Cassell, 1886, $2.

Mr. Chesneau is a first-rate critic, and this book contains much matter which may give valuable suggestions to the student. 707.

Coffin, Wm. A.

THE FINE ARTS AT THE PARIS EXPOSITION OF 1889, in the N. Y. *Nation*, Vol. XLIX., nos. 1259-1268, inclusive (July to October, 1889).

THE FINE ARTS AT THE WORLD'S FAIR, CHICAGO, 1893, in the *Nation*, Vol. LVII., nos. 1466-1471, inclusive (August to September, 1893).

See what is said of this writer in Part II.

Collignon, Maxime.

ARCHÉOLOGIE GRECQUE. (B.E.B.A.) Transl. by J. H. Wright as MANUAL OF GREEK ARCHÆOLOGY. N. Y., Cassell, 1886, $2.

This book and Mr. A. S. Murray's on the same subject contain all that any person except special students need read, except that this author's "Mythology" (Phila., Lippincott, $3), or any similar treatise, should be referred to. 913.38.

Colvin, Sidney.

Article FINE ART. Encyclopædia Britannica, 9th edition.

Full of good sense and just perception. Even what seems fanciful will be found to be suggestive and to help to a right sense of what fine art is. The student should notice an error in speaking of sculpture, etc., as "imitative arts." Fine art should not be said to imitate anything, but only to represent or express what it deals with. Indeed there is no such thing as an imitative fine art or a fine art of imitation.

Article ART. Encyclopædia Britannica, 9th ed.

Should be read with above-named article "Fine Art."

Conway, William A.

DAWN OF ART IN THE ANCIENT WORLD: AN ARCHÆOLOGICAL SKETCH. N. Y., Macmillan, 1891, $1.25.

Valuable for its suggestions as to the probable origin of those artistic types which have become so familiar to the world that it is hard to realize the necessity of accounting for them. In such a book much must be given as probable which cannot be proved in any satisfactory way. This book is to be read as an attempt to bring these probabilities into shape. It is valuable as an encouragement to independent thought on the part of the reader. 913.

De Forest, Julia B.

SHORT HISTORY OF ART. N. Y., Dodd, Mead, & Co., $2.

A popular account of works of art of the better known varieties. It is much sounder in its criticism and more generally trustworthy than some similar compilations, but contains serious errors, such as the general information given as to Della Robbia work, in which the very large and elaborate pieces are ignored, and an unsuitability of the material to these is asserted; and such, also, as the wholly inaccurate account of Gothic vaulting. 709.

Emerson, Alfred.

Editor and reviser. Article ARCHÆOLOGY, Johnson's Universal Cyclopædia. Edition 1893-95.

Fromentin, Eugene.

(See his treatises on painting, Part II., in which the true principles of fine art are admirably explained.)

Gonse, Louis.

L'ART JAPONAIS. (B.E.B.A.) Transl. by M. P. Nickerson as JAPANESE ART. Morrill, Higgins & Co., Chicago, published this book in 1892, at $2. Publishers June, 1895, unknown.

Japanese art is recognized by most European and American artists as having peculiar and very great merit. In fact, the Japanese are the only artistic nation known to us in the sense that European nations were artistic formerly. This is a fairly good book on the subject; there are also others; all, or nearly all, suffer from a lack of real life-long familiarity with the subject on the part of the writers. Mr. E. F. Fenollosa

ments of fact have often been found erroneous, and are frequently corrected in the notes to this translation. **027.**

Watts, Theodore.

Article "POETRY," Encyclopædia Britannica, 9th ed.

Should be read for the comparison of different Fine Arts, as poetry with painting and sculpture, and for the remarks upon thoughts expressible in painting and sculpture though not in words.

GLOSSARIES.

(See Note at Head of Part I.)

Adeline, Jules.

LEXIQUE DES TERMES D'ART. (B.E.B.A.) Transl. as ART DICTIONARY. Authorized and enl. ed. N. Y., Appleton, 1891, $2.25.

So small a book can only give a few of the terms used in art; moreover, the translation of a dictionary is peculiarly difficult, because of the rearrangement necessary. Some terms are used in very different senses in France and in America, as Verandah; and these differences are not always marked in this translation. **703.**

Bryan, Michael.

DICTIONARY OF PAINTERS AND ENGRAVERS. New edition, edited by R. E. Graves. N. Y., Macmillan, 1886, 2 vols., $22.50.

This book, in two large volumes, is more costly than most of the books in this list, but it is the smallest one in English that can be recommended. There are strange omissions in it, but on the whole it is trustworthy. Of course, one does not look to such a book for very critical appreciation of works of art. **750.**

Clement, Clara Erskine, *and* **Hutton, Laurence.**

ARTISTS OF THE NINETEENTH CENTURY AND THEIR WORKS. Bost., Houghton, $3.

A useful book, revised in the latest edition to 1884, and giving brief biographies of artists, with mention of their works. Its space is used up by a great many vague and insignificant critical notices; the preface says that the "average opinion" has been sought for, but it is clear that that can never be found. Ten or twenty lines of "an average opinion" on any artist are absolutely useless. If one man had written all the notices it would at least be possible to get a comparative notion, but, as it is, neither positive nor comparative information is given. **027.**

PART II.

PAINTING AND SCULPTURE.

PRELIMINARY NOTE ON PAINTING.

Most writing about the art of painting has been by persons not very conversant with the actual practice of the art. This is true of all the fine arts; but it is especially true of painting because this art is more popular than others, and also because persons who expect to find literary, narrative, moral or religious sentiment in fine art are naturally led to look for it most in painting. The student should be on his guard against the discussion of this art as if it were closely akin to writing in prose or verse. Painting has its own language and its own set of ideas, which are sufficient for it. See *Prefatory Note.*

PRELIMINARY NOTE ON SCULPTURE.

Very little has been published, in English, on the art of sculpture, except in the form of treatises on Classical Archæology. It is to be noted, however, that much of that avowedly archæological writing is just and discriminating in its dealing with sculpture. The art of sculpture is far less misleading to those who have not especially studied it than painting is; it is much less complicated, it is much more direct and simple in its appeal to the sense of beauty, and in its association with nature. Moreover, it does not appeal so strongly as painting to the popular love of anecdote and incident in art. Those who wish to see stories of battle and adventure, or of domestic sentiment and pathos, will generally choose a collection of pictures rather than a sculpture gallery. Therefore the common writing about fine art, looked at from a literary standpoint, is far less harmful in the case of sculpture than in painting.

Beard, William H.

ACTION IN ART. N. Y., Cassell, 1894. $2.

An interesting book in very simple language, and with many slight illustrations. It would be useful for the student, as calling his attention to some of the conventional resources of the descriptive painter. A great deal may be learned from it of the way in which painter and illustrators work. **707.**

Chesneau, Ernest.

LA PEINTURE ANGLAISE. Transl. by L. M. Etherington, as THE ENGLISH SCHOOL OF PAINTING. With a preface by Prof. Ruskin. N. Y., Cassell, 1895, $2.

See what is said about this writer in Part I. **750.2.**

Child, Theodore.

ART AND CRITICISM: MONOGRAPHS AND STUDIES. N. Y., Harper, $6.

A dozen papers about different detached phases of painting, ancient and modern, and a few words about sculpture. There is a serious lack of exact comprehension of art as a special and peculiar means of expression, and errors occur, hard to account for, but a good general impression can be got in each case. Good and well chosen illustrations. The chapter on the Impressionists is very good. **704.**

Coffin, William A.

AMERICAN ILLUSTRATIONS OF TO-DAY. In *Scribner's Magazine*, January, February, and March, 1892.

These papers contain a great deal of sound discussion of the peculiar character of Illustration as a fine art, and of drawings not strictly Illustration which seem so or are called so because inserted in books and periodicals. See next title.

A WORD ABOUT PAINTING. *Scribner's Magazine*, April, 1894.

Mr. Coffin is one of the very few painters who write about the art which they follow. He is a judicious critic, not the slave of schools or of the opinions of his own allies and friends among artists. His writings may be studied with great profit.

Delaborde, Henri, *l'icomte.*

LA GRAVURE. (B.E.B.A.) Transl. by R. A. M. Stevenson as ENGRAVING: ITS ORIGIN, PROCESSES, AND HISTORY. N. Y., Cassell, 1886, $2.

Treats the subject in a large way, taking up woodengraving and typography; the *criblé* process, etching, engraving with the burin, mezzotint, stipple, printing in color, etc., and an historical account of the art. A very useful book. **701.**

Fromentin, Eugene.

MAITRES D'AUTREFOIS : BELGIQUE, HOLLANDE. Transl. as THE OLD MASTERS OF BELGIUM AND HOLLAND. Bost., Houghton, $3.

An admirable book, full of soundest criticism. The excellence of the critical and analytic writing in this book and the book next named, and the fact that so very little art-writing by artists is available, is the reason for citing them in spite of their high price. **750.0.**

Gonse, N. Louis.

EUGENE FROMENTIN. PAINTER AND WRITER. Transl. by M. C. Robbins. Bost., Houghton, 1883, $3.

This book, although mainly a life of Fromentin, contains long passages of his critical work. In Chap. V. are notes for lectures. **750 0.**

Hamerton, Philip G.

Article DRAWING. Encyclopædia Britannica, 9th ed.

A very instructive paper on the drawing of different epochs and different nations, with valuable critical remarks.

Article ENGRAVING. Encyclopædia Britannica, 9th ed.

Very full and instructive.

These two articles have been brought together with additions, and made into a volume under the title "Drawing and Engraving," which see.

ETCHING AND ETCHERS. Bost., Roberts, $5.

First published in 1866, at a time when the art of etching was being taken up by many painters and many engravers. The first edition, and a third one of 1880, were costly illustrated books. A second and cheaper edition, with illustrations especially meant for students, came out in 1876, but still costs a guinea. It is extremely valuable as at once a treatise on the practice of the art and a history of its development from the 15th century to date. **767.**

THE GRAPHIC ARTS. Bost., Roberts, $2.

A series of descriptive and analytic chapters on the different processes of drawing, painting, and engraving, mainly practical; devoted exclusively to those who wish to learn how those fine arts are practised, what their necessary limitations are, etc.; but these persons only can ever obtain any real sense of fine art. The English edition contains many fine illustrations, and is costly (catalogued, unpriced, by Seeley & Co., London). The Boston edition, without the illustrations, is also valuable. **750.**

MAN IN ART: STUDIES IN RELIGIOUS AND HISTORICAL ART, PORTRAIT AND GENRE. Illustrated by etchings and photogravures. N. Y., Macmillan, $30.

Extends the subject treated in "The Graphic Arts,"

and analyzes the art of different times and nations with reference to the way in which the human body and the human face expressions have been treated. This book is named in the belief that a cheaper edition may appear. **750.**

LANDSCAPE. Bost., Roberts, $2.

Continues the subject treated in "The Graphic Arts," and contains a very full account of landscape art, its purpose and history, and its character as practised by different nations at different times The original edition has about fifty large illustrations (N. Y., Macmillan, $35). **758.**

DRAWING AND ENGRAVING, with Numerous Illustrations. N. Y., Macmillan, $7.

Consists of the author's articles in the Encyclopædia Britannica, 9th ed., with some additions and with plates which greatly increase its value. **700.**

MODERN FRENCHMEN. Bost., Roberts, $2.

Contains biographies of François Rude, the sculptor, and Henri Regnault, the painter : excellent lives of very distinguished men, and useful to the student of art as artists understand and feel it. **924.4.**

LIFE OF J. M. W. TURNER. Bost., Roberts, $2.

In the discussion of the work of this great master many valuable truths about fine art are explained and insisted on. The life of this artist, exclusively devoted to his art, is very instructive. **750.**

Harrison, Jane E.

INTRODUCTORY STUDIES IN GREEK ART. N. Y., Macmillan, $2.25.

Not a history nor a classified account of different schools, but an essay on the spirit and meaning of Greek Sculpture. The author states that she is trying to express the ideality which she finds in Greek Art, but it is a mistake to assume that ideality was unknown in the art of other ancient peoples however superior may have been that of the Greeks. **709.38.**

Havard, Henry.

PEINTURE HOLLANDAISE. (B.E.B.A.) Transl. by G. Powell as THE DUTCH SCHOOL OF PAINTING. N. Y., Cassell, 1885, $2. Out of print.

A very good brief history of that great school of painting upon which English painting is mainly founded, and which has strongly influenced French painting of the 18th and 19th centuries. The critical remarks are generally useful as guides. **759.0.**

Heaton, *Mrs.* **Charles.**

CONCISE HISTORY OF PAINTING. New edition revised by Cosmo Monkhouse. (Bohn.) N. Y., Macmillan, 1893, $1.50.

The most valuable of the older small histories of painting. Mrs. Heaton's book has been entirely revised, both as to matters of fact and date and as to critical appreciation. During the fifteen years between its first appearance and the publication of the present edition both the history and criticism of art had been greatly remade. This new material has been well used by the editor. **750.**

La Farge, John.

LECTURES ON ART. N. Y., Macmillan. (To be published in the autumn of 1895.)

Lectures on painting delivered at the Metropolitan Museum of Art, 1893-94 Of the utmost value as expressing sound and suggestive opinions, and as containing the gathered knowledge of a lifetime of practice in Fine Art. The author is known throughout the art world of America and in France as a painter in oil and water colors of high rank, as a designer of decorations, especially stained glass, in which field he is probably unapproached, and as one of the most experienced and judicious of critics. **750.**

Linton, W. J.

WOOD-ENGRAVING : A MANUAL OF INSTRUCTION. N. Y., Macmillan, $3.

By one of the most able and truly artistic engravers

ments of fact have often been found erroneous, and are frequently corrected in the notes to this translation. 027.

Watts, Theodore.

Article "POETRY," Encyclopædia Britannica, 9th ed.

Should be read for the comparison of different Fine Arts, as poetry with painting and sculpture, and for the remarks upon thoughts expressible in painting and sculpture though not in words.

GLOSSARIES.

(See Note at Head of Part I.)

Adeline, Jules.

LEXIQUE DES TERMES D'ART. (B.E.B.A.) Transl. as ART DICTIONARY. Authorized and enl. ed. N. Y., Appleton, 1891, $2.25.

So small a book can only give a few of the terms used in art; moreover, the translation of a dictionary is peculiarly difficult, because of the rearrangement necessary. Some terms are used in very different senses in France and in America, as Verandah; and these differences are not always marked in this translation. 703.

Bryan, Michael.

DICTIONARY OF PAINTERS AND ENGRAVERS. New edition, edited by R. E. Graves. N. Y., Macmillan, 1886, 2 vols., $22.50.

This book, in two large volumes, is more costly than most of the books in this list, but it is the smallest one in English that can be recommended. There are strange omissions in it, but on the whole it is trustworthy. Of course, one does not look to such a book for very critical appreciation of works of art. 750.

Clement, Clara Erskine, *and* **Hutton, Laurence.**

ARTISTS OF THE NINETEENTH CENTURY AND THEIR WORKS. Bost., Houghton, $3.

A useful book, revised in the latest edition to 1884, and giving brief biographies of artists, with mention of their works. Its space is used up by a great many vague and insignificant critical notices; the preface says that the "average opinion" has been sought for, but it is clear that that can never be found. Ten or twenty lines of "an average opinion" on any artist are absolutely useless. If one man had written all the notices it would at least be possible to get a comparative notion, but, as it is, neither positive nor comparative information is given. 027.

PART II.

PAINTING AND SCULPTURE.

PRELIMINARY NOTE ON PAINTING.

Most writing about the art of painting has been by persons not very conversant with the actual practice of the art. This is true of all the fine arts; but it is especially true of painting because this art is more popular than others, and also because persons who expect to find literary, narrative, moral or religious sentiment in fine art are naturally led to look for it most in painting. The student should be on his guard against the discussion of this art as if it were closely akin to writing in prose or verse. Painting has its own language and its own set of ideas, which are sufficient for it. See *Prefatory Note.*

PRELIMINARY NOTE ON SCULPTURE.

Very little has been published, in English, on the art of sculpture, except in the form of treatises on Classical Archæology. It is to be noted, however, that much of that avowedly archæological writing is just and discriminating in its dealing with sculpture. The art of sculpture is far less misleading to those who have not especially studied it than painting is; it is much less complicated, it is much more direct and simple in its appeal to the sense of beauty, and in its association with nature. Moreover, it does not appeal so strongly as painting to the popular love of anecdote and incident in art. Those who wish to see stories of battle and adventure, or of domestic sentiment and pathos, will generally choose a collection of pictures rather than a sculpture gallery. Therefore the common writing about fine art, looked at from a literary standpoint, is far less harmful in the case of sculpture than in painting.

Beard, William H.

ACTION IN ART. N. Y., Cassell, 1894. $2.

An interesting book in very simple language, and with many slight illustrations. It would be useful for the student, as calling his attention to some of the conventional resources of the descriptive painter. A great deal may be learned from it of the way in which painters and illustrators work. 707.

Chesneau, Ernest.

LA PEINTURE ANGLAISE. Transl. by L. M. Etherington, as THE ENGLISH SCHOOL OF PAINTING. With a preface by Prof. Ruskin. N. Y., Cassell, 1895, $2.

See what is said about this writer in Part I. 750.2.

Child, Theodore.

ART AND CRITICISM: MONOGRAPHS AND STUDIES. N. Y., Harper, $6.

A dozen papers about different detached phases of painting, ancient and modern, and a few words about sculpture. There is a serious lack of exact comprehension of art as a special and peculiar means of expression, and errors occur, hard to account for, but a good general impression can be got in each case. Good and well chosen illustrations. The chapter on the Impressionists is very good. 704.

Coffin, William A.

AMERICAN ILLUSTRATIONS OF TO-DAY. In *Scribner's Magazine,* January, February, and March, 1892.

These papers contain a great deal of sound discussion of the peculiar character of Illustration as a fine art, and of drawings not strictly Illustration which seem so or are called so because inserted in books and periodicals. See next title.

A WORD ABOUT PAINTING. *Scribner's Magazine*, April, 1894.

Mr. Coffin is one of the very few painters who write about the art which they follow. He is a judicious critic, not the slave of schools or of the opinions of his own allies and friends among artists. His writings may be studied with great profit.

Delaborde, Henri, *Vicomte.*

LA GRAVURE. (B.E.B.A.) Transl. by R. A. M. Stevenson as ENGRAVING: ITS ORIGIN, PROCESSES, AND HISTORY. N. Y., Cassell, 1886, $2.

Treats the subject in a large way, taking up wood-engraving and typography; the *criblé* process, etching, engraving with the burin, mezzotint, stipple, printing in color, etc , and an historical account of the art. A very useful book. 701.

Fromentin, Eugene.

MAÎTRES D'AUTREFOIS : BELGIQUE, HOLLANDE. Transl. as THE OLD MASTERS OF BELGIUM AND HOLLAND. Bost., Houghton, $3.

An admirable book, full of soundest criticism. The excellence of the critical and analytic writing in this book and the book next named, and the fact that so very little art-writing by artists is available, is the reason for citing them in spite of their high price. 750.9.

Gonse, N. Louis.

EUGENE FROMENTIN. PAINTER AND WRITER. Transl. by M. C. Robbins. Bost., Houghton, 1883, $3.

This book, although mainly a life of Fromentin, contains long passages of his critical work. In Chap. V. are notes for lectures. 750 0.

Hamerton, Philip G.

Article DRAWING, Encyclopædia Britannica, 9th ed.

A very instructive paper on the drawing of different epochs and different nations, with valuable critical remarks.

Article ENGRAVING, Encyclopædia Britannica, 9th ed.

Very full and instructive.

These two articles have been brought together with additions, and made into a volume under the title "Drawing and Engraving," which see.

ETCHING AND ETCHERS. Bost., Roberts, $5.

First published in 1866, at a time when the art of etching was being taken up by many painters and many engravers. The first edition, and a third one of 1880, were costly illustrated books. A second and cheaper edition, with illustrations especially meant for students, came out in 1876, but still costs a guinea It is extremely valuable as at once a treatise on the practice of the art and a history of its development from the 15th century to date. 707.

THE GRAPHIC ARTS. Bost., Roberts, $2.

A series of descriptive and analytic chapters on the different processes of drawing, painting, and engraving, mainly practical; devoted exclusively to those who wish to learn how those fine arts are practised, what their necessary limitations are, etc.; but these persons only can ever obtain any real sense of fine art. The English edition contains many fine illustrations, and is costly (catalogued, unpriced, by Seeley & Co., London). The Boston edition, without the illustrations, is also valuable. 750.

MAN IN ART: STUDIES IN RELIGIOUS AND HISTORICAL ART, PORTRAIT AND GENRE. Illustrated by etchings and photogravures. N. Y., Macmillan, $30.

Extends the subject treated in "The Graphic Arts,"

and analyzes the art of different times and nations with reference to the way in which the human body and the human face expressions have been treated. This book is named in the belief that a cheaper edition may appear. 750.

LANDSCAPE. Bost., Roberts, $2.

Continues the subject treated in "The Graphic Arts," and contains a very full account of landscape art, its purpose and history, and its character as practised by different nations at different times The original edition has about fifty large illustrations (N. Y., Macmillan, $15). 758.

DRAWING AND ENGRAVING, with Numerous Illustrations. N. Y., Macmillan, $7.

Consists of the author's articles in the Encyclopædia Britannica, 9th ed , with some additions and with plates which greatly increase its value. 700.

MODERN FRENCHMEN. Bost., Roberts, $2.

Contains biographies of François Rude, the sculptor, and Henri Regnault, the painter : excellent lives of very distinguished men, and useful to the student of art as artists understand and feel it. 024.4.

LIFE OF J. M. W. TURNER. Bost., Roberts, $2.

In the discussion of the work of this great master many valuable truths about fine art are explained and insisted on. The life of this artist, exclusively devoted to his art, is very instructive. 750.

Harrison, Jane E.

INTRODUCTORY STUDIES IN GREEK ART. N. Y., Macmillan, $2.25.

Not a history nor a classified account of different schools, but an essay on the spirit and meaning of Greek Sculpture. The author states that she is trying to express the ideality which she finds in Greek Art, but it is a mistake to assume that ideality was unknown in the art of other ancient peoples however superior may have been that of the Greeks. 700.38.

Havard, Henry.

PEINTURE HOLLANDAISE. (B.E.B.A.) Transl. by G. Powell as THE DUTCH SCHOOL OF PAINTING. N. Y., Cassell, 1885. $2. Out of print.

A very good brief history of that great school of painting upon which English painting is mainly founded, and which has strongly influenced French painting of the 18th and 19th centuries. The critical remarks are generally useful as guides. 750.9.

Heaton, *Mrs.* **Charles.**

CONCISE HISTORY OF PAINTING. New edition revised by Cosmo Monkhouse. (Bohn.) N. Y., Macmillan, 1893, $1.50.

The most valuable of the older small histories of painting. Mrs. Heaton's book has been entirely revised, both as to matters of fact and date and as to critical appreciation. During the fifteen years between its first appearance and the publication of the present edition both the history and criticism of art had been greatly remade. This new material has been well used by the editor. 750.

La Farge, John.

LECTURES ON ART. N. Y., Macmillan. (To be published in the autumn of 1895.)

Lectures on painting delivered at the Metropolitan Museum of Art, 1893-94 Of the utmost value as expressing sound and suggestive opinions, and as containing the gathered knowledge of a lifetime of practice in Fine Art. The author is known throughout the art world of America and in France as a painter in oil and water colors of high rank, as a designer of decorations, especially stained glass, in which field he is probably unapproached, and as one of the most experienced and judicious of critics. 750.

Linton, W. J.

WOOD-ENGRAVING: A MANUAL OF INSTRUCTION. N. Y., Macmillan, $3.

By one of the most able and truly artistic engravers

of modern times on his own art, its technicalities and true nature, and its history. Mr. Linton is one of those very few artists who know how to write upon art. In reading his work one learns not only much about wood-engraving but also much about art as the artist sees it. **701.**

Marquand, Allen, *and* **Frothingham, A. L.,** *Jr.*
HISTORY OF SCULPTURE. N. Y., Longmans, $1.50.
Announced for December, 1895; may be expected to be valuable. **730.**

Middleton, J. H.
Article SCHOOLS OF PAINTING. Encyclopædia Britannica, 9th ed.
Gives brief accounts of all the principal schools and names all the greatest masters. Many illustrations. The criticism is generally just.

Article SCULPTURE. Encyclopædia Britannica, 9th ed.
Valuable paper, both technical and historical.

Article WOOD-CARVING. Encyclopædia Britannica, 9th ed.

Article TEMPERA. Encyclopædia Britannica, 9th ed.
Describes the process which was most used in Italy both for wall work and panel painting during the days of the early renaissance.

Moore, George.
IMPRESSIONS AND OPINIONS. N. Y., Scribner, $1.25.
Four essays: "Meissonier and the Salon Julien," "Art for the Villa," "Degas," "New Pictures in the National Gallery." See what is said of this author's book, "Modern Painting." **750.**

MODERN PAINTING. N. Y., Scribner, $2.
Twenty essays on living painters and modern art tendencies, both good and evil, with frequent allusions to old artists, and some account of men who are not painters. Thus the article on Charles Keene, the draughtsman and caricaturist of the London *Punch,* is admirable art criticism. There is some excess of enthusiastic praise of art which he loves and of contempt for artists and critics whom the author looks upon as wholly astray in their aims and work, but the book is almost wholly right in its tendency. It should be read with care by all who really wish to know how artists look at and understand art and how art should be interpreted. **750.**

Morris, William, *and* **Middleton, J. H.**
Article MURAL PAINTING. Encyclopædia Britannica, 9th ed.
Extremely valuable remarks on the principle of fine art used decoratively, as almost all important fine art has been.

Paris, Pierre.
LA SCULPTURE ANTIQUE. (B.E.B.A.) Transl. as MANUAL OF ANCIENT SCULPTURE. Ed. by J. E. Harrison, Phila., Lippincott, 1889, $3.
Treats of the sculpture of the ancient Asiatic nations, of Egypt, of Greece, Etruria, and Rome. It covers, therefore, much the same ground as the chapters on sculpture of the books by Babelon, Collignon, Maspero, and Murray, named in Part I.; it is well to compare the treatment of such subjects by different authors. **732.**

Perkins, Charles C.
HISTORICAL HANDBOOK OF ITALIAN SCULPTURE. N. Y., Scribner, $4.
Devoted chiefly to the sculpture of Central and Northern Italy from about 1300 to about 1600. It contains many errors, and should be wholly revised in the light of modern discoveries, but it can give a good general account of this very important phase of art. **734.**

Poynter, Edward J.
TEN LECTURES ON ART. Lond., Chapman & Hall, 3s. 6d.
Contains very just conclusions as to fine art and very clearly expressed analysis of painting of many schools. The comparisons of Continental painting with English are fair and almost wholly satisfactory. **750.**

Poynter, Edward J., *Editor.*
A series of "ART HANDBOOKS." Illustrated.

Poynter, E. J., *and* **Head, P. R.** PAINTING, CLASSICAL AND ITALIAN. N. Y., Scribner, $2. **759.**

Smith, Gerard W. PAINTING, FRENCH AND SPANISH. N. Y., Scribner, $2. **759.4.**

Buxton, H. J. W., *and* **Poynter, E. J.** GERMAN, FLEMISH, AND DUTCH PAINTING. N. Y., Scribner, $2. **759.**

Redgrave, Gilbert R. HISTORY OF WATER COLOR PAINTING IN ENGLAND. N. Y., Scribner, $2. **759.2.**

Buxton, H. J. Wilmot. ENGLISH PAINTERS: With a Chapter on American Painters by S. R. Koehler. N. Y., Scribner, $2. **759.2.**

These five books may be taken together as forming a history of Painters and Painting in the sense that they tell what Painters have been successful and famous in the different countries of Europe and in the United States before about 1860 ; that they give dates, mention by name the more celebrated pictures, and give prominence to those artists who are esteemed the bringers in of important changes and as founders of new schools. Considered as works of criticism, they fail in that there is a visible attempt to explain what cannot easily be explained in words, except at great length, and that, moreover, they seem to be written rather by scholars familiar with the externals of art, but knowing little of its essential character. In these respects the book on water color in England is much the best, but this is partly because 259 pages are devoted to this small subject ; a space ten times as great as it would occupy in proportion with the others. A brief synoptical history of painting would be best in the form of a biographical dictionary of artists arranged in the order of their schools. If a dictionary such as Bryan's or Seubert's could be rearranged so that the notices would follow one another systematically and not alphabetically, and made accessible by a full alphabetical index, the comparative length of the notices would show the student which were the more important artists, and differences of type and so forth might be utilized. In this way the necessity of keeping up a continuous narrative would be avoided. The author would not attempt to make his story attractive except as to one artist at a time. Something like th s is done in the volume above named on German, Flemish, and Dutch Painting, and this is the most useful of the series. It is probable that books covering so large a field as is the painting of even one great nation are seldom read consecutively ; they are used for reference. Only books on a much larger scale, with much more opportunity for detail and comparison, can be made agreeable reading.

With regard to one volume of this series it should be said that the sketch of American Art does not include the men who have made it what it now is, even artists so long before the public as La Farge, Inness, Chase, and Martin being omitted. Probably it was not meant to include men living when the book was written.

Radcliffe, A. G.
SCHOOLS AND MASTERS OF SCULPTURE. N. Y., Appleton, $3.
A sketch of the History of Sculpture in all ages. There has been a serious attempt to make an interesting

continuous narrative of each chapter, and the attempt is more nearly successful than could be anticipated. The critical value of different chapters varies greatly; thus the account of Gothic sculpture is of little utility, that of sculpture under the Romans is marred by too great willingness to accept as fact what is only assumed, while the account of nineteenth century sculpture is usually good and shows much critical insight. A great deal of space is taken up by mere anecdote; and this has the additional bad result that contemporary gossip about a work of art is allowed to influence opinion as to the work itself and its value. The book ends with two chapters on the museums of Europe and America, but these are far too brief to be of much value as guides to the student. There are about thirty full-page photographic illustrations of representative sculptures. **730.**

SCHOOLS AND MASTERS OF PAINTING. N. Y., Appleton, $3.

Has nearly the same character as the companion volume on sculpture. **750.**

Redford, George.

SCULPTURE: EGYPTIAN, ASSYRIAN, GREEK, AND ROMAN. (Art handbook series.) N. Y., Scribner, $2.

A good general account of ancient sculpture; may be trusted for the general accuracy of its statements. It seems carelessly written, however, as if the exact force of words was not felt. **732.**

Redgrave, Richard *and* Samuel.

A CENTURY OF PAINTERS OF THE ENGLISH SCHOOL. 2d edition. Abridged and illustrated. Lond., Sampson Low, 1890, 7s. 6d.

An account of the English painters from the time of Henry VIII. to the close of the generation which was passing away about 1885. It is very readably written in narrative form. Few books of the kind are as just and sympathetic as this. It does not give the names of those living in 1889. **750.2.**

Redgrave, Samuel.

DICTIONARY OF ARTISTS OF THE ENGLISH SCHOOLS, ETC. New and revised edition. N. Y., Macmillan, $5.

Contains much the same matter as a "Century of Painters," but arranged alphabetically under names of artists, and to this it adds notices of sculptors, architects, etc. **703.**

Reid, George.

Article PAINTING. Encyclopædia Britannica, 9th ed.

Devoted practically to descriptions of different processes, with valuable hints.

Scott, Leader.

SCULPTURE, RENAISSANCE AND MODERN. (Art handbook series.) N. Y., Scribner, $2.

A good cyclopædic account; many names of sculptors and their works, and much brief analysis of their work are given; the material is well arranged and the book is very readable in spite of its compactness. Many remarks on outlying subjects are questionable, as when the Moors are called "finest architects," and where Della Robbia work is denied the name of sculpture, and where Vischer's shrine at Nuremberg is called "late Gothic, almost Romanesque." In short, this, like most of these hastily written English books, is in a general way trustworthy, but rather as a compilation than as a book by a competent critic. **735.**

Stranahan, *Mrs.* C. H.

HISTORY OF FRENCH PAINTING FROM ITS EARLIEST TO ITS LATEST PRACTICE, including an account of the French Academy and its Schools of Instruction. N. Y., Scribner, $3.50.

As the French schools of painting have been for a century and a half the most important body of graphic art in Europe, steadily growing in an orderly sequence, this book, which relates the external history of this growth and appreciates and qualities it very justly, is important to all students. There are errors, but the work is surprisingly accurate in the main, and is full in detail. It includes a careful history of the French government's influence and control of the Fine Arts. See also "Meissonier and the Salon Julien" in George Moore's "Impressions and Opinions" in this list. **750.4.**

Sturgis, Russell.

ARTICLES IN JOHNSON'S UNIVERSAL CYCLOPÆDIA. Ed. 1893-5.

CHIAROSCURO — DRAWING — ENGRAVING — ILLUSTRATION — IMPRESSIONISM — LITHOGRAPHY — PAINTING — SCULPTURE — WOOD CARVING — WOOD ENGRAVING.

See also some of the biographies of artists in the same Cyclopædia.

See also Part I. of this list.

Upcott, L. E.

INTRODUCTION TO GREEK SCULPTURE. N. Y., Macmillan, 1887, $1.10.

One of several books which have been published as companions to a small museum of casts, or a collection of photographs. Valuable in itself as a rather full account of a few important sculptures, pictures of which occur in many books. If it were desired to get a few casts or photographs, they might well be purchased according to the list given, p. 9-12. **733.**

Van Dyke, John C.

ART FOR ART'S SAKE. Seven University Lectures on the Technical Beauties of Painting. N. Y., Scribner, $1.50.

Of much value, because it explains in very simple language and in detail how a painter conceives a picture and goes to work at it, and how he looks at the pictures which he and other artists have produced. Should be read with care as if a text-book of the painter's trade. **750.**

HOW TO JUDGE A PICTURE: Familiar Talks in the Gallery with Uncritical Lovers of Art. N. Y., Hunt & Eaton, 60 c.

A manual containing useful hints, but nothing that is not better given in "Art for Art's Sake." Its general tendency is to be approved. **750.**

HISTORY OF PAINTING. N. Y., Longmans, 1895, $1.50.

For the reader who understands that no man's opinion as to a given painter is of final authority, and that there is indeed no such thing as authority in criticism, this is probably the best brief history of painting accessible. A lover of Michelangelo will feel that the paintings on the vaults of the Sistine Chapel should not be included under works which are not valuable in color. A lover of Turner will feel that the greatest of landscape painters is treated with too little respect. A lover of Florentine religious painting will feel that Paolo Veronese is made too much of. In each of these cases and in many others a well-informed student of painting may agree or disagree with Mr. Van Dyke. Let this be understood, and this little book can do nothing but good, and will then be of great value. **750.**

Viollet-le-Duc, E. E.

HISTOIRE D'UN DESSINATEUR. Transl. as LEARNING TO DRAW; OR, THE STORY OF A YOUNG DESIGNER. N. Y., Putnam, $2.

Under the form of a biography of a young man of natural good ability as a draughtsman and designer, but not of great genius, the right way of studying art practically is considered, and much wise suggestive advice given. **740.**

Waldstein, Charles.

CATALOGUE OF CASTS in the Museum of Classical Archæology of the Fitzwilliam Museum, Cambridge, England. Lond., Macmillan, 1889, 1s. 6d.

A smaller book of the same general character as that of Mr. Upcott. It would be useful in connection with that, or without it. 730.

Wauters, A. J.

PEINTURE FLAMANDE. (B.E.B.A.) Transl. by Mrs. H. Rossel as THE FLEMISH SCHOOL OF PAINTING. N. Y., Cassell, $2.

Out of print. Like all the books of this series, the French original is valuable. 750.0.

Wilson, C. Heath.

Article FRESCO. Encyclopædia Britannica, 9th ed.

PART III.

ARCHITECTURE.

PRELIMINARY NOTE.

Although Architecture is a Decorative Art, and should logically be put under that head (see *Prefatory Note*), it is more convenient to treat it separately, especially because of the enormous number and importance of the books in many languages which are devoted to architecture alone. Of these many fine and costly books but a small number are in English, either in their original form or in translation; and of the books which are in English only a very few, and those not often valuable, are of moderate cost.

The Fine Art of Architecture has a curious history. From the earliest historical times to the 15th century there was a general tendency for styles to develop naturally and spontaneously one out of another. One style would perhaps disappear in a time of conquest and in the ruin of the civilization which had created it; then the conquerors, perhaps after a long time of little artistic production, would evolve a new style. Occasional attempts were made to revive a style of former times, but these were never of much importance. In the 15th century, however, a deliberate attempt was made in Italy to return to the style of the Roman Empire; that is, to the system of architectural decoration seen in the ruined buildings of about the years 50 to 350 A.D., found in Italy and in other countries on the Mediterranean. This was caused less by admiration of the beauty of those structures than by reverence for the mighty traditions of the Roman Empire, and by the revival of classical learning which was going on at the same time. All this is to be studied in treatises upon the Renaissance. The style of architecture so created by deliberate effort was at first in the hands of most able artists, accomplished sculptors and painters, and it had a fresh and original beauty of its own. Soon, however, it grew to be a more nearly exact copying of the ancient structures. In different forms this artificial style went on developing itself through the 16th, 17th, and 18th centuries. During all these years, as in previous times of more natural styles of architecture, no man would build in any other style than the one accepted; but since the French Revolution all has been chaos.

The books and articles on Archæology are apt to contain much information about architecture, but it is to be observed that their writers have generally no experience either in building or in designing buildings.

Architecture is so complex an art that positive and peremptory opinions about it should be mistrusted, from whatever source they come. Nearly all great excellences in the art bring their errors and faults with them ; more than the fine arts proper, architecture is a series of compromises, and *the best* has to be given up very often for the second best.

The attention of students is called to the Avery Architectural Library at Columbia College, New York. Mr. Samuel P. Avery and his wife have founded this library as a memorial to their son, Henry O. Avery, an architect, who died in 1890. Fifty thousand dollars has already been given to this foundation, and expended in books and periodicals on architecture and decorative art. The choice of books has been careful. The library is accessible to all persons, both by day and in the evening, except on Sundays.

Avery ARCHITECTURAL LIBRARY, CATALOGUE OF.

To appear in the autumn of 1895. An excellent catalogue of authors and titles of the Avery Library mentioned above (Part III., Preliminary Note). It is probable that there is no other list, as full and as carefully made as this, of books on architecture and decorative art. 010.700.

Corroyer, Edouard.

L'ARCHITECTURE GOTHIQUE. (B.E.B.A.) Transl. as GOTHIC ARCHITECTURE. Edited by Walter Armstrong. N. Y., Macmillan, 1893, $2.

A very good account of the origin and growth of the great styles of Western Europe, from 1150 to 1500, with useful illustrations. It is the work of a very competent man, and should be studied with care. 723.5.

Fergusson, James.

A HISTORY OF ARCHITECTURE IN ALL COUNTRIES, FROM THE EARLIEST TIME TO THE PRESENT DAY. In 5 vols. 3d edition. Edited by R. P. Spiers. Lond., Murray, 1893.

Two volumes (63 s.) of this work form the history proper, treating the architecture of European peoples and its origin in Western Asia and Egypt, and coming down to the time of the Renaissance. It is important to procure this latest edition. Many serious shortcomings and errors of the original work are supplied and corrected in it. It is the only architectural history of any value in English, and so it is named here in spite of its considerable cost, and of the uncritical character of the original work. Mr. Fergusson was not a builder or designer, and much of his book was written, in the first place, without personal knowledge of the buildings discussed and before the day of abundant photographs. **720.0.**

HISTORY OF THE MODERN STYLES OF ARCHITECTURE. 3d edition. Revised by Robert Kerr. Lond., Murray, 1891, 2 vols., 31s. 6d.

This work forms vols. 3 and 4 of Fergusson's general history ; it is devoted to the styles which began with the Renaissance of the fifteenth century. **720.0.**

HISTORY OF INDIAN AND EASTERN ARCHITECTURE. Lond., Murray, 31s. 6d.

This volume completes the series. It contains the only consecutive account in English of the styles of India, etc., is very inferior and slight. The account of architecture in China, Japan, **720.0.**

Dodd, Mead & Co., N. Y., announce a reprint of the latest edition of the Fergusson series; they now publish an edition not latest.

Freeman, Edward A.

HISTORICAL AND ARCHITECTURAL SKETCHES, CHIEFLY ITALIAN. Lond., Macmillan, 1876, 10s. 6d. (Out of print.)

Interesting papers on ancient cities and their buildings of great historical value to all students of architecture. The author studied architecture all his life, and although wholly out of touch with it as scientific building or as fine art, he saw its value as material for history. **720.4.**

SKETCHES FROM THE SUBJECT AND NEIGHBOR LANDS OF VENICE. Lond., Macmillan, 1881, 10s. 6d.

Similar to the above; a continuation of it, devoted to the little-known country from Treviso and Udine down the Illyrian coast to Cattaro; and also to Trani, Otranto, and the island of Corfu. **045.**

Article NORMANS. Encyclopædia Britannica, 9th ed.

Valuable points on their architecture in England and Sicily.

Freeman, Edward A., *and* Gardiner, Samuel R.

Article ENGLAND, HISTORY. Encyclopædia Britannica, 9th ed.

Mr. Freeman made a life-long study of architecture (see his works mentioned above), and this article contains many valuable passages on the topic, as on p. 300, 310, 317, etc.

Hamlin, A. D. F.

HISTORY OF ARCHITECTURE. N. Y., Longmans, $1.50.

Announced for November, 1895; may be expected to prove very useful. **720.0.**

Article ARCHITECTURE. Johnson's Universal Cyclopædia, ed. of 1893-5.

Lewis, T. Hayter, *and* Street, G. E.

Article ARCHITECTURE. Encylopædia Britannica, 9th ed.

Far less valuable for classical architecture than Mr. Murray's article on Archæology in the same work; shows a lack of clear understanding of styles and essential differences. Mr. Street was an architect in large practice until his death, in December, 1881, but he was exclusively devoted to the Gothic Revival, and although to be exclusive in one's own way is often good for an artist, it is bad for a critic. There are errors in the early part of " Pointed," but the descriptions, as of Chartres Cathedral, are not bad.

Middleton, J. H.

Article ROME. TOPOGRAPHY AND ARCHÆOLOGY, beginning, p. 807, Encyclopædia Britannica, 9th ed.

See what is said of this writer's book on Rome, in Part I.

Morris, William, *and* Middleton, J. Henry.

Article MURAL DECORATION. Encyclopædia Britannica, 9th ed.

Good both in the architecture and the painting. The illustrations are also very valuable.

Papworth, Wyatt.

Article BUILDING. Encyclopædia Britannica, 9th ed.

Valuable in its account of the knowledge necessary to the architect and of the processes of planning and erecting a building. The general principles of construction, except in modern iron and steel building, are well explained.

Reber, Franz Von.

KUNSTGESCHICHTE DES MITTELALTERS. Transl. by J. T. Clarke as HISTORY OF MEDIÆVAL ART. N. Y., Harper, 1887, $5.

Of mediæval fine art Architecture is very much the most important form, and it includes most of the other arts as practiced during the Middle Ages.

This translation is unusual in being the work of a very competent writer. A small glossary of technical terms is added. **709.**

Rosengarten, A.

DIE ARCHITEKTONISCHEN STYLARTEN. Transl. as HANDBOOK OF ARCHITECTURAL STYLES. N. Y., Scribner, $2.50. **720.**

Ruskin, John.

STONES OF VENICE. Chapter on the Nature of Gothic. N. Y., Merrill & Baker, 3 vols., $4.50, and other editions.

Contains an excellent criticism of one side of Gothic Architecture; one of its strongest claims on our attention, viz : its sculpture, at once decorative and expressive in character, and unlike any other sculpture in the world. The structural peculiarities of Gothic are not treated except casually, and the resulting peculiarities of general design are not well explained. Its title should be rather, Gothic Sculpture in its Relations to Building. **020.**

Smith, T. R., *and* Poynter, E. J.

ARCHITECTURE, GOTHIC AND RENAISSANCE. (Art handbooks series.) N. Y., Scribner, $2.

Not inaccurate, nor hard to understand, but vague, discursive ; fails to give clear and connected ideas. It fails also to insist on the most important points. The smaller part, devoted to the Renaissance, is more nearly accurate than that given to the Gothic There is a short glossary of technical terms. **723.**

Smith, T. R., *and* Slater, John.

ARCHITECTURE, CLASSICAL AND EARLY CHRISTIAN. (Art handbooks series.) N. Y., Scribner, $2.

Contains an account of ancient architecture in Egypt, Western Asia—Assyria, Eastern Asia, Greece, the Greek colonies and the Roman Empire; also of Byzantine, Romanesque, and Mohammedan architecture. A good general idea can be obtained from it, but there is in it no sign of intimate acquaintance with the remains described or with the best founded conclusions of modern archæologists. Thus the Roman buildings are said to be of brick, which is the superficial and popular view; the wall being really of small stones laid in mortar and only faced with fine hard bricks. So the question of Grecian Doric temples is treated as if they were all like the Parthenon in general scheme and in material. There is a brief glossary of technical terms. Some of the illustrations are very good. **722.**

Sturgis, Russell.
Article GRECIAN ARCHITECTURE. Johnson's Universal Cyclopædia, ed. 1893-5.
Article HOUSE. Johnson's Universal Cyclopædia, ed. 1893-5.

Viollet-le-Duc, E. E.
ENTRETIENS SUR L'ARCHITECTURE. Transl. by B. Bucknall as DISCOURSES ON ARCHITECTURE. Lond., Sampson Low, 2 vols., 63s.
There is nowhere a more masterly treatise on architectural art. Its inmost secrets are known to this able writer, who sees what is strong and what is weak in every style, and makes it clear to his readers He is also a master of explanatory and descriptive drawing. No such illustrations of architectural subjects as those in his books are known. An edition of this work, published by Ticknor, Boston, 1881, $15, is now out of print. **720.**

PART IV.

MINOR DECORATIVE ARTS: COSTUME, EMBROIDERY, GLASS, INLAY AND MOSAIC, LEATHER WORK, METAL WORK, POTTERY AND PORCELAIN, TEXTILE FABRICS.

These arts, called also the subsidiary arts and by other similar names, differ from architecture only in the comparatively small size and cost and comparatively small importance to mankind of the objects which belong to them. It must be noted that the essence of decorative art is that it adorns some object which is necessary and useful in a practical way. Thus a little independent figure in bronze is sculpture; but the pommel of a sword worked into a similar figure is decoration as well as sculpture, and the whole sword-hilt so adorned is a single work of decorative art. Buildings do not differ from weapons or furniture in this respect.

During the past forty years the literature of these arts has grown to enormous proportions. Few of the good books are in English and still fewer are inexpensive. The selection here given is of books which are essentially artistic. Thus in costume, Fairholt's "Costume in England" [(Bohn) N. Y., Macmillan, 2 vols., $3], and Planché's "History of British Costume" in 2 quarto vols., and also [(Bohn) N. Y., Macmillan, $1.50], are valuable historically, but are not studies of decorative art.

Balfour, Henry.
EVOLUTION OF DECORATIVE ART. N. Y., Macmillan, 1893, $1.25.
An interesting and suggestive account of very primitive forms of ornament, both pre-historic and among savages of our own time. Careful reading of this book throws a good deal of light on many problems of fine art. **740.**

Benson, W. A. S.
ELEMENTS OF HANDICRAFT AND DESIGN. N. Y., Macmillan, $1.60.
Intended for school workshops, but its directions for simple carpenter work and the making of b ok-shelves and tables are excellent, and are illustrated with 94 drawings. The soundest principles of design are explained in simple language and well enforced. This part of the book is important, because there is a strong tendency in our times towards mere taking of designs from old works. This shows how designs are made, originally. The final chapter gives good general ideas as to coloring, and a long bibliography is added. **740.**

Evans, Maria Millington (Lady Evans).
CHAPTERS ON GREEK DRESS. N. Y., Macmillan, 1893, $2.
Of general value as containing an analysis of the most simple and beautiful costume known to us, that of the ancient Greeks; and also as being a key to that important part of sculpture and painting which we call drapery, which, with European artists, is founded on Greek examples. **301.**

INDUSTRIAL ARTS, THE: HISTORICAL SKETCHES: (One of the Art Handbooks of South Kensington Museum). Lond., Chapman & Hall, 3s.
A good general account of the ornamental arts as represented in museums. **600.**

Lefebvre, Ernest.
BRODERIES ET DENTELLES. (B.E.B.A.) Transl. by A. S. Cole as EMBROIDERY AND LACE. Phila., Lippincott, 1888, $3.50. **746.**

Middleton, J. Henry.
Article TEXTILE FABRICS. Encyclopædia Britannica, 9th ed.
Gives much attention to artistic design in stuffs.
Article PLATE. Encyclopædia Britannica, 9th ed.
Article MOSAIC. Encyclopædia Britannica, 9th ed.

Morris, William, *Editor.*
ARTS AND CRAFTS ESSAYS: By Members of the Arts and Crafts Exhibition Society. N. Y., Scribner, 1893, $2.50.
Some excellent papers, such as "Furniture and the Room," by Edward S. Prior, and "The Room and Furniture," by Halsey Ricardo. Mr Morris's preface is also important. "Modern Embroidery," by Mary E. Turner, is one of the papers which have peculiar value. Contains also "Decorative Printing and Designing," by Walter Crane; "Bookbinding," by Cobden Sanderson, and "Dyeing," by William Morris. **602.**

Muntz, Eugene.
LA TAPISSERIE. (B.E.B.A.) Transl. by Miss L. J. Davis as SHORT HISTORY OF TAPESTRY. N. Y., Cassell, $2. **746.**

Rudler, F. W.
Article ENAMEL. Encyclopædia Britannica, 9th ed.
A very full paper, and valuable.

Sturgis, Russell.
Articles, Johnson's Universal Cyclopædia, Edition 1893-5:
"Costume," "Decorative Art," "Embroidery," "Enamel," "Furniture," "Glass in Artistic Design," "Lacquer," "Metal Work," "Porcelain," "Pottery," "Tapestry," "Textile Fabrics," and many shorter articles.

MUSIC.

A SELECTION FROM ITS LITERATURE, WITH NOTES BY

HENRY E. KREHBIEL,
Musical Editor New York "Tribune."

New York, June, 1895.

Ambros, A. W.

THE BOUNDARIES OF MUSIC AND POETRY: A STUDY IN MUSICAL ÆSTHETICS. Transl. from the German by J. H. Cornell. N. Y., Schirmer, 187 p., $2.

Entertaining as well as suggestive. An answer to Hanslick's "The Beautiful in Music," which see. Free from the ordinary obscurities of metaphysical writing, and full of illustrations drawn from the other arts. It combats the notion that feelings are neither the aim nor the content of music, but points out the limitations of musical expression and warns against the extravagances of descriptive, or programme, music. 780.

GESCHICHTE DER MUSIK. MIT ZAHLREICHEN NOTENBEISPIELEN UND MUSIKBEILAGEN. Dritte Auflage. Leipsic, F. E. C. Leuckart, 1892, 3 vols., 584, 596, 640 p., $11.

In every respect the most thorough and scholarly history of music yet written. Unfortunately the author died while giving the finishing touches to the fourth volume, which brings the story of musical development down to the culmination of the *a capella* style in Palestrina. The revision of the manuscript of the last volume was accomplished by G. Nottebohm. In the third edition the first volume, devoted to the music of ancient Greece and the Orient, has been entirely rewritten by H. von Sokolowsky to make it conform with the more recent discoveries and theories of Rudolph Westphal and F. A. Gevaert in this department. The second volume was revised by Heinrich Reimann, the third by Otto Kade. A necessary companion to the first edition is the index (*Namen und Sachregister*), prepared by Wilhelm Bäumker, and published as a separate volume by Leuckart in 1882. In the third edition each volume has its own index. 780.9.

Apthorp, William F.

HECTOR BERLIOZ: Selections from His Letters and Æsthetic, Humorous, and Satirical Writings. Transl., with biographical sketch of the author. N. Y., Holt, 427 p., $2.

A readable translation of well-chosen extracts from Berlioz's French writings, "First Journey to Germany," "Musical Grotesques," and "A Travers Chants." In an appendix are M. Guillaume's discourse at the funeral of Berlioz and a catalogue of Berlioz's compositions. 780.

MUSICIANS AND MUSIC LOVERS, AND OTHER ESSAYS. N. Y., Scribner, 346 p., $1.50.

Criticism with an agreeable literary flavor, the reflections and conclusions of a studious man and an experienced judge. Two of the essays discuss the relationship between the art, the musician, the critic, and the public. The remainder are mostly critical biography, the subjects being Bach, Meyerbeer, Offenbach, Franz, Dresel, and Dwight. 748.0.

Banister, Henry C.

MUSIC. N. Y., Holt, 325 p., 80 c.

A handbook, most admirably arranged, with definitions at once terse and luminous. It ought to be at the elbow of every reader of musical criticism or analysis. 780.4.

Benedict, *Sir Julius.*

WEBER. (Great Musicians series of biographies, edited by Francis Hueffer.) Lond., Sampson Low, 176 p., $1.

A well-written and authoritative book which derives special interest from the fact that the author was a pupil of Weber. A valuable feature is the descriptive catalogue of Weber's compositions. 780.

Ehlert, Louis.

FROM THE TONE WORLD: A SERIES OF ESSAYS. Transl. from the German by Helen D. Tretbar. 2d edition. N. Y., C. F. Tretbar, 397 p., $1.50.

Criticism by one of the most delightful writers on music that Germany has produced—a musician of keen discernment, of warm love for his art, and withal a master of a poetical and sympathetic literary style. The second, undated, edition was published in 1893, and contains essays on Brahms, Wagner's "Parsifal," and Liszt as a *littérateur*, which are not in the first edition. Of special value are the essays on "Tristan und Isolde," the Bayreuth festival, "Parsifal," "Schumann and His School," "Chopin," and "Brahms." 780.4.

Fillmore, John Comfort.

PIANOFORTE MUSIC, its history, with biographical sketches and critical estimates of its greatest masters. Phila., Theodore Presser, 245 p., D. $1.50.

Unnecessarily extended in its biographical department, but valuable, especially to the younger pianoforte students, in its exposition of the growth of the mechanics of pianoforte playing. 786.

Finck, Henry T.

WAGNER AND HIS WORKS: the Story of His Life, with Critical Comments. With portraits. N. Y., Scribner, 2 vols., 460, 530 p., $4.

The biographical portion remarkably complete, clearly, and forcibly written, with agreeable variety and picturesqueness. Facts carefully sifted and well ordered. The polemical and critical portions marred by uncompromising radicalism of statement and frequent instances of imperfect literary taste. 782.2.

Grove, *Sir George.*

DICTIONARY OF MUSIC AND MUSICIANS (A.D. 1450-1889), by eminent writers, English and foreign. Illustrated. Appendix edited by J. A. Fuller Maitland. N. Y., Macmillan, 5 vols., $25.

The only really comprehensive encyclopædia of music in English. Frequently faulty in statement (the appendix is chiefly occupied with corrections) and not always well balanced in its estimate of the musical activities of the different peoples of the world; yet an indispensable book of reference to the serious student. 780 3.

Hadow, W. H.

STUDIES IN MODERN MUSIC. With portraits. N. Y., Macmillan, 2 vols., 335, 312 p., $4.50.

Chiefly taken up with critical biography, written with discernment, independence, and forcefulness, and in an agreeable style. The first series treats of Berlioz, Schumann, and Wagner; the second of Chopin, Dvořák, and Brahms. The opening essay of the first series is devoted to Music and Musical Criticism, of the second to a study of the Outlines of Musical Form. These essays are ingenious efforts to discover a basis for judgment on musical art-works, and are valuable for their suggestiveness. **780.4.**

Hanslick, Eduard.

THE BEAUTIFUL IN MUSIC: a Contribution to the Revisal of Musical Æsthetics. Transl. from the 7th edition by Gustav Cohen. N. Y., Novello, Ewer & Co., 174 p., $2.50.

One of the most gracefully written as well as keenest discussions of the nature and essence of music extant. Dr. Hanslick contends that music possesses no means for representing definite feelings. The beautiful in music, therefore, does not depend on emotional expression. The content of music is the musical idea, which is not only an object of intrinsic beauty but also an end in itself, not a means for representing feelings or thoughts. In reply see Ambros's "The Boundaries of Music and Poetry" in this list. **780.1.**

Henderson, W. J.

PRELUDES AND STUDIES: Musical Themes of the Day. N. Y., Longmans, 245 p., $1.25.

A book of criticisms, suggestive, instructive, and filled with the charm of good literature. About half the volume is devoted to Wagner and his latter-day works; the rest to a study of the evolution of pianoforte music and a sympathetic essay on Schumann and the programme symphony. **780.4.**

Hunt, H. G. Bonavia.

CONCISE HISTORY OF MUSIC FROM THE COMMENCEMENT OF THE CHRISTIAN ERA TO THE PRESENT TIME. N. Y., Macmillan, 184 p., 90 c.

Designed for the use of schools, and to that end provided with a list of examination questions. Section I, chiefly a chronological and biographical record; Section II, a series of tables of musicians and musical events; Section III, a summary in which the growth of the art is traced. An excellent book for systematic study, but also helpful for quick reference. **780.9.**

Jahn, Otto.

LIFE OF MOZART. Transl. from the German by Pauline D. Townsend, with a preface by George Grove, D.C.L. With portraits and fac-simile reproductions of autographs. N. Y., Novello, Ewer & Co., 3 vols., 431, 478, 443 p., $10.

In its way the last word on Mozart. The biographical part is exhaustive and all the chief works of Mozart are interestingly analyzed. A monumental work. **780.**

Jullien, Adolphe.

RICHARD WAGNER, HIS LIFE AND WORKS. Transl. from the French by Florence Percival Hall. Introduction by B. J. Lang. Illustrated with 14 phototypes from originals drawings by Fantin-Latour, 15 portraits of Richard Wagner, and 113 text cuts; scenes from his operas; views of theatres, autographs, and numerous caricatures. Bost., J. B. Millet Co., 2 vols., $10.

A critical biography, written in a sprightly and entertaining vein by a distinguished French writer, who is an enthusiastic admirer of Wagner's music and a calm and discriminating judge of his personal character. There are evidences in the translation of unfamiliarity with French musical terminology and Wagner's works. **782.2.**

Lampadius, W. A.

LIFE OF FELIX MENDELSSOHN-BARTHOLDY. Transl. by W. A. Gage. Bost., O. Ditson & Co., $1.25.

A standard work, written in a spirit of affectionate sympathy. **780.**

Langhans, W.

HISTORY OF MUSIC IN TWELVE LECTURES. Transl. from the German by J. H. Cornell. New and enlarged edition. N. Y., Schirmer, $1.50.

A good translation of the lectures delivered by Dr. Langhans in the *Neue Akademie der Tonkunst*, at Berlin. The author belongs to the new romantic school, and devotes his last lecture to Wagner: it is biographical and expository rather than critical. The preceding chapters are not overburdened with biographical detail, and trace the development of music through its principal phases in an interesting and instructive manner. **780.9.**

Macfarren, G. A.

MUSICAL HISTORY BRIEFLY NARRATED AND TECHNICALLY DISCUSSED, with a roll of the names of musicians and the times and places of their births and deaths. Lond., A. & C. Black, 220 p., 6s.

A reprint, with amplifications of the article "Music," in the 9th edition of the Encyclopædia Britannica. A model of encyclopædic writing in clearness, terseness, and comprehensiveness. Touching the questions of modern musical polemics the author's attitude is extremely conservative. His Roll of Names is defective from an American point of view. **780.9.**

Marx, Adolph Bernhard.

LUDWIG VAN BEETHOVEN, LEBEN UND SCHAFFEN. In zwei Theilen mit Chronologischem Verzeichniss der Werke und Autographischen Beilagen. Dritte Auflage, mit Berücksichtigung der neuesten Forschungen durchgesehen und vermehrt von Dr. Gustav Behncke. Berlin, Otto Janke, 14 marks (N. Y., B. Westermann, $4.65). 2 vols., 365, 456 p., paper.

A critical biography written with ardent sympathy and in a sanely poetical style, with analyses of the larger compositions of Beethoven which give it a place not filled by any English biography. **780.**

Niecks, Frederick.

FREDERICK CHOPIN AS A MAN AND MUSICIAN. N. Y., Novello, Ewer & Co., 2 vols., 340, 375 p., $10.

A standard work, the ablest yet written on the subject, though unduly extended by dissertations on unessential topics. Contains appreciative and intelligent analyses and criticisms, and a well-compiled and annotated list of Chopin's published compositions. **780.**

Nohl, Louis.

LIVES OF BEETHOVEN, HAYDN, LISZT, MOZART, AND WAGNER. Transl. by George P. Upton and John J. Lalor. With portraits. Chic., A. C. McClurg & Co., 5 vols., 75 c. each. **927.8.**

Parry, C. Hubert H.

THE ART OF MUSIC. N. Y., Appleton, 374 p., $4.

A series of thoroughly admirable essays on the art of music and its historical growth, free from biographical detail, scientific in spirit and sound. **780.**

Reissmann, August.

LIFE AND WORKS OF ROBERT SCHUMANN. Transl. from 3d edition of the German by Abby Langdon Alger. Lond., George Bell & Co., 276 p., 3s. 6d.

A critical biography, with intelligent discussions of Schumann's principal compositions. **780.**

Rockstro, W. S.

GENERAL HISTORY OF MUSIC FROM THE INFANCY OF THE GREEK DRAMA TO THE PRESENT PERIOD. New edition. Lond., Sampson Low, 14s.

Correct and comprehensive, but not always well balanced. It includes Wagner's work, but the chapter devoted to the poet-composer smacks of polemics rather than history. **780.0.**

LIFE OF GEORGE FREDERICK HANDEL. With introductory notice by George Grove, D.C.L. N. Y., Macmillan, 452 p., $2.50.

Trustworthy and serviceable. Contains a valuable catalogue of Handel's works and a genealogical tree. **780.**

Spitta, Philipp.

JOHANN SEBASTIAN BACH: His Work and Influence on the Music of Germany, 1685-1750. Transl. from the German by Clara Bell and J. A. Fuller Maitland. N. Y., Novello, Ewer & Co., 3 vols., 656, 721, and 419 p., $12.

A monumenta example of German thoroughness and devotion. **780.**

Stainer, Sir John, *and* **Barrett, W. A.**

DICTIONARY OF MUSICAL TERMS. N. Y., Novello, Ewer & Co., 456 p., $3.

A standard authority and the best work of its kind in English. **780.3.**

Thayer, Alexander Wheelock.

LUDWIG VAN BEETHOVEN'S LEBEN. Nach dem Original Manuscript, deutsch bearbeitet. Berlin, W. Weber, 21 marks (N. Y., B. Westermann, $7). 3 vols. 384, 416, 519 p., paper.

The court of last resort for all questions touching the man Beethoven; there is no discussion, beyond the historical, of his compositions. Written in English by an American, and translated by Dr. H. Deiters. The three volumes published respectively in 1866, 1872, and 1879 bring the life of Beethoven down to the end of 1816. A fourth volume is yet to come. The work represents thirty-five years of labor and its authority is indefectible. **780.**

Upton, George P.

THE STANDARD CANTATAS: their stories, music, and composers.

THE STANDARD OPERAS: their plots, music, and composers.

THE STANDARD ORATORIOS: their stories, music, and composers.

THE STANDARD SYMPHONIES: their stories, music, and composers. Chic., A. C. McClurg & Co., 4 vols., $1.50 each. **780.4.**

Weitzmann, C. F.

HISTORY OF PIANOFORTE PLAYING AND PIANOFORTE LITERATURE. With Musical Appendices and a Supplement containing the History of the Pianoforte according to the latest researches. Illustrated. With a biographical sketch of the author and notes by Otto Lessmann. Transl. by Dr. Th. Baker. N. Y., Schirmer, 379 p., $2.50.

An accepted authority. Contains specimens of compositions for keyed instruments from the 16th, 17th, and 18th centuries, and an exposition of the old ornaments and graces. **780.**

EDUCATION.

THE KINDERGARTEN.

A SELECTION FROM ITS LITERATURE,

ANNOTATED BY

ANGELINE BROOKS,

Professor of Kindergarten Methods and Director of the Kindergarten, Teachers' College, New York.

New York, June, 1895.

Barnard, Henry, *Editor.*
KINDERGARTEN AND CHILD CULTURE PAPERS. Bost., Journal of Education, $2.50.
A valuable collection of papers containing more on Kindergarten subjects than any other one book published. 372.2.

Blow, Susan E.
SYMBOLIC EDUCATION. (International Education series.) N. Y., Appleton, $1.50.
A commentary on the Mother Play and Nursery Songs of Froebel. 372.2.

Brooks, Angeline.
KINDERGARTEN PAPERS. Springfield, Mass., Milton Bradley Co., 25 c.
Practical papers on vital questions. 372.2.

Buckland, Anna.
USE OF STORIES IN THE KINDERGARTEN. N. Y., E. Steiger & Co., 25 c.
Full of valuable suggestions. 372.2.

Emerson *and* **Brown,** *Misses.*
STORIES IN SONG. Bost., O. Ditson & Co., 75 c.
Contains not only songs for the Kindergarten, but a supplement for primary schools. 372.

Froebel, Friedrich.
THE EDUCATION OF MAN. Transl. by W. N. Hailman. (International Education series.) N. Y., Appleton, 1887, $1.50.
A standard work, published in 1824, containing a full exposition of Froebel's philosophy. Dr. W. T. Harris says: "This book deserves a thorough annual study by every teacher's reading club in the land." 370.

THE MOTHER PLAY AND NURSERY SONGS. Transl. by Miss Jarvis. Bost., Lee & Shepard, $2.
Froebel said that whoever understood this book understood his philosophy. Two thoughts furnish the key to it: the importance of infancy as the germ stage of life, and the symbolism of all material things. 372.2.

Harrison, Elizabeth.
CHILD NATURE. Chicago, Kindergarten College, $1.
A helpful and instructive book. It has been read with great benefit by thousands of mothers. 372.

Hubbard, Clara Benson.
MERRY SONGS AND GAMES. St. Louis, Mo., Balmer, Weber Music Co., $2.
A book of practical songs, much used in kindergartens. 372.2.

Kindergarten Stories. Bost., J. L. Hammett, 60 c.
Carefully selected ; the result of practical work with children. 372.2.

Marenholtz-Bulow, *Baroness* **Bertha Von.**
CHILD AND CHILD-NATURE. Syracuse, N. Y., C. W. Bardeen, $1.50.
A very satisfactory presentation of Froebel's philosophy is given in this work. 372.

REMINISCENCES OF FRIEDRICH FROEBEL. Bost., Lee & Shepard, $1.50.
A graphic account of the last years of Froebel's life; written by the gifted woman through whom he first obtained recognition by the leading educators of Germany. 370.

Meyer, Bertha.
FROM THE CRADLE TO THE SCHOOL. N. Y., E. Steiger & Co., $1.
A wise unfolding of the principles that should govern child-life. 372.

Page, Annie L.; Brooks, Angeline; Putnam, *Mrs.* **H. H. ;** *and* **Peabody,** *Mrs.* **Mary H.**
THE KINDERGARTEN AND THE SCHOOL. Springfield, Mass., Milton Bradley Co., 75 c.
Originally written for teachers' reading circles and containing much in condensed form. By four active workers. 372.2.

Peabody, Elizabeth P.
LECTURES TO KINDERGARTNERS. Bost., D. C. Heath & Co., $1.
One of the most valuable books for mothers and kindergartners ever written. 372.2.

Poulsson, Emilie.
FINGER PLAYS FOR NURSERY AND KINDERGARTEN. Springfield, Mass., Milton Bradley Co., $1.25.
Truly a work of genius. All the plays are in harmony with Froebel's philosophy. 372.2.

In the Child's World. Springfield, Mass., Milton Bradley Co., $2.

A choice collection of short stories, entirely suited to little children, with suggestions for additional reading on the subjects presented. **372.**

Shirreff, Emily.

Home Education in Relation to the Kindergarten. Lond., Chapman & Hall, 1s. 6d.

Pronounced valuable by leading kindergartners. **372.2.**

Short Sketch of the Life of Froebel. Lond., Chapman & Hall, 2s.

Should be read by every one who wishes to be informed about the founder of the New Education. **370.**

Walker, Gertrude, *and* Jenks, Harriet S.

Songs and Games for Little Ones. Bost., O. Ditson & Co., $2.

A valuable collection, much used in kindergartens. **372.**

Wiltse, Sara E.

Stories for Kindergarten and Primary School. Bost., Ginn & Co., 40 c.; boards, 30 c.

Miss Wiltse has devoted much time to the subject of story-telling: this book is the result of her best thought. **372.**

NOTES.

See Psychology for W. Preyer's "Mental Development in the Child," and F. Tracy's "Psychology of Childhood."

E. Steiger & Co., New York, and Milton Bradley Co., Springfield, Mass., manufacture in great variety material for kindergartners.

KITCHEN AND COOKING-GARDEN.

Huntington, Emily.

Children's Kitchen-Garden Work; adapted from the original, with additional songs. N. Y., J. W. Schermerhorn & Co., 1893, 74 p., D. boards, 30 c.

Contents: Uses of wood and paper; table-setting and dish-washing; bed-making and sweeping; clothes-washing; dinner-setting; songs.

A primer setting forth a brief outline of the lessons in the next book.

Kitchen Garden: Object Lessons in Household Work; including songs, plays, exercises and games, with illustrations and music. N. Y., J. W. Schermerhorn & Co., 1893, 133 p., Q. $3.

Author originated the kitchen garden which applies kindergarten methods to teaching little girls to sweep, dust, answer the door, lay the table, and other simple household duties. Miss Huntington's classes have been successfully conducted for years at the Wilson Mission, Avenue A and St. Mark's Place, New York.

The Cooking Garden: a systematized course of cooking for pupils of all ages, including plan of work, bills of fare, songs, and information. N. Y., J. W. Schermerhorn & Co., 1885, 198 p., Q. $3.

A manual which carries kitchen gardening one step farther than the preceding book, to cooking. The lessons are so contrived as heartily to interest young pupils. They have been tested far and wide, and warmly approved.

NOTE.

J. W. Schermerhorn & Co., N. Y., manufacture a variety of material for use in kitchen and cooking gardens.

EDUCATION AS A SCIENCE AND AN ART.

DRAWING; PENMANSHIP; SHORTHAND; GRAMMAR; COMPOSITION; RHETORIC;
ELOCUTION; LANGUAGE; MATHEMATICS; BOOK-KEEPING; ASTRONOMY;
PHYSICS (INCLUDING ELECTRICITY).

A SELECTION FROM THEIR LITERATURE,

ANNOTATED BY

EDWARD R. SHAW,
Professor of Pedagogy, New York University.

New York, July, 1895.

EDUCATION AS A SCIENCE AND AN ART.

The reader interested in the correlation of studies should read : The Report of the Committee of Fifteen in *Educational Review*, March, 1895 ; N. Y., Holt & Co., 35 c. The First Year-Book of the Herbart Society ; Normal, Ill., 1895, 50 c.: Dr. De Garmo's article on the correlation, concentration and co-ordination of studies in this book is very able, readjusts the whole discussion, introducing new conceptions of the problem. Dr. Van Liew's article on the Culture Epochs is the first extended treatment of this subject in English. The paper in form, unfortunately, is largely influenced by German models, and though it needs to be condensed and rearranged, is a scholarly treatment of the subject.

Those interested in the scientific investigation of educational questions should read the *Pedagogical Seminary*, edited by G. Stanley Hall. Worcester, Mass., J. H. Orpha, $1.50 a no.; $4 a vol.; nos. appear irregularly.

A Descriptive Bibliography of Education, useful though tentative in character, was edited by G. Stanley Hall and John M. Mansfield in 1886. Bost., D. C. Heath & Co., 325 p., $1.50.

The American Society for the Extension of University Teaching, Edward T. Devine, Ph.D., Secretary, 111 South 15th St., Philadelphia, Pa., issues a large variety of circulars, syllabi and other pamphlets and books in advocacy and pursuance of its aims.

Browning, Oscar.
ASPECTS OF EDUCATION. N. Y., E. L. Kellogg & Co., 1894, 63 p., D. 25 c.
Gives an excellent idea of humanism, realism, and naturalism, their rise and how they have affected educational thought and practice. 370.4.

Compayré, Gabriel.
HISTORY OF PEDAGOGY. Bost., Heath, 1886, 598 p., D. $1.75.
Up to the present the fullest and most comprehensive history of education in English. 370.9.

De Garmo, Charles.
HERBART AND THE HERBARTIANS. (Great Educators series.) N. Y., Scribner, 1895, 268 p., D. $1.
Gives an exposition of the theory of education as advanced by Herbart, and modified by his followers. Discusses the concentration and correlation of studies, giving each of the Herbartian educator's point of view, with criticisms. Chronicles the spread of Herbartian ideas in America. Proposes a feasible plan for the co-ordination of studies. 370.

Fitch, Joshua G.
LECTURES ON TEACHING. With preface by an American Normal teacher. N. Y., Macmillan, 1885, 436 p., D. $1.
Not a manual of methods, but a book filled with practical comment and suggestion, written in a very pleasing style. One of the first books the novice in teaching should read. The chapters on discipline and the teacher and his attitude towards his vocation are notably strong and wholesome—sounding the note that true character is what will influence character. 371.

Lange, Helene.
HIGHER EDUCATION OF WOMEN IN EUROPE. (International Education series.) N. Y., Appleton, 1890, 36+186 p., D. $1.
After preface on higher education of women in America, argues for the higher education of women in Germany, compares woman's opportunities in Germany with those in England and other countries. Many suggestions to teachers of girls and of boys are to be found in the chapter on Moral Education in England and Germany. 370.

Lange, Karl.
APPERCEPTION. Edited by Charles De Garmo. Bost., Heath, 1895, 279 p., D. $1.
A translation of one of the best German books on teaching. Will give the English reading teacher new ideas. Destined to exert great usefulness in advancing teaching to a higher plane in America. Makes an exhaustive examination of the theory of apperception, or mental apprehension and assimilation, and then points out its varied application to teaching, and its value. Gives at the close of the book a succinct history of the rise and growth of the idea of apperception. A book to be studied closely. 370.

MacVicar, Malcolm.

PRINCIPLES OF EDUCATION. Bost., Ginn & Co., 1892, 178 p., D. 70 c.

Matter presented in uninviting form, but the book contains in the parts devoted to the period of childhood, the period of youth, the principles of the pupil's work, the principles of the teacher's work, the general and special principles of teaching, and the means to be used, some of the most strongly presented, soundest, and most valuable material that has thus far been written by an American teacher. 370.1.

McMurry, Charles A.

GENERAL METHOD. Bloomington, Ill., Pub. School Pub. Co., 1895, 201 p., D. 75 c.

A simple and interesting presentation of the aim of education, the relative value of studies, the doctrine of interest, the culture epochs theory of arranging studies, the concentration of studies, and apperception from the point of view of the followers of Herbart. An excellent book for introduction to the study of the Herbartian pedagogy. 371.

Painter, F. V. N.

HISTORY OF EDUCATION. (International Education series.) N. Y., Appleton, 1886, 16+335 p., D. $1.50.

A graphical but brief account of educational movements and reformers from early times down to the present. 370.0.

Payne, Joseph.

LECTURES ON THE SCIENCE AND ART OF EDUCATION. Syracuse, N. Y., C. W. Bardeen, 1885, $1.

The work of an able, enthusiastic teacher and a close student of education. Sets forth the principles of teaching as well as the art. Shows how Nature teaches and the defects of her method. States the essentials of good methods. Finds a basis for all method in the proposition that learning is self-teaching. Lays stress upon action and things as factors contributing greatly to the pupil's mental development. A most stimulating book for the teacher. 370.

Quick, Robert H.

ESSAYS ON EDUCATIONAL REFORMERS. (International Education series.) New edition, revised and enlarged. N. Y., Appleton, 1890, 34+560 p., D. $1.50.

Interesting sketches of the men and the schools that have affected educational thought and practice with exposition of their theories and principles. Contents include Sturm, Schools of the Jesuits, Rabelais, Montaigne, Ascham, Mulcaster, Ratichius, Comenius, Locke, Rousseau, Basedow, Pestalozzi, Froebel, Jacotot, Spencer, Thoughts and Suggestions, The Schoolmaster's Moral and Religious Influence. 370.0.

Spencer, Herbert.

EDUCATION. N. Y., Appleton, $1.25; E. L. Kellogg & Co., $1.

Discusses, What knowledge is of most worth, Intellectual Education, Moral Education, and Physical Education. The chapter on intellectual education is the most important for its elucidation of the principles of education and as showing their application. 370.

DRAWING.

Thompson, L. S.

MANUAL TRAINING SERIES OF DRAWING. Nos. 1 and 2. 60 p. each. Illus. Bost., D. C. Heath & Co., 1895, 25 c. each.

Treat of clay modelling of objects and in relief, paper folding and cutting, color, construction of geometrical solids, etc. Directions clear, exercises and illustrations excellent. For class use or self-instruction. 740.

MODEL AND OBJECT SERIES OF DRAWING. Nos. 1, 2, 3, 15 c. each, $1.75 per doz.

Manual, 35 c. Illus. Bost., D. C. Heath & Co., 1895.

A system of drawing from objects, progressive, practical, philosophical. The manual states clearly the principles of model drawing. For class use or self-instruction. 741.

PENMANSHIP: SHORTHAND.

Jackson, John.

THEORY AND PRACTICE OF HANDWRITING. Illus. N. Y., Wm. Beverley Harison, 160 p., $1.25.

Sets forth the claims of vertical writing and gives forms of capital and small letters and directions for teaching the vertical hand. Presents a brief history of the former use of upright handwriting, its decay and revival. 052.

Pitman, Isaac.

COMPLETE PHONOGRAPHIC INSTRUCTOR. N. Y., Isaac Pitman & Sons, 250 p., D. $1.50.

The standard text-book, used in the public schools of New York City. Shorthand, it should be remembered, is best and most rapidly acquired with the aid of a teacher.

I. Pitman & Sons, N. Y., issue a "Phonographic Dictionary," $1.50; the "Phonographic Teacher," 20 c.; "Manual of Phonography," 40 c.; "Phonographic Reporter," 60 c.; "Phonographic Phrase Book," 35 c.; "Business Correspondence in Shorthand," nos. 1 and 2, 30 c. each. 053.

Witherbee, J. V.

SYSTEM OF VERTICAL PENMANSHIP: The Common Sense Copy Books. N. Y., A. Lovell & Co., 1895, 7 nos. for 40 c.

The best system of vertical writing yet issued. Size of book and directions in accordance with the hygienic requirements of vertical writing. 052.

GRAMMAR.

Salmon, David.

LONGMAN'S SCHOOL GRAMMAR. New edition. Longmans, 1893, 264 p., 75 c.

Begins with parts of speech instead of analysis of sentences. Leads up to definitions inductively, and then gives admirable exercises to test and fix the learner's idea. Very clear in presentation and arrangement of subject-matter. A book well planned to elicit the interest of the learner. 372.0.

COMPOSITION, RHETORIC, ELOCUTION.

"The thorough study of a few good authors of the highest excellence, writing upon subjects within the grasp of a young person's mind, frequent practice in forms of composition which do not demand original thought, and remorseless criticism by the teacher and the writer—these seem to be some of the points most needing attention by young students of English literature and language."— *Literary World.*

Bell, A. Melville.

PRINCIPLES OF ELOCUTION, with Exercises and Notations. Washington, D. C., A. Melville Bell, 1893, 240 p., O. $1.50.

One of the best manuals on the subject. The outgrowth of years of careful study, close observation and analysis. Extended treatment of Articulation, Inflexions, Modulation of Voice, Emphasis and Gesture. Leads the student to determine what his special faults of delivery are, then directs him how to overcome these. Great variety and number of exercises for practice. Specially adapted for self-teaching.

Prof. Hiram Corson, in his "Aims of Literary Study" (N. Y., Macmillan, 1895, 75 c), argues that good literature is best understood when properly read aloud. He commends Dr. James Rush's " Philosophy of the Human Voice " (Phila., Lippincott, $3). **808.5.**

Genung, John F.

OUTLINES OF RHETORIC. Bost., Ginn, 1895, 331 p., D. $1.10.

An interesting, original and lucid presentation of the principles of rhetoric, with well-chosen illustrative examples. **808.**

Hill, Adams S.

FOUNDATIONS OF RHETORIC. N. Y., Harper, 1894, 372 p., O. $1.

A book indispensable to whoever wishes to become a writer of good English. A marked feature is the arrangement of sentences and paragraphs in parallel columns, thus contrasting good with bad usage. In this manner the choice of words and their collocation in sentences, the varieties of sentence structure, the qualities of style and the formation of paragraphs are treated. **808.**

Lewes, George Henry.

PRINCIPLES OF SUCCESS IN LITERATURE. Edited, with introduction and notes, by Prof. F. N. Scott. Bost., Allyn & Bacon, 1893, 159 p., S. 50 c.

A book of the utmost value to writers. Clearness, sincerity, and beauty are discussed as the principles of success in literature: all three are admirably exemplified in the book itself. **808.**

Luce, Robert.

WRITING FOR THE PRESS. 4th edition revised. Bost., Writer Pub. Co., 1891, $1.

By a practical journalist, who tells how to prepar printer's copy; warns against common errors in grammar, phraseology, and construction; gives useful hints for condensation, telegraph correspondence, reporting testimony, etc. **808.**

Morton, Agnes H.

LETTER WRITING: Suggestions, Precepts, and Examples for Business and Social Correspondence. Phila., Penn Pub. Co., 1894, 222 p., S. 50 c.

An unpretending little book, which can aid the inexperienced. **808.0.**

Newcomer, Alphonso G.

PRACTICAL COURSE IN ENGLISH COMPOSITION. Bost., Ginn & Co., 1895, 249 p., O. 90 c.

An excellent book, to be used conjointly with Hill's "Foundations of Rhetoric," as it directs the student where to find interesting and varied material for composition. Deals with narrative, description, essays, criticism, debate, oratory, and miscellaneous forms of composition, as news, reviews, letters, etc. **808.**

Shaw, Edward R.

ENGLISH COMPOSITION BY PRACTICE. Illus. N. Y., Holt, 1895, 203 p., D. 80 c.

This book carries forward a study, by means of observation, comparison, and inference, of the principles observed generally by good writers, and at the same time gives actual practice in writing connected English. The use of the conventional detached sentence in exercises is abandoned, and the learner is put to work upon wholes. Stress is thus laid upon sequence of thought and unity and fluency in writing. A knowledge of punctuation is developed in an entirely new way. Diction is treated at the end of the book after the learner by his efforts in composing has acquired an appreciation of it. A chapter is devoted to common errors. Based on five years of experiment and test in the class-room. **808.**

NOTE.

While studying composition the student may with profit read the great masters of literature. See FICTION and LITERATURE.

LANGUAGE: PHILOLOGY.

Lounsbury, Thomas R.

HISTORY OF THE ENGLISH LANGUAGE. Revised and enlarged edition. N. Y., H. Holt & Co., 1894, 14+505 p., D. $1.12.

The best book of the kind. Part I. A clear and concise account of the Roman, Teutonic, Norman, and other influences which formed the English language; with a review of its changes from within. Part II. History of the inflections of the noun, adjective, pronoun and verb: this Part is less adapted to the general reader than to the special student. Author is Professor of English at Yale University. **420.9.**

Müller, F. Max.

SCIENCE OF THOUGHT. N. Y., Scribner, 1887, 2 vols., 18+325, 331 p., D. $4.

A discursive consideration of language from a somewhat metaphysical point of view. Maintains in opposition to Darwin that there is "no reason without language, no language without reason"—language being defined as articulate speech. See Darwin's "Descent of Man." For criticism see W. D. Whitney's "Max Müller's Science of Language" in this list. **400.**

Whitney, William Dwight.

LIFE AND GROWTH OF LANGUAGE : an Outline of Linguistic Science. (International Scientific series.) N. Y., D. Appleton & Co., 1875, 326 p., D. $1.50.

Though written in 1875, may serve as an authoritative introduction to the science of language. Clear and interesting in style. Author was Professor of Sanskrit and Comparative Philology at Yale University, and superintended the preparation of the Century Dictionary. See also his article on " Language " in Johnson's New Cyclopædia, 1894. **401.**

MAX MÜLLER'S SCIENCE OF LANGUAGE. N. Y., D. Appleton & Co., 1893, 79 p., O. paper, 50 c.

A severe criticism, maintaining that while thought is vastly indebted to language, thought is often independent of language, and that articulate speech has arisen naturally, many steps of the process being evident. **400.**

NOTE.

Language as a distinctive human faculty is traced by George John Romanes in its probable development in " Mental Evolution in Animals " and " Mental Evolution in Man " (N. Y., D. Appleton & Co., $3 each) In the Proceedings of the American Association for the Advancement of Science for 1886, p. 279, Horatio Hale has a paper of sterling value on " The Origin of Language, and the Antiquity of Speaking Man "; the volume is to be found in the larger public libraries, and is published at Salem, Mass. See works under Evolution in NATURAL HISTORY and HUMAN EVOLUTION, under ANTHROPOLOGY and under PSYCHOLOGY.

MATHEMATICS.

Bradbury, William F.

THE ACADEMIC GEOMETRY. Bost., Thompson, Brown & Co., 1893, 366 p., O. $1.25.

Treats the subject of demonstrative geometry in the

usual way, but has some superior points. Practical problems are placed at the foot of the pages, which point out application of the theorems learned. The theorems at the end of each book for original demonstration are carefully chosen, are progressive in character, and give review of truths gained. Diagrams strong and clear in outline. Matter placed openly and attractively on page. By ingenious use of various type the learner is able to distinguish readily hypothesis, demonstration, and conclusion. The nature of the different kinds of reasoning used is carefully explained to learner. 513.

Hill, G. A.

GEOMETRY FOR BEGINNERS. Illus. Bost., Ginn & Co., 1893, 314 p., O. $1.10.

A book constructed in accordance with the principles of pedagogy. Designed by the variety of its exercises to make geometry easy and interesting. All theorems and generalizations are led up to by the solution of concrete problems. Very thoughtfully graded. The accompanying illustrations give many ideas of the application of geometrical truths. 513.

Smith, Charles, *and* Stringham, Irving.

ELEMENTARY ALGEBRA, for the use of Preparatory Schools. N. Y., Macmillan, 1895, 584 p., O. $1.10.

Very carefully elaborated development of principles. The treatment in this respect new rather than conventional. Deals with simple equations and simultaneous equations of the first degree before taking up factoring. Introduces simple quadratic equations in factoring. Then treats H. C. Factor and L. C. Multiple, Fractions. Requires strong powers of generalization. Suited to the needs of those who wish a thorough knowledge of the elements of algebra. An excellent book for final review. 512.

Wentworth, G. A.

GRAMMAR SCHOOL ARITHMETIC. Bost., Ginn & Co., 1895, 348 p., D. 65 c.

Extremely clear and simple presentation of the subject. The plan is to lead learners by the solution of problems within their capacity and comprehension to a knowledge of the principles involved instead of by the application of rules and formulæ. Nearly all examples drawn from the demands of ordinary every-day life—not invented to test the application of principles and formulæ. Furnishes a large number of examples for oral solution. An appendix gives rules and principles clearly, concisely, and philosophically stated. Well suited for self-instruction. 511.

SCHOOL ALGEBRA. Bost., Ginn & Co., 1895, 362 p., O. $1.12.

For its grade, one of the best books yet offered on this subject. The treatment is clear, the matter carefully graded, the arrangement logical, the problems, upon the whole, new. Suited to those who wish to gain a knowledge of elementary algebra from one book. 512.

BOOK-KEEPING.

Meservey, A. B.

BOOK-KEEPING, SINGLE AND DOUBLE ENTRY. Bost., Thompson, Brown & Co., 1889, 222 p., O. 80 c.

Method of presentation clear, making acquirement of subject easy. Adapted to self-instruction or class use. The wide use of this work proves its merits. 057.

Packard, S. S., *and* Bryant, H. B.

BRYANT AND STRATTON'S COUNTING HOUSE BOOK-KEEPING. N. Y., Am. Book Co., $2.

A work developed in the practice of leading business colleges. Adapted to the higher grades of public and private schools and to self-instruction when the learner has had some practical experience.

The Am. Book Co., N. Y., publishes blanks and blank-books for learners in book-keeping.

ASTRONOMY.

Bowen, Eliza A.

ASTRONOMY BY OBSERVATION. Illus. N. Y., Am. Book Co., 1890, 94 p., D. $1.

An excellent book for beginners. Leads the learner to study at the outset the reality itself instead of diagrams. By following in order, diurnal motion of stars, annual motion, the ecliptic, the earth as moving, the moon and her motions, motions of the planets, it builds up a knowledge of these by direct observation and record of observations by drawings. The three pages on Talks with Observers especially good. Large star maps and explicit directions make the finding of constellations and stars very easy. Part II. Descriptive Astronomy, merely conventional treatment. 520.7.

Clarke, James Freeman.

HOW TO FIND THE STARS: with an account of the Astronomical Lantern. Bost., D. C. Heath & Co., paper, 15 c.

Brief directions for finding the principal star-groups. Accompanies the author's Astronomical Lantern (sold by these publishers at $4.50), provided with 17 slides, giving 22 constellations, an admirable means of becoming familiar with the principal stars and nebulæ. 523.80.

Newcomb, Simon, *and* Holden, Edward S.

ASTRONOMY: Briefer Course. (American Science series.) Illus. N. Y., Holt, 1895, 338 p., O. $1 25.

A clear elementary presentation of the subject. Requires a slight knowledge of algebra and geometry. An excellent book to follow "Astronomy by Observation." 520.

Serviss, Garrett P.

ASTRONOMY WITH AN OPERA-GLASS. With maps and directions to facilitate the recognition of the constellations and the principal stars visible to the naked eye. N. Y., Appleton, $1.50.

Shows in a most captivating way what may be learned by studying the heavens with an opera-glass magnifying 3.6 diameters. Takes up the aspect of the stars as to color and position. Brings up much of entertaining mythology with reference to the constellations and particular stars. Gives interesting fa is relative to each bright star. Points out the solstitial and equinoctial points, the nebulæ and the Milky Way. Directs to careful study of surface of moon, Jupiter and his satellites, and what may be seen of the other planets. Does not treat of planetary motions. Involves no knowledge of mathematics. 520.

Young, Charles A.

TEXT-BOOK OF GENERAL ASTRONOMY. Illus. Bost., Ginn & Co., 551 p., O. $2.50.

Regarded the best exposition of the facts, principles, and methods of astronomy, giving latest knowledge on unsettled points. Suited for the general reader as well as the student. May with advantage follow Newcomb and Holden's "Astronomy." 520.

PHYSICS: ELECTRICITY.

Barnard, Charles.

FIRST STEPS IN ELECTRICITY. N. Y., Maynard, Merrill & Co., 1894, 133 p., D. 60 c.

A good primer for young people. Illustrates simple experiments. 537.1.

Electricity in Daily Life: a popular account of the application of electricity to everyday uses. By Cyrus F. Brackett, Franklin L. Pope, Joseph Wetzler, Henry Morton, Charles L. Buckingham, Herbert L. Webb, W. S. Hughes, John Millis, A. E. Kennelly, M. Allen Starr. With 120 illustrations. N. Y., Scribner, 1891, 17+288 p., O. $3.

Thoroughly interesting chapters on Electricity in the Service of Man; the Electric Motor; the Electric Railway; Electric Lighting; the Telegraph; Making and Laying a Cable; Electricity in Warfare, in the Household, in Relation to the Human Body. 537

Houston, Edwin J.

DICTIONARY OF ELECTRICAL WORDS, TERMS, AND PHRASES. New and revised edition. Illus. N. Y., W. J. Johnston Co., 1894, 669 p., O. $5.

F. B. Crocker, Professor of Electrical Engineering, School of Mines, Columbia College, New York, says: "This is the most complete electrical dictionary in any language. Defines almost every existing electrical term, whether highly scientific or slang. Important facts are explained quite fully. It is a book of reference on all branches of electricity. Suited to the needs of everybody, from the general reader to the advanced electrical engineer." **537.**

Shaw, Edward R.

PHYSICS BY EXPERIMENT. Illus. N. Y., Maynard, 1895, 320 p., D. $1.

Elementary in character—a book for beginners. The learner by means of explicit directions is given experiments to perform, and through actual observation is led inductively to the law involved. The book encourages self-development and begets interest. Develops manual skill. Whole treatment of magnetism and of voltaic and dynamic electricity extremely simple. Explanation of the generation of electricity by a dynamo new and very easy to comprehend. **530.7.**

Poyser, A. W.

MAGNETISM AND ELECTRICITY. N. Y., Longmans, 1895, 250 p., D. 80 c. **537.**

Taylor, John E.

THEORETICAL MECHANICS, including Hydrostatics. N. Y., Longmans, 1894, 7+262 p., D. 80 c. **531.**

Wright, Mark R.

SOUND, LIGHT, AND HEAT. N. Y., Longmans, 1895, 269 p., D. 80 c. **530.**

These excellent manuals give a much more extended treatment of elementary physics than "Physics by Experiment," and are of suitable grade to follow that book.

Thompson, Sylvanus P.

ELECTRICITY AND MAGNETISM. New edition. Illus. N. Y., Macmillan, 1892, 456 p., S. $1.25.

Prof. F. B. Crocker says: "This is a very good elementary treatment of fundamental principles. Extensively and successfully used as a text-book for students beginning the study of electricity. Suited for the general reader, the practical worker, and the engineer not electrical." **537.**

CHEMISTRY.

A SELECTION FROM ITS LITERATURE,

ANNOTATED BY

H. CARRINGTON BOLTON, Ph.D.,

Lecturer on the History of Chemistry, Columbian University, Washington, D. C.

Washington, D. C., June, 1895.

Buckley, Arabella B.

A SHORT HISTORY OF NATURAL SCIENCE, and of the progress of discovery from the time of the Greeks to the present day; for the use of schools and young persons. 5th edition, revised and rearranged. N. Y., Appleton, 1895, 29+509 p., D. $2.

This simply written and admirable little work gives to chemistry its share of space in the history of science. It can be cordially recommended to all who wish to read of the mutual relations of the sciences, and their growth from earliest times. 500.

Cooke, Josiah Parsons.

THE NEW CHEMISTRY. (International Scientific series.) Revised edition. N. Y., Appleton, 1884, 400 p., D. $2.

Written in popular style; aims to develop the general principles of the new chemistry in systematic order; substances and processes are described only so far as necessary to illustrate principles. To enjoy this work fully the reader should know the elements of chemistry. 540.4.

Faraday, Michael.

CHEMICAL HISTORY OF A CANDLE, with a Lecture on Platinum. Delivered before a Juvenile Auditory, 1860-61. Edited by William Crookes. N. Y., Harper, 1874, 224 p., D. 85 c.

In no work on chemistry have the phenomena of combustion, the nature of the atmosphere, and the chemistry of coal-gas been more clearly presented. The work is a little old-fashioned, but its fundamental statements are sound, and the absence of technicalities will always make it charming. 540.4.

Johnston, James F. W.

CHEMISTRY OF COMMON LIFE. New edition revised and enlarged by Arthur Herbert Church. Illus. N. Y., Appleton, 1879, 592 p., D. $2.

Contents: The Air we breathe; the Water we drink; the Soil we cultivate; the Plant we rear; the Bread we eat; the Beef we cook; the Beverages we infuse (teas, coffees, cocoas); the Sweets we extract (grape and cane sugars, manna and milk sugar); the Liquors we ferment (beers, wines, brandies); the Narcotics we indulge in (tobacco, hops, poppy, lettuce, Indian hemp, betel-nut, pepperwort, coca, etc.); the Poisons we select; the Odors we enjoy (volatile oils and fragrant resins); the Smells we dislike (natural and those produced by chemical art); the Colors we admire; what we Breathe and breathe for; the Body we cherish; what, how, and why we Digest; the Circulation of Matter, (a recapitulation).

A popular exposition touching the daily life of man which reveals to the reading public a new world of interest. The book is most attractive in style and thoroughly accurate. 542.

Meyer, Ernst von.

HISTORY OF CHEMISTRY FROM EARLIEST TIMES TO THE PRESENT DAY, being also an introduction to the study of the science. Transl. by George M'Gowan. N. Y., Macmillan, 1891, 556 p., O. $4.50.

An ably written, condensed history, covering the entire period of chemistry, and from a modern standpoint. The progress of the science since Lavoisier is treated particularly fully. This is unqualifiedly the best history of chemistry in the English language. 540.0.

Meyer, Lothar.

OUTLINES OF THEORETICAL CHEMISTRY. Transl. by P. Phillips Bedson and W. Carleton Williams. N. Y., Longmans, 1888, 587 p., O. $2.50.

Presents a summary of the most recent theories of chemical philosophy; it is better adapted for advanced students than for the general reader. A standard work. 540.1.

Muir, M. M. Pattison.

TREATISE ON THE PRINCIPLES OF CHEMISTRY. 2d edition. N. Y., Macmillan, 1884, $4.

A well-written work, abreast of the times, suitable for advanced students. 540.1.

Remsen, Ira.

ELEMENTS OF CHEMISTRY: a Text-Book for Beginners. (American Science series.) N. Y., Holt, 1892, 272 p., D. 80 c.

A rational text-book, comprising something more than mere statements of fact, of experiments, and of rules. So arranged as to help the pupil to think as well as to see, to reason as well as to observe, and to understand why he performed given experiments, and the lessons to be learned from them. The language is not technical, the experiments selected are for the most part simple, and questions connected with experiments will lead students to draw their own inferences. Only about twenty-five pages are given to compounds of carbon, and those wishing to pursue the study further are referred to the following work. 540.1.

INTRODUCTION TO THE STUDY OF THE COMPOUNDS OF CARBON, OR ORGANIC CHEMISTRY. Bost., Heath, 1885, 362 p., D. $1.20.

Without a rival as an introduction to the study of organic chemistry for beginners. *Nature*, an English scientific journal of the highest character, began its review of it with: "This is Chemistry." 547.

Richards, *Mrs.* Ellen H.

CHEMISTRY OF COOKING AND CLEANING. Bost., Estes, 1882, D. 50 c.

An excellent little manual by a woman who knows her subject and sympathizes with her readers. It assumes an elementary knowledge of chemistry. 542.

Venable, F. P.

SHORT HISTORY OF CHEMISTRY. Bost., Heath, 1894, 171 p., D. $1.

Forms a good brief survey of the growth of chemistry from earliest times to the present day. 540.0.

NOTES.

Those wishing fuller information as to the literature of chemistry should consult Prof. H. Carrington Bolton's " Select Bibliography of Chemistry," 1492-1892 (Washington, D. C., Smithsonian Institution, 1893, $1.50). It contains over 12,000 titles of books and periodicals in 24 languages. The author is engaged on a Supplement to be issued in 1896.

The American Chemical Society, a national organization with 850 members at the end of 1894, issues a monthly journal and other publications, all of which are sent free to members. All chemists are eligible for membership; the dues are $5 per annum; no initiation fee. Albert C. Hale, General Secretary, 551 Putnam Ave., Brooklyn, N. Y.

GEOGRAPHY.

Frye, Alexander Everett.

PRIMARY GEOGRAPHY. Illus. Bost., Ginn & Co., 1895, 137 p., D. 75 c.

Appeals to the child's interests, and is suited to his capacity and needs. Begins with home features, makes the earth the whole to which all is related, emphasizes child's own country. Aims to build up in the child's mind an apperceptive series of geographical ideas rich in content.—EDWARD R. SHAW, *Professor of Pedagogy, New York University.* **551.4.**

COMPLETE GEOGRAPHY. Bost., Ginn & Co., 1895, 7+184 p., Q. $1.55.

A book on new lines, written by an educator, and incomparably superior to any geography heretofore issued for school-room use. Begins with typical forms of land and water, gives geological reasons for the formation of shores, plains, valleys, mountains, volcanoes, lakes, seas, etc., and shows their relation to industry and commerce. Bases study of continents upon relief forms. In study of continents and parts of continents, uses maps with few details, which are supplemented at the end of the book by 28 pages of full, clear, and beautiful reference maps. Emphasizes the commercial relations between nations and sections. Very full treatment of industrial regions of the United States. Finely illustrated. Choice, selection, and arrangement of pictures, which are nearly all engraved from photographs, especially to be commended. A work which can be read and studied at home with profit.—EDWARD R. SHAW, *Professor of Pedagogy, New York University.* **551.4.**

Mill, Hugh Robert.

THE REALM OF NATURE: An Outline of Physiography. (University Extension series.) Illus. N. Y., Scribner, 1895, 366 p., D. $1.50.

A most interesting, clearly written, scientific, and condensed account of the structure of the earth, its physical phenomena, and the relations these bear to its life. Brings together the latest knowledge bearing upon the physical geography of the earth. A book of very wide range. Nineteen maps of especial beauty elucidate the text.—EDWARD R. SHAW, *Professor of Pedagogy, New York University.*

GEOLOGY.

A SELECTION FROM ITS LITERATURE:

WITH ANNOTATIONS BY

EDWARD S. BURGESS,

Professor of Natural Science, Normal College, New York.

New York, June, 1895.

"Without demonstration in the field it is impossible to use geology as an educational instrument in a profitable way."—*Nation.*

Dana, James D.

MANUAL OF GEOLOGY. 4th edition. N. Y., Am. Book Co., 1895, 1087 p., O. $5.

The most recent and extensive treatise on North American geology, and on historical geology in general. Devotes less attention to structural geology, but is indispensable to the student who would be up to date in the historical geology of the United States and Canada. Leading American geologists have supplied the results of their recent labors and added vitally to its value. Simple and clear in arrangement and terminology. Adapted to the advanced student. 550.2.

Dawson, *Sir* John William.

GEOLOGICAL HISTORY OF PLANTS. (International Scientific series.) N. Y., Appleton, 1888, 290 p., D. $1.75.

The best brief descriptive work in English on that part of historical geology which relates to fossil vegetation. It is, however, too little illustrated, and gives but little prominence to the evolutionary history of plant life. Represents best the plant-forms of Canadian rocks, omitting many which are of great importance in the United States. Adapted to the fairly advanced student. 580.

HANDBOOK OF GEOLOGY FOR THE USE OF CANADIAN STUDENTS. Montreal, Dawson Bros., 1889, 250 p., D. $3.

The best treatment of Canadian geology; written largely from the author's own investigations; and presenting in clear summary the results of the very active and scholarly work of the Canadian Geological Survey. It is authoritative and definite, and at the same time descriptive and readable. Adapted to teachers and fairly advanced students. 550.

Geikie, *Sir* Archibald.

TEXT-BOOK OF GEOLOGY. 3d edition, revised and enlarged. N. Y., Macmillan, 1893, 1147 p., O. $7.50.

The best book of its kind. Written from a scholarly standpoint; with a comprehensive and masterly view of the subject, applied to the world at large. Compared with Dana's "Manual," it presents a broader view of geology as a whole; especially of structural and of dynamic geology. It excels also in its descriptions of rocks, giving more attention to physical and obvious characteristics. Its disadvantages are that its arrangement is more cumbersome; its terminology less simple and less in accord with American usage; it is designed especially for use in Great Britain, and its illustrations are chiefly British. Dana's much more detailed treatment of historical geology makes his work a necessity, but this is needed as its complement. Adapted to the advanced student. 550.2.

Le Conte, Joseph.

ELEMENTS OF GEOLOGY: a Text-Book for Colleges and for the General Reader. New and enlarged edition. N. Y., Appleton, 1886, $4.

An excellent general work for the student of moderate development. Its strength is its clear treatment of dynamical and structural geology, unencumbered by great detail; its close and systematic paragraphing fitting it for college use; its luminous illustrations. Not up to date, however, in American earlier geology, especially Cambrian, and in western representation of later periods. Gives but scant treatment of general metamorphism, of mountain building, and of European glacial history. 550.2.

Shaler, Nathaniel Southgate.

FIRST BOOK IN GEOLOGY. Bost., D. C. Heath & Co., 1884, 255 p., D. $1.10.

An excellent introduction to geology; chiefly dynamic. Treating the action of the forces which have shaped the earth; considering the formation and history of pebbles, sand, mud and soils; the making of rocks and coal; the work of air and water, volcanoes and earthquakes; the formation of mineral veins and caverns, hills and mountains, valleys and lakes. A brief sketch follows of the fossil contents of the rocks, the appearance of species, and development of organic life. A short description of the most important rocks is added. Simple in statement, flowing and narrative in style. Presupposes no geologic knowledge. Adapted to the beginner or general reader; may be used as a primer for earliest class-work; may be read together with the same author's "Story" or as preliminary to Le Conte's "Elements." 550.7.

THE STORY OF OUR CONTINENT. Bost., Ginn & Co., 1891, 278 p., D. 75 c.

A plain and simple treatment of the physiography and the geological history of North America. Elementary and descriptive in style. Its object is to show how the present and past physical features of the continent have been successively developed. It shows the connection between the geology and the geography of the United States, and the causes which have aided to determine regional and national development. Adapted to the beginner. May serve as introduction to the author's "Nature and Man in America." 550.

NATURE AND MAN IN AMERICA. N. Y., Scribner, 1891, 290 p., D. $1.50.

Eight readable and descriptive chapters on the influence of environment on organic life; the first four show how the "whips of necessity" have driven organisms up and on towards higher planes; the second half treats of the geographic influence on man in America. Gives latest views on the effects of geologic changes, physical conditions, and geographic features, on the successive characteristics of Indians and of colonial settlements, and on the distribution and development of American nationality. In pleasing colloquial style. No illustrations. Adapted to the general reader. May be read as intermediate in scope between the author's "The Story of Our Continent" and "Aspects of the Earth." **550.**

ASPECTS OF THE EARTH: a Popular Account of Some Familiar Geological Phenomena. N. Y., Scribner, 1889, 344 p., D. $2.50.

A more extended series of papers on geologic subjects; presented in attractive and entertaining style, while maintaining scientific accuracy. Separate chapters treat of the Stability of the Earth, Volcanoes, Caverns, Rivers, Winds, Forests, Origin of Soils. Especially interesting from its reducing general geological principles to familiar experience, giving many examples. Illustrations numerous and particularly valuable, because taken from photographs of actual geologic features. Adapted to the fairly advanced student and the general reader. **550.**

Winchell, Alexander.

WALKS AND TALKS IN THE GEOLOGICAL FIELD. Meadville, Pa., Flood & Vincent, 1887, 329 p., O. $1.

A series of interesting talks, addressing children and youth. Describes simple observations, beginning with the home neighborhood, extending to field, lake, stream, and mountain; then glancing at historical geology, the nebular hypothesis, and reviewing cosmical development to the present time. Conversational in style. No illustrations. Adapted to use as reading for beginners. **550.**

METEOROLOGY.

Russell, Thomas, *U. S. Assistant Engineer.*

METEOROLOGY: Weather and Methods of Forecasting, Description of Meteorological Instruments and River Flood Predictions in the U. S. Illus. N. Y., Macmillan, 1895, 277 p., O. $4.

. . . Prof. Russell, having paid especial attention to these matters while in the Weather Bureau, now gives the fullest account of the methods employed that is to be found in our language.—*Nation.* **551.5.**

BOTANY.

A SELECTION FROM ITS LITERATURE,

ANNOTATED BY

D. P. PENHALLOW,

Professor of Botany, McGill University, Montreal.

Montreal, June, 1895.

The comparative fulness of this list of books is due to the conviction that botany furnishes the most attractive gateway to the field of science. It takes the observer out of doors, it appeals to the sense of beauty in an uncommon degree, it tempts to sketching—so that the hand confirms and preserves what is seen by the eye; when the services of insects and birds to flowers and fruits are noticed, the position of botany as a department of natural history is more strongly emphasized.

Under COUNTRY OCCUPATIONS see works on Agriculture, Floriculture and Gardening.

Bailey, W. W.

BOTANICAL COLLECTOR'S HANDBOOK. Illus. Salem, Mass., George A. Bates, 1881, 139 p., $1.50.

A comprehensive handbook for the collection and preservation of plants of all kinds, with useful information as to published works on the floras of different countries, and notes on the principal herbaria of the United States. Adapted to the practical botanist. 580.7.

Bessey, Charles E.

BOTANY: Advanced Course. Revised. Illus. N. Y., Holt, 1892, 611 p., $2.20.

A clear and comprehensive summary of the structure, development, and classification of vegetable organisms. Adapted to the general reader and to the advanced student. 580.7.

Chapman, A. W.

FLORA OF THE SOUTHERN UNITED STATES. 2d edition. N. Y., Am. Book Co., 1884, 698 p., $3.60.

A practical manual, with glossary of terms. A standard work for the recognition of flowering plants and Pteridophytes south of Virginia and Kentucky, and east of the Mississippi River. Adapted to the field botanist in that region. 581.07.

Cooke, M. C.

BRITISH FRESH WATER ALGÆ. Illus. Lond., Williams & Norgate, 1882-84. 2 vols., 329, 130 p., Parts 2-10, 78s.

A standard work for the recognition of the fresh water algæ, with plates in natural colors. Applicable to the determination of the more common algæ of the United States. Adapted to the working algologist. 580.3.

Coulter, J. M.

MANUAL OF THE FLORA OF THE ROCKY MOUNTAINS. N. Y., Am. Book Co., 1885, 452+28 p., $1.62.

A practical manual with glossary of terms. The standard work for the recognition of Phanerogams and Pteridophytes within the Rocky Mountain region, from the British boundary to New Mexico. Adapted to the field botanist within that region. 581.07.

Dana, *Mrs.* William Starr.

HOW TO KNOW THE WILD FLOWERS. New edition, revised and enlarged. Illus. N. Y., Scribner, 1895, 372 p., D. $1.75.

Gives directions for use of the book and collection of plants; chapters on fertilization of flowers, explanation of terms used and discussion of some of the most important plant families. Common and scientific names of plants, together with full description and popular account of each species. Illustrations accurate and excellent. Plants grouped by color of flowers, without attempt at scientific classification. Aims at popularizing the knowledge of plants. Technical terms few. One of the best works of the kind extant. Well adapted to the lover of wild flowers who wishes to become better acquainted with them without special training. 580.

Darwin, Charles.

FERTILIZATION OF ORCHIDS BY INSECTS. 2d edition. Illus. N. Y., Appleton, 1884, 300 p., D. $1.75.

One of the most important contributions to our knowledge of the relations between insects and plants, based upon extended personal observation. Adapted to the general reader and to the special student. 581.10.

INSECTIVOROUS PLANTS. Illus. N. Y., Appleton, 1875, 462 p., D. $2.

The best general work on a most attractive and remarkable phase of plant life, derived from personal observation. Adapted to the general reader and the special student. 580.

POWER OF MOVEMENT IN PLANTS. Illus. N. Y., Appleton, 1880, 592 p., D. $2.

A philosophical exposition of the movements manifested by plants, as derived from personal observation. Adapted to the general reader and to the special student. 581.1.

Dawson, *Sir* John William.

GEOLOGICAL HISTORY OF PLANTS. (International Scientific series.) Illus. N. Y., Appleton, 1888, 290 p., $1.75.

A clear, authoritative, and popular digest of the relations of plant life to the various geological epochs. Adapted to the general reader and advanced student. **580.**

De Bary, A.

COMPARATIVE ANATOMY OF THE VEGETATIVE ORGANS OF THE PHANEROGAMS AND FERNS. Transl. from the German. Illus. Oxford, Clarendon Press, 1884, 659 p., O. 22s. 6d.

The standard authority on the anatomy of the higher plants. Adapted to advanced and special students. **581.1.**

COMPARATIVE MORPHOLOGY AND BIOLOGY OF THE FUNGI, MYCETOZOA, AND BACTERIA. Transl. from the German. Illus. Oxford, Clarendon Press, 1887, 525 p., O. 22s. 6d.

The best general summary. Adapted to the advanced and special student. **581.4.**

De Candolle, Alphonse.

ORIGIN OF CULTIVATED PLANTS. (International Scientific series.) N. Y., Appleton, 1884, 468 p., D. $2.

The standard authority on the origin of cultivated plants. Adapted to the general reader. **580.**

Dyer, T. F. Thiselton.

FOLK-LORE OF PLANTS. N. Y., Appleton, 1889, 328 p., D. $1.50.

An admirable, concise, and systematic summary, with illustrative cases. Adapted to the general reader. **398.**

Goebel, K.

OUTLINES OF CLASSIFICATION AND SPECIAL MORPHOLOGY. Transl. from the German and revised. Illus. N. Y., Macmillan, 1887, 515 p., O. $5.25.

An advanced text-book, giving a comprehensive summary of the morphology of plants based on modern lines of research. Adapted to the advanced student and general reader. **580.1.**

Goodale, George L.

PHYSIOLOGICAL BOTANY. (Gray's Series of Text Books, II.) Illus. N. Y., Am. Book Co., 1888, 478+36 p., D. $2.

One of the best works on the minute anatomy and physiology of plants, with directions for the practical student. Clear, concise, comprehensive. Adapted to advanced students and to the general reader. **581.1.**

WILD FLOWERS OF AMERICA. 51 colored plates by Isaac Sprague. Bost., Bradlee Whidden, 1886, 210 p., Q. $7.50.

The best popular work on the wild flowers of America. Accurate illustrations in color from nature. Text scientific and trustworthy. Adapted to the general student and to every lover of flowers. **581.07.**

Gray, Asa.

SCHOOL AND FIELD BOOK OF BOTANY. Revised by L. H. Bailey. Illus. N. Y., Am. Book Co., 1895, 226, 519 p., D. $1.80.

Part I.—A very useful summary of the structure and classification of plants, with a full glossary of terms. Adapted to beginners.

Part II.—A manual for the recognition of the more widely known introduced and cultivated plants. Adapted to gardeners and to field botanists as a companion to Gray's "Manual." **580.2.**

MANUAL OF THE BOTANY OF THE NORTHERN UNITED STATES. 6th edition. Illus. N. Y., Am. Book Co., 1760 p., D. $2.

The standard manual for the recognition of Phanerogams, Pteridophytes, and Hepaticæ east of the Mississippi River and north of North Carolina and Tennessee, with a glossary of terms. Adapted to the field botanist within that region. **581.97.**

STRUCTURAL BOTANY. 6th edition. Illus. N. Y., Am. Book Co., 1880, 442 p., D. $2.

The leading text-book on the general morphology of the phanerogams. It contains, also, an important outline of the history and principles of classification. Adapted to the general reader and to the students of high schools. **581.4.**

Hardinge, E. M.

WITH THE WILD FLOWERS. Illus. N. Y., Baker & Taylor Co., 1894, 271 p., S. $1.

A pleasantly written book, containing many interesting facts relative to plant life. Devoid of systematic treatment, style popular, technical terms few. Adapted as a reader to beginners, but of no value for the recognition of plants. **580.**

Mathews, F. Schuyler.

FAMILIAR FLOWERS OF THE FIELD AND GARDEN. Illus. N. Y., Appleton, 1895, 308 p., D. $1.75.

A popular description of wild flowers arranged in chronological sequence, illustrated by well-drawn figures; with a systematical index giving family, color, locality, environment, and date of blooming. Scientific and common names are given; technical terms few. Aims at popularizing the study of plants. Adapted to stimulate a wider knowledge of the plants about us, but of limited value for the recognition of species. Chiefly useful for those who have little time or inclination for scientific study. **580.**

Miller, Ellen, *and* Whiting, Margaret Christine.

WILD FLOWERS OF THE NORTHEASTERN STATES: Drawn and Described from Life. N. Y., Putnam, 1895, 11+622 p., Q. $4.50.

Comprises 308 flowers, given in large and free illustrations. The families are arranged in the order laid down in Gray's "Manual." The descriptions are given in simple and clear language. **580.**

Müller, Hermann.

FERTILIZATION OF FLOWERS. Illus. Transl. from the German by D'Arcy W. Thompson; with preface by Charles Darwin. Lond., Macmillan, 1883, 669 p., O. 21s.

A comprehensive and authoritative discussion of the various external agencies by which fecundation in plants is accomplished. Adapted to the advanced student and the general reader. **581.10.**

Newell, Jane H.

OUTLINES OF LESSONS IN BOTANY. Bost., Ginn & Co., 1893. Part I., From Seed to Leaf. Illus. 150 p., 50 c. Part II., Flower and Fruit. Illus. 393 p., 80 c.

A concise, clear, and attractive presentation of some of the more prominent facts in the structure and growth of familiar plants. Emphasizes the importance of study in the field. Treatment devoid of excessive technicalities. Full glossary of terms. Specially adapted to the young either for special reading or general study. **580.7.**

A READER IN BOTANY. Bost., Ginn & Co., 1893. Part I., From Seed to Leaf. Illus. 209 p., 60 c. Part II., Flower and Fruit. Illus. 179 p., 60 c.

An admirable compilation of some of the more salient features in the structure and economy of plant life. Specially adapted as readers for young pupils, to whom this and the preceding book would bring a new interest in the study of plant life. **580.7.**

Penhallow, D. P.

BOTANICAL COLLECTOR'S GUIDE. Illus. Montreal, E. M. Renouf, 1891, 125 p., 75 c.

A handy pocket guide to the collection and preservation of Phanerogams and Pteridophytes, with samples of labels, drying and mounting paper, etc. Emphasizes the need of practical study and observation in the field. Adapted to beginners and pupils of high schools. **580.7.**

Sachs, Julius von.
History of Botany (1530-1860). Transl. from the German and revised. N. Y., Macmillan, 1890, 563 p., O. $2.50.

The most philosophical and trustworthy work on the history of botanical science. Adapted to the general reader and advanced student. **580.0.**

Smith, John.
Dictionary of Economic Plants. N. Y., Macmillan, 1882, 457 p., O. $3.50.

A useful compendium of the popular names of plants which supply the natural and acquired wants of man in all matters of domestic and general economy; their history, products, and uses. Adapted to the general student. **580.3.**

Spaulding, Volney M.
Introduction to Botany. Bost., D. C. Heath & Co., 1893, 246 p., D. 80 c.

A convenient, reliable, and useful guide to the study of plants in their broader botanical aspects. Contains directions to student and teacher, list of reference works, and specifications for a simple laboratory outfit. A book to arouse interest and enthusiasm. Admirably adapted to grammar schools and to students working independently, but for the latter no wholly satisfactory work can be named, as much must be left to the discretion and intelligence of properly qualified teachers. **580.7.**

Trouessart, E. L.
Microbes, Ferments, and Moulds. (International Scientific series.) Illus. N. Y., Appleton, 1886, 314 p., D. $1.50.

The best popular summary concerning some of the most important forms of plant life. Adapted to the general student. **580.0.**

Vines, S. H.
Lectures on the Physiology of Plants. Illus. N. Y., Macmillan, 1886, 710 p., $5.

A clear and reliable exposition of the functions of plants. Adapted to the advanced student and general reader. **581.1**

Weed, Clarence Moores.
Ten New England Blossoms and Their Insect Visitors. Illus. Bost., Houghton, 1895, 8+142 p., D. $1.25.

The ten blossoms, familiar also in Canada, are the glaucous willow, mayflower, spring beauty, purple trillium, jack-in-the-pulpit, showy orchis, pink lady's-slipper (fringed polygala, Canada lily, and common thistle. A charming book for children, richly illustrated. It brings young observers to the ground common to the studies of flowers and of insects. **581.16**

NATURAL HISTORY AND HUMAN EVOLUTION.

A SELECTION FROM THEIR LITERATURE,

ANNOTATED BY

OLIVE THORNE MILLER,

Author of "Bird Ways," "In Nesting Time," etc.

Brooklyn, N. Y., June, 1895.

Agassiz, Elizabeth C. *and* **Alexander.**
SEA SIDE STUDIES IN NATURAL HISTORY. Illus. Bost., Houghton, $3.
A treatise on the marine creatures common to our coast, more particularly that of Massachusetts Bay. Too scientific for the beginner, but useful to more advanced students as a manual. **500.7.**

Agassiz, Louis.
METHODS OF STUDY IN NATURAL HISTORY. Bost., Houghton, $1.50.
A charming work in Agassiz's simple and attractive style, untechnical in manner, and broadening and inspiring to the reader. It aims to give hints to young students in the best method of arriving at scientific truth, and includes a sketch of the history of Science. It was written as a protest against the Darwinian theory, and naturally is not brought down to date. **500.7.**

Ballard, Harlan H.
THREE KINGDOMS: Handbook of the Agassiz Association. N. Y., Writers' Pub. Co., 75 c.
An outgrowth of the Agassiz Association, being answers to the questions asked for years by students of Natural History throughout the country. Organizing a society, conducting a meeting, starting a museum, collecting and preserving plants, seaweed, insects, birds and eggs, minerals, etc., are considered. A list of recommended books is given. At the end of this department see note on Agassiz Association. **590.7.**

Bamford, Mary A.
UP AND DOWN THE BROOKS. Illus. (Riverside library for young people.) Bost., Houghton, 250 p., S. 75 c.
An interesting and trustworthy introduction to the study of insect life in and about fresh-water streams. **500.7.**

Bates, Henry W.
A NATURALIST ON THE RIVER AMAZONS. Bost., Roberts, $2.50. With memoir of the author by Edward Clodd. N. Y., Appleton, $5.
A record of personal adventures, combined with the observations of a trained student on the great river, the country through which it flows, and the marvels of insect and animal life which abound there. It is written in clear and simple style ; is interesting to the general reader as well as to the naturalist. It has long been a favorite. **590.**

Birds. *See* Ballard, Burroughs, Coues, Gibson, Grant, Keyser, Merriam, Miller, Thompson, Torrey, Treat, Willcox, Wright.

Buckley, Arabella C.
WINNERS IN LIFE'S RACE, OR THE GREAT BACK-BONE FAMILY. Illus. N. Y., Appleton, $1.50.
A popular treatise on the early history of mammals, intended to introduce and interest the reader in the study of Natural History. Graphically written and good for beginners. **590.**

Burroughs, John.
WAKE ROBIN. WINTER SUNSHINE. FRESH FIELDS. LOCUSTS AND WILD HONEY. PEPACTON. SIGNS AND SEASONS. RIVERBY. Bost., Houghton, 7 vols., $1.25 each.
Essays on Nature and Bird life, extending over many years, in Mr. Burroughs' well-known delightful style. **590.**

Chapman, Frank M.
HANDBOOK OF THE BIRDS OF EASTERN NORTH AMERICA. N. Y., Appleton, 1895, 421 p., D. $3.
An exhaustive manual of the five hundred species of birds to be found in the area designated. Useful to the student of Ornithology studying the bird in the hand, as well as to the bird-lover who wishes to "name the birds without a gun." **508.2.**

Clodd, Edward.
A PRIMER OF EVOLUTION. N. Y., Longmans, 1895, 185 p., D. 75 c.
An abridgment of the author's "Story of Creation," a condensed statement, and a good general view of the Theory of Evolution, beginning with elements or atoms, and proceeding systematically to social evolution. Written in remarkably clear, simple, and attractive style, easily understood by the unscientific reader, and an excellent introduction to the more elaborate works on the subject. **575.**

Comstock, John Henry, *and* **Comstock, Anna Botsford.**
MANUAL FOR THE STUDY OF INSECTS. Ithaca, N. Y., Comstock Pub. Co., 1895, 700 p., $3.75.
A general work on entomology, with analytical keys to the orders and families ; devoted especially to insects, their lives and transformations ; describing the common species, and very fully illustrated. Written in clear, untechnical language, interesting to the general reader. A feature helpful to the beginner is the pronunciation of the Latin names. **505.7.**

Coues, Elliot.
KEY TO NORTH AMERICAN BIRDS. 4th revised edition. Illus. Bost., Estes, $7.50.
A standard key to all the birds of North America. Valuable as a manual of reference. Written in Dr. Coues' delightful, untechnical style, and fully illustrated. **508 2.**

Darwin, Charles.

DESCENT OF MAN AND SELECTION IN RELATION TO SEX. N. Y., Appleton, $3.

An exposition of the theory that man is descended from ape-like animals, with arguments and evidences in its favor. **573.2**

ORIGIN OF SPECIES. Revised, with the latest additions and corrections. N. Y., Appleton, 1 vol., $2; 2 vols., large print, $4.

This work is the corner-stone of the theory of evolution as extended to organic life. **575.8**

Drummond, Henry.

THE ASCENT OF MAN. N. Y., James Pott & Co., 1894, 9+346 p., D. $2.

An able and interesting work surveying the whole process of human evolution. The author lays stress on the struggle for the life of others which, beginning in motherhood, has enormously qualified the struggle for self emphasized by Darwin. **573.2**

Evolution, Human. *See* Clodd, Darwin, Drummond, Hartmann, Morgan, Romanes, Wallace, Weismann. For **Evolution in General,** *see* under PHILOSOPHY IN GENERAL, Collins, Fiske, and Spencer.

Fishes. *See* Agassiz, Elizabeth C., and Goode, G. B.

Gibson, William Hamilton.

SHARP EYES. N. Y., Harper, 1892, 322 p., O. $5.

Published first as chapters in Harper's *Young People*, and well calculated to interest young persons in insect life. Written in simple style and exquisitely illustrated by the author. **500.4**

Goode, G. Brown.

AMERICAN FISHES. Illus. N. Y., Standard Book Co., 1889, 12+496 p., O. $5.

A popular and interesting treatise upon the game and food fishes, with especial reference to their habits and the methods of capturing them. Author is assistant secretary of the Smithsonian Institution, Washington, D. C. **507**

Grant, John B.

OUR COMMON BIRDS AND HOW TO KNOW THEM. Illus. N. Y., Scribner, 1891, 216 p., T. $1.50.

Helpful to beginners in the study of birds. The color key is useful, but the plates from mounted birds are not very accurate. It has a calendar of dates at which birds may be expected. **508.2**

Hartmann, Robert.

ANTHROPOID APES. (International Scientific series.) N. Y., Appleton, 1886, 325 p., D. $1.75.

Beginning with a brief history of our acquaintance with the apes, the author proceeds to give a popular account of their structure, varieties, and distribution, devoting a chapter to their life in captivity, and another to their position in the Zoological System. **500.8**

Hudson, C. H.

THE NATURALIST IN LA PLATA. Illus. N. Y., Appleton, 1892, 388 p., D. $4.

Charmingly written and trustworthy accounts of some of the little-known birds, mammals, and insects of Patagonia, with suggestive essays on the death-feigning instinct and other subjects of interest. Untechnical and attractive to the general reader as well as to the specialist. **500**

Insects. *See* Ballard, Bamford, Comstock, Lubbock, Manton, McCook, Packard, Treat.

Keyser, Leander S.

BIRD-DOM. Bost., Lothrop, 1891, 226 p., D. $1.

Popularly written accounts of bird life in Ohio, intended particularly to interest young persons in the study, and full of fresh observations and suggestions. Will serve for all Middle Western States in its observations; written in pleasing style. **508.2**

Lubbock, Sir John.

ANTS, BEES, AND WASPS. (International Scientific series.) N. Y., Appleton, 1882, 448 p., D. $2.

A pleasantly written record of experiments with the insects named during a period of ten years. Treating of their habits and manners, their relations to plants, to other animals, to their relatives, their power of communication, their senses, and their general intelligence. **505.7**

Manton, W. P.

INSECTS: HOW TO CATCH AND HOW TO PREPARE THEM FOR THE CABINET. Bost., Lee & Shepard, 1881, 32 p., D. 50 c.

Full of capital directions and hints, in simple and easily understood language. No directions for identification or classifying. It is eminently practical, and requires no expensive outfit. **505.7**

McCook, Henry C.

TENANTS OF AN OLD FARM. Illus. N. Y., Fords, 1886, 460 p., D. $1.50.

A pleasantly written work, connected by a thread of story, on insect life and manners, particularly spiders, on which Dr. McCook is a well-known authority. Fully illustrated, and in addition supplied with grotesque cuts by Dan Beard, which do not enhance its value, but do add to its fun. **505.4**

Merriam, Florence A.

BIRDS THROUGH AN OPERA GLASS. (Riverside library for young people.) Bost., Houghton, 1889, 223 p., S. 75 c.

An introduction to the study of ornithology. Not too scientific for the beginner, yet giving some idea of classification. Almost wholly original. **508.2**

Miller, Olive Thorne.

BIRD WAYS. IN NESTING TIME. LITTLE BROTHERS OF THE AIR. A BIRD LOVER IN THE WEST. Bost., Houghton, 4 vols., $1.25 each.

Untechnical but trustworthy studies of bird life, both in freedom and captivity. Original observations. **508.2**

OUR HOME PETS: How to Keep Them Well and Happy. N. Y., Harper, $1.25.

A practical treatise on the selection and care of pets, especially birds, but embracing also dogs, cats, and nearly all our more common captives. **500**

Morgan, C. Lloyd.

ANIMAL LIFE AND INTELLIGENCE. Illus. Bost., Ginn, 1891, 512 p., D. $4.

Contents: The Nature of Animal Life. The Process of Life. Reproduction and Development. Variation and Natural Selection. Heredity and the Origin of Variations. Organic Evolution. The Senses of Animals. Mental Processes in Man. Mental Processes in Animals: Their Powers of Perception and Intelligence. The Feelings of Animals: Their Appetences and Emotions. Animal Activities: Habit and Instinct. Mental Evolution.

A work for the advanced student, being a special study of the mental processes of the lower animals, the first part a careful consideration of organic evolution. It is written in a clear style, intended for, and in general easily comprehended by, the ordinarily intelligent reader. **591.5**

Morse, Edward S.

FIRST BOOK OF ZOOLOGY. N. Y., Am. Book Co., 188 p., D. 87 c.

Prepared for pupils wishing to gain a general knowledge of the structure, habits, and modes of growth of lower animals, such as snails, insects, spiders, crustaceans, worms, etc. Directions are given for collecting and preserving specimens, for observing habits, etc. It treats of American forms only, and is fully illustrated. **590.**

Nicholson, H. Alleyne.

MANUAL OF ZOOLOGY. N. Y., Appleton, 1880, 571 p., O. $2.50.

An exhaustive treatise on the whole animal kingdom, from the protozoa to man. It is technical in treatment, but supplied with a glossary. Intended for advanced students, and perfectly trustworthy, but, in these days of rapid advance in science, perhaps not fully up to date. **590.**

Packard, A. S., *Jr.*

ENTOMOLOGY FOR BEGINNERS. 3d edition revised. N. Y., Holt, 1888, $1.40.

Popularly written for beginners and useful to advanced students. Contains directions for collecting, preserving, forming cabinets, mounting for the microscope, preparing insects for study, and a guide to the books describing species. **505.7.**

Romanes, George John.

ANIMAL INTELLIGENCE. (International Scientific series.) N. Y., Appleton, 1883, 520 p., $1.75.

A popularly written treatise on the evidences of intelligence in animals. Its scope includes insects, fish, reptiles, birds, and mammals; numerous interesting anecdotes are given in proof of the author's position. **501.5.**

DARWIN AND AFTER DARWIN: I. The Darwinian Theory. Illus. Chic., Open Court Pub. Co., 1892, 450 p., D. $2.

The best brief exposition of Darwinism, carefully prepared for popular use by the assumption of perfect ignorance of Natural Science on the part of the reader. A sequel, " Post-Darwinian Questions," edited by Prof. C. Lloyd Morgan, same pub'ishers, $1.50.

EXAMINATION OF WEISMANNISM. Chic., Open Court Pub. Co., 1893, 209 p., D. $1.

In this volume Romanes treats of Weismann's theories, leaving the assumption of non-transmissibility of acquired characters, upon which they are based, for consideration in a future (and unwritten) volume. See Weismann's " Essays Upon Heredity." **575.**

Stokes, Alfred C., *M.D.*

MICROSCOPY FOR BEGINNERS. N. Y., Harper, 1887, 308 p., D. $1.50.

This book aims to stimulate the interest of the beginner by helping him to learn the names of some of the common fresh-water microscopical organisms, both animal and vegetable. It is simple and direct in method, and the subject is made very attractive. The keys for identification are excellent, and the glossary explains the technical terms unavoidably employed. Probably the best book of its kind. **578.**

Thompson, Maurice.

BYWAYS AND BIRD-NOTES. N. Y., John B. Alden, 1885, 179 p., S. 75 c.

Original and delightfully recounted observations on birds, especially those of the Southern States. **598.2.**

Thomson, T. Arthur.

STUDY OF ANIMAL LIFE. (University series.) N. Y., Scribner, 1892, $1.50.

One of the manuals prepared for the University Extension work. It teaches the natural method of study, first interesting the student in the object, the animal in its every-day life and natural surroundings, thence leading to the study of its internal activities, its structure, and lastly to the theories of animal life. The subject is simply and popularly presented in an inspiring way. **500 7.**

Thoreau, Henry D.

WALDEN; OR, LIFE IN THE WOODS. Bost., Houghton, 357 p., O. $1.50.

A well known, but always interesting story of the author's attempt to solve the problem of simple living by building and occupying a small house in the woods, with many keen observations on animals, plants, and birds.

Thoreau's Works, 11 vols., are published by Houghton, Boston, $1.50 each. They include " A Week on the Concord and Merrimac Rivers," " The Maine Woods," " Cape Cod," and " Excursions." **590.**

Torrey, Bradford.

BIRDS IN THE BUSH. THE RAMBLER'S LEASE. THE FOOT-PATH WAY. Bost., Houghton, 3 vols., $1.25 each.

Chiefly studies of birds in rambles in various parts of New England. They are among the best literature concerning birds. **598.2.**

Treat, *Mrs.* **Mary.**

HOME STUDIES IN NATURE. Illus. N. Y., Harper, 253 p., D. $1.50.

Original studies in bird, insect, and plant life. Part I. is observations on birds; Part II., the habits of insects, especially the burrowing spiders; Part III., plants that consume animals, of which author has made close study; Part IV., flowering plants. **590.**

Wallace, Alfred Russel.

CONTRIBUTIONS TO THE THEORY OF NATURAL SELECTION, TROPICAL NATURE, and other essays. N. Y., Macmillan, $1.75.

Essays on descriptive and theoretical biology in pleasing and popular style. The author was co-discoverer with Charles Darwin of the law of natural selection. He here sets forth original observations and arguments in its support. **575.4.**

DARWINISM. Illus. N. Y., Macmillan, 1890, 14+494 p., D. $1.75.

An exposition of the theory of Natural Selection, bringing the subject down to 1889, in Mr. Wallace's well-known lucid and pleasing style. Objections to Darwinism are discussed with the result that Mr. Wallace deems it in the main confirmed by thirty years' observation and criticism. **575.**

Weismann, D. Auguste.

ESSAYS UPON HEREDITY AND KINDRED BIOLOGICAL PROBLEMS. N. Y., Macmillan, 1889. Vol. I., 448 p., $2; Vol. II., 1892, 222 p., $1.30.

These volumes set forth Weismann's theories based upon the idea that there can be no inheritance of characters acquired by the individual. See Romanes' " Examination of Weismannism." **575.**

Willcox, M. A.

POCKET GUIDE TO THE COMMON LAND BIRDS OF NEW ENGLAND. Bost., Lee & S., 1895, 158 p., D. 60 c.

Prepared by Prof. Willcox for her students in Wellesley College. Gives a simple and very easily mastered color key for the identification of ninety of the most common birds of New England—which are those of the Middle States as well—and a short, untechnical account of each. A valuable introduction to the study of birds. **598.2.**

Wright, Mabel Osgood.

BIRDCRAFT. N. Y., Macmillan, 1895. 315 p., D. $3.

An excellent, untechnical manual for the use of persons wishing to learn the names and something of the habits of birds. It treats in a charming manner of two hundred of the most common species, and identification is made simple by a color key to the species. **598.2.**

NOTES.

The Agassiz Association, Pittsfield, Mass., was founded in 1875 by its present president, Harlan H. Ballard. Its purpose is to encourage the personal observation of Nature, and to stimulate and direct that sort of original scientific study pursued by Louis Agassiz. Its local branches, or "chapters," collect the minerals, plants, or animals of their immediate neighborhood, learn what they can regarding their collections, or study together some branch of science. There are family and school chapters, and chapters of young or of adult persons only. Entrance fee for a chapter, $1. Individuals can join the Association as Corresponding Members: entrance fee, 50c. The Association publishes "Three Kingdoms," mentioned in foregoing list; "The World of Matter: a Guide to the Study of Chemistry and Mineralogy," by Harlan H. Ballard, $1; also *The Observer*, its official journal, $1 a year.

The National Science Club for Women, Mrs. Laura O. Talbott, General Secretary, 927 P St., Washington, D. C., has a membership throughout the United States. Its sections, each with a chairman, include Archæology, Ornithology, Ichthyology, Psychology, Botany, Geology, Mineralogy, Astronomy, Meteorology, Forestry, Microscopy, Hygiene, Medical Science, Economics. Fee for active membership, $1 annually.

ANTHROPOLOGY.

Clodd, Edward.

THE STORY OF PRIMITIVE MAN. (Library of useful stories.) Illus. N. Y., Appleton, 1895, 184 p., S. 40 c.

A good primer, in simple language. 572.

Mason, Otis Tufton.

WOMAN'S SHARE IN PRIMITIVE CULTURE. Illus. (Anthropological series, edited by Prof. Frederick Starr, University of Chicago.) N. Y., Appleton, 1894, 9 + 295 p., D. $1.75.

Written in exemplification of the fact that the beginnings of all the great industrial arts are due to woman. . . . It was the gradual pressure of her insistence upon the value of the product of her first planted food-grains which turned mankind from the nomadic savage into the settled tiller of the soil. Only after the necessity of warfare had grown less urgent . . . did the arts of peace become the province of men. . . . The more than equal share played by woman in the invention and spread of language has not been elsewhere set forth with so much clearness.—*Nation.*

Author is Curator of the Department of Ethnology, National Museum, Washington, D. C. 572.

Tylor, Edward B.

ANTHROPOLOGY: an Introduction to the Study of Man and Civilization. Illus. (International Scientific series.) N. Y., D. Appleton & Co., 1891, xv. + 448 p., D. $2.

Much the best introductory work. In clear and simple language prehistoric man is described, and his first steps toward civilization as a maker and user of tools, as the discoverer of fire, are traced. Language, in its successive stages of sign-making, gesture, and articulate speech, is next passed under review. Writing as gradually mastered is sketched. The arts of life and the sciences are outlined from their beginnings. Chapters on the spirit-world, the relations of history and mythology, and society close the work. For fuller treatment see this author's "Primitive Culture" (N. Y., Holt, 1889, 2 vols., $7), and Sir John Lubbock's "Origin of Civilization and the Primitive Condition of Man" (N. Y., Appleton, $5). Mr. Tylor is president of the Anthropological Society of England. 572.

PSYCHOLOGY.

A SELECTION FROM ITS LITERATURE, WITH NOTES, BY

E. W. SCRIPTURE, Ph.D. (Leipzig),
Director of the Yale Psychological Laboratory.

New Haven, Conn., July, 1895.

Holmes, Oliver Wendell.

MECHANISM IN THOUGHT AND MORALS. In Vol. VIII. ("Pages from an old volume of life," p. 260.) Riverside Edition of Holmes' Works. Bost., Houghton, $1.50.

    Written in charming style twenty-five years ago, this may still serve as an introduction, from the literary side, to the new psychology.   150.

James, William.

PSYCHOLOGY: Briefer Course. N. Y., Holt, 1892, 13+478 p., D. $2.

    Based on Prof. James's "Principles of Psychology" (see note thereon). About two-fifths of this book are either new or rewritten. Omits the polemics, history, and pure speculation of the advanced work. Directly available for the class-room or the general reader who has some elementary knowledge of the subject.   150.

PRINCIPLES OF PSYCHOLOGY: Advanced Course. N. Y., Holt, 2 vols., 10+689, 6+704 p., O. $6.

    A brilliant and suggestive work. Author is not an experimental psychologist. As a whole, the volumes are for the advanced student, but the chapters on "Habit" and "Memory" can be enjoyed by every reader. See note on Prof. James's "Briefer Course."   150.

Ladd, George Trumbull.

PRIMER OF PSYCHOLOGY. N. Y., Scribner, 1894, 15+224 p., D. $1.

    A very pleasant and readable account of the fundamental problems of psychology.   150.

Morgan, C. Lloyd.

INTRODUCTION TO COMPARATIVE PSYCHOLOGY. N. Y., Scribner, 1894, 14+382 p., D. $1.25.

    Interesting account of observations on acts of animals. The facts related are subjected to critical examination, an advance over previous books on the same subject. Compare with Wundt.   150.

Preyer, W.

MENTAL DEVELOPMENT IN THE CHILD. N. Y., Appleton, 1894, 170 p., D. $1.

    A book that should be read by all mothers, kindergartners, and primary teachers. The best introduction to the important subject of child-study. Traces the development of the senses in the order of their unfolding, the growth of the notions of space, time, and causality, the advent of language, the development of self-consciousness. The book has a valuable introduction by Dr. Wm. T. Harris. Prof. Preyer can be regarded as the founder of "Child-Study."   150.

Ribot, Th.

GERMAN PSYCHOLOGY OF TO-DAY, with introduction by James McCosh, D.D. N. Y., Scribner, 1886, $2.

    A translation by Prof. J. M. Baldwin of a well-known French work. Ribot is one of the best friends of the new, or experimental, psychology, although he makes the mistake of confusing it with physiology of the brain. The book contains an excellent account of the achievements of Herbart, Fechner, and Wundt.   150.

Sanford, Edmund C.

COURSE IN EXPERIMENTAL PSYCHOLOGY. Bost., Heath, 1894, 183 p., D. 90 c.

    Very elementary set of experiments, which can be performed by everybody, based upon work in the laboratory of Clark University, Worcester, Mass. Only a part of the first section (on the senses) yet published; Part II. in press (July, 1895).   150.

Scripture, E. W.

THINKING, FEELING, DOING. Meadville, Pa., Flood & Vincent, Chautauqua Century Press, 1895, 304 p., D. $1.50.

    Elementary work, first book in the English language on the new psychology, based exclusively on experiment. No long words. Special attention to practical applications in every-day life. Copiously illustrated.   150.

Tracy, Frederick.

PSYCHOLOGY OF CHILDHOOD. Bost., Heath, 1895, 183 p., D. 90 c.

    A clear account of all that has been done by others in this new field of psychology, so that the work is a useful bibliography, while it records some important original observations, especially on the evolution of the faculty of speech. Treats of infancy rather than childhood.   150.

Wundt, William.

HUMAN AND ANIMAL PSYCHOLOGY. N. Y., Macmillan, 1892, 454 p., O. $4.

    Prof. Wundt, of the University of Leipzig, is the greatest psychologist of the age; founder of the first psychological laboratory. Gives in this book a general view of psychology and its methods, with brief accounts of the main lines of experiment and their results. Complete and clear treatment of all the fundamental problems of the science. Although the translation uses unnecessarily long words, this is the best handbook on the subject in the English language.   150.

ECONOMIC, SOCIAL AND POLITICAL SCIENCE.

A SELECTION FROM ITS LITERATURE BY

GEORGE ILES.

New York, July, 1895.

For a full bibliography, published in 1891, see "The Reader's Guide in Economic, Social and Political Science." Edited by R. R. Bowker and George Iles. N. Y., G. P. Putnam's Sons, cloth, $1; paper, 50 c.

POLITICAL ECONOMY: GENERAL.

Walker, Francis Amasa.

POLITICAL ECONOMY: Briefer Course. N. Y., Holt, 1892, 8+415 p., D. $1.50.

Prof. E. R. A. Seligman, of Columbia College, says: "A condensation of the author's 'Advanced Course.' The best introduction to political economy in the English language." 330.1.

POLITICAL ECONOMY: Advanced Course. N. Y., Holt, 1890, 537 p., O. $2.50.

Prof. E. R. A. Seligman, of Columbia College, says: "General Walker is the acknowledged head of the American economists. Eminently clear and logical, suggestive and stimulating. Advances new theories of distribution and makes a break with the older doctrines. This work is accepted as a text-book in England." 330.1.

LAND AND RENT.

George, Henry.

PROGRESS AND POVERTY. N. Y., Henry George, $1.

The author's proposal of a "single tax" equal to ground-rent has called forth world wide discussion. For criticism see last chapter John Rae's "Contemporary Socialism" (N. Y., Scribner, $2.50). 333.

Walker, Francis A.

LAND AND ITS RENT. Bost., Little, Brown & Co., 1883, 229 p., S. 75 c.

Reviews the doctrines of Carey, Bastiat, Mill, Leroy, Beaulieu, and George as to rent. The best American book on the subject from the conservative standpoint. 333.

CAPITAL AND LABOR.

Atkinson, Edward.

THE INDUSTRIAL PROGRESS OF THE NATION: Consumption limited, Production unlimited. N. Y., Putnam, 1890, 395 p., O. $2.50.

Contents: The Distribution of Products; The Food Question; The Relative Strength and Weakness of Nations; What Shall be Taxed; What Shall be Exempt; A Single Tax on Land; Slow-burning Construction. Timely themes treated in a masterly and interesting way. 330.4.

Dexter, Seymour.

CO-OPERATIVE SAVINGS AND LOAN ASSOCIATIONS. N. Y., Appleton, 1889, 300 p., D. $1.25.

Clear and full description of typical forms of Building and Loan Associations, Mutual Savings and Loan Associations, and Co-op-rative Banks Gives history of their growth in the United States, discussion of the advantages of different forms, and description of mode of organization under New York law. 334.1.

Ely, Richard T.

THE LABOR MOVEMENT IN AMERICA. N. Y., T. Y. Crowell & Co., 1886, 373 p., D. $1.50.

A history which includes the platforms of the principal labor organizations. 331.87.

Gilman, Nicholas Paine.

PROFIT-SHARING BETWEEN EMPLOYER AND EMPLOYEE. Bost., Houghton, 1889, 460 p., O. $1.75.

The one comprehensive book on this subject. Mr. Gilman edits a small quarterly, "Employer and Employed," published for the Association for the Promotion of Profit-Sharing by Geo. H. Ellis, 141 Franklin St., Boston, Mass., 40 c a year. 334.6.

Gladden, Washington.

TOOLS AND THE MAN: property and industry under Christian law. Bost., Houghton, 1893, 308 p., D. $1.25.

Applies moral tests to the institution of property, the system of wage earning, the process of competition, and the existing organization of society. Inquires how the industrial system can be Christianized.... The book will not fail to clarify the view of those who are willing to work for society and are seeking direction.—JOHN B. CLARK, in *Political Science Quarterly*. 331.1.

Lowell, Josephine Shaw.

INDUSTRIAL ARBITRATION AND CONCILIATION. N. Y., Putnam, 1893, 116 p., D. cloth, 75 c.; paper, 40 c.

Presents the various methods of successful labor arbitration employed since 1860 in England, Belgium, and the United States. A concise and interesting statement. 331.1.

Mallock, William H.

LABOR AND THE POPULAR WELFARE. N. Y., Macmillan, 1894, 357 p., D. 90 c.

Undertakes to show the enormous additions which mind, as distinguished from manual labor, has made to the wealth of the world Of all expositions of the kind, this is the most cogent, detailed, and the best fortified. Its importance can hardly be overrated.—*Nation*. 331.1.

Toynbee, Arnold.

INDUSTRIAL REVOLUTION IN ENGLAND. N. Y., Humboldt Pub. Co., 1890, cloth, $1; paper, 60 c.

A sympathetic review of the introduction of machinery within the past century, and the result of increased dependence of labor on capital. 331.1.

Webb, Sidney, *and* **Cox, Harold.**

EIGHT HOURS DAY. N. Y., A. Lovell, 272 p., D., paper, 50 c.

Clear and well-balanced arguments for and against an eight hours day. Shows that the general result of past reductions in hours has been beneficial to both capital and labor, also that experience shows legislation to be the only efficient way of securing such limitation. The chapter on practical proposals is especially valuable. **331.81.**

Wells, David A.

RECENT ECONOMIC CHANGES, and their effect on the production and distribution of wealth, and the well-being of society. N. Y., Appleton, 1889, 12+493 p., D. $2.

A graphic recital of the betterment wrought by modern invention and enterprise. The increased buying power of a dollar is proved to be due to new and improved machinery, transportation, and methods of doing business. A storehouse of facts admirably digested. The author is the leading authority on American taxation. **331.1.**

Wood, Henry.

THE POLITICAL ECONOMY OF NATURAL LAW. Bost., Lee & Shepard, 1894, 305 p., D. $1.25.

An attempt by a conservative to show how far economic forces express natural, and therefore irresistible, law. Includes a survey of competition and co-operation, strikes and lockouts, trusts, socialism, monetary theories, free trade and protection. A book of uncommon value, simply and clearly written. **331 1.**

MONEY: CURRENCY: BANKING.

Brough, William.

NATURAL LAW OF MONEY. N. Y., Putnam, 1894, 168 p., D. $1.

One of the most meritorious of recent publications upon monetary science. In a remarkably clear and lucid style Mr. Brough shows that the tendency to substitute credit in place of material substances is the distinctive mark of progress in the art of effecting exchanges ... Gold has now become the standard money of international trade, but its use as currency is decreasing as compared with that of credit.—*Nation.* **332.**

Harvey, William H.

COIN'S FINANCIAL SCHOOL. Chic., Coin Pub. Co.; N. Y., Am. News Co., 1895, cloth, $1; paper, 25 c., or 50 c.

A widely circulated argument in favor of free and unlimited coinage of silver by the United States. See, for reply, Horace White's "Coin's Financial Fool." **332.42.**

White, Horace.

COIN'S FINANCIAL FOOL. N. Y., J. S. Ogilvie Co., 1895, paper, 25 c.

A reply to "Coin's Financial School," with illustrations by Dan. Beard. An unillustrated pamphlet edition is published by the Sound Currency Committee, Reform Club, 52 William St., N. Y., 5 c. **332.42.**

MONEY AND BANKING: illustrated by American history. Bost., Ginn & Co., 1895, 488 p., D.

The latest and best book on the subject. Reviews the various developments of paper and silver currency and gives the experience of Europe with the gold standard. Explains what a bank does, describes the successive phases of American banking, and forecasts its probable future. Among the appendices are "The Baltimore Plan," "Secretary Carlisle's Plan," and "Recent Bimetallist Movements in Germany." Mr. White is an uncompromising upholder of the gold standard, and an able critic of American currency and banking systems. He is editor of the *New York Evening Post*, and an acknowledged authority in finance. **332.**

NOTE.

The Sound Currency Committee of the Reform Club, 52 William St., New York, issues *Sound Currency* semi-monthly; each number gives in pamphlet form a valuable discussion of some phase of the currency question. Among these issues are Horace White's "State and National Banks," and "Coin's Financial Fool"; W. M. Trenholm's "The People's Money"; L. Carroll Root's "Canadian Bank Note Currency"; John De Witt Warner's "The Currency Famine of 1893." $1 a year; clubs of ten, 50 c.; clubs of twenty-five, 40 c.; single copies, 5 c.; a discount is allowed for lots of 100.

RAILROADS: TRUSTS: PROTECTION. FREE TRADE.

Hadley, Arthur T.

RAILROAD TRANSPORTATION: its history and its laws. N. Y., Putnam, 1885, 269 p., D. $1.50.

The best book on the subject. Author is Professor at Yale University. **385.**

Halle, Ernst Von.

TRUSTS, OR INDUSTRIAL COMBINATIONS AND COALITIONS IN THE UNITED STATES. N. Y., Macmillan, 1895, 350 p., D. $1.25.

Gives in concise, intelligible form all that an industrious collector of facts can find out concerning Trusts. The arrangement of facts is excellent. There is little bias in the treatment; the author considers it too early yet to form any decision.—*Nation.*

Contains the best extant bibliography on the subject, and the agreements and by-laws of several leading combinations. **338.8.**

Lloyd, Henry D.

WEALTH AGAINST COMMONWEALTH. N. Y., Harper, 1894, 4+563 p., O. $2.50.

Chiefly a history of the Standard Oil Combination, taken from court records and testimony presented to State legislative and Congressional committees. The author does not hide his hatred of "Trusts"; he has studied them since their birth. **338.8.**

Sumner, William Graham.

PROTECTIONISM THE ISM WHICH TEACHES THAT WANT MAKES WEALTH. N. Y., Holt, 1885, 172 p., S. $1.

An able and severe criticism of Protection, by a Professor of Yale University. **337.1.**

Thompson, Robert Ellis.

PROTECTION TO HOME INDUSTRY. N. Y., Appleton, 1886, $1.

Lectures advocating Protection delivered at Harvard University. **337.3.**

SOCIALISM AND SOCIAL QUESTIONS.

Bellamy, Edward.

LOOKING BACKWARD, 2000 – 1887. Bost., Houghton, 1890, 470 p., D. cloth, $1; paper, 50 c.

This famous socialistic and Utopian romance gave rise to the Nationalist movement. **335.**

Bonar, James.

MALTHUS AND HIS WORK. N. Y., Macmillan, 1888, 430 p., O. $4; N. Y., Harper, 1885, 224 p., S. paper, 25 c.

Presents Malthus's contributions to political economy, and traces his influence upon recent economic thought. Reviews his critics. The best survey of the discussion on population. **312.**

Booth, Charles, *Editor.*

LIFE AND LABOR OF THE PEOPLE IN LONDON.

N. Y., Macmillan, 1895, 6 vols., I. to IV., $1.50 each; V. and VI., $3 each.
A faithful house-to-house study, not only of great interest for its facts, but as the one perfect example of the thoroughness and sympathy which should characterize social inquiry. **331.8.**

Ely, Richard T.

SOCIALISM AND SOCIAL REFORM. N. Y., Crowell, 1894, 11+449 p., D. $1.50.
Both as expositor and a critic Dr. Ely shows fairness and breadth of judgment; his position throughout being neither that of a hard and fast conservative, nor that of an extreme radical, but rather that of a social reformer. He deals with "Socialism as a Scheme of Production" very fully, . . . but his treatment of "Socialism as a Scheme for the Distribution and Consumption of Wealth" is most superficial. . . . —LINDLEY M. KEASBEY in *Political Science Quarterly*. **335.**

Kidd, Benjamin.

SOCIAL EVOLUTION. New and enlarged edition. N. Y., Macmillan, 1894, 7+374 p., D. cloth, $1.50; paper, 25 c.
At the end of an able review in the *Political Science Quarterly*, December, 1894, Prof. Franklin H. Giddings says: "Altogether, then, Mr. Kidd's book is a curious mixture of truth and fallacy. But it is an interesting book, and stimulating. It will make a great many people do more serious thinking in sociology than they have ever done before." **335.**

Malthus. *See* Bonar.

Rae, John.

CONTEMPORARY SOCIALISM. Revised and enlarged edition. N. Y., Scribner, 1892 10+508 p., O. $2.50.
States and criticises in a masterly way the principles of Lassalle, Marx, Karl Marlo, the Socialists of the Chair, the Christian Socialists, the Russian Nihilists, and Henry George; with a general chapter on Socialism and the Social Question. **335.**

Smith, Richmond Mayo.

EMIGRATION AND IMMIGRATION. N. Y., Scribner, 1890, 316 p., D. $1.50.
An historical and statistical survey. Discusses the political and social effects of immigration, as also the economic gain derived from it. A bibliography is appended. An able and suggestive book, much the best on the subject. **325.1.**

Spencer, Herbert.

THE STUDY OF SOCIOLOGY. (International Scientific series.) N. Y., Appleton, 1880, 14+426 p., D. $1.50.
Explains the scope of the science, its utility and method, and gives some of its more important general principles. Author is the foremost sociologist living. In style this is the most attractive of Mr. Spencer's books. **307.**

CHARITIES.

Gilman, Daniel C., *Editor.*

THE ORGANIZATION OF CHARITIES: a report of the sixth section of the International Congress of Charities, Corrections and Philanthropy, Chicago, June, 1893. Balt., Johns Hopkins Press, 1894, 32+400 p., O. $1.50.
Essays on Charity Organization in the United States, Great Britain, Germany, France, Italy, and Russia. A very excellent collection of original material, full of interest for persons engaged in active work or in study in connection with one of the most pressing problems of practical sociology.—RICHMOND MAYO SMITH in *Political Science Quarterly*. **301.**

Henderson, Charles Richmond.

INTRODUCTION TO THE STUDY OF THE DEPENDENT, DEFECTIVE, AND DELINQUENT CLASSES. Bost., D. C. Heath & Co., 1893, 287 p., D. $1.50.
Contains nothing positively new to the tolerably well-informed student of such subjects, but as this branch of sociology is not generally studied, it may serve as a real introduction for many well-disposed but as yet unenlightened persons. Authorities for study and illustration are introduced directly at the point of discussion; a copious bibliography is thus presented exactly where it applies.—*Nation*.
Author is Associate Professor of Sociology, Divinity School, University of Chicago. **300.**

Warner, Amos G.

AMERICAN CHARITIES: a study in Philanthropy and Economics. N. Y., Crowell, 1895, 8+430 p., D. $1.75.
A review of current methods of American charities, with informed and sensible criticism. An admirable book for the practical worker. **300.**

LIQUOR QUESTION.

Cyclopædia of Temperance and Prohibition. N. Y., Funk & Wagnalls, 1891, 671 p., O. $3.50.
An exhaustive work from the Prohibition standpoint, though written with the aim of making an authoritative rather than a partisan presentation. Most useful to students of the Liquor Question. **178.**

AMERICAN GOVERNMENT.

Bailey, Edmund (Edmund Alton).

AMONG THE LAW-MAKERS. Illus. N. Y., Scribner, 1886, 308 p., D. $1.50.
Author when a boy was page in the U. S. Senate. Describes and illustrates the three Departments of the Federal Government in an interesting way. **342.730.**

Bryce, James.

THE AMERICAN COMMONWEALTH. New edition, revised and enlarged; with new chapters on The Tammany Ring in New York City; The Home of the Nation; The South Since the War; Present and Future of the Negro. N. Y., Macmillan, 1895, 2 vols., 724, 904 p., O. $4.
Prof. J. W. Burgess, Dean of the Faculty of Political Science, Columbia College, says of this work in the *Political Science Quarterly*: "It is the most comprehensive and exhaustive work in any language on the public law and political institutions of the United States." **342.730.**

Macy, Jesse.

FIRST LESSONS IN CIVIL GOVERNMENT. Bost., Ginn, 1894, 13+229 p., D. 60 c.
Arranged for school use by an accomplished teacher. The beginner, not at school, will find it helpful. **342.730.**

OUR GOVERNMENT. Bost., Ginn, 1894, 318 p., D. 75 c.
Admirably adapted to young people. Gives a concise account of the origin of our government, describes local and federal governments, and the administration of justice. Discusses the national and state constitutions. Gives the Articles of Confederation and the Constitution of the United States. Deservedly the most popular book of its kind. **342.730.**

BRITISH AND CANADIAN GOVERNMENTS.

Bourinot, John George.

HOW CANADA IS GOVERNED. Illus. Toronto, Canada, Copp, Clark & Co., 1895, 358 p., D. $1.
A concise account of the growth of the Canadian Constitution; the Dominion, Provincial, municipal

and school governments of Canada. The Imperial control over Canada is described and the Constitution of the Dominion is appended. Author is Clerk of the Canadian House of Commons. **342.971.**

MANUAL OF THE CONSTITUTIONAL HISTORY OF CANADA. Montreal, Dawson Bros., 1888, 238 p., D. $1.25.

By the chief authority on Canadian Constitutional questions. **342.071.**

Douglas, James.

CANADIAN INDEPENDENCE, ANNEXATION AND BRITISH IMPERIAL FEDERATION. (Questions of the Day series.) N. Y., Putnam, 1894, 7+114 p., D. 75 c.

By a Canadian for twenty years engaged in large mining enterprises in the United States. In Chapter V. points the Maritime provinces to self-help. Takes a conservative view, favorable to Imperial Federation. **071.**

Feilden, H. St. Clair.

SHORT CONSTITUTIONAL HISTORY OF ENGLAND. 3d edition. Bost., Ginn & Co., 1895, 378 p., D. $1.35.

This edition of the late Mr. Fielden's work has been in part rewritten by W. Gray Etheridge, so as to include recent discussions of disputed subjects. The best brief introduction. **342.42.**

Freeman, Edward A.

THE GROWTH OF THE ENGLISH CONSTITUTION FROM THE EARLIEST TIMES. 4th edition. N. Y., Macmillan, 1884, 234 p., D. $1.75.

A useful sketch by one of the first historians of his time. **342.42.**

See HISTORY also for important books on this subject.

Smith, Goldwin.

CANADA AND THE CANADIAN QUESTION. N. Y., Macmillan: Toronto, Hunter, Rose & Co., 1891, 325 p., D. $2.

A masterly sketch by an eminent English historian long resident in Canada. He argues for annexation to the United States. For an opposite view see G. R. Parkin's "The Great Dominion" (N. Y., Macmillan, 1895, $1.75). **071.**

WOMAN SUFFRAGE.

Jacobi, Mary Putnam.

COMMON SENSE APPLIED TO WOMAN SUFFRAGE. N. Y., Putnam, 1894, 136 p., D. 50 c.

A plea to the Constitutional Convention of New York, 1894. Argues that women should have the suffrage because men have; that they will do good if they vote; that they will do no harm if they do not vote.—*Critic.* **324.3.**

Stanton, Elizabeth Cady; Anthony, Susan B.; and Gage, Matilda J., *Editors.*

HISTORY OF WOMAN SUFFRAGE. Rochester, N. Y., Susan B. Anthony, 1882, 3 vols., $10.

By leaders in the movement for Woman Suffrage. Describes the work done by and for women during the half-century preceding the writing of this work. Gives 47 portraits of leading Woman Suffragists. **324.3.**

NOTES.

The National-American Woman Suffrage Association expects in November, 1895, to establish National headquarters in Philadelphia, whence publications will be issued.

An Association to oppose the movement for Woman Suffrage has been formed in New York; Mrs. M. Eleanor Phillips, 169 East 60th St., Secretary. It publishes Woman Suffrage, Goldwin Smith; Some of the Reasons Against Woman Suffrage, Francis Parkman; The Wrongs of Suffrage, Heloise Jamison; Woman and the Law, Francis M. Scott; The Relation of the Sexes to Government, Prof. A. Cope; The Blank Cartridge Ballot, Rossiter Johnson; Letter of Hon. Abram S. Hewitt; Speech of Francis M. Scott; Should We Ask for the Suffrage?, Mrs. Schuyler Van Rensselaer; Letter on Woman Suffrage from one Woman to Another, Mrs. Richard Watson Gilder. All at 10 c. each.

MUNICIPAL GOVERNMENT.

Conkling, Alfred R.

CITY GOVERNMENT IN THE UNITED STATES. N. Y., Appleton, 1894, 11+227 p., D. $1.

A comprehensive survey, with suggestions for reform, by an ex-alderman of New York. **352.**

Shaw, Albert.

MUNICIPAL GOVERNMENT IN GREAT BRITAIN. N. Y., Century Co., 1895, 8+385 p., D. $2.

Gives a good description of municipal government in Great Britain at the present time. . . . Apart from its comparison of English with American conditions, and apart from the evident desire to apply the English system to American conditions, the book is deserving of great praise.—F. J. GOODNOW in *Political Science Quarterly*. **352.**

PARLIAMENTARY PRACTICE.

Cushing, L. S.

MANUAL OF PARLIAMENTARY PRACTICE. Bost., Thompson, Brown & Co., 1885, 75 c.

The standard authority. **328.1.**

NOTES.

The American Economic Association, Jeremiah W. Jenks, Secretary, Ithaca, N. Y., meets annually during the Christmas holidays. It publishes a variety of economic monographs of high value. Annual subscription, $3; life membership, $50.

The National Civil Service Reform League, William Potts, Secretary, 56 Wall St., New York, is an organization of the local Civil Service Reform Association throughout the Union. It issues a variety of publications in the interest of Civil Service Reform.

The American Social Science Association, F. B. Sanborn, Secretary, Concord, Mass., meets every August at Saratoga, N. Y.; it issues the *Journal of Social Science*, containing its transactions. Annual subscription, $5.

SERIES.

Books of interest and weight are published in "Questions of the Day" series, N. Y., G. P. Putnam's Sons. Swan Sonnenschein & Co., London, issue an important "Social Science" series, 2s. 6d. per vol.; sold by C. Scribner's Sons, N. Y., $1.

PHILOSOPHY.

HISTORY OF PHILOSOPHY: PHILOSOPHY IN GENERAL: LOGIC AND SCIENTIFIC METHOD: ETHICS.

A SELECTION WITH NOTES BY

J. CLARK MURRAY,

Professor of Philosophy, McGill University, Montreal.

Montreal, June, 1895.

HISTORY OF PHILOSOPHY.

Erdmann, J. E.

HISTORY OF PHILOSOPHY. Translation edited by W. S. Hough, Professor of Philosophy in the University of Minnesota. N. Y., Macmillan, 3 vols., $10.50.

Published since the work of Lewes, and more useful, for all purposes, than any of the previous histories, to which he refers as supplementing his own. No history, even in German, combines the same fulness of detail with compactness in treatment. 100.

Lewes, George Henry.

BIOGRAPHICAL HISTORY OF PHILOSOPHY from its Origin in Greece down to the Present Day. N. Y., Routledge, 650 p., D. $1.40.

Adapted to give a more interesting view of the whole field than any other original work in English. Written, indeed, with the purpose of proving, as its motto from Goethe implies, that "man is not born to solve the problem of existence"; yet its biographical character gives it a peculiar human interest. The predominance of this interest, however, obliges the author to omit a multitude of details, for which he refers his readers to "more comprehensive histories previously published." 100.

PHILOSOPHY IN GENERAL.

Collins, Howard.

EPITOME OF THE SYNTHETIC PHILOSOPHY: with a preface by Herbert Spencer. N. Y., Appleton, $2.50.

An epitome of Spencer's nine volumes (N. Y., Appleton, $18). Useful as a guide to students, but, of course, lacking the interest attaching to the illustrations in which Spencer traces evolution throughout nature and life. 102.8.

Fiske, John.

OUTLINES OF COSMIC PHILOSOPHY, based on the Doctrines of Evolution, with Criticisms on the Positive Philosophy. Bost., Houghton, 1875, 2 vols., $6.

By no means a mere reproduction of Spencer's philosophy, but an independent exposition of Evolutionism, showing originality, especially in regard to social evolution and the relation of religion and science. 140.0.

Louis of Poissy.

ELEMENTARY COURSE OF CHRISTIAN PHILOSOPHY, based on the principles of the best Scholastic Authors, adapted from the French of Brother Louis of Poissy by the Brothers of the Christian Schools. N. Y., P. O'Shea, 1893, 538 p., D. $1.50.

A convenient handbook for those who wish to form some idea of the system of philosophy taught in Roman Catholic institutions of higher education. 180 4.

Philosophical Classics. Phila., Lippincott, $1.25 per vol.

A series of admirable monographs by eminent writers of our day. Already published are the volumes on Bacon, Berkeley, Butler, Descartes, Fichte, Hamilton, Hegel, Hobbes, Hume, Kant, Leibnitz, Locke, Spinoza, and Vico. 104.

Spencer, Herbert.

FIRST PRINCIPLES OF A NEW SYSTEM OF PHILOSOPHY. N. Y., Appleton, 559 p., D. $2.50.

Contains the general principles which underlie the author's "System of Synthetic Philosophy," recently completed, of which his nine volumes (N. Y., Appleton, $18) are the detailed illustration. Commonly accepted as the most systematic exposition of the philosophy involved in prevalent theories of Agnostic Evolutionism. 102.8.

Watson, John.

COMTE, MILL, AND SPENCER: an Outline of Philosophy. N. Y., Macmillan, 1895, 302 p., D. $1.75.

Valuable for those who wish to see the opposite side of philosophy from that of the works by Spencer and Fiske. A critique of the experimental Agnosticism represented by Comte, Mill, and Spencer, it is also a compact exposition of the Idealism of our day in its application to the various sciences. Its leading doctrine is to prove "that we are capable of knowing reality, and that reality when so known is absolutely rational." 104.

LOGIC: SCIENTIFIC METHOD.

Harris, William T.

HEGEL'S LOGIC: a Book on the Genesis of the Categories of Thought: a Critical Exposition. Chic., S. C. Griggs & Co., 1890, 433 p., D. $1.50.

Designed, like Wallace's prolegomena, to help English readers to an understanding of "Hegel's Logic." 103.5.

Jevons, William Stanley.

ELEMENTARY LESSONS IN LOGIC, Deductive and Inductive. With copious Questions and Examples, and a Vocabulary of Logical Terms. New edition. N. Y., Macmillan, 40 c.

Continues, notwithstanding numerous additions to

the literature of Logic, probably the most useful book for beginners. Peculiarly free from the illustrations by which the science has often been degraded to a sort of systematic intellectual trifling. 100.

THE PRINCIPLES OF SCIENCE: a Treatise on Logical and Scientific Method. New edition, revised. N. Y., Macmillan, $2.75.

May be taken up with advantage after the "Elementary Lessons" by those who wish to advance to the higher problems of Logic. The first chapters are comparatively uninteresting; they are followed by the best extant exposition of the principles underlying scientific generalization and discovery; illustrations are drawn from many and diverse modern triumphs of science. 100.

Mill, John Stuart.

A SYSTEM OF LOGIC, RATIOCINATIVE AND INDUCTIVE: being a connected View of the Principles of Evidence and the Methods of Scientific Investigation. Revised edition. N. Y., Routledge, $1.40; Harper, $2.50.

Formed a new epoch in the literature of Logic, especially by its luminous exposition of the methods of experimental inquiry, and its interesting illustration of these in the achievements of modern science. 100.

Wallace, William.

THE LOGIC OF HEGEL. 2d edition, revised and augmented. Oxford, Clarendon Press, 1894, 2 vols., 21s.

With Hegel began a new departure in philosophy. He held that the laws of thought, which Logic investigates, are also the laws of reality. This view is compactly expounded in his smaller treatise on Logic, translated, with explanatory notes, in Vol. II. of this work. Vol. I. contains prolegomena to the study of Hegel. Both prolegomena and notes are very helpful. 103.5.

ETHICS.
Adler, Felix.

THE MORAL INSTRUCTION OF CHILDREN. (International Education series.) N. Y., Appleton, 1892, 270 p., D. $1.50.

Designed not only for professional teachers, but for all who are called to direct the education of children. Without the presuppositions of religion. For its purpose there is no better book in English. Author is Founder and Leader of the Society for Ethical Culture, New York. 170.7.

Everett, C. C.

ETHICS FOR YOUNG PEOPLE. Bost., Ginn & Co., 1891, 185 p., S. 50 c.

Intended for minds advanced beyond childhood, and likely to be inquisitive about the reasons why duty should be done. Adapted therefore to introduce such minds to the *science* of Ethics. 170.7.

Gilman, Nicholas Paine.

LAWS OF DAILY CONDUCT. Bost., Houghton, 1891, 149 p., D. $1. **Jackson, Edward Payson.** CHARACTER-BUILDING: a Master's Talks with his Pupils. Same publishers, 230 p., D. $1.

These two books may be had separately, or in one volume ($1.50). They were both adjudged a prize offered by the American Secular Union for a book to aid public school teachers in giving moral instruction to their pupils apart from religious doctrine. The authors are both friendly to religion, though not obtruding it either as a speculative foundation or as a practical motive of morality. 170.7.

Green, Thomas Hill.

PROLEGOMENA TO ETHICS. 3d edition, edited by A. C. Bradley. N. Y., Macmillan, $3.25.

Admits the natural evolution of the moral life, but interprets the process of evolution from the idealistic point of view. By far the ablest exposition of Ethical Idealism in the English language. Not a book for beginners. 171.

Jackson, E. P. *See* Gilman, N. P.

Schurman, Jacob Gould.

ETHICAL IMPORT OF DARWINISM. N. Y., Scribner, 1887, 264 p., $1.50.

More popular than Green's "Prolegomena"; a clear and interesting exposition of the difficulties connected with the explanation of moral life on the common theory of evolution. 171.7.

Seelye, Julius H.

DUTY: a Book for Schools. Bost., Ginn & Co., 1892, 71 p., S. 30 c.

Bases morality on the *universal* principles of religion, but without reference to the distinctive dogmas of particular sects. 170.7.

Sidgwick, Henry.

OUTLINES OF THE HISTORY OF ETHICS FOR ENGLISH READERS. 2d edition. N. Y., Macmillan, 1888, 278 p., D. $1.25.

An admirable historical sketch of the various phases of ethical speculation. 170.9.

Spencer, Herbert.

PRINCIPLES OF ETHICS. N. Y., Appleton, 2 vols., $4.

Part of the author's "System of Synthetic Philosophy," specially designed to illustrate the laws of evolution in the sphere of man's moral life. 171.7.

PHYSICAL CULTURE.

HYGIENE: SANITATION: NURSING AND EMERGENCIES.

SELECTED BY

AUGUSTA H. LEYPOLDT,
Editor Literary News, New York.

New York, August, 1895.

PHYSICAL CULTURE.

Bissell, Mary Taylor, *M.D.*

PHYSICAL DEVELOPMENT AND EXERCISE FOR WOMEN. (Portia series.) N. Y., Dodd, Mead & Co., 1891, 5+108 p., D. $1.25.

Dr. Bissell has much practical experience in the field of which she writes, and her book is consequently a sensible and useful one. The brief explanations of the laws of growth, and of the influence of environment (including dress) upon growth, are a logical introduction to the enumeration of the ways in which growth and development are promoted by exercise. The last chapter, profusely illustrated, explains how such exercise may be taken, often by surprisingly simple means. . . . Dr. Bissell not only sanctions cricket, but urges swimming, rowing, riding, and other delightful forms of outdoor exercise.—*Nation.*
613.7.

Blaikie, William.

HOW TO GET STRONG AND HOW TO STAY SO. Illus. N. Y., Harper, 1879, 296 p., S. $1.

Prescribes gymnastic exercises for physical development, and gives simple directions for the care of the body. 613.7.

Call, Anna Payson.

POWER THROUGH REPOSE. Bost., Roberts, 1891, 169 p., D. $1.

To nervous, overworked, worried and worrying people we commend this book. . . . It maintains that one can train oneself to absolute relaxation in times of rest, and to the employment of just enough force—and not too much—in times of labor—so as to double the possibilities of life.—*Literary World.*

In the same vein the author has written " As a Matter of Course." Bost., Roberts, 1894, $1. 613.70.

Checkley, Edwin.

NATURAL METHOD OF PHYSICAL TRAINING. N. Y., Baker & Taylor Co , 1890, 152 p., D. $1.50.

A system of exercise to form muscle and to reduce flesh, without dieting or apparatus. Illustrated. 613.7.

Huxley, Thomas Henry.

LESSONS IN ELEMENTARY PHYSIOLOGY. Illus. New edition; revised by Dr. Foster. N.Y., Macmillan, 1885, $1.10.

QUESTIONS ON FOREGOING. Same publishers, 40 c.

A capital introduction, by one of the greatest men of science of our time, to the formal study of physiology. 612.

La Grange, Fernand, *M.D.*

PHYSIOLOGY OF BODILY EXERCISE. (International Scientific series.) N. Y., Appleton, 1892, 16+395 p., $1.75.

Contents: Muscular work, Fatigue, Habituation to work, Exercise, Results of exercise, Office of the brain in exercise.

An able and systematic review from the standpoint of a physiologist of authority. For the student rather than the general reader. 613.72.

Posse, Nils, *Baron.*

SWEDISH SYSTEM OF EDUCATIONAL GYMNASTICS. Bost., Lee & S., 1890, 5+275 p., O. $2.

An exposition of merit. Illustrated. 613.71.

HYGIENE: SANITATION.

Allen, Chillian B., *M.D.,* **and Mary A.,** *M.D.*

MAN WONDERFUL IN THE HOUSE BEAUTIFUL: an allegory, teaching the principles of physiology and hygiene and the effects of stimulants and narcotics; for home reading, also adapted as a reader for schools. 6th ed. N. Y., Fowler & Wells Co., 1888, $1.50.

Useful as an introduction to the facts of physiology and the essentials of hygiene; pleasantly written in an allegorical narrative style. This work is largely used as a school text-book, and is well worth reading. Fully illustrated. 613.

Clarke, Edward H.

BUILDING OF A BRAIN. Bost., Houghton, 1874, $1.25.

Intended chiefly for teachers and parents. Sets forth clearly the necessity of rest and economy of strength among girl students and women engaged in brain work. Should be read in conjunction with the author's " Sex in Education." 613.7.

SEX IN EDUCATION; or, A Fair Chance for Girls. Bost., Houghton, 1873, $1.25.

The necessity of periodic rest is the point urged by Dr. Clarke. 613.70.

Davis, Irenæus P., *M.D.*

HYGIENE FOR GIRLS. N. Y., Appleton, 1883, 210 p., D. $1 25.

Contents: Nerves and nervousness, Habit and association, Sympathy and imagination, Organs peculiar to women, Feminine employment, Amusements, Social customs, Harmony and elements of beauty, Hygienic morals.

Brief chapters, simply and interestingly written, on matters of the utmost moment to girls and women. .613.

Galbraith, Anna M., *M.D.*

HYGIENE AND PHYSICAL CULTURE FOR WOMEN. N. Y., Dodd, Mead & Co., 1895, 8+294 p., D. $1.75.

Describes the body, the exercises conducing to health and beauty, the benefits of good air, water and food. Discusses fashionable dress and sensible dress, work, rest, recreation, sleep, and the disabilities peculiar to women. The author writes from observation and experience ; her style is clear and interesting. Illustrations good.

" I have examined the manuscript of this book with some care. I think it contains sound doctrine, well expressed. In my opinion, its wide circulation among the women of this country will be of service to their physical condition, and I cheerfully commend it to their favorable consideration."—D. B. ST. JOHN ROOSA, *President New York Academy of Medicine.* 613.

Herrick, Christine Terhune.
CRADLE AND NURSERY. N. Y., Harper, 1889, 7+298 p., S. $1.
A clear, popular, and pleasant treatise on the nursing, clothing, and feeding of little children. For popular reading. **640.**

Jacobi, Abraham, *M.D.*
INFANT DIET. Rev., enl., and adapted to popular use by Mary Putnam Jacobi, M.D. (Putnam's handy-book series.) N. Y., Putnam, 50 c.
Covers a wide field with clearness and minuteness of direction. Popular in style. An authority.
Admirably simple and comprehensive.—*N. Y. Tribune.* **640.**

Newsholme, Arthur, *M.D.*, and **Scott, Margaret E.**
DOMESTIC ECONOMY: COMPRISING THE LAWS OF HEALTH in their application to home life and work. 3d edition. Illus. Lond., Swan Sonnenschein & Co., 1894, 3s. 6d.
One of the most valuable books for general reference that the housekeeper can possess. It comprises: Personal and domestic hygiene; Domestic management; and Home nursing. Every detail of these subjects is treated clearly, simply, and precisely; there is not a superfluous line or theoretical proposition in the book. **613.**

Plunkett, *Mrs.* **H. M.**
WOMEN, PLUMBERS AND DOCTORS; or household sanitation. Illus. N. Y., Appleton, 1885, 248 p., D. $1.25.
In popular and easy style, and well adapted for general reading. **628.6.**

Prudden, T. Mitchell, *M.D.*
DRINKING WATER AND ICE. N. Y., Putnam, 1892, 75 c.
Plainly sets forth the relations of good and bad water, and of ice, to health and disease.—*Critic.*
Dr. Prudden is director of the Physiological and Pathological Laboratory, College of Physicians and Surgeons, New York. **613.32.**

DUST AND ITS DANGERS. N. Y., Putnam, 1891, 75 c.
Tells of the dangers of disease, especially consumption, which lurk in dust, and how these dangers may be avoided.—*Literary World.* **614.71.**

THE STORY OF THE BACTERIA. N. Y., Putnam, 1890, 75 c.
The relation of bacteria to health and to disease is told in a very plain, sensible, and trustworthy manner.—*Literary World.* **610.01.**

Reynolds, Ernest S., *M.D.*
PRIMER OF HYGIENE. N. Y., Macmillan, 1894, 164 p., S. 35 c.
Contents: Parasites; Air and water and their impurities; Food, cooking and beverages; Personal health; The house; Infectious diseases and their prevention; Medical and surgical emergencies; Hints on sick nursing.
The best primer of health. Author is an eminent English physician. His book is written for higher grade school children and is provided with series of questions, but can be read with profit by everybody. The copious illustrations include ventilating gas-fixtures and other important devices. **,613.**

Starr, Louis, *M.D.*
HYGIENE OF THE NURSERY. Phila., P. Blakiston, Son & Co., 1892, $1.
The aim of the author is to point out a series of hygienic rules which, if applied to the nursling, can hardly fail to maintain good health, give vigor to the frame, and so lessen susceptibility to disease. Dr. Starr is an eminent authority. **613.**

Strahan, S. A. K , *M.D.*
MARRIAGE AND DISEASE. N. Y., Appleton, 1892, 6+326 p., D. $1.25.
A popular study of heredity and of inherited disease. Author is none too emphatic in his exhortation to those contemplating marriage to consider the probabilities of health and disease in their offspring. For awakening the attention of the thoughtless we know few books better than this.—*Literary World.* **613.9.**

Terhune, *Mrs.* **Mary V. H.** (Marion Harland).
EVE'S DAUGHTERS; OR, COMMON SENSE FOR MAID, WIFE, AND MOTHER. N. Y., Scribner, 1889, 6+454 p., D. $1.50.
Full of wise and kindly counsel regarding education, culture, courtship, marriage, the family and the home. The work of an accomplished author, who writes out of long and successful experience. **613.**

Tracy, Roger S., *M.D.*
HANDBOOK OF SANITARY INFORMATION FOR HOUSEHOLDERS. N. Y., Appleton, 1895, 114 p., S. 50 c.
Treats of air, drainage, disinfection, adulterations of food, water and filters. The author is Sanitary Inspector of the New York City Health Department; he gives in detail the plan of house drainage recommended by the Board of Health of New York City. Appendix presents priced lists of disinfectants and plumbers' materials. **613.5.**

Uffelmann, Julius, *M.D.*
MANUAL OF THE DOMESTIC HYGIENE OF THE CHILD; for the use of students, physicians, sanitary officials, teachers and mothers. Transl. by Harriet R. Milinowski and edited by Mary Putnam Jacobi, M.D. N. Y., Putnam, 1891, 239+10 p., D. $1.75.
Scientific and comprehensive. For trained readers. **649.**

NURSING AND EMERGENCIES.

Doty, Alvah H., *M.D.*
PROMPT AID TO THE INJURED. Illus. N. Y., Appleton, 1889, 224 p., D. $1.50.
Directions are plain and sound. Well arranged, clear and concise.—*Critic.* **614.88.**

Hampton, Isabel Adams.
NURSING, ITS PRINCIPLES AND PRACTICE. Illus. Phila., W. B. Saunders, 1893, 7+484 p., D. $2.
A very complete and well written book, containing much valuable information for those employed as trained nurses, either in hospitals or in private life. The author had extended experience as Superintendent of Nurses in Johns Hopkins Hospital, Baltimore. **610.73.**

Mitchell, S. Weir, *M.D.*
DOCTOR AND PATIENT. Phila., Lippincott, 1888, 177 p., D. $1.50.
Contents: The physician; convalescence; pain and its consequences; the moral management of sick and invalid children; nervousness and its influence on character; out-door and camp-life for women.
Much can be learned from this little book.—*Literary World.*
The author, a Philadelphian, is one of the most eminent living physicians. **610.4.**

SELF-CULTURE

ETIQUETTE: CLUBS FOR WOMEN AND GIRLS.

SELECTED BY

AUGUSTA H. LEYPOLDT,
Editor Literary News, New York.

New York, August, 1895.

SELF-CULTURE.

Chester, Eliza.

GIRLS AND WOMEN. (Riverside Library for Young People.) Bost., Houghton, 1890, 238 p., D. 75 c.
In clearness and force, in temperance, in wisdom, and in elevation of feeling, a very remarkable book. It is rather by contagion with a fine nature than by direct argument that books aimed at changes of character accomplish their work. In this book, however, the cogency of presentation is no less remarkable than its persuasiveness.—*Nation.*
Discusses health, occupation, culture, and society. Written for girls of possible leisure and advanced education; the style is adapted to the average girl. 374.

CHATS WITH GIRLS ON SELF-CULTURE. (Portia series.) N. Y., Dodd, Mead & Co., 1891, 213 p., D. $1.25.
Devoted to inward and spiritual culture as Dr. Bissell's "Physical Development and Exercise" is to physical. Brightly and entertainingly written. Particularly valuable are the chapters on How shall we learn to observe? How shall we learn to think?—*Nation.* 374.

THE UNMARRIED WOMAN. (Portia series.) N.Y., Dodd, Mead & Co., 1892, 253 p., D. $1.25.
Bright and sensible chapters on why some women do not marry; dependence; freedom; problems; opportunities; success; business, and other phases of the unmarried woman's life. 370.

Craik, Dinah Maria (Miss Mulock).

ABOUT MONEY AND OTHER THINGS. N. Y., Harper, 1887, 234 p., D. 90 c.
Unambitious and slight as these pages are, their simple, direct moral teaching, their sound reflections on the common things of life, with the gracious womanliness which is felt pervading them, combine to make this excellent home reading.—*Nation.* 374.

Dodge, Grace H.

BUNDLE OF LETTERS TO BUSY GIRLS ON PRACTICAL MATTERS. N. Y., Funk & Wagnalls, 1887, 139 p., S. 50 c.
Written to those girls who have not time or inclination to think and study about the many important things which make up life and living.—*The author.*
Filled with practical advice to young girls.—*Literary World.* 374.

Dodge, Grace H., *Editor.*

THOUGHTS OF BUSY GIRLS. N. Y., Cassell & Co., 1892, 9+137 p., D. 50 c.
Written on a wide variety of practical subjects by some fifty members of working-girls' clubs. These papers prove that those busy girls who find, as their editor puts it, little time for study but much for thinking, are learning to think justly, and some of them to write vividly.—*Nation.* 374.

Hamerton, Philip G.

HUMAN INTERCOURSE. Bost., Roberts, 1884, 12+430 p., D. $2.
Graceful discussions of the rights of the guest, friendship, love, marriage, and much else. The author rightly deems that life owes much to the thoughtful and just cultivation of the social feelings. 824.80.

Kay, David.

MEMORY: WHAT IT IS AND HOW TO IMPROVE IT. (International Education series.) N. Y., Appleton, 1888, 26+334 p., D. $1.50.
The best popular work on memory. See also chapter XVI. in vol. I., James's "Psychology," Advanced Course. 154.

Legouvé, Ernest.

ART OF READING. Phila., Penn Pub. Co., 50 c.
An agreeable primer on the art of reading aloud with intelligence, and hence with expression. Author is senior member of the French Academy. See A. M. Bell's "Elocution" under EDUCATION. 808.5.

Mahaffy, J. P.

ART OF CONVERSATION. N. Y., Putnam, 1888, 9+174 p., S. 75 c.; Phila., Penn Pub. Co., 50 c.
Mr. Mahaffy is interested in improving the natural social gifts of men and women, and in getting them to talk together with more pleasure. He warns them of the shoals and reefs on which conversation is commonly wrecked in small and large companies.—*Nation.* 374.1.

Ruskin, John.

PEARLS FOR YOUNG LADIES: Letters and Advice on Education, Dress, Marriage, Influence, Work, Rights, etc.; collected and arranged by Mrs. L. C. Tuthill. N. Y., Merrill & Baker, 1887, 50 c., $1, and upwards.
A selection of beautiful thoughts and apothegms from the greatest living master of English prose. 824.80.

Willard, Frances E.

HOW TO WIN: A BOOK FOR GIRLS. N. Y., Funk & Wagnalls, 1886, 5+125 p., D. $1.
By the founder of the Women's Christian Temperance Union. Addressed rather to the development of character than to specific modes of bread-winning. 374.

ETIQUETTE.

Hall, Florence Howe.

SOCIAL CUSTOMS. Bost., Estes, $1.75.
A sensible treatise on etiquette and the forms of social observance. Helpful for home-makers, young and old, because founded on common sense. 305.

Jackson, Helen Hunt (H. H.).
BITS OF TALK ABOUT HOME MATTERS. Bost., Roberts, 1887, $1.

A book that ought to have a place of honor in every household. As we read it, we laugh and cry with the author.—*Harriet Prescott Spofford.*

Hardly treats of etiquette, strictly speaking, but of home relations and the courtesies of life. **396.**

Sherwood, *Mrs.* **John M.**
MANNERS AND SOCIAL USAGES. N. Y., Harper, 1887, 487 p., S. $1.25.

By a lady who has for many years moved in the best society of New York. **395.**

CLUBS FOR GIRLS AND WOMEN.

Jones, Mary Cadwalader.
WOMEN'S OPPORTUNITIES IN TOWN AND COUNTRY. Chap. XVI., Vol. II. Woman's Book. N. Y., Scribner, 1894, 2 vols., $7.50.

A sprightly presentation of out-of-door studies; village improvement societies; travel, book, and report clubs; the work of cooking-schools, college-settlements, kindergartens, day nurseries, Girls' Friendly Societies, Young Women's Christian Associations, Working-girls' Clubs, hospital visiting. **396.**

Miller, Harriet M. ("Olive Thorne Miller").
THE WOMAN'S CLUB. N. Y., Lovell, Coryell, 1891, 116 p., D. $1.

A very good practical guide and handbook for women who desire to form a club of almost any sort.—*Literary World.*

The author writes from large and satisfactory experience. **367.**

Stanley, Maude.
CLUBS FOR WORKING-GIRLS. New edition. N. Y., Macmillan, 1890, 276 p., D. $1.50.

Gives details of the management of English clubs for working girls, with descriptions of these clubs by the girls themselves, as also of their excursions to the country in summer. Miss Grace Dodge gives an account of working-girls' clubs in New York. . . . A book which one cannot read without a feeling of profound admiration.—*Nation.* **367.**

Shattuck, Harriette R.
WOMAN'S MANUAL OF PARLIAMENTARY LAW: with practical illustrations especially adapted to women's organizations. Bost., Lee & Shepard, 1892, 12+248 p., S. 75 c.

By the President of the Boston Political Class. Planned for women's clubs and other organizations. Full and clear. **328.1.**

USEFUL ARTS: LIVELIHOODS.

CHOSEN BY

AUGUSTA H. LEYPOLDT,
Editor Literary News.

New York, August, 1895.

GENERAL.

Croly, *Mrs.* **J. C.** (Jennie June, *pseudonym*).
THROWN ON HER RESOURCES; OR, WHAT GIRLS CAN DO. N. Y., T. Y. Crowell & Co., 1891, $1.
Read as a series of familiar talks, the volume will be interesting to many. The book needs decidedly more matter and more art in presentation.—*Nation.* 300.

Hubert, Philip G., Jr.
OCCUPATIONS FOR WOMEN. Vol. I., Chap. I., Woman's Book. N. Y., Scribner, 1894, 2 vols., $7.50.
Discusses Art Study, Architecture, Teaching, Typewriting, Stenography, Women's Exchanges, Trained Nursing, Medicine, Law, Journalism, Dressmaking, Millinery, Work at Home, Acting, Photography, How Women are Swindled. Sensibly written and informing. In the paragraph on Libraries Mr. Hubert's statement as to there being a Library School at Columbia College is wrong. There are Library Schools at the State Library, Albany, N. Y.; Pratt Institute, Brooklyn, N. Y.; Drexel Institute, Philadelphia; and in Summer at Amherst College, Amherst, Mass.
See also in Vol. II., p. 277, of the same work Supplementary Information, including reference to many important magazine articles. 300.

Meyer, Anna Nathan.
WOMAN'S WORK IN AMERICA. N. Y., Holt, 1891, 457 p., D. $1.50.
Contents: Introduction, Julia Ward Howe.—Woman in Education: In the East, Mary F. Eastman; In the West, May Wright Sewall; In the South, Christine Ladd Franklin.—Woman in Literature, Helen Gray Cone.—Woman in Journalism, Susan E Dickinson.—Woman in Medicine, Dr. Mary Putnam Jacobi.—Woman in the Ministry, Rev. Ada C. Bowles.—Woman in the State, Mary A. Livermore.—Woman in Law, Ada M. Bittenbender.—Woman in Industry, Alice Hyneman Rhine.—Woman in Philanthropy: Care of Poor, Josephine Shaw Lowell; Care of Sick, Edna D. Cheney; Care of Criminals, Susan Barney; Care of Indians, A. H. Quinton; Work of the W. C. T. U., Frances Willard; Work of the Red Cross, Clara Barton; Anti-Slavery Movement, Lillie B. Chace Wyman.
The editor's intent is to describe the fields of labor which contain evidences of woman's progress, those in which women, if entrance were not absolutely denied to them, were at least not welcomed nor valued. A book which needs and deserves thorough revision.—*Literary World.* 300.

Stoddard, William O.
WOMEN IN THEIR BUSINESS AFFAIRS. Vol. I., Chap. II., Woman's Book. N. Y., Scribner, 1894, 2 vols., $7.50.
Capital advice on Keeping Accounts, the Rights of Married Women, Signatures, Real Estate and its Care, Business Papers, Personal Property, Banking, Building and Loan Associations, Investments, Insurance, Wills.
See also Vol. II., p. 279, of the same work for supplementary information. 300.

Walker, Alfred.
HINTS TO WOMEN ON THE CARE OF PROPERTY. N. Y., Harper, 1878, paper, 20 c.
Full of sensible advice. Written some years ago, before the field of investment was as difficult as it is to-day. 332.

White, Sallie Joy.
BUSINESS OPENINGS FOR GIRLS. Bost., D. Lothrop Co., 1891, 75 c.
It would be difficult to find anywhere else encouragement at once so sound and so genial to girls and women to seek happiness and dignity in honest work.... To "newspaper-workers" Mrs. White speaks out of the fulness of 20 years' experience on the staff of the Boston *Herald.*—*Nation.* 300.

Woman's Book, dealing practically with the modern conditions of home-life, self-support, education, opportunities, and everyday problems. N. Y., Scribner, 1894, 2 vols., 400, 397 p., Q. $7.50.
Contents: Vol. I. Occupations for women, P. G. Hubert; Women in their business affairs, W. O. Stoddard; Principles of housekeeping, Lillian W. Betts; Society and social usages, Constance C. Harrison; Æsthetics of dress, Eva W. McGlasson; Dress from a practical standpoint, by several writers; Hygiene in the home, J. W. Roosevelt, M.D.; Training of children, Kate Douglas Wiggin; Education of women, Lyman Abbott; Books and reading, T. W. Higginson; Art of travel, Elizabeth Bisland. Vol. II. Home grounds, Samuel Parsons, Jr.; Flower garden, John N. Gerard; House building, Helen C. Candee; House decoration and furnishing, Mary G. Humphrey; Supplementary information; Women's opportunities in town and country, Mary C. Jones; Woman's handiwork, Constance C. Harrison.
The purpose is to give practical information and helpful suggestions touching all the subjects which concern the American women of to-day. The different writers have been carefully chosen, and have done excellent work. There is a valuable appendix, and a full index. Illustrated.—*Critic.* 300.

BOOKBINDING: PORCELAIN PAINTING: WOOD-CARVING: AND OTHER MINOR ARTS.

See also concluding titles and notes under FINE ART.

Leland, Charles G.
MANUAL OF WOOD-CARVING. Revised by John J. Holtzapffel. N. Y., Scribner, $1.75.
Arranged as twenty lessons, giving practical and exact instruction. Although it is impossible for printed instruction to take the place of a teacher, especially in explaining a handicraft, an ingenious girl or boy might take up wood-carving with the aid of this manual alone, and have a very fair chance of success. *Literary World.* 730.

MINOR ARTS, PORCELAIN PAINTING, WOODCARVING, STENCILING, MODELLING, MOSAIC WORK, etc. Illus. N. Y., Macmillan, 1880, 148 p., D. 90 c.
Simple and practical, and for use of elementary classes.—*Pratt Institute Library, Brooklyn, N. Y.* 740.

REPOUSSÉ WORK: embossing on sheet brass. Illus. N. Y., Art Interchange Co., 1883, 12 p. Q. 35 c. 739.

Painting on Silk, Satin, and Plush. Illus. N. Y., Art Interchange Co., 1885, 15 p., Q. 35 c. **750**.

Zaehnsdorf, J. W.

ART OF BOOKBINDING. Illus. N. Y., Macmillan, 1890, 187 p., D. $1.50.
Describes the various processes of binding in a clear and practical manner, giving directions for trade binding, and also for more elaborate and artistic work. Of value to those who are in the trade, as well as to amateurs.—*Pratt Institute Library, Brooklyn, N. Y.* **080**.

DRAWING: DESIGN.

See also titles and notes under FINE ART.

Jackson, Frank G.

LESSONS ON DECORATIVE DESIGN: an Elementary Text-Book. Lond., Chapman & Hall, 1891, 173 p., O. 7s. 6d.
Presents concisely and correctly the principles which underlie decorative design.—*Critic.*
Used as a text-book at Pratt Institute, Brooklyn, N. Y. **745**.

Martineau, Gertrude.

A VILLAGE CLASS FOR DRAWING AND WOODCARVING. N. Y., Longmans, 75 c.
A helpful little handbook for the use of teachers in freehand or object drawing and geometrical drawing. Arranged in lessons, profusely illustrated. **740**.

White, Gleeson, *Editor.*

PRACTICAL DESIGNING: a Handbook on the Preparation of Working Drawings. Illus. N. Y., Macmillan, 1893, 327 p., D. $2.50.
Aims to aid students in making practical designs for carpets, woven fabrics, floor cloths, etc. Explains from manufacturers' standpoint the limitations and requirements imposed by the material.—*Pratt Institute Library, Brooklyn, N. Y.* **740**.

PHOTOGRAPHY.

Abney, William de W.

PHOTOGRAPHY. N. Y., Longmans, 1878, $1.25.
Capt. Abney is one of the foremost photographers of the day, and this treatise is a standard work though published several years ago.—*Committee on Literature, Camera Club, N. Y.* **770**.

Adams, W. I. L.

AMATEUR PHOTOGRAPHY: a Practical Guide for the Beginner. N. Y., Baker & Taylor Co., 1893, 90 p., D. cloth, $1; paper, 50 c.
A brief, simple, and trustworthy guide, by the editor of the *Photographic Times*, N. Y. **770**.

Adams, W. I. L., *and* **Ehrmann, Charles.**

PHOTOGRAPHIC INSTRUCTOR FOR THE PROFESSIONAL AND AMATEUR. 3d ed. Illus. N. Y., Scovill & Adams Co., 1891, 215 p., O. $1.25.
A practical text-book on photography; fuller than 'Amateur Photography.' Contains a series of 24 lessons as given by Prof. Ehrmann at the Chautauqua School of Photography, which have been revised and enlarged, also an appendix on the nature and use of the various chemicals and substances employed in photographic practice. Amateurs will gain practical skill in the making of good photographs if they follow closely and exactly the instructions given.—*Pratt Institute Library, Brooklyn, N. Y.* **770**.

Meldola, Raphael.

THE CHEMISTRY OF PHOTOGRAPHY. (Nature series.) N. Y., Macmillan, 1891, 382 p., D. $2.
A series of lectures delivered to a class of advanced students by a celebrated English professor of chemistry. The author is the discoverer of several important chemical products used in photography. The work is a valuable one to the chemist who seeks knowledge about the chemistry of the art.—*Committee on Literature, Camera Club, N. Y.* **771**.

NEEDLEWORK: EMBROIDERY.

Croly, *Mrs.* **J. C.** (Jennie June, *pseudonym*), *Editor.*

LADIES' FANCY WORK: Embroidery, Needlework, Knitting, Painting on Silk, etc. N. Y., A. L. Burt, 1886, 150 p., Q. paper, 50 c.
A capital book, with 200 illustrations. **746**.

NEEDLEWORK: a Manual of Stitches and Studies in Embroidery and Drawn-Work. N. Y., A. L. Burt, 1885, 126 p., O. paper, 50 c.
Chiefly a compilation, with original additions, all excellent in quality and liberally illustrated. **746**.

Glaister, E.

NEEDLEWORK. (Art at Home series.) N. Y., Macmillan, 1880, 11+124 p., D. 90 c.
Contains many useful hints, and the remarks upon color, stitches, and materials are good and suggestive. The author describes the many sources from which a design may be culled, and the proper design to be used for particular objects.—*Nation.* **746**.

Hapgood, Olive C.

SCHOOL NEEDLEWORK: a course in sewing designed for use in schools. Bost., Ginn, 1893. Pupils' edition, 162 p., 60 c. Teachers' edition, 244 p., 85 c.
An excellent book for giving modern methods of teaching and learning sewing. The instructions are clear and stimulating. In Teachers' Edition, besides the needlework, short talks are given on the making of the material and instruments in use in sewing.—MARY SCHENCK WOOLMAN, *Instructor in Sewing, Teachers' College, New York.* **046**.

Kirkwood, L. J.

ILLUSTRATED SEWING PRIMER, with Songs and Music. N. Y., Am. Book Co. 1883, 67 p., D. 30 c.
Adapted for young pupils: full of suggestions for sewing school teachers. Author is a teacher of long and successful experience.—*Pratt Institute Library, Brooklyn, N. Y.* **046**.

Lefébure, Ernest, *and* **Cole, A. S.**

EMBROIDERY AND LACE, Their Manufacture and History from the Remotest Antiquity to the Present Day. Illus. Phila., Lippincott, 1888, 336 p., O. $3.50.
A handbook giving in detail the history of embroidery and lace-making; well illustrated, and aims to stimulate among women an interest in artistic work along these lines. Not a work of instruction.—*Pratt Institute Library, Brooklyn, N. Y.* **746**.

Leland, Charles G.

OUTLINE EMBROIDERY. N. Y., Art Interchange Co., 1892, 21 p., Q. paper, 35 c. **746**.

Rosevear, Elizabeth.

NEEDLEWORK, KNITTING AND CUTTING OUT. N. Y., Macmillan, 1894, $1.75.
A valuable and practical book of teaching methods

of sewing and draughting in English schools. It is filled with illustrations, and is accurate and clear in style.—MARY SCHENCK WOOLMAN, *Instructor in Sewing, Teachers' College, N. Y.*   040.

Woolman, Mary Schenck.

A SEWING COURSE FOR SCHOOLS. N. Y., Teachers' College. 1895. Without models, $3.50; with 45 models, $20.

A progressive course of sewing for the use of teachers in this branch of manual training. The instructions are short and to the point and the book is filled with matters helpful to the teacher. It is adapted for schools, mission-work, and private classes, and is text-book and model book combined, having bristol board pages inserted with the text. The instructions are sufficiently plain for those who wish to make their own models. Author is Instructor in Sewing, Teachers' College, New York and this course is now in use in the Domestic Department of the College.   040.

NOTE.

The "Butterick Publishing Co., New York, issue "Art of Crocheting," 143 p., an elementary book; "Fancy and Practical Crocheting," an advanced book; "Art of Drawn-Work," 117 p.; "Art of Knitting," 174 p.; and "Art of Lace-making," 134 p. Each book in large pages, bound in paper, and generously illustrated, 50c. All are clear and practical in their instructions, and all but "Fancy and Practical Crocheting" are suited to beginners as well as experts.

TYPE-WRITING.

Humphrey, F. S.

MANUAL OF TYPE-WRITING, Business Letter-Writing, and Exercises for Phonographic Practice. N. Y., Baker & Taylor Co., 1886, 185 p., O. $1.50.

Of special value to phonographers. Very full and helpful in its models of business correspondence, law forms, and specifications for engineers and builders. Not nearly so complete in its directions for manipulation as Torrey's book—next in this list.   652.

Torrey, Bates.

PRACTICAL TYPEWRITING BY THE ALL-FINGER METHOD. 3d edition, revised and enlarged. N. Y., Fowler & Wells Co., 1894, 174 p., O. $1.50.

A graduated series of exercises on the typewriter, arranged for self-instruction and school use. Insists on the use of all the fingers of both hands. No other work is so well and fully illustrated in directing the learner. The instruction is applied to all the leading machines. Many useful general hints are given.   652.

TELEGRAPHY: TELEPHONY.

Houston, Edwin J.

DICTIONARY OF ELECTRICAL WORDS, TERMS, AND PHRASES. 3d edition. Illus. N. Y., W. J. Johnston Co., 1894, 667 p., O. $5.

The most complete electrical dictionary in any language. Defines almost every existing electrical term, whether highly scientific or slang. Important facts are explained quite fully. It is a book of reference on all branches of electricity. Suited to the needs of everybody, from the general reader to the advanced electrical engineer.—F. B. CROCKER, *Prof. of Electrical Engineering, Columbia College, N. Y.*   537.

Lockwood, Thomas D.

PRACTICAL INFORMATION FOR TELEPHONISTS, N. Y., W J. Johnston Co., 1888, 192 p., D. $1.

Takes up various appliances and explains their use in simple language. Useful and practical.—*Pratt Institute Library, Brooklyn, N. Y.*   054.0.

Maver, William, *Jr.*

AMERICAN TELEGRAPHY. N. Y., J. H. Bunnell & Co., 1892, 563 p., il. Q. $3.50.

A clear and complete description of the various kinds of telegraph systems and apparatus. An excellent book of reference on telegraphy, brought right down to date. For the practical and practical advanced student, the engineer, electrical or not electrical.—F. B. CROCKER, *Prof. of Electrical Engineering, Columbia College, N. Y.*   054.

Poole, Joseph.

PRACTICAL TELEPHONE HANDBOOK AND GUIDE TO THE TELEPHONIC EXCHANGE. N. Y., Macmillan, 1891, 225 p., D. $1.

A practical manual which treats of the recent methods of telephonic working; fully illustrated. Somewhat more technical than Lockwood.   054.0.

JOURNALISM: AUTHORSHIP.

Dixey, Wolstan.

TRADE OF AUTHORSHIP. Brooklyn, N. Y., 73 Henry St., Wolstan Dixey, 1890, 128 p., D. $1.

Contents: The Author's Market, Trade, and Life. The liveliest and most readable book on its theme; it has no superior for good sense and comprehensiveness of information.—*Literary World*   020.6.

Luce, Robert.

WRITING FOR THE PRESS; a Manual for editors, reporters, correspondents and printers. Bost., Writer Pub. Co., 1891, 95 p., $1.

Contents: Preparing copy; words and phrases; noting common errors; use of titles; condensation; errors of arrangement; punctuation; proof-reading; newspaper writing; telegraph correspondence; reports of testimony; head-lines.

A capital book. Author was on the staff of the Boston *Globe*.   020.6.

BOOKSELLING.

Growoll, Adolf.

THE PROFESSION OF BOOKSELLING; a handbook of practical hints for the apprentice and bookseller. In 3 pts. Pt. 1. N. Y., Office of *The Publishers' Weekly*, 1893, 10+65 p. bds., $2.

Puts in accessible form, direction and information of a practical kind that may be of service to the young recruit in the ranks of the book trade, as well as suggestive to those who may already have worked their way along without assistance of any kind. The author, who is managing editor of *The Publishers' Weekly*, has submitted each chapter to the revision of one, in many cases to the revision of several authorities on the subject, so that the work is not the expression of an individual but the composite opinion of several masters. The chapter "Bibliography of Literature," is excellent reading for those who would become familiar with the literatures of the world. The second part, which will be issued shortly, contains an admirably condensed description of bookbinding from a practical point of view, as well as a history of bibliopegic art from its earliest beginning to the present; illustrated with 16 representative bindings. The third part, in preparation, will contain matter of interest chiefly to the antiquarian bookseller and stationer. Parts II. and III. will be $2 each.   055.50.

COUNTRY OCCUPATIONS.

THE FARM: ORCHARD, KITCHEN AND MARKET GARDEN: DAIRY: POULTRY: BEE KEEPING: FLOWER GARDEN: LANDSCAPE GARDENING: BY

L. H. BAILEY,

Professor of Horticulture, Agricultural College, Cornell University, Ithaca, N. Y., and B. M. Watson, Jr., Instructor Bussey Institution of Harvard University, Jamaica Plain, Mass.

June, 1895.

Mr. Watson's notes are those on the books of P. Barry, P. Henderson, S. W. Johnson, W. Robinson, L. R. Taft, and Mrs. S. Van Rensselaer. All other notes are by Prof. L. H. Bailey.

See BOTANY for Gray's "Manual" and other works useful in this department.

THE FARM.

Aikman, C. M.

MANURES AND THE PRINCIPLES OF MANURING. Lond., W. Blackwood & Sons, 1894, 592 p., D. $2.25.

The most recent account of the theory and practice of enriching the land, considering the question in all its aspects. **631.**

Johnson, S. W.,

HOW CROPS FEED. N. Y., Orange Judd Co., 1894, $2.

"A treatise on the atmosphere and the soil as related to the nutrition of agricultural plants." A companion volume to "How Crops Grow." Taken together, they form a very complete statement of the methods of growth in plants, and their relation to soil and air. By their aid many of the common operations of husbandry are explained. Adapted to all who take a more than cursory interest in plant life. Requires an elementary knowledge of chemistry. **630.2.**

HOW CROPS GROW. New and rev. ed. Illus. N. Y., Orange Judd Co., 416 p., D. $2.

"A treatise on the chemical composition, structure, and life of a plant." Designed for students of agricultural chemistry, and adapted to all who wish information on the composition, structure, modes of development, organization and use of the different parts of a plant. **630.2.**

Waring, Geo. E., *Jr.*

ELEMENTS OF AGRICULTURE: a Book for Young Farmers. N. Y., O. Judd Co., 251 p., D. $1.

A plain synoptical account of the way in which the plant lives and grows, of the soil, of manures, mechanical cultivation, and the like. Discusses the whole field of the underlying principles of agriculture. **630.2.**

ORCHARD AND KITCHEN GARDEN.

Bailey, L. H.

AMERICAN GRAPE TRAINING. N. Y., Rural New Yorker, 1893, 95 p., O. 75 c.

The only work devoted to the training of American grapes. Illustrated with photo-engravings directly from the vines. It treats all the leading systems. **634.**

HORTICULTURIST'S RULE-BOOK. 3d edition. N. Y., Macmillan, 1895, 75 c.

A Compendium of Useful Information for Fruit-Growers, Truck-Gardeners, Florists, and Others. A condensed manual of all rules and recipes and figures used by horticulturists; as insecticides, fungicides, means of combating all the important insects and fungi, planting-tables, dates of planting, yields, estimates for heating greenhouses, greenhouse rules of practice, tables of weights and measures, legal and customary standards, grafting waxes, methods of packing and storing fruits and vegetables, and thousands of other useful facts. **634.**

Barry, P.

FRUIT GARDEN. New edition. Illus. N. Y., O. Judd Co., 516 p., D. $2.

A thoroughly practical treatise on all kinds of fruit-growing carried on in this country. The various details of preparation of the soil, propagation and cultivation are explained; the general arrangement and management of permanent plantations are given; there are complete lists and descriptions of our numerous varieties of fruits, with chapters on gathering, packing, shipping, and preserving. Insects and fungous pests are considered. Good lists of the better varieties of fruits are made, which are valuable to novices. **634.**

Burpee, W. Atlee.

HOW AND WHAT TO GROW IN A KITCHEN GARDEN OF ONE ACRE. Phila., W. Atlee Burpee & Co., 1888, 198 p., D. 50c.

A brief handbook advising a selection of soils and varieties, and methods of cultivation and treatment, for a home or mixed vegetable garden. **035.**

Biggle, Jacob.

BIGGLE BERRY BOOK. Phila., Farm Journal, 1894, 126 p., D. 50 c.

A little book giving summary statements of many growers concerning the best methods and varieties in growing strawberries, raspberries, blackberries, currants, and gooseberries, etc. Fullest on strawberries. Has colored plates of varieties. **634.**

Greiner, T.

HOW TO MAKE THE GARDEN PAY. Phila., Wm. Hy. Maule, 1890, 272 p., D. $2.

A complete illustrated manual of vegetable gardening, for both amateurs and market gardeners. It is a concise and reliable exposition of the entire subject for field culture, with advice on forcing structures. **035.**

Henderson, Peter

GARDENING FOR PROFIT. New and enlarged

edition. Illus. N. Y., O. Judd Co., 376 p., D. $2.

Although written for market gardeners, this book is invaluable to any one who wishes to grow good vegetables. Preparation of soil and manures, cultivation in all phases, lists and descriptions of different vegetables are given. This is the book of a practical man, one of the best gardeners and horticultural writers we have had. It is adapted to the use of everybody who desires a vegetable garden. **035.**

Rawson, W. W.

SUCCESS IN MARKET GARDENING. Bost., W. W. Rawson, 1892, $1.

A condensed manual of commercial vegetable growing, under glass and in the field, in New England. **035.**

Roe, E. P.

SUCCESS WITH SMALL FRUITS. N. Y., Dodd, Mead & Co., 1881, 388 p., D. $1.50; illus., $2.50.

A pleasant, readable account of the best practices of growing and selling the berry fruits, as strawberries, raspberries, currants, gooseberries, etc. **634.**

Sempers, F. W.

INJURIOUS INSECTS AND THE USE OF INSECTICIDES. Phila., W. Atlee Burpee & Co., 1894, 216 p., D. 50 c.

A practical and profusely illustrated handbook of all common insect pests, with means of combating them. It is designed wholly as a practical manual. **632.**

Terry, T. B., and Root, A. I.

HOW TO GROW STRAWBERRIES. Medina, Ohio, A. I. Root, 1890, 144 p., D. 40 c.

The most explicit manual of strawberry growing. A chatty record of experiences. **634.**

THE DAIRY.

Gurler, H. B.

AMERICAN DAIRYING. Chic., Breeders' Gazette, 1894, 267 p., D. $1.

A practical manual, specifying the feeding and care of a dairy herd, and the actual operations in the manufacture of milk products and the care of a creamery. **637.**

Russell, H. L.

OUTLINES OF DAIRY BACTERIOLOGY. Madison, Wis., H. L. Russell, 1894, 156 p., D. $1.

Discusses the latest phases of the rôle of microbes and fermentation in the modification of milk, butter, and cheese. **637.**

POULTRY.

Collingwood, H. W.

THE BUSINESS HEN. N. Y., Rural New Yorker, 1892, 150 p., D. paper, 50 c.

A handbook of methods and management of poultry for profit, comprising feeding and marketing the product. The chapters are contributed by various poultrymen. Gives little attention to fancy breeds. **030.5.**

Felch, I. K.

POULTRY CULTURE. Chic., Donohue, Henneberry & Co., 1885, 430 p., D. $1.50.

Discusses the subject from a fancier's standpoint. Very full upon mating and breeding thoroughbred fowls, and upon scoring and judging. **030.5.**

Wright, Lewis.

PRACTICAL POULTRY KEEPER. N.Y., O. Judd Co., 243 p., D. $2.

Chiefly a description of breeds and varieties, and their origin, with only short accounts of methods of management and feeding. Preface dated 1867. **030.5.**

BEE-KEEPING.

Cook, A. J.

BEE-KEEPER'S GUIDE; OR, MANUAL OF THE APIARY. Chic., Thomas G. Newman, 1881, 302 p., D. $1.50.

Part I. comprises the natural history of the honey bee, and the anatomy and physiology of the insect. Part II. is a detailed manual of the most approved operations in apiculture, being full upon all practical points of the business. **038.**

FLOWER-GARDEN.

Ellwanger, H. B.

THE ROSE. N. Y., Dodd, Mead & Co., 1882, 293 p., D. $1.25.

A full account of the tribes and types of roses, and a manual of their cultivation, both in the open and under glass. Particularly full on varieties. **716.**

Heinrich, Julius.

WINDOW FLOWER-GARDEN. N. Y., Orange Judd Co., 75 c.

A commendable little book. **716.**

Henderson, Peter.

PRACTICAL FLORICULTURE. New and enlarged edition. Illus. N. Y., O. Judd Co., 1893, 325 p., D., $1.50.

Plain, practical directions for growing tender plants and flowers. Originally written for men who make this their business, it is, nevertheless, by far the best book obtainable for the amateur. Both this book and "Gardening for Profit" contain chapters on cold frames and pits, hot-beds, and simple greenhouse construction. Adapted to all who wish to obtain the best up-to-date methods. **716.**

Hunt, M. A.

HOW TO GROW CUT FLOWERS. N. Y., Florists' Exchange; Chic., American Florist, 1893, 228 p., D. $2.

A practical manual by a successful florist, comprising excellent chapters on greenhouse or forcing house construction, with explicit directions for growing roses, carnations, chrysanthemums, violets, mignonette, bulbs, and orchids. **710.**

Mathews, F. Schuyler.

THE BEAUTIFUL FLOWER GARDEN. Phila., W. Atlee Burpee & Co., 1894, 50 c.

Treats flowers and flower-growing from the artists' point of view, and it is profusely illustrated with excellent pen sketches by the author. It is the only American handbook which treats the subject from this standpoint. Directions are also given for the growing of the common flowers. **710.**

Robinson, W.

ENGLISH FLOWER-GARDEN. 3d edition. Lond., John Murray, 1893, 751 p., O. 15 s.

Well suited for American use, although written for the climatic conditions of Great Britain. Deals with hardy plants, herbaceous perennials in particular, some annuals, and some flowering trees and shrubs. The opening chapters give good advice on laying-out, and the general care of gardens. There are copious lists of different classes of plants for special purposes. The bulk of the book is devoted to an alphabetical list of hardy plants for garden use, with description and important directions for culture. The reader must remember that the English climate is less exacting than the American, and that some plants here set down as hardy are tender in America. The illustrations are numerous and much better in quality than usual in gardening books. **716.**

Taft, L. R.
GREENHOUSE CONSTRUCTION. Illus. N. Y., O. Judd Co., 1894, 208 p., D. $1.50.

A thoroughly good book for any one planning to build a greenhouse. Contains descriptions of all the new and improved methods of construction and equipment. Written for amateurs as well as florists. Methods particularly adapted to American climate. **710.3**.

LANDSCAPE GARDENING.

Kemp, Edward.
LANDSCAPE GARDENING ; OR, HOW TO LAY OUT A GARDEN. American edition. N. Y., John Wiley & Son, 1880, 403 p., D. $2.50.

Probably the best single handbook which aims to cover the entire field of theory and practice of landscape gardening. It introduces the subject with an excellent discussion of the principles of the art, and the rules of design follow as suggestions therefrom.
710.

Parsons, Samuel, *Jr.*
LANDSCAPE GARDENING. N. Y., Putnam, 1891, 329 p., Q. $3.50.

Considers the subject from the side of plants and planting effects, rather than from the side of design. An artistic volume of the greatest interest to students of plant forms and their artistic expressions. Author has contributed " The Home Grounds," Chap. XII., Vol. II., Woman's Book, N. Y., Scribner, 2 vols., $7.50.
710.

Van Rensselaer, *Mrs.* **Schuyler.**
ART OUT-OF-DOORS. N. Y., Scribner, 1893, 399 p., D. $1.50.

A most readable and instructive book for all who own land and attempt its cultivation. Without being a practical treatise on landscape gardening, it contains a great deal of excellent advice about all matters pertaining to ornamental planting in its different forms. Adapted to all who wish to improve or embellish country places. In appendix is a list of standard books on landscape gardening. **710.**

DOMESTIC ECONOMY.

CHOSEN BY

AUGUSTA H. LEYPOLDT,
Editor Literary News.

New York, August, 1895.

ARCHITECTURE.

See also under FINE ART.

Brunner, A. W.
  COTTAGES: Hints on Economical Building. N. Y., W. T. Comstock, 1884, 78 p., D. $1.
  Gives 24 designs for inexpensive country houses, planned by good architects. With a chapter by W. Paul Gerhard on Water Supply, Drainage, Heating, and Ventilation. 728.

Candee, Helen Churchill.
  HOUSE-BUILDING. Vol. II., Chap. XIV., Woman's Book. N. Y., Scribner, 1894, 2 vols., $7.50.
  A thoroughly helpful chapter from the point of view of the woman who occupies a house, and who, with no undue awe of the architect, desires the house to be wholesome, cheery, convenient, and not too dear. 390.

Gibson, L. H.
  CONVENIENT HOUSES, with 50 plans for the housekeeper, architect, and housewife; a journey through the home; practical house-building for the owner; business points in building; how to pay for a home. N. Y., Crowell, 1889, 321 p., O. $2.50.
  One of the most practical books of the kind. The author is a practising architect, who writes with knowledge, clearness, and sense. Plans are given for fifty houses, mostly of a very modest kind, with exteriors of several. The amateur house-builder should get a good deal of useful instruction and many sensible suggestions from this book —*Nation.* 728.

Osborne, C. Francis.
  NOTES ON THE ART OF HOUSE-PLANNING. N. Y., W. T. Comstock, 1888, 106 p., D. $1.
  A useful book on arranging the rooms of a house in the most convenient way, without wasting space. 728.

Sturgis, Russell, *and Others.*
  HOMES IN CITY AND COUNTRY. Illus. N. Y., Scribner, 1893, 8+214 p., O. $2.
  Contents: The City House in the East and South, by Russell Sturgis; The City House in the West, by John W. Root; The Suburban House, by Bruce Price; The Country House, by Donald G. Mitchell ["Ik Marvel"]; Small Country Places, by S. Parsons, Jr ; Building and Loan Associations—a clear and interesting explanation—by W. A. Linn—with pictures of houses at $1050, and upward, built by Associations. The other illustrations represent American architecture from Colonial times to the present day. The architects who contribute chapters are among the foremost in America. 728.

Suburban and Country Homes: forty-five designs for houses of moderate cost. N. Y., Wm. T. Comstock, 1894, cloth, $2; paper, $1.
  The designs are by various practising architects of standing. Includes "Suggestions on House Building," by Albert Winslow Cobb; and "How to Plumb a Suburban House," by Leonard D. Hosford—two useful chapters. 728.

HOUSE DECORATION AND FURNISHING.

Brunner, Arnold W., *and* **Tryon, Thomas.**
  INTERIOR DECORATION. Illus. N. Y., Wm. T. Comstock, 1891, 65 p., Q. cloth, $2; paper, $1.50.
  Authors are architects; they offer decorations suited to the hall, staircase, library, parlor, dining-room, study, and bedrooms, both for city and country houses. Many good hints are given for altering and bettering old work, and on furnishing. A book which will suggest many points for discussion before the practising architect and decorator are called upon. 740.

Eastlake, *Sir* **Charles L.**
  HINTS ON HOUSEHOLD TASTE. Edited by C. C. Perkins. Illus. Bost., Houghton, 1881, $3.
  By the famous designer. His book, though written in 1878, is a classic, and can be gainfully consulted to-day. 740.

Garrett, Rhoda *and* **Agnes.**
  SUGGESTIONS FOR HOUSE DECORATION, in Painting, Woodwork and Furniture. Phila., Porter, 1877, $1.
  Written from the artist's point of view, and requiring some means and previous knowledge to carry out its ideas. 740.

Girl's Room, A. With plans and designs for work up stairs and down, and entertainments for herself and friends. Bost., D. Lothrop Co., 1886, 236 p., D. $1.
  A chatty book about furnishing and decorating a girl's room in good taste at little cost. The directions for making odds and ends and for recreations are capital. 740.

Harrison, Constance Cary.
  WOMEN'S HANDIWORK IN MODERN HOMES. N. Y., Scribner, 1881, 12+242 p., O. $2.
  Treats of embroidery, painting, and wood-carving, and gives practical hints for the decoration of modern homes. Contains five colored plates and numerous illustrations. 740.

Humphreys, Mary Gay.
  HOUSE DECORATION AND FURNISHING. Vol. II., Chap. XV., Woman's Book. N. Y., Scribner, 1894, 2 vols., $7.50.
  Discusses the subject as it appeals to women of purse and good taste. Women who earn their bread by decorative art will find some valuable hints here.
  See also in the same volume, page 336, "Practical House Furnishing" by Lida Rose McCabe. 390.

Wheeler, Candace, *Editor.*
  HOUSEHOLD ART. (Distaff series.) N. Y., Harper, 1893, 204 p., S. $1.
  Contents: The philosophy of beauty applied to house interiors, Candace Wheeler; the development of American homes, Mrs. M. G. Van Rensselaer; some work of the Associated Artists, Mrs. Burton Harrison;

wall-papers, ceilings and dados, Susan N. Carter; the progress of American decorative art, Mary Gay Humphreys; the limits of decoration, Lucia Gilbert Runkle; about furnishings, Florence Morse; decorative and applied art, Candace Wheeler.
Brief and sketchy papers of interest. 740.

HOUSEKEEPING: GENERAL.

See under PHYSICAL CULTURE for Hygiene, Sanitation, Nursing, and Emergencies: *see* under USEFUL ARTS for Needlework.

Betts, Lillian W.
THE PRINCIPLES OF HOUSEKEEPING. Vol. I., Chap. III., Woman's Book. N. Y., Scribner, 1894. 2 vols., $7.50.
A thorough survey of the duties of housekeeping, and of recent labor-saving inventions, including the Aladdin oven and the electric cooker. Discussing popular cook-books, Mrs. Betts points out their deficiencies and inconsistencies, declaring them to be "good servants, but bad mistresses."
See also Vol. II., page 307, of this work for supplementary information. 306.

Butler, Edward A.
OUR HOUSEHOLD INSECTS. Illus. N. Y., Longmans, 1893. 10+344 p., D. $2.
An excellent book, which any housewife may read with profit, and every entomologist will find convenient for reference. Although primarily written for English readers, it is equally available for America. It is not a book of remedies for pests, but those who intelligently read it will be far better able to cope with their tormentors than ever before.—*Nation.* 591.05.

Goodholme, Todd D., *Editor.*
DOMESTIC CYCLOPÆDIA OF PRACTICAL INFORMATION. New edition. Illus. N. Y., Scribner, 1889. 650 p., O. $5.
A book of reference on all household subjects. Includes Drainage, the Garden, and the Dairy, by George E. Waring, jr.; Locating, Building, and Repairing, by Calvert Vaux and Thomas Wisedell; Warming and Ventilation, by Lewis Leeds; Decoration as applied to Walls, Floors, and Furniture, by Geo. Fletcher Babb; Domestic Chemistry—disinfecting, cleaning, and dyeing, by Elwyn Waller; Dietetics and Alcoholic Beverages, by Austin Flint, M.D.; Diseases and Hygiene of Children, by Abr. Jacobi, M.D.; General Medicine, by Wm. T. Lusk, M.D.; Cooking and Domestic Management, by Mrs. Elizabeth S. Miller and Giuseppi Rudmani; Business Forms and Legal Rules, by Johnson T. Platt. The *Nation* calls it "an indispensable book in every well-regulated family." 640.

Herrick, Christine Terhune.
HOUSEKEEPING MADE EASY. N. Y., Harper, 1888. 7+313 p., S. $1.
Gives minute directions for every important duty of the household, beginning with renting, furnishing and settling the house, and engaging the maid. Then follows the routine for each day of the week; the care of cellar, kitchen and pantry; the war on dust and dirt; gathering up fragments; marketing, dressmaking and much else.
"Housekeeping done thoroughly" would have better defined this book. The writer is a sensible woman, with a practical knowledge of her subject.—*Nation.*
640.

Nitsch, Helen. (Catherine Owen, *pseudonym.*)
TEN DOLLARS ENOUGH: Keeping house well on ten dollars a week. Bost., Houghton, 1887. 9+279 p., D. $1.
A narrative of the struggles and triumphs of a young wife. Its simple story gives a personal interest to household matters, and offers good receipts not found in formal cook-books. 640.

FOOD: COOKING: SERVING.

Abel, Mary Hinman.
PRACTICAL SANITARY AND ECONOMIC COOKING, adapted to persons of moderate and small means. Rochester, N. Y., American Public Health Assoc., 1890. 11+190 p., D. 40 c.
This little volume is more than a collection of recipes. Mrs. Abel states simply and clearly the underlying principles of wholesomeness of diet and sensible cookery. She suggests many expedients that make for health and economy. Her receipts are practical, and many of them inexpensive.—HELEN KINNE, *Instructor in Cooking, Teachers' College, N. Y.* 641.

Atkinson, Edward.
THE SCIENCE OF NUTRITION. 4th edition, revised and enlarged. Bost., Damrell & Upham, 1895. 247 p., D. $1.
Mr Atkinson in this book tells in clear and simple language all that he knows about cooking nutritious and toothsome food with the least possible trouble and at the lowest cost. His invention, the Aladdin Oven, for cooking at lower temperatures than common, and within non-conducting walls so as not to cook the cook, is fully described, with all the instructions for use the inventor can give. The Aladdin Oven (or Atkinson Cooker) is manufactured by the Asbestos Paper Co., 71 Kilby St., Boston, Mass., $12. With full equipment, namely, Mr. Atkinson's "Science of Nutrition," lamp, cooking thermometer, an extra metallic table, two vegetable pans, and one roasting-pan with grates, $20. The Oven is adapted for oil or gas. 641.

Bostwick, Lucy W.
MARGERY DAW'S HOME CONFECTIONERY. N. Y., Brentano, 50 c.
Describes how to prepare cooked and uncooked candies of all kinds, many of them good and inexpensive. 642.

Canned Foods and How to Use Them.
N. Y., Ward, Lock & Bowden, 1893, $1.
Several hundred receipts, many of them new, are given for the preparation of tinned foods for camping and excursion parties, and for meals at home. Canned foods so largely enter into the modern bill of fare that this book is a welcome addition to the kitchen shelf. 641.

Corson, Juliet.
PRACTICAL AMERICAN COOKERY AND HOUSEHOLD MANAGEMENT. N. Y., Dodd, Mead & Co., 1886, 22+591 p., D. $1.50.
Full of excellent receipts. Includes the care of children and invalids, and careful instructions for marketing and carving.—*Critic.*
Good, but somewhat elaborate. Miss Corson's methods are decidedly French. She is one of the best teachers of her art in America. 641.

Henderson, Mary F.
DIET FOR THE SICK: a Treatise on the Values of Foods, their application to special conditions of health and disease, and on the best methods of their preparation. Illus. N. Y., Harper, 1885, $1.50.
A comprehensive and reliable book. Its bills of fare for invalids are adapted to a wide variety of cases. 641.

Herrick, Christine Terhune.
CHAFING-DISH SUPPER. N. Y., Scribner, 1894, 75 c.
Practical suggestions as to the choice and use of chafing-dishes, with receipts for toothsome dishes, and half-a-dozen menus for Sunday night teas. 641.

LIBERAL LIVING UPON NARROW MEANS, Bost., Houghton, 1890, $1.
A menu well planned and economically considered is offered for every day of a week during each month of the year. Includes valuable hints for avoiding waste.—*Critic.* 641.

THE LITTLE DINNER. N. Y., Scribner, $1.

Helpful to young housekeepers who wish to entertain simply, yet want something more elaborate than the every day dinner.—HELEN KINNE, *Instructor in Cooking, Teachers' College, N. Y.* 041.

Lemcke, Gesine.

DESSERTS AND SALADS, European and American, economical and dainty. 5th edition. N. Y., C. T. Dillingham & Co., 1892, 296 p., O. $1.25.

A comprehensive and trustworthy guide: its receipts are clearly written. 041.

EUROPEAN AND AMERICAN CUISINE. N. Y., Appleton, 1895, 600 p., O. $2.

Directions include receipts for more than 200 soups and 300 modes of cooking fish—branches commonly neglected in cook-books. Other departments, excepting desserts and salads (see foregoing book), are equally full. Quantities, time and method are stated with the clearness and accuracy of an accomplished teacher. 041.

Lincoln, *Mrs.* **D. A.**

BOSTON COOK-BOOK. What to do and what not to do in cooking. Bost., Roberts Bros., 1890, 14+536 p., D. $2.

A trustworthy guide in practical cookery. The arrangement of the topics is systematic, and the directions for work so concise and exact that a novice in following them is able to obtain good results. A book for well-to-do people. Though not a scientific treatise, it gives a useful outline of the chemistry and physiology of food.—HELEN KINNE, *Instructor in Cooking, Teachers' College, N. Y.* 041.

BOSTON SCHOOL KITCHEN TEXT-BOOK, lessons in cooking for the use of classes in public and industrial schools. Bost., Roberts Bros., 1888, 232 p., D. $1.

Just what its name implies; a study of food, and explanation of general principles in cooking; adapted for practical use in the classes of public and industrial schools.—*Critic.*
Specially good for chemistry of foods. 041.

CARVING AND SERVING. Bost., Roberts Bros., 1887, 52 p., S. 60 c.

Plain practical directions designed to teach women how to carve with ease and grace. 043.

Nitsch, *Mrs.* **Helen.** (Catherine Owen, *pseud.*)

LESSONS IN CANDY-MAKING. Springfield, Mass., C. W. Bryan & Co., 1887, 70 p., D. 50 c.

Practical receipts for making candy, with directions for coloring it. Intended for women wishing to earn money at their homes. Emphasizes the importance of making the candy equal in all respects to that of confectioners.—*Pratt Institute Library, Brooklyn, N. Y.* 042.

Parloa, Maria.

FIRST PRINCIPLES OF HOUSEHOLD MANAGEMENT AND COOKERY: a Text-book for Schools and Families. New and enlarged edition. Bost., Houghton, 1885, 12+176 p., S. 75 c.

A practical little text-book in clear language. Discusses the chemical composition of foods, and outlines a series of twelve lessons. Adds many simple and economical receipts, which are the result of the author's experience in teaching classes of women. Offers valuable suggestions for diet for the sick.—*Pratt Institute Library, Brooklyn, N. Y.* 041.

KITCHEN COMPANION: a Guide for all who wish to be good housekeepers. Bost., Estes & Lauriat, 1887, $2.50.

An exhaustive culinary treatise; everything from building the kitchen to placing ferns on the table is explained.—*Critic.* 041.

Richards, Amy G.

COOKERY. Montreal, Canada, E. M. Renouf, 1895, 436 p., D. $1.25.

A very complete and useful book. Many of the receipts are new; all are well chosen. Miss Richards is an exponent of the Canadian school, one in which the best elements of English and French cookery are combined. 041.

Rorer, *Mrs.* **S. T.**

CANNING AND PRESERVING. N. Y., O. Judd Co., 40 c.

Full and easy directions for canning and preserving fruits and vegetables; making jellies, syrups, and catsups; drying herbs and fruits. 041.

PHILADELPHIA COOK BOOK. Phila., Arnold & Co., 1886, $1.75.

Comprehensive and reliable. Brief introductions explain the chemistry and the mode of selecting the viands. 041.

Springsteed, Anne Frances.

THE EXPERT WAITRESS. N. Y., Harper, 1894, 131 p., D. $1.

Explains in minute detail the method of laying and serving the table at all meals; also gives clear directions for the performance of the other duties required of a waitress in private families The housekeeper who does not have a waitress will find useful hints in this book. 047.

Terhune, *Mrs.* **Mary V. H.** (Marion Harland, *pseud.*).

BREAKFAST, LUNCHEON, AND TEA. N. Y., Scribner, 1883, $1.75.

COMMON SENSE IN THE HOUSEHOLD: a manual of practical housewifery. Majority edition, revised. N. Y., Scribner, 1892, 7+546 p., D. $1.50. 640.

Chiefly a cookery book, including dishes for the nursery and sick-room. A few directions for washing, cleaning, and the like are added.

Mrs. Terhune's cookery is distinctively American, of the Southern school; her receipts are trustworthy, and the directions sufficiently clear to be followed successfully by the inexperienced housewife. Some of her dishes, notably the desserts, are too rich, but every cook modifies the receipts she uses. There is a decided charm in the cordial tone of the little talks interspersed through Mrs. Terhune's household books. 041.

DINNER GIVING. N. Y., Scribner, 1883, 713 p., D. $1.75.

A simple bill of fare for every day in the year, with full directions for cooking and serving; twelve elaborate menus are also given. 041.

Thompson, *Sir* **Henry,** *M.D.*

FOOD AND FEEDING. 5th edition, revised and enlarged. N. Y., Warne, 1887, 174 p., D. $1.25.

Contents include: Choice of food, suggestions as to cooking—with some recipes, arrangement and combination of meals. Rebukes the general habit of eating too much meat and fat.—*Literary World.* 043.

White, Sallie Joy.

COOKERY IN THE PUBLIC SCHOOLS. Bost., D. Lothrop Co., 1890, 173 p., D. 75 c.

Sketches the origin and growth of industrial education for girls; argues for public cooking schools on the ground of their success in Boston; gives a course of lessons on cooking based on those of the Boston schools. Lays stress on cleanliness, economy, and attractive service. Girls desirous of studying cookery with a view to becoming class-teachers will here learn something of the requirements demanded for the position. 641.

Williams, W. Mattieu.
CHEMISTRY OF COOKERY. N. Y., Appleton, 1885, 328 p., D. $1.50.
Explains in simple terms the chemistry of boiling, roasting, grilling, frying, and stewing. Discusses the nourishing qualities of various foods and how these qualities are affected by cooking. Has a word of sense on vegetarianism. The author was a chemist of eminence, and his chapters are based on experiment and experience. The reader need know little more than the barest rudiments of chemistry to get much good from this book. 641.

LAUNDRY: SCOURING: DYEING.

Calder, F. L., and Mann, E. E.
TEACHERS' MANUAL OF ELEMENTARY LAUNDRY WORK. N. Y., Longmans, 1891, 76 p., S. 30 c.
As useful at home as at school. Describes washing materials, utensils and their uses, and preparation for washing. Gives capital receipts for washing, starching, bleaching, ironing, and removing stains. Both authors are English; one is a teacher. There is no American book on this subject. 648.

Hurst, George H.
HANDBOOK OF GARMENT DYEING AND CLEANING. Lond., C. Griffin & Co.; Phila., Lippincott, 1895, 180 p., D. $1.75.
A thoroughly practical work by an English chemist. Besides dyeing and cleaning garments, it treats of bleaching and finishing fabrics, of scouring and dyeing skin rugs and mats, cleaning and dyeing feathers, glove cleaning and dyeing, and straw bleaching and dyeing. Fully illustrated. 667.2.

Rothery, G. C.
HANDBOOK OF LAUNDRY MANAGEMENT. Illus. Lond., Crosby Lockwood & Son, 1889, O. 2s. 6d.
Part I., devoted to operations and processes, is quite worth the price of the volume to the housewife. Part II., dealing with building and machinery, would only interest those who pursue laundering as a trade. The high grade of intelligence required in the commercial laundry of to-day by the introduction of machinery adds one more to the list of profitable employments open to women. 648.

DRESS.

Davis, Jeannette E.
ELEMENTS OF MODERN DRESS-MAKING. N. Y., Cassell & Co., 1894, 12+193 p., D. $1.
A handbook for the use of students, amateur or professional, and of those qualifying to teach dressmaking in public schools. Goes thoroughly into the subjects of bodice and skirt making, fitting, finishing, etc., and gives valuable information concerning standard dress fabrics and the linings and other materials used in the construction of a gown. Written in plain, simple language, with illustrative diagrams. Much to be commended. 640.

Dress from a Practical Standpoint.
By several writers. Vol. I., Chap. VI., Woman's Book. N. Y., Scribner, 2 vols., $7.50.
Hints for dress for infants, young children, schoolgirls and adults. Describes sensible articles of dress in detail, wedding trousseaux, furs and mourning, and the care of clothes. Tells about dressmaking and millinery at home and at school. 390.

Ecob, Helen Gilbert.
THE WELL-DRESSED WOMAN: a study in the practical application to dress of the laws of health, art, and morals. N. Y., Fowler & Wells Co., 1893, 8+262 p., D. $1.
A sensible and useful account of the harm done to modern women by tight-fitting garments and heavy skirts. It is capable of raising from apathy those who feel indifferent to the subject, and helping the woman who wants to know the truth but has little time to study for herself.—MARY SCHENCK WOOLMAN, *Instructor in Sewing, Teachers' College, N. Y.* 646.

Hill, Georgiana.
HISTORY OF ENGLISH DRESS. Lond., R. Bentley & Son, 1893, 2 vols., 322, 342 p., O. 30s.
From the Roman occupation of Great Britain to the present day. Well illustrated. Concludes with an excellent chapter on taste in dress and the secret of good dressing. 646.

McGlasson, Eva Wilder.
ÆSTHETICS OF DRESS. Vol. I., Chap. V., Woman's Book. N. Y., Scribner, 1894, 2 vols., $7.50.
Treats of taste, sincerity, simplicity, unity, appropriateness, textile fabrics, colors, line, hygiene, conventionality, individuality, originality, picturesqueness, eccentricity. A good chapter. 390.

Steele, Frances Mary, and Adams, E. L. S.
BEAUTY OF FORM AND GRACE OF VESTURE. N. Y., Dodd Mead & Co., 1892, 7 + 231 p., D, $1.75.
Contains suggestions for the making of a healthful and artistic style of garment for women. Dress is considered as a means of expression, and the desire is to make the expression sensible and worthy.—MARY SCHENCK WOOLMAN, *Instructor in Sewing, Teachers' College, N. Y.* 640.

AMUSEMENTS AND SPORTS.

CHOSEN AND ANNOTATED BY

ALICE B. KROEGER,
Librarian, Drexel Institute, Philadelphia.

Philadelphia, June, 1895.

GENERAL.

Bartlett, George B.
NEW GAMES FOR PARLOR AND LAWN. N. Y., Harper, 1882, 227 p., S. $1.
 Contains proverbs in action, illustrated poems, magic, and other interesting amusements. 700.

Beard, Lina *and* **Adelia B.**
AMERICAN GIRLS' HANDY BOOK: How TO AMUSE YOURSELF AND OTHERS. N. Y., Scribner, 1893, 474 p., D. $2.
 Gives directions more or less precise and praiseworthy for the observance of holidays, the giving of parties and picnics, for games, for work both useful and ornamental. For youthful readers.—*Literary World.* 700.

Champlin, John Denison, Jr., *and* **Bostwick, Arthur E.**
YOUNG FOLKS' CYCLOPÆDIA OF GAMES AND SPORTS. Illus. N. Y., Holt, 1890, 831 p., O, $2.50.
 Describes games, sports, and amusements of all kinds for boys and girls. It is written from the American standpoint, with illustrations and historical information, and is arranged alphabetically. The best general reference book. 700.

Gomme, Alice Bertha.
CHILDREN'S SINGING GAMES: With the Tunes to Which They Are Sung. N. Y., Macmillan, 1894. First series and Second series, 70 p., Q. $1.50 each.
 These English games, some of which are played in modified forms by American children, afford charming amusement, because the natural outgrowth of national life, free from the instructiveness or setness of invented games for little children. The editor is an author of mark in the field of folk-lore; these games have been collected by herself and her friends, partly from their value as illustrating ancient customs otherwise unrecorded. Both volumes are illustrated with rare and sympathetic skill by Winifred Smith. 700.

Hale, Lucretia Peabody.
FAGOTS FOR THE FIRESIDE. New edition. Illus. Bost., Houghton, 1894, 334 p., D. $1.25.
 More than 150 entertaining games for evenings at home and social parties. These range from ingenious games of words and proverbs and games of pure sport; they are new and old, and make every demand, from the least to the greatest, upon the mental agility of the player.—*Literary World.* 700.

Hoffmann, Prof. Louis (*pseud.* of Angelo John Lewis).
PARLOR AMUSEMENTS AND EVENING PARTY ENTERTAINMENTS. Illus. N. Y., Routledge, 504 p., D. $1.50.
 Gives detailed instructions for many kinds of games of action, games with pen and pencil, "catch" games, forfeits, card games, miscellaneous amusements, amateur theatricals, tableaux, living wax-work exhibitions, shadow pantomimes, etc. 790.

Newell, William Wells.
GAMES AND SONGS OF AMERICAN CHILDREN. Illus. N. Y., Harper, 1883, 242 p., O, $1.50.
 A collection, with history, of the games of the children of America, and a comparison with those of other countries. 790.

Pollard, Josephine.
PLAYS AND GAMES FOR LITTLE FOLKS. Illus. N. Y., McLoughlin, 128 p., O. $1.
 Sports of all kinds, fireside fun and singing games for very young people. 700.

Ruutz-Rees, Janet E.
HOME OCCUPATIONS. (Appleton's Home books.) N. Y. Appleton, 1883, 135 p., D. 60 c.
 Clear instructions as to the uses of tissue-paper, card-board, beads, etc., for decorative purposes. Adapted to young girls. 700.

Sherwood, *Mrs.* **Mary Elizabeth (Wilson).**
HOME AMUSEMENTS. (Appleton's Home books.) N. Y., Appleton, 1884, 152 p., D. 60 c.
 Brief chapters on private theatricals, games, outdoor recreations and other amusements. 700.

Smiley, *Mrs.* **Annie E.**
FIFTY SOCIAL EVENINGS FOR EPWORTH LEAGUES AND THE HOME CIRCLE. N. Y., Hunt & Eaton, 1894, 70 p., S. 25 c.
 Bright and interesting games suitable for church entertainments and home parties. 700.

What Shall We Do To-Night? or, Social Amusements for Evening Parties. N. Y., Dick & Fitzgerald, 366 p., D. $2.
 An excellent compilation, offering twenty-six varied entertainments for social gatherings and festivals. 700.

PUZZLES.

Bellamy, William.
A CENTURY OF CHARADES. Bost., Houghton, 1894, 101 p., S. $1.
 Contains 100 bright and entertaining charades, not for acting. Incomparably the best collection extant. 703.

Howard's Book of Conundrums and Riddles. N. Y., Dick & Fitzgerald, boards, 50 c.; paper, 30 c.

CARDS: CHECKERS: CHESS.

Coffin, Charles Emmet.
GIST OF WHIST: a Concise Guide to the Modern Scientific Game. 4th edition revised. N. Y., Brentano's, 1895, 109 p., S. 75 c.
 Contents: Fundamental principles; American leads; Conventional plays; Practical precepts, including the laws of whist and of duplicate whist. A capital summary, clearly and attractively presented. 704.

Dick, William Brisbane.
GAMES OF PATIENCE; OR, SOLITAIRE WITH CARDS. N. Y., Dick & Fitzgerald, 1883, 154 p., D. $1; boards, 75 c.
 Includes 64 games, with illustrations. This attractive game of cards for one player has often proved a delightful pastime for the invalid and a mental relief for the tired and overworked. 705.

Amusements and Sports.

THE AMERICAN HOYLE; OR, HANDBOOK OF GAMES. N. Y., Dick & Fitzgerald, 1892, 514 p., D. $1.50.
An important authority on all card games, checkers, chess and dominoes. Especially valuable for its rules for whist, collated from the various works by "Cavendish." **704.**

Dunne, Frank.

DRAUGHT-PLAYER'S GUIDE AND COMPANION. N. Y., Dick & Fitzgerald, 152 p., D. $1.50.
An authoritative book, suited to beginners and advanced players. **704.**

Modern Whist. N. Y., Dick & Fitzgerald, 72 p., S. paper, 25 c.
Contains complete rules and instructions, the American leads, and much other information. Compiled from "Cavendish." The best cheap manual. **704.**

CONJURING.

Hoffmann, *Prof.* **Louis** (*pseud.* of Angelo John Lewis).

MODERN MAGIC: a practical treatise on the art of conjuring. Illus. N. Y., Routledge, 563 p., D. $1.50.
Includes card tricks, tricks with coin, with jewelry and other sleight-of-hand performances, which make an interesting feature of an evening's entertainment. **703.**

TABLEAUX: AMATEUR THEATRICALS: CHARADES.

Frost, S. A.

PARLOR ACTING CHARADES. N. Y., Dick & Fitzgerald, 152 p. S. boards, 50 c.; paper, 30 c.
Short parlor comedies and farces, requiring no expensive scenery or setting. **703.**

Nugent, Edmund C.

BURLESQUE AND MUSICAL ACTING CHARADES. N. Y., Dick & Fitzgerald, 175 p., S. boards, 50 c.; paper, 30 c.
Twelve charades with music and pianoforte accompaniments. With hints for performance. **703.**

Pollard, Josephine.

ARTISTIC TABLEAUX; with diagrams and descriptions of costumes. N. Y., Dick & Fitzgerald, 1884, paper, 30 c. **793.**

Weldon's Fancy Costumes. N. Y., Dick & Fitzgerald, 114 p., S. paper, 30 c.
Contains more than fifty illustrations of historical, national, and emblematic costumes, with directions for making them. **703.**

BILLIARDS.

Garnier, Albert.

SCIENTIFIC BILLIARDS, and Practice Shots, With Hints to Amateurs, and 106 diagrams in colors. N. Y., Appleton, $3.50.
The standard authority. **704.**

DANCING.

Dick's Quadrille Call-Book and Ball-Room Prompter. N. Y., Dick & Fitzgerald; boards, 75 c.; paper, 50 c.
A compilation which includes all the popular dances, more than a hundred figures for the "German," and the rules of deportment and etiquette in the ballroom. **703.**

Dodworth, Allen.

DANCING AND ITS RELATIONS TO EDUCATION AND SOCIAL LIFE. New ed. Illus. N. Y., Harper, 1888, 302 p., D. $1.50.
The author writes on American dancing and gives full instructions for learning the different kinds of dances. **703.**

OUTDOOR SPORTS.

Camp, Walter.

BOOK OF COLLEGE SPORTS. Illus. N. Y., Century Co., 1893, 329 p., O. $1.75.
Includes track athletics, rowing, football, and baseball. These are fully explained for the benefit of the spectator of games, and much sound advice is given to participants.—*Literary World.* **796.**

Dwight, James.

PRACTICAL LAWN-TENNIS. Illus. N. Y., Harper, 1893, 168 p., S. $1.25.
A comprehensive little volume, covering the whole matter from the preparation of the ground to the regulation of tournaments.—*Literary World.* **776.**

Ford, Horace.

THEORY AND PRACTICE OF ARCHERY. New edition, revised by W. Butt. N. Y., Longmans, 1887, $4.50.
We can recommend this book as a thoroughly comprehensive work on practical archery. Especially valuable to those who take more than a superficial interest in the subject, and to whom the ordinary manuals are unsatisfactory.—*Nation.*
Mr. Ford was for ten years champion archer of England. **706.**

Thompson, Maurice.

WITCHERY OF ARCHERY: a Complete Manual. New edition. Illus. N. Y., Scribner, 1879, 269 p., S. $1.50.
Historical and practical information on the subject, with a chapter on English archery practice. **796.**

HORSEMANSHIP.

DeHurst, C., *pseud.*

HOW WOMEN SHOULD RIDE. Illus. N. Y., Harper, 1892, 248 p., S. $1.25.
Aids women to acquire a practical knowledge of how to manage the horse under saddle and in harness. **708.**

Mead, Theodore H.

HORSEMANSHIP FOR WOMEN. N. Y., Harper, 1887, 160 p., D. $1.25.
Instruction in amateur training, etiquette in the saddle, leaping, and buying a saddle-horse. **798.**

CYCLING.

Clyde, Henry.

PLEASURE-CYCLING. Bost., Little, Brown & Co., 1895, 180 p., S. $1.
A stirring plea for the cycle as a means of health and joy for young and old, with useful hints for choosing a machine, and for riding with safety and comfort. Dress for men is prescribed by the author, dress for ladies by a lady. A capital manual for the beginner, and available, too, as a "discourager of hesitancy." **796.**

Porter, Luther H.

CYCLING FOR HEALTH AND PLEASURE. Illus. N. Y., Dodd, 1895, 195 p., S. $1.
Gives advice to learners and tourists, tells how to prevent accidents, philosophizes on the relation of speed to gearing, pictures and describes many forms of cycling costumes, and has quite an encyclopædia of practical points.—*Critic.* **796.**

Richardson, *Sir* **Benjamin Ward,** *M.D.*

WHAT TO AVOID IN CYCLING. N. Y., *North American Review,* August, 1895, 50 c.
The writer, an eminent English physician, heartily commends cycling. He regards it as unsuitable for those too young and those of weak hearts. He condemns overstrain in ordinary riding no less than in racing.

WORKS OF REFERENCE.

A SELECTION ANNOTATED BY

HELEN KENDRICK JOHNSON,
Editor American Woman's Journal.

New York, June, 1895.

Allusions, Familiar.

Edited by WILLIAM A. and CHARLES G. WHEELER. Bost., Houghton, $2.

Explains thousands of allusions likely to be met with in reading—names of celebrated pictures, statues, ruins, palaces, churches, and curiosities, historical events, etc. **025.5.**

American Literature, Library of.

Edited by EDMUND CLARENCE STEDMAN and ELLEN MACKAY HUTCHINSON. N. Y., W. E. Benjamin. 11 vols. $30 and upwards.

A carefully edited work, giving specimens from 1200 American authors, from early colonial times to the present, with many portraits. **810.8.**

Anecdote, A Century of.

JOHN TIMBS. (Chandos Classics series.) N. Y., Warne, 75 c., or $1.

Mr. Timbs, who did much admirable compilation, has here made a careful and well-chosen selection of famous *bon mots* and incidents. **828.**

Archæology, Sacred.

MACKENZIE, E. C. WALCOTT. Lond., L. Reeve & Co., 18s.

A popular dictionary of ecclesiastical art, institutions, and customs. **220.93.**

Art Dictionary, Adeline's.

N. Y., Appleton, 1891, $2.25.

Translated from a standard French work. **703.**

Art, Handbook of Legendary and Mythological.

CLARA ERSKINE CLEMENT. Bost., Houghton, $3.

Mrs. Clement brings enthusiasm as well as exact knowledge to her task, and the illustrations are a great help. **700.**

Atlases.

For a large atlas, the RAND-MCNALLY INDEXED ATLAS OF THE WORLD is perhaps the best. It is thoroughly indexed, so that any town, village, mountain, island, lake, or stream can be found at once. N.Y., and Chic., Rand, McNally & Co., 2 vols., $18.50. The SCRIBNER-BLACK ATLAS OF THE WORLD is also good, and has a ready-reference index. N. Y., Scribner, $22.50. The same may be said of APPLETON'S LIBRARY ATLAS OF MODERN GEOGRAPHY, which is equally well indexed. N. Y., Appleton, $17.50. All these contain a great deal of matter besides the maps. For some purposes, the RAND-MCNALLY BUSINESS ATLAS, which has a peculiarly convenient method of indicating railroads, is especially valuable. Issued annually. $7.50. **912.**

Authors, Dictionary of.

S. AUSTIN ALLIBONE. Phila., Lippincott, 5 vols., $37.50.

The first volume was published in 1854; the second and third in 1871; the fourth and fifth (which are largely supplementary) in 1891. The work is not only a catalogue of British and American authors and their books, but a collection also of biographical and critical notes, some original and some quoted from standard reviews. **011.**

Authors, Handbook of American; and Handbook of English.

OSCAR FAY ADAMS. Bost., Houghton, 2 vols., 75 c. each.

Very convenient for quick reference. **011.**

Bible, Concordances to the.

WALKER'S COMPREHENSIVE CONCORDANCE. Bost., Congregational S. S. and Publishing Soc., 1895, $2.

Trustworthy: Cruden's, which is cheaper (N. Y., Routledge, $1), is very faulty. Strong's Exhaustive Concordance (N. Y., Hunt & Eaton, $7) is the best if the very fullest work is required. **220.2.**

Classical Antiquities, Schreiber's Atlas of.

From the German of Th. Schreiber. Edited by Prof. W. C. F. Anderson. N. Y., Macmillan, $6.50.

Exceedingly useful in the study of classical archæology and for those who seek to know the material surroundings of the Greeks and Romans. The work has 2500 illustrations representing the manners, customs, lives, and recreations of the ancients. **013.38.**

Classical Antiquities, Dictionary of.

Mythology, Religion, Literature, and Art. From the German of Dr. Oskar Seyffert. Edited with additions by Prof. Henry Nettleship, M.A., and Dr. J. E. Sandys. 450 illustrations. N. Y., Macmillan, 716 p., O. $3.

An excellent modernized translation of a high German authority, treating of Greek and Roman mythology, philosophy, history, literature, painting, sculpture, music, and the drama. The learned English editors have included the results of the latest researches. **013.38.**

CYCLOPÆDIAS:

THE AMERICAN, when issued in its revised edition, 20 years ago, was by far the best general cyclopædia in the market; it is still very valuable. N. Y., Appleton, 16 vols., $80.

THE ENCYCLOPÆDIA BRITANNICA is mainly a collection of admirable dissertations on great subjects, minor topics being to a large extent omitted, and all biographies of living persons excluded. (Authorized Americanized edition.) N. Y., Scribner, 25 vols., $125 and upwards.

CHAMBERS'S ENCYCLOPÆDIA, in its new edition, 1892, is by far the best of the cheap cyclopædias. Phila., Lippincott, 10 vols., $30.

JOHNSON'S CYCLOPÆDIA, new and revised edition, 7 vols. published, 1 vol. to be published Oct., 1895, has the advantage of being the latest, and is in many important respects the best. N. Y., Appleton, and A. J. Johnson Co., 8 vols., $48, or $56.

APPLETON'S ANNUAL CYCLOPÆDIA (1 vol. yearly) is a history of the world for the year represented. It is arranged topically and alphabetically, and forms an admirable supplement to any cyclopædia. N. Y., Appleton, $5.

CASSELL'S MINIATURE CYCLOPÆDIA, N. Y., Cassell, 1888, $1, is a marvel of condensation, fairly accurate, and handy for quick reference. 030.

THE CYCLOPÆDIA OF AMERICAN BIOGRAPHY is the only extensive work on this subject that is published complete. Accurate, and illustrated with hundreds of portraits. N. Y., Appleton, 6 vols., $30.

LIPPINCOTT'S BIOGRAPHICAL DICTIONARY is American and foreign. Phila., Lippincott, $12. 920.

GOODHOLME'S DOMESTIC CYCLOPÆDIA is an excellent book for household use. N. Y., Scribner, $5. *See* under HOUSEKEEPING, GENERAL, for contents.

THE YOUNG FOLKS' CYCLOPÆDIAS OF COMMON THINGS, and of PERSONS AND PLACES, by John D. Champlin, are full of accurate information, in simple language. N. Y., Holt, 2 vols., $2.50 each. 030.

THE CYCLOPÆDIA OF PAINTERS AND PAINTINGS, by John D. Champlin, Jr., and Charles C. Perkins, gives brief records of painters and their works, illustrated with more than 2000 portraits, autographs, and outline pictures. N. Y., Scribner, 4 vols., $20. 750.

DICTIONARIES, ENGLISH.

The largest complete dictionary is the CENTURY, which is very full, well edited and beautifully printed. N. Y., Century Co., 1891, 6 vols., $60 and upwards. Uniform with this work and supplementary to it is the CENTURY CYCLOPEDIA OF NAMES in geography, biography, history, ethnology, art, archæology, fiction, etc. N. Y., Century Co., 1894, $10 and upwards. A little later than the Century Dictionary, and containing more words, though not so bulky, is the STANDARD. This also has been carefully edited and beautifully illustrated. N. Y., Funk & Wagnalls, 1894, 1 vol., $12; 2 vols., $15 and upwards. THE INTERNATIONAL, formerly known as WEBSTER'S UNABRIDGED, Springfield, Mass., G. & C. Merriam Co., 1890, $10, is an excellent work for ready reference, though a little older than those mentioned above, and not so well illustrated. The differences that originally existed between WEBSTER'S and WORCESTER'S have constantly diminished in successive editions, until now they are hardly important. WORCESTER'S, Phila., Lippincott, $10, is undergoing revision. THE ACADEMIC DICTIONARY, abridged from the INTERNATIONAL, is perhaps the best dictionary at a low price: it is illustrated, N. Y., Am. Book Co., 1895, $1.50. THE DICTIONARY OF TERMS, PHRASES, AND QUOTATIONS is made on the principle of defining only such words as need defining for the ordinary reader. N. Y., Appleton, $3.

DICTIONARIES OF FOREIGN AND DEAD LANGUAGES.

French;

DE LORME, WALLACE AND BRIDGEMAN'S. Bost., D. C. Heath & Co., 1152 p., D. $1.50. 443.

German;

WEIR'S. Bost., D. C. Heath & Co., 1126 p., D. $1.50. 433.

Greek;

LIDDELL & SCOTT'S LEXICON, 7th edition, revised and enlarged, $10. INTERMEDIATE LEXICON, founded on the foregoing, $4; ABRIDGED EDITION, $1.25. N. Y., Harper. 483.

Italian;

MEADOW'S, new and revised edition. N. Y., Appleton, $2. 453.

Latin;

HARPER'S LATIN DICTIONARY. N. Y., Harper, $6.50; LEWIS'S ELEMENTARY LATIN DICTIONARY. N. Y., Harper, $2. 473.

Spanish;

SLOANE'S NEUMAN AND BARETTI, ABRIDGED BY VELAZQUEZ. N. Y., Appleton, $1.50. 463.

ENGLISH LITERATURE.

Cyclopædia of:

Edited by ROBERT CHAMBERS. Phila., Lippincott, 2 vols., $7.

An admirable book, especially for brief study of the earlier authors. Not to be looked to for very recent literature. 820.2.

Dictionary of:

A Comprehensive Guide to English Authors

and Their Works. By W. DAVENPORT ADAMS. N. Y., Cassell, 776 p., D. $2.50.

Embraces the standard names in English and American literary biography, with lists of the authors' chief works, and occasional brief critical opinions. Another feature of value is the references to notable characters in books, first lines of many poems, songs and ballads, etc. For practical purposes the work may supply the place of Allibone. **820 3.**

Familiar Short Sayings of Great Men.

SAMUEL A. BENT. Bost., Houghton, $2.

Not only records the saying, but gives context and explanatory notes. **808.8.**

Fiction, Noted Names of.

WILLIAM A. WHEELER. New edition, with appendix, by C. G. WHEELER. Bost., Houghton, $2.

Convenient for quick reference and short explanation. The same matter appears as one of the appendices in the International Dictionary. **803.**

Gazetteer of the World, Lippincott's.

If more geographical information is required than can be found in the atlases, this Gazetteer is the best book in which to look for it. Phila., Lippincott, $12. **910.3.**

Haydn's Dictionary of Dates.

BENJAMIN VINCENT. 20th edition. N. Y., Putnam, 1892, 1136 p., O. $6.

An English budget of universal information relating to all ages and nations, with dates. A standard and useful work. **030.**

Hazell's Annual.

A Cyclopædic Record of Men and Topics of the Day. Issued annually. Lond., Hazell, Watson & Viney, 3s. 6d.; N. Y., Scribner, Brentano, and other book importers, $1.50.

An exceedingly useful survey of the important topics of the year, compiled in large measure, however, for British reference, dealing mainly with English, Colonial, and foreign affairs, though discussing general questions of the time, such as religious, industrial, political, and social movements, education, art, science, music and literature, etc., etc. **030.**

Historical Literature, Manual of.

Brief descriptions of the more important Histories in English, French, and German, with practical suggestions as to Methods and Courses of Study. By Chas. Kendall Adams, LL.D. N. Y., Harper, 720 p., D. $2.50.

Very helpful to the historical student and general reader. **002.**

History, Dictionary of English.

Edited by SIDNEY J. LOW and F. S. PULLING. N. Y., Cassell, $6.

English history treated topically, in generally brief articles, arranged alphabetically. **042.**

History for Ready Reference.

J. N. LARNED. Springfield, Mass., C. A. Nichols & Co., 1895, 5 vols, $25.

Condenses on the dictionary plan extracts from the foremost writers. A capital work for either the general reader or the student. **008.**

Initials and Pseudonyms.

WILLIAM CUSHING. N. Y., Crowell, 2 vols., $8.

One section enters writers by their pen names, and the other by their real names. **014.**

Literary Curiosities, Handbook of.

WILLIAM S. WALSH. Phila., Lippincott, $3.50.

An interesting collection of oddities, with many erudite notes. **828.**

Quotations, Dictionary of.

Compiled by JAMES WOOD. From Ancient and Modern, English and Foreign Sources, including Phrases, Mottoes, Maxims, Proverbs, Aphorisms, etc. N. Y., Warne & Co., 659 p., D. $3.

A really good and comprehensive cyclopædia of the wisdom of the world's great minds. The arrangement of its 30,000 references is alphabetical. Translations of the classical and modern foreign maxims are, of course, supplied. Fuller than Bartlett's book in quotations from authors not American or English. **808.8.**

Quotations, Familiar.

JOHN BARTLETT. 9th and enlarged edition. Bost., Little, Brown & Co., $3.

By far the best book of its kind for references to English and American literatures. Other literatures are meagrely represented. **808.8.**

Quotations, Familiar, Translated.

RAMAGE'S.

From French and Italian authors.
" German and Spanish authors.
" Greek authors.
" Latin authors.
With English translations and lives of the authors.
From British authors, by J. C. Grocott, with parallel passages from various Writers, ancient and modern, and an appendix containing quotations from American authors, by Anna L. Ward. 5 vols. N. Y., Routledge, $2 each.

An excellent and comprehensive collection. **808.8.**

Readers' Handbook of Allusions, References, Plots, and Stories.

E. COBHAM BREWER. Lippincott, $3.50.

Answers many daily recurring questions. **828.**

Shakespeare, Concordances to.

JOHN BARTLETT'S gives in every instance the whole line as well as the word. N. Y., Macmillan, $14. Less full, but excellent, is CHARLES AND MARY COWDEN CLARKE'S CONCORDANCE. N. Y., Scribner, $7.50. Briefer, and less desirable, is W. DAVENPORT ADAMS' CONCORDANCE TO THE PLAYS. N. Y., Routledge, $1.50. **822.33.**

Shakespeare, Index to Works of.

EVANGELINE M. O'CONNOR. N. Y., Appleton, 1887, 419 p., D. $2.

Refers, by topics, to notable passages; with brief histories of the plays, mention of all characters, and sketches of the principal ones. Explains obscure allusions and obsolete expressions. A useful supplement to a concordance. **822.33.**

Statesman's Year-Book.

A Statistical and Historical Annual of the States of the World for each year. Edited by J. Scott Keltie and I. P. A. Renwick. N. Y., Macmillan, 1150 p., D. $3.

Published yearly. An invaluable treasury of statistical reference, from official returns, concerning every Empire, State, and Dependency in the World. Its topics embrace constitution and government, area and population, commerce, defence, finance, production and industry, of the several countries, with a mass of general information of high practical value. **003.**

Synonyms and Antonyms, Complete Dictionary of.

SAMUEL FALLOWS, D.D. N. Y., F. H. Revell Co., 1886, 512 p., D. $1.

Contains an appendix of Briticisms, Americanisms, grammatical uses of prepositions, foreign phrases, and other useful information. **424.**

Synonyms Discriminated.

CHARLES JOHN SMITH. N. Y., H. Holt & Co., 1889, 781 p., D. $1.50.

Illustrated, with quotations from standard writers. Fuller in synonyms than Bishop Fallows' book. **424.**

Thesaurus of English Words and Phrases.

New edition, enlarged and improved, by Peter Mark Roget. N. Y., Longmans, $3 ; Crowell, $1.50.

A dictionary of synonyms which has long enjoyed high repute. The work is arranged topically, on an elaborate and rather complex plan, though a word-index gives facility of reference. **424.**

Woman's Book.

N. Y., Scribner, 1894, 2 vols., $7.50.

A work by some twenty writers of mark, who treat every phase of woman's work and duty, with much valuable information as to the more recently established means of livelihood for women. Admirably illustrated in black and white, and in colors. See USEFUL ARTS, GENERAL, for contents. **306.**

LIST OF PERIODICALS.

The first price in this list is for a year; the price for a single copy is given in case a sample is desired. When several different periodicals are ordered together through a bookseller or publisher, a discount is usually granted. So also when five or more subscriptions for one publication are sent together.

AGRICULTURE: DAIRYING: GARDENING.

AMERICAN GARDENING: semi-monthly. New York, A. T. De La Mare Printing and Pub. Co., $1 (1 copy, 5 c.).
CULTIVATOR AND COUNTRY GENTLEMAN: weekly. Albany, N. Y., Luther Tucker & Son, $2.50 (1 copy, 5 c.).
FARM AND FIRESIDE: semi-monthly. Springfield, O., Mast, Crowell & Kirkpatrick, 50 c. (1 copy, 5 c.).
FARM JOURNAL: monthly. Philadelphia, Pa., Wilmer Atkinson Co., 50c. (1 copy, 5 c.).
GARDEN AND FOREST: weekly. New York, Garden and Forest Pub. Co., $4 (1 copy, 10 c.).
HOME AND FARM: semi-monthly. Louisville, Ky., Home and Farm Pub. Co., 50 c. (1 copy, 3 c.).
RURAL NEW YORKER: weekly. New York, Rural Publishing Co., $1 (1 copy, 3 c.).

ARCHITECTURE.

AMERICAN ARCHITECT AND BUILDING NEWS: weekly. Boston, Mass., American Architect and Building News Co., $6 (1 copy, 15 c.).
ARCHITECTURE AND BUILDING: weekly. New York, William T. Comstock, $6 (1 copy, 15 c.).

ART: DECORATION: FURNITURE.

ART AMATEUR: monthly. New York, Montague Marks, $4 (1 copy, 35 c.).
ART INTERCHANGE: monthly. New York, Art Interchange Co., $4 (1 copy, 35 c.).
ART JOURNAL, LONDON: monthly. New York, Chicago, Washington, Brentano's, $6 (1 copy, 50 c.).
DECORATOR AND FURNISHER: monthly. New York, Art Trades Pub. and Printing Co., $2 (1 copy, 20 c.).

BOOKS: LIBRARY.

LIBRARY JOURNAL: monthly. New York, R. R. Bowker, $5 (1 copy, 50 c.).
LITERARY DIGEST: weekly. New York, Funk & Wagnalls Co., $3 (1 copy, 10 c.).
LITERARY NEWS: monthly. New York, R. R. Bowker, $1 (1 copy, 10 c.).
PUBLISHERS' WEEKLY. New York, R. R. Bowker, $3 (1 copy, 10 c.).

CHILDREN AND YOUNG PEOPLE.

HARPER'S ROUND TABLE, formerly HARPER'S YOUNG PEOPLE: weekly. New York, Harper & Bros., $2 (1 copy, 5 c.).
ST. NICHOLAS: monthly. New York, Century Co., $3 (1 copy, 25 c.).
YOUTH'S COMPANION: weekly. Boston, Mass., Perry Mason & Co., $1.75 (1 copy, 5 c.).

DRESS: FASHIONS.

DELINEATOR. monthly. New York, Butterick Pub. Co., $1 (1 copy, 15 c.).
HARPER'S BAZAR: weekly. New York, Harper & Bros., $4 (1 copy, 10 c.).

EDUCATION.

EDUCATION: monthly, except July and August. Boston, Mass., Kasson & Palmer, $2 for first year; afterward $3 (1 copy, 35 c.).
EDUCATIONAL REVIEW: monthly, except July and August. New York, Henry Holt & Co., $3 (1 copy, 35 c.).
PRIMARY EDUCATION: monthly. Boston, Mass., Educational Publishing Co., $1 (1 copy, 10 c.).
SCHOOL JOURNAL: weekly. New York, E. L. Kellogg & Co., $2.50 (1 copy, 6 c.).

HISTORY.

AMERICAN HISTORICAL REVIEW: quarterly. New York, Macmillan & Co., $3 (1 copy, $1).
MAGAZINE OF AMERICAN HISTORY: monthly. New York, Historical Publication Co., $5 (1 copy, 50 c.).

HOUSEHOLD.

BABYHOOD: monthly. New York, Babyhood Pub. Co., $1 (1 copy, 10 c.).
GOOD HOUSEKEEPING: monthly. Springfield, Mass., Clark W. Bryan & Co., $2 (1 copy, 20 c.).
LADIES' HOME COMPANION: semi-monthly. Springfield, O., Mast, Crowell & Kirkpatrick, $1 (1 copy, 5 c.).
LADIES' HOME JOURNAL: monthly. Philadelphia, Pa., Curtis Pub. Co., $1 (1 copy, 10 c.).

ILLUSTRATED WEEKLIES.

HARPER'S WEEKLY. New York, Harper & Bros., $4 (1 copy, 10 c.).
ILLUSTRATED LONDON NEWS: weekly. New York Agency in Pulitzer Building, $6 (1 copy, 15 c.). Midsummer and Xmas nos., $1 extra.
LESLIE'S ILLUSTRATED WEEKLY. New York, Arkell Weekly Co., $4 (1 copy, 10 c.).

LITERARY JOURNALS.

CRITIC: weekly. New York, Critic Co., $3 (1 copy, 10 c.).
DIAL: semi-monthly. Chicago, Dial Co., $2 (1 copy, 10 c.).
LITERARY WORLD: bi-weekly. Boston, Mass., E. H. Hames & Co., $2 (1 copy, 10 c.).
NATION: weekly. New York, Evening Post Pub. Co., $3 (1 copy, 10 c.).

WEEK: weekly. Toronto, Canada, Week Publishing Co., $3 (1 copy, 10 c.).

MAGAZINES.

AMERICAN WOMAN'S JOURNAL: monthly. New York, American Journal Pub. Co., $1 (1 copy, 10 c.).
ATLANTIC MONTHLY. Boston, Mass., Houghton, Mifflin & Co., $4 (1 copy, 35 c.).
CANADIAN MAGAZINE: monthly. Toronto, Canada, Ontario Pub. Co., $2.50 (1 copy, 25 c.).
CENTURY MAGAZINE: monthly. New York, Century Co., $4 (1 copy, 35 c.).
CONTEMPORARY REVIEW: monthly. American reprint. New York, Leonard Scott Publication Co., $4.50 (1 copy, 40 c.).
COSMOPOLITAN: monthly. Irvington, N. Y., John Brisben Walker, $1.20 (1 copy, 10 c.).
FORTNIGHTLY REVIEW: monthly. American reprint. New York, Leonard Scott Publication Co., $4.50 (1 copy, 40 c.).
FORUM: monthly. New York, Forum Pub. Co., $3 (1 copy, 25 c.).
HARPER'S NEW MONTHLY. New York, Harper & Bros., $4 (1 copy, 35 c.).
LIPPINCOTT'S: monthly. Philadelphia, J. B. Lippincott Co., $3 (1 copy, 25 c.).
MCCLURE'S MAGAZINE: monthly. New York, Samuel S. McClure, $1 (1 copy, 10 c.).
NINETEENTH CENTURY: monthly. American reprint. New York, Leonard Scott Publication Co., $4.50 (1 copy, 40 c.).
NORTH AMERICAN REVIEW: monthly. New York, Lloyd Bryce, $5 (1 copy, 50 c.).
REVIEW OF REVIEWS: monthly. New York, Albert Shaw, $2.50 (1 copy, 25 c.).
SCRIBNER'S: monthly. New York, C. Scribner's Sons, $3 (1 copy, 25 c.).

MUSIC.

MUSICAL COURIER: weekly. New York, Musical Courier Co., $4 (1 copy, 10 c.).

PHOTOGRAPHY.

PHOTOGRAPHIC TIMES: monthly. New York, Photographic Times Pubg. Assoc., $4 (1 copy, 35 c.).
SUN AND SHADE: including photography in colors: monthly. New York, New York Photo-Gravure Co., $5 (1 copy, 50 c.).

PROHIBITION.

UNION SIGNAL: weekly. Chicago, Ill., Women's Temperance Publication Assoc., $1 (1 copy, 5 c.).
VOICE: weekly. New York, Funk & Wagnalls Co., $1 (1 copy, 3 c.).

SCIENCE.

AMERICAN NATURALIST: monthly. Philadelphia, Pa., Edwards & Docker Co., $4 (1 copy, 35 c.).
NATURE: weekly. London and New York, Macmillan & Co., $6 (1 copy, 15 c.).
POPULAR SCIENCE MONTHLY. New York, D. Appleton & Co., $5 (1 copy, 50 c.).
SCIENCE: weekly. New York, 41 E. 49th St., $5 (1 copy, 15 c.).
SCIENTIFIC AMERICAN: weekly. New York, Munn & Co., $3 (1 copy, 8 c.).

WOMAN SUFFRAGE.

WOMAN'S JOURNAL: weekly. Boston, Mass., C. H. Simonds, 1 year on trial, $1.50; afterward, $2.50 a year (1 copy, 5 c.).

HINTS FOR A GIRLS' CLUB

WITH A HOME OF ITS OWN.

See books under CLUBS FOR GIRLS AND WOMEN, p. 122.

1. NUMBER. A score of girls, not all bread-winners, nor all of the leisure class, can form a club better than a larger number. They will first of all discuss the project among their acquaintances and friends, find out whether a club is really wanted, about how many are likely to join it, what its aims in response to local needs should be, and where it had best make its home.

2. HOUSING. The home of the club should be near the homes of its members. In a city, if the club-rooms can be easily reached without paying car-fare, so much the better. It is well to choose the rooms in a quiet street just off a central thoroughfare. In the country, where rents are low, there is more freedom of choice. Wherever the club makes its home, it should avoid a neighborhood where loafers congregate. In a city it may be possible to reduce the rent by sub-letting the rooms during the day for a kindergarten, or for other classes. The rent may have to be guaranteed for six or twelve months by some well-to-do member or other friend of the club. This only when there is a certainty that the club will be able to pay the rent.

3. GIFTS. While the club should plan nothing it cannot pay for, it should always be glad to accept aid from friends. Delicacy here is required on both sides: wherever possible donors should be known only to the club-officers.

4. FURNISHING. Cheery and cosy rooms help to make a club attractive to its members, and serve to win additions to its ranks. Strong and simple stuffs are best in furnishing; they can easily be chosen in attractive colors and patterns. A handsome rug, which can be had for a few dollars, is more wholesome and less costly than a carpet. Next to durability and convenience, simplicity of form in furniture is the most desirable quality—it means the least possible labor in dusting and cleaning. In adorning the club-rooms quality rather than quantity is desirable. Simplicity is always the mark of good taste. A few carefully chosen pictures, a good plaster cast or two, give a room an air of refinement denied to many a parlor profusely and expensively adorned. In furnishing and fitting up, no gift should be accepted which is unsuitable. Sometimes tables, carpets, and the like, quite out of keeping with the club, are offered.

5. INAUGURAL RECEPTION. As soon as a club is settled in its home it is customary to hold a reception, to which the members invite their friends, and all others whom they think will be interested in the aims of the club. A brief address on the outlook of the club, and an invitation to join its ranks, may very properly be given at this reception.

6. ARRANGEMENT OF ROOMS. When possible, the club should have two adjoining rooms, leaving the larger one nearly empty, with only folding chairs, and perhaps a small table against the wall. This gives space for dancing, drills, classes, and business meetings. The smaller room can be a pretty library and sitting-room.

7. BACK-YARD. A back-yard is always desirable. Hammocks can be swung there in summer, flowers planted and tended, with incidental study of botany.

8. FOOD. It is advantageous, when the club-rooms are in a house where a janitress, or a friend of the club, has a kitchen for the preparation of simple meals. Here lessons in cooking can be given, refreshments for parties can be made ready, and inexpensive suppers provided for members who come directly from their work to the club.

9. SUPERVISION. The rooms should at all times be scrupulously clean, thoroughly lighted and ventilated, and well warmed in cold weather. It is advisable to appoint a senior member who will be responsible for these matters, say for a week or a month, and who will be present every evening of her term.

10. MUSIC. As music affords the recreation most enjoyed, a piano of good tone should be one of the first things secured by the club.

11. BOOKS. As soon as a club is able it should begin to form a library. This LIST will give hints for purchases, or for borrowings from public libraries. In New York the State Library at Albany sends a desired assortment of twenty-five or more books as a "travelling library" to any club or person in the State who will become responsible for the return of the volumes within a year. The sole expense is for carriage both ways. As a help to the club librarian there is nothing better than Miss Mary W. Plummer's "Aid for Small Libraries," published by the Pratt Institute Library, Brooklyn, N. Y., at 25 cents. If the club is sufficiently large and prosperous to buy fittings for its library specially designed, it should correspond with the Library Bureau, 146 Franklin St., Boston, manufacturers of all kinds of shelving, desks, and drawers for catalogue-cards and other supplies for libraries. This LIST OF BOOKS numbers each book according to the Decimal Classification—set forth in full in a volume at $5, in condensed form at $2 [Library Bureau, Boston]. This classification is excellent for libraries whose shelves are open to readers, who thus find together the books on a special subject. For a library the books of which are not on shelves accessible to readers, a strictly alphabetical arrangement by authors is perhaps best. This is the plan in the Mercantile Library, New York, any one of whose 250,000 volumes can be had in a minute or less. The practice of permitting

readers full and inviting access to books is steadily growing in large and small libraries. Wherever feasible it is much to be commended. A club library should have a printed classified catalogue, and also a card-catalogue kept up to date and open to all readers. The books should have removable, washable linen covers —which cost 3 to 5 cents each. *See* under A LITERARY CLUB OF GIRLS OR WOMEN, paragraphs 5 and 6.

12. PERIODICALS. As soon as possible a club should have periodicals for a reading-table. The selection, of course, should begin with the leading local newspapers, and extend, as means permit, to weekly journals and monthly magazines. *See* LIST OF PERIODICALS. All but the latest issues of the magazines may be circulated among the members for home reading. If a library is established, these magazines, duly bound, will prove very popular.

13. RECREATIONS in the way of music, recitations, and the like, should be judiciously arranged as far ahead as possible. If one or two evenings in the week are statedly set apart for entertainment it will save the trouble of giving notices for each occasion. If any member or friend of the club has talent in original story-telling this should be drawn upon and will prove delightful. Entertainments of a somewhat elaborate kind, to which friends are invited, or for which a small fee is charged, can be given as often as they prove really interesting, not oftener.

14. INSTRUCTION. Classes for instruction in cooking, dressmaking, and other useful arts should be formed as soon as desired by the members and when any needed outlay is guaranteed. Paid teachers of approved skill in their work, of evident power to interest a class, should be engaged. They know more about the latest and best methods than volunteers usually do, and the fact of payment insures their responsibility. A good teacher never omits to take a broad view of her subject, and in explaining how to bake a loaf, or how to dye a garment, her class may be surprised to find that they have long been chemists without suspecting it. If a competent lady will conduct literary classes gratis, her services should be gladly accepted from motives of economy and to promote the spirit of co-operation among friends of the club.

15. HEALTH. Health talks are always interesting and helpful. A woman physician may be engaged by the club for, say, two hours each week for consultation. In this way the beginnings of a malady may be discovered in time to treat it successfully, the injury due to a special form of employment pointed out, and the general conditions for health to be observed by each individual made clear. The same physician may be engaged by the club, in cases of illness among members, and at some saving of cost. A similar engagement of a dentist is, perhaps, also advisable.

16. CO-OPERATION. As opportunity may offer, it is well for a club to enjoy other advantages of co-operation. If among its members five or ten conclude to buy sewing-machines, bicycles, suites of furniture, or make other considerable purchases at one time and place, a material saving can be effected. So also in the matter of subscribing for magazines, buying books, and, perhaps, insurance. Not the least gain in a club is the way in which it brings to the attention of the young and inexperienced the methods of building associations and other approved means of saving and investment.

OUTLINE CONSTITUTION AND BY-LAWS FOR A GIRLS' CLUB.

I. NAME.—The name of this Club shall be "The ———— Club."

II. OBJECTS.—The objects of this Club are, by union, to promote the happiness and usefulness of its members, and to create a centre of enjoyment, friendship, and culture.

III. OFFICERS.—The officers of this Club shall be a President, Vice-President, Treasurer, and Secretary. (In small clubs one officer may be both Secretary and Treasurer.) They shall be *ex-officio* members of the Council. They shall be elected by ballot at the annual meeting of the Club in each year, and shall hold the office for one year thereafter and until their successors are elected.

IV. PRESIDENT.—The President shall preside at all meetings of the Club and of the Council, shall be *ex-officio* member of all committees, and shall perform such other duties as the Council or the Club shall authorize.

V. VICE-PRESIDENT.—The Vice-President shall share the responsibilities of the President, and fulfil the duties of the latter when the President is absent.

VI. TREASURER.—The Treasurer shall have charge of all moneys of the Club, shall attend to the collection of initiation fees, fines, and monthly dues, shall read out and post the names of non-paying members, and notify them, in accordance with By-Law XII., shall pay bills, and render monthly accounts to the Club.

VII. SECRETARY.—The Secretary shall give notice of all regular meetings of the Club and the Council, and shall keep minutes of such meetings. She shall conduct the correspondence of the Club, and keep the records of the Club and the Council.

VIII. COUNCIL.—1. There shall be a Council to consist of eight members, including the four officers. It shall have general charge, management, and control of the affairs, funds, and property of the Club, and, with the knowledge and consent of the Club, shall authorize and control all expenditures. It shall be the duty of the Council to prepare plans of action to be laid before the Club at its monthly meetings, and to carry out the wishes of the Club as then expressed, and as provided in these By-Laws.

2. At the annual meeting of the Club, to be held on the first Monday of each December, four members shall be elected by ballot, who shall, with the officers of the Club, constitute the Council of eight members. The four members who are not officers shall divide themselves into two classes of two members each. The terms of these classes shall be respectively one and two years.

Thereafter at each annual meeting of the Club two members to replace the out-going class shall be elected by ballot as members of the Council, and their term of office shall be two years. In such elections a majority of the votes cast shall be necessary to elect. Vacancies which shall occur in either class shall be filled by the Council.

3. The Council shall submit at each annual meeting a general report of the affairs of the Club, and an estimate of income and outlay for the ensuing year.

4. The Council shall meet once a month. Special meetings may be called by order of the President or three members of the Council. A majority of its members shall constitute a quorum of the Council.

5. An absence on the part of a member of the Council from three consecutive regular meetings thereof, without satisfactory reasons being given, shall be deemed a resignation therefrom.

6. In respect to all questions of construction of these By-Laws the decision of the Council shall be final.

IX. MEETINGS AND ELECTIONS.—1. There shall be a regular monthly meeting of the Club on the first Monday of every month.

2. The order of business shall be: (1) Reading of the Minutes and the Secretary's Report. (2) Report of Treasurer. (3) Reports of Committees. (4) Notices and remarks from officers or other members of the Council. (5) General business.

3. The order of business at the annual meeting shall be the same as at the monthly meeting, with the exception that after clause 4 the members shall proceed to the election of officers for the ensuing year and members of the Council to replace the outgoing class.

4. One-third (or, one-half) the members shall constitute a quorum at any meeting of the Club.

X. COMMITTEES.—The President shall appoint, with the consent of the Council, a Committee on Hospitality, on the Library, and such other committees as she shall see fit, and shall appoint one of the members of the Council to serve on each committee.

All committees shall be under the direction and subject to the advice of the Council.

XI. MEMBERS.—1. Members must be over fourteen years of age.

2. They shall have free access to the rooms of the Club whenever open, shall be entitled to enter classes, draw books from the library, use the piano, and have a vote at all elections, and a vote upon all matters of business that shall be presented to the Club by the Council.

XII. DUES.—1. Members shall pay an initiation fee of (25) cents, and monthly dues of (10) cents, payable in advance.

2. Initiation fee shall cover dues for month of joining.

3. Any member who fails to pay her dues before or on the 15th of the month shall be fined five cents, unless she can show just cause why she has not paid before.

4. The names of members who owe dues for two months shall be read aloud by the Treasurer at the business meeting at the beginning of the third month of their indebtedness, and such names shall be posted on the Bulletin Board, where they shall remain until the beginning of the fourth month, upon which the Treasurer shall notify such members that unless their back dues are paid, or just cause for non-payment shown, before the 15th of the same month, their membership shall cease.

Such persons may not again become members of the Club within one year from the time when they ceased to pay their Club dues, unless they have paid all arrears to the Club or offered an excuse satisfactory to the Treasurer. [At the discretion of the Council this rule may be modified in special cases.]

XIII. AMENDMENT OF BY-LAWS.—These By-Laws can be amended by a two-thirds vote of the members present at a regular meeting, provided due notice has been given of the proposed change.

A LITERARY CLUB OF GIRLS OR WOMEN.

1. NUMBER. Ten, or thereabouts, is a good number with which to form a literary club. It may grow to twenty-five, and usually cannot with advantage exceed that number.

2. OFFICERS. At the first stated meeting a president and secretary-treasurer should be chosen for a year, and a constitution and by-laws, as simple as possible, adopted. [Hints therefor will be found at the end of the article A GIRLS' CLUB.] Club business at meetings should have the utmost despatch if members are not to be wearied.

3. PLACE OF MEETING. Should the club decide to meet at the houses of members in succession, or in a church-building, the matter of expense will be of little moment. The only charge need be for postal-cards bearing notices of meetings.

4. THEMES. The themes of a club will, of course, depend on the interests of its members. Hence the more diverse these interests the better for the club. A collector of portraits, a student of French history, a traveller familiar with Italian cities, can bring her friends to new and charming fields of study and exploration. In many clubs it is customary to read a paper of about half an hour's length at each meeting, and devote to discussion another half hour, or an hour, closing with quite informal talk. In such cases it is well to draw up a program in advance, and include mention of the subject of a paper in the notice of a meeting. Thus members come prepared to question, to offer comment, or to add illustration. Often a member is so very familiar with a special mode of living, or of bread-winning, that she shuns it as the theme of a paper. Yet the division of labor in a factory, or a hotel, with its daily routine; the construction and the good and bad points of a great apartment-house, the revelation of character to a teacher in a public school, the management of a department-store, can be made of vivid interest to friends ignorant of these matters. If a part, or the whole of the themes during a season can be given connection, so much the better. In trying to avoid desultory work there is, however, some risk of sticking to a single theme after its interest is worn out.

5. TALKS. A club is sure to number among its members, or friends who are not members, men and women who will be glad to give a brief talk, perchance on a subject that has engaged the interest of a lifetime. Such a talk may prove better and is easier to get than a formal paper. No program should be so rigid as to exclude the opportunity to hear good talk of this kind, especially when it comes from an unheralded visitor from afar.

6. BOOKS AND STUDY. Many books of pure literature, history, and fiction can mean more when read by the members of a club than by others. The privilege often enjoyed in a club of consulting or questioning a better informed reader than oneself is of great value. In other departments of literature, those dealing with the useful and fine arts, for example, advantages even more important arise from club membership. A reader, by herself, is tempted to glance idly through the illustrations of a volume on wild-flowers and resist its persuasions to go a-field and form acquaintance with buds, blossoms and their manifold insect ministry. In a club with the impulse of companionship and the direction of an informed and enthusiastic leader, the author of a sterling flower-book becomes a living voice with a story to tell of absorbing interest. And many a worker who at home, or elsewhere, alone, is contented with her own experience, may in the realm of her toil deem books of little use to her. With the wholesome emulation of a club, with a good teacher to solve difficulties that never occurred to the author's mind, this young woman finds that a good book on an art, or a trade, or on household management, is simply the record of much fuller experiences than her own, which can immensely improve her daily practice and, it may be, lift pressing burdens from her shoulders. A word in season is golden when it lightens toil.

7. TEACHERS. In the formal study of a great poet—Shakespeare, Dante, Goethe—or of a foreign tongue, a club opens the way for many women who desire thorough instruction and cannot get it either at home or at college. A club enables a competent teacher to be engaged at a reasonable charge, it keeps a student steadily at her work, it provides her with congenial friends of kindred aims. Efforts otherwise desultory are given connection, purpose, fruitage.

A WOMAN'S CLUB.

Olive Thorne Miller's "The Woman's Club," published by Lovell, Coryell & Co., New York, at $1, is a practical guide and handbook which renders unnecessary here any hints for the establishing or management of women's clubs. Mrs. Miller begins with an enthusiastic argument for the woman's club as evolved from the home, as supplementing it helpfully and delightfully. Next, she describes clubs of widely different types—Sorosis, of New York; the New England Woman's Club, of Boston; the Fortnightly and the Women's Club, of Chicago; the New Century, of Philadelphia; the Saturday, of Columbus, O.; the Seidl Society, of Brooklyn, and others. Drawing upon her large experience, Mrs. Miller suggests how clubs may best be founded and conducted, pointing out common defects in rules, discipline, and spirit. A model constitution and code of by-laws in full detail are added, with wise comment.

NOTES.

THE CHAUTAUQUA LITERARY AND SCIENTIFIC CIRCLE plans a four years' course of home-reading, each year's of which is complete in itself. The five books prescribed for 1895–96, with the *Chautauquan*, a monthly magazine, can be had for $7, from Hunt & Eaton, 150 Fifth Avenue, New York. The membership fee in addition is 50 c. yearly, sent to John H. Vincent, Buffalo, N. Y. Individual readers are recommended to form Local Circles and to report to John H. Vincent. Chautauqua has been a pioneer in the work of making reading systematic, of breaking the bread of science to the plain people. Its Summer School is the most important and influential in the world.

THE SOCIETY TO ENCOURAGE STUDIES AT HOME has its work done by women for women, all over the country, wholly by correspondence. Any woman over seventeen may ask the Secretary, 41 Marlborough St., Boston, Mass., for a circular giving rules and subjects of study. Further information is obtained in the same way. Students procure books from the Society's Library for a small charge, or they buy or borrow them. Each one is directed by her assigned correspondent, as if she were a private pupil; and the work is done in a sympathetic spirit, to encourage thorough study, either elementary or advanced. The fee is $3 for the term, but for those really unable to pay it, a few scholarships are provided. The Society is twenty-two years old, and many students have persevered ten or more years under its direction, continuing one subject, or changing, as they pleased.

THE ROUND ROBIN READING CLUB, which was founded less than two years ago, brings together the person who desires to know and the person best qualified to inform. It has no books of its own, but uses the best literature; it dictates no subject, leaving its members to select what they need or like. The work is done by means of original schedules and personal correspondence. In classes, as with single readers, the personal character of the work is never lost. To students in the library it is invaluable as a guide to not merely a subject, but to the important critical, biographical, or historical work connected with it. It is endorsed by such men as Howells, Hale, Stockton, E. J. James, Gilder, Mabie, and others, and has on its lists of examiners university professors and thoroughly trained literary men and women. Terms and other information can be obtained from the Director, Miss Louise Stockton, 4213 Chester Ave., Philadelphia, Pa.

LIST OF PUBLISHERS.

Alden, John B., 12 Vandewater St., New York.
Allyn & Bacon, 172 Tremont St., Boston.
American Book Co., Washington Square, New York.
American Florist, 322 Dearborn St., Chicago.
American News Co., 39 Chambers St., New York.
American Public Health Ass'n, P. O. Drawer 289, Rochester, N. Y.
American Publishing Co., 424 Asylum St., Hartford, Ct.
American Tract Soc., 10 E. 23d St., N. Y.
Anthony, Susan B., 17 Madison St., Rochester, N. Y.
Appleton, D., & Co., 72 5th Ave., New York.
Arena Publishing Co., Pierce Bldg., Copley Square, Boston.
Armstrong, A. C., & Son, 51 E. 10th St., N. Y.
Arnold & Co., 420 Library St., Philadelphia.
Arrowsmith, J. W., Bristol, England.
Art Interchange Co., 152 W. 23d St., New York.
Baker & Taylor Co., 7 E. 16th St., New York.
Balmer & Weber Music House Co., 908 Olive St., St. Louis, Mo.
Bardeen, C. W., 406 S. Franklin St., Syracuse, N. Y.
Belford, Clarke & Co. Out of business.
Bell, A. Melville, 1525 35th St., Washington, D. C.
Bell, George, & Sons, York St., Covent Garden, London.
Benjamin, William E., 10 W. 22d St., New York.
Bentley, R., & Sons, New Burlington St., W., London.
Black, A. & C., 4 Soho Sq., W., London.
Blackwood, W., & Sons, 37 Paternoster Row, London.
Blakiston, P., Son & Co., 1012 Walnut St., Philadelphia.
Bonner's, Robert, Sons, 182 William St., New York.
Bowen-Merrill Co., 11 W. Washington St., Indianapolis, Ind.
Bradley, Milton, Co., 47 Willow St., Springfield, Mass.
Breeders' Gazette, 358 Dearborn St., Chicago.
Brentano's, 31 Union Sq., New York; 204 Wabash Ave., Chicago; 1015 Penn. Ave., Washington, D. C.
Briggs, William, 33 Richmond St., W., Toronto.
Bryan, Clark W., Springfield, Mass.
Bunnell, J. H., & Co., 76 Cortlandt St., New York.
Burpee, W. Atlee, & Co., 475 N. 5th St., Philadelphia.
Burt, A. L., 97 Reade St., New York.
Butterick Pub. Co., 9 W. 14th St., New York.
Cassell Publishing Co., 31 E. 17th St., New York.
Catholic Publication Soc. Co., out of business: address W. J. Hennessy, 114 5th Ave., New York.
Century Co., 33 E. 17th St., New York.
Chapman & Hall, 11 Henrietta St., W. C., London.
Chatto & Windus, 214 Piccadilly, London.
Chautauqua Century Press, Meadville, Pa.
Clarendon Press, Oxford, England.
Coates, Hy. T., & Co., 1326 Chestnut St., Philadelphia.
Coin Publishing Co., 115 Monroe St., Chicago.
Comstock Publishing Co., Ithaca, N. Y.
Comstock, Wm. T., 23 Warren St., New York.
Congregational S. S. and Publishing Soc., Congregational House, Boston.
Contemporary Publishing Co., 5 Beekman St., New York.
Copp, Clark & Co., 9 Front St., West, Toronto, Canada.
Crowell, T. Y., & Co., 46 E. 14th St., New York.
Damrell & Upham, 283 Washington Street, Boston.
Dawson Bro's. (W. Foster Brown, successor), 2323 St. Catherine St., Montreal, Canada.
De Wolfe, Fiske & Co., 365 Washington St., Boston.
Dick & Fitzgerald, 18 Ann St., New York.
Dillingham, C. T., & Co., 764 Broadway, New York.
Dillingham, G. W., 33 W. 23d St., New York.
Ditson, Oliver, Co., 451 Washington St., Boston.
Dixey, Wolstan, 73 Henry St., Brooklyn, N. Y.
Dodd, Mead & Co., 151 Fifth Ave., New York.
Donohue, Henneberry & Co., 407 Dearborn St., Chicago.
Dutton, E. P., & Co., 31 West 23d St., New York.
Estes & Lauriat, 301 Washington St., Boston.
Farm Journal, Wilmer Atkinson Co., 1024 Race St., Philadelphia.
Flood & Vincent, Meadville, Pa.
Florists' Exchange, 2 Duane St., New York.
Fords, Howard & Hulbert, 47 E. 10th St., New York.
Fowler & Wells Co., 27 E. 21st St., New York.
Funk & Wagnalls Co., 30 Lafayette Pl., New York.
Gebbie & Co., 910 Walnut St., Philadelphia.
George, H., & Co., now Sterling Pub. Co., 106 Fulton St., New York.
Ginn & Co., 13 Tremont Pl., Boston.
Griggs, S. C., & Co., 262 Wabash Ave., Chicago.
Hammett, J. L., 352 Washington St., Boston.
Hardwick & Bogue, London. Out of business.
Harison, Wm. Beverley, 59 5th Ave., New York.
Harper & Bros., Franklin Sq., New York.
Hazel, Watson & Viney, 1 Creed Lane, E. C., London.
Heath, D. C., & Co., 110 Boylston St., Boston.
History Co., 721 Market St., San Francisco.
Holt, Henry, & Co., 29 W. 23d St., New York.
Home Publishing Co., 3 E. 14th St., New York.
Houghton, Mifflin & Co., 4 Park St., Boston, and 11 E. 17th St., New York.
Hovendon Co., 318 6th Ave., New York.
Humboldt Publishing Co., 64 5th Ave., New York.
Hunt & Eaton, 150 5th Ave., New York.
Hunter, Rose & Co., 25 Wellington St., W., Toronto, Canada.
Hurst & Co., 135 Grand St., New York.
Hutchinson, O., 25 E. 14th St., New York. Out of business.
Innes, A. D., & Co., Bedford St., W. C., London.
International News Co., 83 Duane St., New York.
Ivers, M. J., & Co., 379 Pearl St., New York.
James, Davis L., 131 W. 7th St., Cincinnati.
Johns Hopkins Press, Baltimore, Md.

Johnston, W. J., Co., 253 Broadway, New York.
Journal of Education, New England Pub'g Co., 3 Somerset St., Boston.
Judd, Orange, Co., 52 Lafayette Pl., New York.
Kellogg, E. L., & Co., 61 E. 9th St., New York.
Keppler & Schwarzman, 39 E. Houston St., New York.
Kindergarten College, 10 Van Buren St., Chicago.
Leach, Shewell & Sanborn, 202 Devonshire St., Boston.
Lee & Shepard, 10 Milk St., Boston.
Leuckart, F. E. C., Johannisgasse, 4, Leipsic, Germany.
Lippincott, J. B., Co., 715 Market St., Philadelphia.
Little, Brown & Co., 254 Washington St., Boston.
Lockwood, Crosby, & Son, 7 Stationers' Hall Court, E. C., London.
Longmans, Green & Co., 15 E. 16th St., N. Y.
Lothrop Publishing Co., 92 Pearl St., Boston.
Lovell, A., & Co., 3 E. 14th St., New York.
Lovell, Coryell & Co., 318 6th Ave., N. Y.
Low, Sampson, Marston & Co., Fetter Lane, E. C., London.
McClurg, A. C., & Co., 117 Wabash Ave., Chicago.
McKay, David, 23 S. 9th St., Philadelphia.
McLoughlin Bros., 874 Broadway, New York.
Macmillan & Co., 66 5th Ave., New York.
Macmullen & Co., Brockville, Ont., Canada.
Maule, W. H., 1711 Filbert St., Philadelphia.
Maynard, Merrill & Co., 47 E. 10th St., N. Y.
Merriam, G. & C., Co., Springfield, Mass.
Merrill & Baker, 74 5th Ave., New York.
Millet, J. B., Co., 6 Hancock Ave., Boston.
Morrill, Higgins & Co. Out of business.
Moulton, C. W., 20 Main St., Buffalo, N. Y.
Munro, George, 27 Vandewater St., N. Y.
Munro, Norman L., 24 Vandewater St., New York.
Murray, John, 50A Albemarle St., W., London.
Newman, T. G., 147 S. Western Ave., Chicago.
Nichols, C. A., Co., 202 Main St., Springfield, Mass.
Novello, Ewer & Co., 21 E. 17th St., New York.
Nutt, David, 270 Strand, W. C., London.
Ogilvie, J. S., & Co., 57 Rose St., New York.
Open Court Pub. Co., 324 Dearborn St., Chicago.
O'Shea, Patrick, 19 Barclay St., New York.
Penn Publishing Co., 1020 Arch St., Philadelphia.
Pitman, Isaac, & Sons, 33 Union Sq., West, New York.
Poet-Lore Co., 196 Summer St., Boston.
Porter & Coates, now Henry T. Coates & Co., 1326 Chestnut St., Philadelphia.
Pott, James & Co., 114 5th Ave., New York.
Pratt Institute Library, Brooklyn, N. Y.
Presser, Theodore, 1708 Chestnut St., Philadelphia.
Public School Publishing Co., Bloomington, Ill.
Publishers' Weekly, 59 Duane St., New York.
Puritan Publishing Co., 36 Bromfield St., Boston.

Putnam's, G. P., Sons, 27 W. 23d St., New York; 27 King William St., Strand, London.
Rand, McNally & Co., 166 Adams St., Chicago.
Rawson, W. W., 34 S. Market St., Boston.
Reeve, L., & Co., Henrietta St., W. C., London.
Religious Tract Society, 56 Paternoster Row, London.
Renouf, E. M., 2238 St. Catherine St., Montreal, Canada.
Revell, Fleming H., Co., 112 5th Ave., New York.
Roberts Bros., 3 Somerset St., Boston.
Root, A. I., Medina, Ohio.
Routledge, George, & Sons, 29 W. 23d St., New York.
Rowsell & Hutchinson, 76 King St., E., Toronto, Canada.
Rural New Yorker, 409 Pearl St., New York.
Russell, H. L., Madison, Wis.
Saunders, Walter B., 913 Walnut St., Philadelphia.
Schermerhorn, J. W., & Co., 3 E. 14th St., N. Y.
Schirmer, now Kenkel, F. P., 35 Union Sq., New York.
Schulte, F. J., & Co., 334 Dearborn St., Chicago.
Scott, Walter, Warwick Lane, E. C., London.
Scovill & Adams Co., 423 Broome St., New York.
Scribner's, Charles, Sons, 157 Fifth Ave., New York.
Silver, Burdett & Co., 110 Boylston St., Boston.
Simpkin, Marshall & Co., Stationers' Hall Court, E. C., London.
Smith, Elder & Co., Waterloo Place, London.
Smithsonian Institution, Washington, D. C.
Sonnenschein, Swan & Co., 6 White Hart St., E. C., London.
Standard Book Co. Out of business.
Steiger, E., & Co., 25 Park Pl., New York.
Stone & Kimball, 334 Dearborn St., Chicago.
Tait, J. S., & Sons, 65 Fifth Ave., New York.
Taylor, J. A., & Co. Out of business.
Teachers' College, W. 120th St., Morningside Heights, New York.
Thompson, Brown & Co., 23 Hawley St., Boston.
Tretbar, C: F., 109 E. 14th St., New York.
United States Book Co., 318 6th Ave., N. Y.
Unwin T. Fisher, Paternoster Buildings, E. C., London.
Ward & Drummond, 164 Fifth Ave., New York.
Ward, Lock & Bowden, 15 E. 12th St., New York.
Warne, Frederick, & Co., 3 Cooper Union, 4th Ave., New York.
Westermann, B., & Co., 812 Broadway, N. Y.
Whidden, Bradlee, 18 Arch St., Boston.
Wiley, John, & Son, 53 E. 10th St., New York.
Williams & Norgate, 14 Henrietta St., W. C., London.
Woman's Temperance Publishing Ass'n, 161 La Salle St., Chicago.
Writer Publishing Co., 282 Washington St., Boston.
Writers' Publishing Co.; out of business: address H. D. Newson, 331 Pearl St., New York.

INDEX.

Abandoned claim, Loughead, 25.
Abbott, E. A., 74.
Abbott, L. *See* Woman's book, 123.
Abel, M H , 134.
Abney, W. de W., 174.
About money, Craik, 121.
Absentee, Edgeworth, 12.
Academic dictionary, 136.
Accomplished gentleman, Sturgis, 35.
Acland and Ransome, 52.
Acting. *See* Hubert, 123. *See also* Amateur theatricals, 134.
Adam Bede, Eliot, 13.
Adam, G. Mercer, annotator, 60.
Adams, C. K., 137
Adams, E. L S. *See* Steele, F. M., and Adams, E. L. S., 132.
Adams, H. B., 54.
Adams, J: and A., 41.
Adams' manual of hist. literature, 54.
Adams, O. F., 135.
Adams, W. D , 74, 136.
Adams, W. I. L., 121.
Addison, D. D , 4°.
Addison, J., 61; life of, Johnson, 43-44.
Adeline, J., 84, 135.
Adirondack stories, Deming, 10.
Adler, F., 118.
Adventures of Caleb Williams, 15.
Adventures of Captain Horn, Stockton, 34.
Adventures of Philip, Thackeray, 36.
Adventures of Sherlock Holmes, Doyle, 12.
Æneid. *See* Morris, 71.
Africa, Baedeker, 55; Martin, 57: Stanley, 58 ; Vincent, 59.
After twenty years, Sturgis, 35.
Afterwhiles, Riley, 73.
Agassiz Association, 111.
Agassiz, E. C and A., 108.
Agassiz, L., 108
Agatha Page, Henderson, 20.
Agatha's husband, Craik, 9
Agincourt, James, 22.
Agnes, O'iphant, 28.
Agriculture, Waring, 126. *See also* Farm and farming, 126.
Aguilar, G., 1
Airy, fairy Lilian, Hungerford, 21.
Aladdin oven. *See* Atkinson, 130.
Alaska, Scidmore, 58.
Alcott, L. M., works, 1-2; life of, Cheney, 42.
Aldrich, T B , tales, 2; poems, 61.
Alec Forbes, MacDonald, 26.
Alexander, Mrs. (*pseud.*). *See* Hector, Mrs. A. F., 19.
Alexander's feast, Dryden, 65
Algæ, British fresh water, Cooke, 105.
Algebra, Smith and Stringham, 99; Wentworth, 93
Alice Lorraine, Blackmore, 6.
Alice's adventures in Wonderland, Dodgson, 11.
Allan Quatermain, Haggard, 16.
Allan's wife, Haggard, 16.
Allen, C. B. and A., 119.
Allen, J. L., 2
Allen, W. F , 52, 54. *See also* Myers, P. V. N , and Allen, W. F., 52.
Allibone, S. A., 135.
All sorts and conditions of men, Besant, 4.
Allusions, familiar, Wheeler, 135.
Alone, Terhune, 35.
Altiora Peto, Oliphant, 28.
Alton Locke, Kingsley, 23.
Amateur theatricals Weldon, 134.
Amazon River, Bates, 55, 108.
Ambitious woman, Fawcett, 14.
Ambros, A. W., 91.
Amelia, Fielding, 14.

America, discovery of, Fiske, 47; history of, Winsor, 49, 50 ; Mackenzie, 50; Bancroft, 49; labor movement in, Ely, 4); social life in, Trollope, 59.
American Association for the Advancement of Science, 98.
American Chemical Society, 101.
American commonwealth, Bryce, 47.
American commonwealth series, 47, 115.
American cyclopædia, 135.
American Economic Association, 116.
American Folk-Lore Society, 79.
American girl in London, Cotes, 9.
American girls' handy book, Beard, 131.
American Historical Association, 49.
American Historical Register, 49.
American men of letters series, 46, 49.
American notes, Dickens, 11.
American religious leaders series, 46.
American revolution, Fiske, 48; Sloane, 49.
American Social Science Association, 116.
American Society for the Extension of University Teaching, 96.
American statesmen series, 46, 49.
Americans, domestic manners of, Trollope, 59.
Amicis, D', E., 55.
Among the law-makers, Bailey, 115.
Amusements and sports (department), 131-135.
Ancient mariner, Coleridge, 64.
Anderson, H. C., 41.
Anecdotes, century of, Timbs, 135.
Anglomaniacs, Harrison, 18.
Angola, folk-tales of, Chatelain, 77.
Animals, domestic. *See* Miller, 109.
Annals of a quiet neighborhood, MacDonald, 26.
Anne, Woolson, 40.
Anstey, F. (*pseud.*). *See* Guthrie, T. A., 16.
Anthologies, 60.
Anthropology, 111.
Antiquary, Scott, 32.
Antiquities, of Great Britain, Brand, 78 ; Greek, Collignon, 81; English, Jewitt, 82; Oriental, Babelon, 81; Roman, Ramsay and Lanciani, 81; atlas of, Schreiber, 135; dict. of, Seyffert, 135.
Antonyms, Fallows, 137.
Ants *See* Insects
Apes, Hartmann, 109.
Apperception, Lange, 95.
Appledore farm, Macquoid, 26.
Appleton's annual cyclopædia, 136.
Appleton's encyclopædia of Am. biography, 41, 43
Appleton's guide-books, 55.
Appreciations, Pater, 71.
April hopes, Howells, 21.
Apthorp, W. F , 91.
Arblay, *Mme.* F. B. de, 2.
Archæology, Emerson, 81 ; Murray, 82 ; Oriental, Babelon, 81; Greek, Collignon, 81 ; sketch of, Conway, 81; Roman, Helbig and Lanciani, 82 ; Middleton, 82 ; Egyptian, Maspero, 84 ; Petrie, 81; Greek, Murray, 83 ; Fitzwilliam, museum of, Waldstein, 87 ; dict. of, Mackenzie, 135.
Archery, Ford, 114 ; Thompson, 134.
Archibald Malmaison, Hawthorne, 19.
Archie Lovell, Edwardes, 12
Architects, lives of, Vasari, 81.
Architecture (department), 89-90, 170. *See also* Hubert, 123; Woman's book, 123.

Arctic regions, Greely, 56; Nansen, 58 ; Nordenskiold, 58; Peary, 58.
Argentina, Child, 56.
Argles, *Mrs* M. H. *See* Hungerford, *Mrs.* M. H , 21.
Ariadne Florentina, Ruskin, 83.
Aristocracy, 2.
Arkman, C. M., 126.
Armadale, Collins, 8.
Armazindy, Riley, 173.
Armorel of Lyonesse, Besant, 4.
Armourer's prentices, Yonge, 40.
Army tales, Stannard, 33.
Arnold, M , 61.
Around the world in the yacht *Sunbeam*, Brassey, 55-56.
Art, 81-87, Reber, 89; industries, 90; historical sketches of, 90; handbook of, 90; Clement, 135; dict. of, Adeline, 135. *See also* Decorative arts
Art out of doors, Van Rensselaer, 128.
Art study. *See* Hubert, 123.
Arthur Mervyn, Brown, 6.
Artist, education of the, Chesneau, 81.
Artists of the 19th century, Clement and Hutton, 84 ; dict. of, Redgrave, 87.
Arts and crafts essays, Morris, 90.
Arundel motto, Hay, 19.
As a matter of course, Call, 119.
As it was written, Harland, 17.
Ascent of man, Drummond, 109.
Asia, Baedeker, 55.
Asphodel, Maxwell, 26.
Astoria, Irving, 48.
Astronomy, 99.
At her mercy, Payn, 29.
At odds, Tautphœus, 35.
At the red glove, Macquoid, 26.
Atherton, *Mrs.* G. F., 2.
Athletics. *See* Camp, 134.
Atkinson, E., 113, 130.
Atlases, 135; Lippincott's gazetteer, Attaché, Haliburton, 17.
137.
Auld licht idylls, Barrie, 4.
Aunt Diana, Carey, 8.
Aurelian, Ware, 38.
Aurora Floyd, Maxwell, 26.
Austen, J., novels, 2-3 ; life of, Smith, 45.
Austin Elliot, Kingsley, 23.
Austin, *Mrs* J G , 3.
Australian ballads and rhymes, Sladen, 69.
Authors, sketches of, Brandes, 41; Cone and Gilder, 42; Fields, 43; dict. of, Allibone, 135; handbook of, Adams, 135.
Authorship, Dixey, 125.
Autobiography of a slander, Lyall, 25.
Autobiography of Mark Rutherford, White, 38.
Average man, Grant, 16.
Average woman, Balestier, 3.
Avery Architectural Library, catalogue of 88
Aztec treasure-house, Janvier, 22.

Babelon, E , 81.
Babylonia, Sayce, 83.
Baby's grandmother, Walford, 37.
Bach, J. S , Spitta, 93.
Bacon, A. M , 55.
Bacon, F., 61. *See also* Philosophical classics, 117
Bacteria, De Bary, 106; Prudden, 120 ; Russell, 127. *See also* Microbes.
Baedeker's guide-books, 55.
Bailey, E., 115.
Bailey, L. H , annotator, 126.
Bailey, W. W., 105.

Balcony stories, King, 23.
Balestier, C. W., 3.
Balfour, H., 90.
Ball, J. D., 53.
Ballads and barrack-room ballads, Kipling, 69.
Ballard, H. H., 108.
Bamford, M. A., 108.
Bancroft, G., 49.
Bancroft, H. H., 49.
Bangs, J. K., 3.
Banister, H. C., 91.
Banking, 114.
Barchester towers, Trollope, 37.
Baring-Gould, S., history, 53; mythology, 78.
Barlow, J., 3.
Barnaby Rudge, Dickens, 11.
Barnard, C., 99.
Barnard, H., 94.
Barney, S. *See* Meyer, 123.
Baroness, Peard, 29.
Barr, *Mrs.* A. E., 3.
Barrack-room ballads, Kipling, 69.
Barras, *Comte de*. *See* Napoleon, 45.
Barrett, W. A. *See* Stainer, *Sir* J., *and* Barrett, W. A., 93.
Barrie, J. M., 3-4.
Barriers burned away, Roe, 31.
Barry, P., 126.
Bar sinister, Walworth, 37.
Bartlett, G. B., 133.
Bartlett, J., 74, 137.
Barton, C. *See* Myer, 123.
Baseball. *See* Camp, 134.
Bates, H. W., 55, 108.
Baylor, F. C., 4.
Bayly, A. E. *See* Lyall, E., (*pseud.*), 25.
Beaconsfield, B. D., *Earl of*. *See* Disraeli, B., 4.
Beard, L. *and* A. B., 133.
Beard, W. H., 84.
Beauchamp's career, Meredith, 27.
Beauty, personal. *See* Dress, 132.
Beauty's daughters, Hungerford, 21.
Bébée, De la Ramé, 10.
Beckford, W., 4.
Bee-keeping, Cook, 127.
Bee-man of Orn, Stockton, 34.
Bees, Lubbock, 109.
Beethoven, L. v., Marx, 92; Nohl, 92; Thayer, 93.
Before the Gringo came, Atherton, 2.
Beggar on horseback, Payn, 29.
Beggars all, Dougall, 11.
Begum's daughter, Bynner, 7.
Belinda, Edgeworth, 12.
Bell, A. M., 97.
Bell, Currer (*pseud.*). *See* Brontë, C.
Bell, Ellis (*pseud.*). *See* Brontë, E.
Bellamy, E., 4, 114.
Bellamy, W., 133.
Belles-lettres. *See* Literature (department), 60-80.
Benedict, *Sir* J., 91.
Benefits forgot, Balestier, 3.
Ben-Hur, Wallace, 37.
Benjamin S. G. W., 55.
Benson, W. A. S., 90.
Bent, S. A., 136.
Berdoe, E., 62
Berkeley. *See* Philosophical classics, 117.
Berkeleys and their neighbors, Seawell, 32.
Berlioz, H., Apthorp, 91.
Berris, Macquoid, 26.
Besant, *Sir* W., 4.
Beside the bonnie brier bush, Watson, 38.
Bessey, C. E., 105.
Betts, L. W., 130. *See also* Woman's book, 123.
Betty Alden, Austin, 3.
Between whiles, Jackson, 21.
Beulah, Wilson, 39.
Beyond recall, Sergeant, 32.
Beyond the dreams of avarice, Besant, 4.
Beyond the gates, Ward, 7.
Bible, Cook, 61; concordances to, 135.
Bible in Spain, Borrow, 55.
Bicycling. *See* Cycling, 134.
Bigelow, J., 63.
Biggle, J., 126.
Billiards, Garnier, 134.
Biography (department), 41-46.

Birds, Burroughs, 108; Chapman, 108; Coues, 101; Grant, 109; Key-Osgood, 110; Thompson, 110; Torser, 109; Merriam, 109; Miller, 103; rey, 110; Willcox, 110.
Birds' Christmas Carol, Wiggin, 39.
Birrell, A., 41.
Bishop, W. H., 4-5.
Bisland, E., 55. *See also* Woman's book, 123.
Bissell, M. T., 119.
Bits of talk about home matters, Jackson, 122.
Bittenbender, A. M. *See* Meyer, 123.
Black, W., novels, 5; life of Goldsmith, 66.
Black sheep, Yates, 40.
Blackmore, R. D., 5.
Blaikie, W., 119.
Blanche, Lady Falaise, Shorthouse, 33.
Bleak house, Dickens, 11.
Blind, M., 41.
Blow, S. E., 94.
Blue fairy book, Lang, 24.
Blue pavilions, Couch, 9.
Blumner, H., 52.
Boldrewood, Rolf (*pseud.*). *See* Browne, T. A., 6.
Bolton, H. C., annotator, 101.
Bolton, S. K., 41.
Bonar, J., 114.
Bonny Kate, Tiernan, 36.
Bookbinding, Zaehnsdorf, 124.
Book-keeping, Meservey, 99; Packard *and* Bryant, 99.
Bookselling, Growoll, 125.
Booth, C., 114.
Bootles' baby, Stannard, 33.
Boots and saddles, Custer, 56.
Borrow, G., 55.
Bostonians, James, 22.
Bostwick, A. E. *See* Champlin, J. D., *and* Bostwick, A. E., 133.
Bostwick, L. W, 130.
Boswell, J., 41.
Botany (department), 105-108.
Bourinot, J. G., 49-50, 115.
Bourrienne, L. A. F. de. *See* Napoleon, 45.
Bowen, E. A., 93.
Bowker, R. R., 113.
Bowles, A. C. *See* Meyer, 123.
Bow of orange ribbon, Barr, 3.
Boyesen, H. H., novels, 5; history, 54.
Boys of '76, Coffin, 49.
Bracebridge Hall, Irving, 21.
Brackett, C. F., 99.
Bradbury, W. F., 98.
Braddon, M. E. *See* Maxwell, *Mrs.* M. E., 26.
Brand, J., 78.
Brandes, G., 41, 55.
Brandrum, S., 75.
Brassey, A. A., 55.
Brave lady, Craik, 9.
Bravo, Cooper, 9.
Brazil, Hates, 55.
Bread-winners (The), 5.
Breakfast-table series, Holmes, 67.
Brewer, E. C., 54, 137.
Bricks without straw, Tourgee, 36.
Bride of Lammermoor, Scott, 32.
Bridgman, Laura D., life of, Lamson, 44.
Brinton, D. G., 78.
Brontë, C., novels, 5-6; life of, Birrell, 41.
Brontë, E., 6.
Brooke, S. A., 60, 77.
Brooks, A., annotator, 94.
Brooks, E. S., 41-42.
Brother to dragons, Chanler, 8.
Brough, W., 114.
Broughton, R., 6.
Brown. *See* Emerson *and* Brown, 94.
Brown, C. B., 6.
Browne, T. A., 6.
Browne, W. H. *See* Johnson, R. M., *and* Browne, W. H., 44.
Brownell, W. C., 81.
Browning, E. B., 62; essay on, Stedman, 75.
Browning, O., 96.
Browning, R., 62; works on, Defries, 62; Kingsland, 62; Corson, 62; Orr, 62; Cooke, 62; Berdoe, 62.
Brueton's Bayou, Habberton, 16.

Brunner, A. W, 129.
Bryan, M., 84.
Bryant *and* Stratton's book-keeping, Packard *and* Bryant, 99.
Bryant, H. B. *See* Packard, H. S., *and* Bryant, H. B., 93.
Bryant, W. C., 62; life of, Bigelow, 63.
Bryce, J., 47, 53, 115.
Buchanan, R. W., 6.
Buckingham, C. L., 99.
Buckland, A., 94.
Huckley, A. B., 101, 108.
Building. *See* Architecture.
Building and loan associations, Dexter, 113. *See also* Stoddard, 123; Sturgis 129.
Building of a brain, Clarke, 119.
Building the nation, Coffin, 49.
Bulwer-Lytton, E. G. E. L., 6.
Bundle of letters to busy girls, Dodge, 121.
Bundle of life, Craigie, 9.
Bunner, H. C., 6.
Bunyan, J., 7.
Burgess, E. S., annotator, 105.
Burgess, J. W, 49.
Burke, E., life of, Morley, 71.
Burnett, *Mrs.* F. H., 7.
Burney, F. *See* Arblay, *Mme.* F. B. d', 2.
Burnham, *Mrs.* C. L., 7.
Burns, R., 63; life of, Shairp, 63.
Burpee, W. A., 126.
Burroughs, J., 108.
Burton, J. H, 51.
Business, women in, Stoddard, 123; White, 123. *See also* Woman's book, 123.
But a Philistine, Townsend, 36.
But yet a woman, Hardy, 17.
Butler. *See* Philosophical classics, 117.
Butler, E. A., 130.
Button's inn, Tourgee, 36.
Buxton, H. J. W., 86.
Bynner, F. C., 7.
Byron, G. G. N., 63; life of, Nichol, 63; Moore, 71.
By the Tiber, Tincker, 36.
Byways and bird notes, Thompson, 110.

Cable, G. W., 7.
Cabot, J. E., 42, 66.
Cæsar, Froude, 43, 52.
Caine, T. H. H., 7.
Calder, F. L., 132.
Call, A. P., 119.
Called back, Fargus, 13.
Calmire, 7.
Cambridge, A., 8.
Camp, W, 134.
Campbell, D., 48.
Canada, 49-50; Baedeker, 55; Appleton, 55; Parkin, 58; Warner, 59; Bourinot, 115.
Canadian poems and lays, Lightall, 60.
Candee, H. C., 129. *See* Woman's book, 123.
Candle, history of a, Faraday, 101.
Candy-making, Hostwick, 130; Nitsch, 131.
Canned foods and how to use them, 130.
Canning and preserving, Rorer, 131.
Canoe and the saddle, Winthrop, 39.
Cantatas, Upton, 91.
Canterbury tales, Chaucer, 64.
Can you forgive her?, Trollope, 37.
Cape Cod, Thoreau, 110.
Cape Cod folks, Greene, 16.
Capital and labor, 113.
Captain Bonneville's adventures, Irving, 48.
Carbon, compounds of, Remsen, 101.
Card games, 134.
Carey, R. N, 8.
Carletons, Grant, 16.
Carlotta's intended, Stuart, 34.
Carlyle, T., histories, 53; essays, 63; life of, Garnett, 63; correspondence, 66.
Carroll, Lewis (*pseud.*). *See* Dodgson, C. L., 11.
Carving and serving, Lincoln, 131.
Cary, E., 65.
Cassell's miniature cyclopædia, 136.

Cassell's new biographical dictionary, 42.
Casting away of Mrs. Leeks and Mrs. Aleshine, Stockton, 34.
Castle Blair, Shaw, 33.
Castle Daly, Keary, 24.
Castle of Otranto, Walpole, 19.
Castle Rackrent, Edgeworth, 12.
Cathedral courtship, Wiggin, 39.
Catherine Furze, White, 38.
Catherwood, *Mrs.* M. H., 8.
Cato, Addison, 61.
Caxtons, Bulwer-Lytton, 6.
Cecil Dreeme, Winthrop, 39.
Cecilia, Arblay, 2.
Celestial passion, Gilder, 66.
Century cyclopædia of names, 136.
Century dictionary, 81, 116.
Century of roundels, Swinburne, 76.
Chadwick, J. W., 65.
Chafing-dish supper, Herrick, 130.
Chamberlain, B. H., 56.
Chambers, R., 136.
Chambers' encyclopædia, 135-136.
Champlin, J. D., 133, 136.
Chance acquaintance, Howells, 20.
Chanler, *Mrs.* A. R., 8.
Channing, E. See Higginson, T. W., and Channing, E., 51.
Channings, Wood, 40.
Chapman, A. W., 103.
Chapman, F. M., 108.
Character, Jackson, 118; Willard, 121. See also Ethics, 118.
Charades, Bellamy, 133; Frost, 134; Nugent, 134.
Charities, 115. See also Meyer, 123.
Charles, *Mrs* E. R., 8.
Charles O'Malley, Lever, 25.
Chatelain, H., 79.
Chaucer, G., 63-64; life of, Ward, 64; works on, Lounsbury, 64; Haweis, 64; Ward, 64.
Chautauqua Literary and Scientific Circle, 145.
Checkers, Dunne, 134.
Checkley, E., 119.
Chemistry (department), 101.
Cheney, E. D., 42. See also Meyer, 123.
Chesneau, E., 81, 84.
Chester, E., 121.
Child, T., 56, 84.
Childe Harold's pilgrimage, Byron, 63.
Children, Harrison, 94; Marenholtz-Bulow, 94; Preyer, 112; Tracy, 112; Adler, 118; Herrick, 120; Jacobi, 120; Starr, 120; Uffelmann, 120. See also Woman's book, 123; Goodholme, 130.
Children of destiny, Seawell, 32.
Children of Gibeon, Besant, 4.
Children of the abbey, Roche, 31.
Children of the ghetto, Zangwill, 40.
Child's history of England, Dickens, 11.
Chili, Child, 56.
China, Ball, 55; Smith, 58.
Chita, Hearn, 18.
Chopin, F., Niecks, 92.
Choy Susan, Bishop, 5.
Christabel, Coleridge, 64.
Christie Johnstone, Reade, 30.
Christie's Faith, Robinson, 31.
Christine, Sergeant, 32.
Christmas hirelings, Maxwell, 26.
Christmas wreck, Stockton, 34.
Chronicles of Carlingford, Oliphant, 28.
Chronicles of Mr. Bill Williams, Johnston, 23.
Chronicles of the Schönberg-Cotta family, Charles, 8.
Church, *Mrs.* R. See Lean, *Mrs.* F. M., 24.
Cigarette-maker's romance, Crawford, 9.
Ciphers, Kirk, 24.
Circuit rider, Eggleston, 12.
Citoyenne Jacqueline, Keddie, 23.
Clarissa Harlowe, Richardson, 30.
Clarke, C., 74, 137.
Clarke, E. H., 119.
Clarke, J. F., 92.
Clarke, M. C., 74, 75, 137.
Claudia Hyde, Baylor, 4.
Clay, H., Schurz, 45.

Cleaning, chemistry of, Richards, 101; handbook of, Hurst, 132.
Clemens, S. L., 8.
Clement, C. E., 84, 135.
Clockmaker, Haliburton, 17.
Clodd, E., 108, 111.
Cloister and the hearth, Reade, 30.
Cloth of gold, Aldrich, 61.
Clubs for girls and women, 122; hints on forming 141-142, 144-145; outline constitution for, 143.
Clyde, H., 134.
Coates, H. T., 60.
Cobbe, F. P., 42.
Cobbleigh, Tom (*pseud.*). See Raymond, W., 30.
Cœur d'Alene, Foote, 14.
Coffee and repartee, Bangs, 3.
Coffin, C. C., 42, 49.
Coffin, C. E., 133.
Coffin, W. A., 81, 84.
Coin's financial fool, White, 114.
Coin's financial school, Harvey, 114.
Cole, A. S. See Lefevre, E., and Cole, A. S., 124.
Coleridge, S. T., 64.
College settlements. See Jones, 122.
Collignon, M., 81.
Collingwood, H. W., 127.
Collins, H., 117.
Collins, W. W., 8.
Colonel Carter of Cartersville, Smith, 33.
Colonel Cheswick's campaign, Shaw, 31.
Colonel's daughter, King, 23.
Colonies, American, Thwaites, 47; and dependencies, Cotton and Payne, 50; European, Payne, 50; Lucas, 60.
Color studies, Janvier, 22.
Columbus, life of, Irving, 43; Seelye, 45; Winsor, 46.
Colvin, S., 82, 69, 81.
Cometh up as a flower, Broughton, R., 6.
Coming race, Bulwer-Lytton, 6.
Compayré, G., 96.
Composers, lives of, Dole, 42.
Composition, Morton, 98; Newcomer, 98; Shaw, 98.
Comstock, J. H., and A. B., 108.
Comte, Watson, 117.
Concord and Merrimac rivers, Thoreau, 110.
Cone, H. G., 42. See also Meyer, 123.
Confectionery. See candy-making.
Confessions of a frivolous girl, Grant, 16.
Confessions of an opium-eater, De Quincey, 62.
Conjuring, Hoffmann, 134.
Conkling, A. R., 116.
Conspiracy of Pontiac, Parkman, 48.
Conundrums. See Puzzles.
Conversation, art of, Mahaffy, 121.
Conway, Hugh (*pseud.*). See Fargus, F. J., 13.
Conway, W. A., 81.
Cook, A. J., 127.
Cook, A. S., 61.
Cooke, G. W., 62.
Cooke, J. P., 101.
Cooke, M. C., 105.
Cooke, R. T., 8.
Cooking, 130-132; chemistry of, Richards, 101. See also Goodholme, 130.
Cooking garden, 95; Huntington, 95.
Cooking schools. See Jones, 122.
Cooper, J. F., 9.
Co-operative savings associations, Dexter, 113.
Cope, A., 116.
Copperhead, Frederic, 15.
Cord and creese, De Mille, 10.
Coren, Griffis, 56.
Corelli, Marie. See Mackay, M., 26.
Corroyer, E., 88.
Corson, H., 62, 74.
Corson, J., 130.
Costume, Greek, 90; Sturgis, 90; Evans, 90. See also Dress.
Cotes, *Mrs.* S. J. D., novels, 9; travel, 56.
Cotton *and* Payne, 50.
Couch, A. T. Q., 9.
Coues, E., 108.
Coulter, J. M., 105.
Counsel of perfection, Harrison, 18.

Countess Eve, Shorthouse, 33.
Countess Radna, Norris, 28.
Count Frontenac and New France under Louis XII., Parkman, 48.
Country cousin, Peard, 29.
Country doctor, Jewett, 22.
Country occupations (department), 126-128.
Courting of Mary Smith Robinson, 31.
Cousin Stella, Jenkin, 22.
Cowper, W., 64; life of, Smith, 64.
Cox, G. W., 78.
Cox, H. See Webb, S., *and* Cox, H., 114.
Craddock, Charles Egbert (*pseud.*). See Murfree, M. N., 27.
Cradle and nursery, Herrick, 120.
Craigie, *Mrs.* ——, 9.
Craik, *Mrs.* D. M., 9, 121.
Craik, H., 60.
Crane, T. F., 78.
Cranford, Gaskell, 15.
Crawford, F. M., 9.
Creighton, *Mrs.* L., 53.
Criticisms on contemporary thought, Hutton, 67.
Crocheting, Butterick Pub., 125.
Crockett, S. R., 10.
Croly, *Mrs.* J. C., 123, 124.
Crops. See Farm and farming, 126.
Cross, J. W., 42.
Cross, *Mrs.* M. E. See Eliot, George, 12.
Crown of wild olive, Ruskin, 73.
Cruger, *Mrs.* J. G. S., 10.
Cruise of the *Midge*, Scott, 32.
Crusades, Michaud, 52.
Cryptogram, De Mille, 10.
Cuckoo in the nest, Oliphant, 28.
Culin, S., annotator, 78.
Culture and anarchy, Arnold, 61.
Cummins, M. S., 10.
Currency, 114.
Curtis, G. W., 10, 64-65; biographies, Cary, 65; Chadwick, 65.
Cushing, L. S., 116.
Cushing, W., 137.
Cushman, C., Stebbins, 45-46.
Custer, *Mrs.* E. B., 56.
Customs and myths, Lang, 79.
Cycling, 134.
Cyclopædias, 135-136; of temperance, 115; of practical [household] information, Goodholme, 130; Century, 136; of Eng. literature, Chambers, 136.

Da capo, Ritchie, 31.
Dairying, 127.
Daisy chain, Yonge, 40.
Daisy Miller, James, 22.
Dakota, life in, Custer, 56.
Dana, C. A., 60.
Dana, J. D., 103.
Dana, R. H., 56.
Dana, *Mrs.* W. S., 105.
Dancing, Dick, 134; Dodworth, 134.
Danesbury house, Wood, 39-40.
Daniel Deronda, Eliot, 12.
Dante, Ward, 46.
Danube from the Black Forest to the Black Sea, Millet, 58.
D'Arblay, *Mme.* F. B. See *under* Arblay, 2.
Darkness and dawn, Farrar, 13.
Darnley, James, 22.
Darwin, C., 105, 109; life and letters of, Darwin, F., 42; journal, 56; teachings of, Romanes, 110; Wallace, 110; Schurman, 118.
Darwin, F., 42.
Daughter of Fife, Barr, 3.
Daughter of Heth, Black, 5.
Daughter of the south, Harrison, 18.
Daughter of to-day, Cotes, 9.
Daughters of the Revolution, Coffin, 49.
David Alden's daughter, Austin, 3.
David Balfour, Stevenson, 34.
David Copperfield, Dickens, 11.
David Grieve, Ward, 38.
Davis, I. P., 119.
Davis, R. H., 10.
Dawson, *Sir* J. W., 103, 105.
Dawson, S. E., 77.
Day at Laguerre's, Smith, 33.
Days of yore, Keddie, 23.
Deacon's week, Cooke, 8.
Dead secret, Collins, 8.

Dearly bought, Burnham, 7.
De Bary, A , 106.
Debenham's vow, Edwards, 12.
De Candolle, A., 106.
Decorative arts, 90–91. *See also* Art; House decoration.
Decmster, Caine, 7.
Deephaven, Jewett, 22.
Deerslayer, Cooper, 9.
Defence of Guenevere, Morris, 71.
Defoe, D., 10.
De Forest, J. B., 81.
Defries, E. P., 62.
De Garmo, C., 96.
De Hurst, C. (*pseud*.), 134.
Delaborde, H., 85.
Deland, *Mrs. M.*, 10.
De la Ramé, L., 10.
Delectable duchy, Couch, 9.
De Mille, J., 10.
Deming, P., 10.
Democracy, 11.
Denzil Quarrier, Gissing, 15.
De Quincey, T., 65.
Descartes. *See* Philosophical classics, 117.
Descent of man, Darwin, 109.
Deserted village, Goldsmith, 66.
Design, Benson, 90. *See also* Decorative arts; Drawing.
Desmond hundred, Austin, 3.
Despot of Broomsedge Cove, Murfree, 27.
Destiny, Ferrier, 14.
Detmold, Bishop, 4.
Dexter, S , 113.
Diana of the crossways, Meredith, 27.
Diary of a man of fifty, James, 22.
Diary of Kitty Trevelyan, Charles, 8.
Dick, W. H., 134
Dick's wanderings, Sturgis, 35.
Dickens, C., 11; life of, Forster, 11.
Dickinson, S E. *See* Meyer, 123.
Dictator, McCarthy, 25.
Dictionaries, English, French, German, Greek, Italian, Latin, Spanish, 136; Century, 81, 136: International, 81, 136; of [Eng.] national biography, 41, 184; of painters and engravers, Bryan, 84; of artists, Clements *and* Hutton, 84; of art, Adeline, 84, 135; of music and musicians, Grove, 91; of musical terms, Stainer *and* Barrett, 93; of electrical words, Houston, 100, 125; of economic plants, Smith, 107; of archaeology, 135; of authors, Allibone, 135; of classical antiquities, Seyffert, 135; of biography, Lippincott, 136; Standard, 136; Worcester, 136; Academic, 136; of Eng. literature, Adams, 136; of dates, Haydn, 136 ; of Eng. history, Low *and* Pulling, 137; of quotations, 137; of synonyms and antonyms, Fallows, 137.
Diet, infant, Jacobi, 120; invalid, Henderson, 130.
Dinner-giving, Herrick, 131; Terhune, 131. *See also* Cooking.
Diplomat's diary, Cruger, 10.
Disraeli, B., 11.
Divina commedia, Dante. *See* Longfellow, 69.
Dixey, W., 125.
Dr. Claudius, Crawford, 9.
Dr. Le Baron and his daughters, Austin, 3.
Dr. Sevier, Cable, 7.
Doctor Thorne, Trollope, 37.
Doctor Zay, Ward. 38.
Doctor's family, Oliphant, 28.
Dodge, G. H., 121.
Dodge, L. *See* Preston, H. W., *and* Dodge, L., 53.
Dodgson, C. L., 11.
Dodworth, A., 134.
Dole, N. H., 42.
Domestic economy (department), 129–132. *See also* Newsholme, 120.
Don John, Ingelow, 21.
Don Orsino, Crawford, 9.
Donovan, Lyall, 25.
Dora, *Sister*, Lonsdale, 44.
Dorcen, Lyall, 25.
Dorothy Foster, Besant, 4.
Doty, A. H., 120.
Dougall, L., 11.
Douglas, A. M., 12.
Douglas, J., 116.

Douglass, F., 42.
Dove in the eagle's nest, Yonge, 40.
Dowden, E., 74.
Doyle, A. C., 12.
Drainage. *See* Goodholme, 130.
Drake, S. A., 49.
Drawing, 124; Hamerton, 85 ; Viollet-le-Duc, 87; Thompson, 97. *See also* Art.
Draytons and the Davenants, Charles, 8.
Dream life and real life, Schreiner, 32.
Dreams, Schreiner, 32.
Dress, 132. *See also* Woman's book, 123; Costume.
Dress-making, Davis, 132. *See also* Hubert, 123.
Drumbeat of the nation, Coffin, 49.
Drummond. H., 109.
Dryden. J., 65; life of, Johnson, 43–44; Saintsbury, 65.
Duchess (*pseud*.). *See* Hungerford, *Mrs.* M. H., 18.
Dufferin and Ava, *Marchioness* of, 56.
Duffy, B., 42.
Dukesborough tales, Johnston, 23.
Du Maurier, G., 12.
Duncan, S. J. *See* Cotes, *Mrs.* S. J. D., 9.
Dunne, F., 134.
Duruy, V., 52, 53.
Dusantes, Stockton, 34.
Dust, Prudden, 120.
Duty, Seelye, 118. *See also* Ethics.
Dwight, J., 134.
Dyeing, Hurst, 132.
Dyer, T. F. T., 78, 106.

Earth, aspects of the, Shaler, 104. *See also* Geography.
Earthly paradise, Morris, 71.
East and west, Harte, 67.
East Angels, Woolson, 40.
Eastlake, *Sir* C. L., 129.
East Lynne, Wood, 39.
Eastman, M. F. *See* Meyer, 123.
Easy chair, Curtis, 65.
Ebb tide, Stevenson, 34.
Ecob, H G., 120.
Economic, social, and political science (department), 113–17.
Edgeworth, M., novels, 12; life and letters, Hare, 43.
Education (department), 94–100.
Educational reformers, essays on, Quick, 97.
Edwards, *Mrs.* A., 12.
Edwards, A. B., novels, 12; travel, 56; archæology, 82.
Edwin Brothertoft, Winthrop, 39.
Eggleston, E., 12.
Eglantine, Stephenson, 33.
Egoist, Meredith, 27.
Egypt, Edwards, 56; Petrie, 83; Maspero, 82; Redford, 87.
Ehlert, L., 91.
Ehrmann, C. *See* Adams, W. I. L., *and* Ehrmann, C., 124.
Eight cousins, Alcott, 2.
Eleanor's victory, Maxwell, 26.
Electricity, Barnard, 99; Brackett, *and others*, 99; Houston, 100; Thompson, 100.
Elia, essays of, Lamb, 69.
Eliot, George, novels, 12–13 ; life and letters. Cross, 42 ; poems and essays, 65-66.
Elliott, S. B., 13.
Ellwanger, H. B., 127.
Elocution, Bell, 97. *See also* Reading.
Elsie Venner, Holmes, 20.
Elsket, Page, 28.
Ely, R. T., 49, 113, 115.
Embossing, Leland, 123.
Embroidery, 90, 124–125; Lefebure, 90; Sturgis, 90; Harrison, 129.
Emergencies, 120.
Emerson, A., 81.
Emerson *and* Brown, 94.
Emerson, R. W., 42, 66 ; correspondence, 66; memoirs of, Cabot, 42, 66; Holmes, 66.
Emerton, E., 52.
Emigrant ship, Russell, 31.
Emigration and immigration, Smith, 115.

Emma, Austen, 3.
Enamel, Rudler, 90 ; Sturgis. 90.
Encyclopædia Britannica, 135.
Encyclopædia of games and sports, Champlin *and* Bostwick, 133.
Encyclopædias. *See* Cyclopædias, 135.
Endymion, Disraeli, 11.
England, 50–52; Dickens, 11; Hawthorne, 57; Smith, 58; Winter, 59.
English humorists, Thackeray, 77.
English novel. Lanier, 69.
Engravers, dictionary of, Bryan, 84.
Engraving, Delaborde, 85; Hamerton, 85; Linton, 85.
Entomology, Packard, 110. *See also* Insects.
Eothen. Kinglake, 57.
Epicurean, Moore, 71.
Epochs of American history, Hart, Thwaites, Wilson. 47.
Epochs of ancient history series, 54.
Epochs of modern history series, 54.
Erdmann, J. E , 117.
Erema, Blackmore, 5.
Eric, Farrar, 13.
Eskimo life, Wanser, 58.
Essay on man, Pope, 72.
Esther Vanhomrigh, Woods, 40.
Etching and etchers, Hamerton, 85.
Ethics, 118.
Ethics of the dust, Ruskin, 73–74.
Ethnology and folk-lore, Gomme, 78–79.
Etiquette, 121–122. *See also* Woman's book, 123.
Eugene Aram, Bulwer-Lytton, 6.
Europe, 52–54 ; Duruy, 52 ; Emerton, 52; Fyffe, 52 ; Myers, 52 ; Seebohm, 52 ; Baedeker, 55.
Evans, M. M., 90.
Evelina, Arblay, 2.
Everett. C. C., 118.
Eve's daughters, Terhune, 120.
Eve's ransom, Gissing, 15.
Evolution, Clodd, 108 ; Darwin, 109; Drummond, 109. *See also* Natural history, 109.
Excursions, Thoreau, 110.
Exercise. *See* Physical culture.
Exiles, Davis, 10.
Experiences of a lady-help, Stannard, 33.
Expiation, French, 15.
Exploration. *See* Travel, 55.
Explorers, Greely, 43 ; Higginson, 57.

Face to face, Francillon, 14.
Faerie queene, Spenser, 75.
Fagots for the fireside, Hale, 133.
Fair barbarian, Burnett, 7.
Fair god, Wallace, 37.
Fairy tales, science of, Hartland, 79. *See also* Lang, 24.
Faith doctor, Eggleston, 12.
Faith Gartney s girlhood, Whitney, 39.
Fallen fortunes, Payn, 29.
Fallows, S., 137.
Familiar short sayings of great men, Bent, 136.
Family tree, Matthews, 26.
Famous types of womanhood, Bolton, 41.
Famous women series, 46.
Fancy work. *See* Needlework.
Faraday, M., 101.
Far from the madding crowd, Hardy, 17.
Fargus, F. J., 13.
Farjeon, B. L., 13.
Farm and farming, 126.
Farrar, F. W., 13.
Fated to be free, Ingelow, 21.
Faucit, H., 75.
Fawcett, E., 13–14.
Fawcett, M. G , 43.
Feilden, H. St. C., 116.
Felch, J. K., 127.
Felix Holt, Eliot, 13.
Felmeres, Elliott, 13.
Fenton's quest, Maxwell, 26.
Fergusson, J., 88–89.
Ferns. *See* Botany, 105–108.
Ferrier, S. E., 14.
Fichte. *See* Philosophical classics, 117.
Fiction (department), 1–40.
Fiction, noted names of, Wheeler, 136–137; lists of, Griswold, 1, 54.

Fielding, H., 14.
Fields, J. T., 43.
Fillmore, J. C., 91.
Finck, H. T., 56, 91.
Fine art (department), 80-91. *See also* Art, Decorative arts, Drawing, Design.
Finger-play for nursery and kindergarten, Poulsson, 94.
First violin, Fothergill, 14.
Fisher, G. P., 47, 49.
Fisherman of Auge, Macquoid, 26.
Fishes, Agassiz, 108; Goode, 109.
Fiske, J., 47, 48, 117.
Fitch, J. G., 96.
Five books of song, Gilder, 66.
Fletcher, J. C., 14.
Flitters, Tatters, and the Counsellor, Hartley, 18.
Flock of girls, Perry, 29.
Flora of the southern U. S., Chapman, A. W., 105; of the Rocky Mountains, Coulter, 105.
Florence, Hare, 57.
Floriculture. *See* Flower garden.
Flower and thorn, Aldrich, 61.
Flower-garden, 127. *See also* Woman's book, 123.
Flower of forgiveness, Steel, 33.
Flowers. *See* Botany, 105-108.
Flute and violin, Allen, 2.
Foes of her household, Douglas, 12.
Folk-lore, science of, Cox, 78; of plants, Dyer, 78, 106; of women of Turkey, Garnett *and* Stuart Glennie, 78; ethnology of, Gomme, 78-79; handbook of, Gomme, 79; of Angola, Chatelain, 79; of Louisiana, Fortier, 79.
Folk-Lore Society, 79.
Food, 130-132.
Fool's errand, Tourgee, 36.
Football. *See* Camp, 134.
Foote, *Mrs.* M. H., 14.
Footpath way, Torrey, 110.
For faith and freedom, Besant, 4.
For the major, Woolson, 40.
Ford, H., 134.
Ford, P. L., 14.
Ford, W. C. *See* Washington, G., 46.
Foregone conclusion, Howells, 20.
Forster, J., 11.
Fortier, A., 79.
Fortune's fool, Hawthorne, 19.
Fortunes of Margaret Weld, Gardner, 15.
Fortunes of Nigel, Scott, 32.
Fortunes of Sir Thomas Upmore, Blackmore, 5.
Fothergill, J., 14.
Foul play, Reade *and* Boucicault, 8.
Four Georges, Thackeray, 77.
Fowler, W. W., 52.
Foxglove Manor, Buchanan, 6.
Framley Parsonage, Trollope, 37.
France, Duruy, 53; Montgomery, 53; Creighton, 53; Lacombe, 53; Guizot, 53.
Francillon, R. E., 14.
Francis, M. E., 14.
Frank Hilton, Grant, 16.
Frankenstein Shelley, 33.
Franklin, B., 43; life of, Morse, 45.
Franklin, C. L. *See* Meyer, 123.
Frederic, H., 15.
Frederick II., Carlyle, 53.
Free trade, 114
Freedom triumphant, Coffin, 49.
Freeman, E. A., histories, 50 54, 89, 116; art, 89.
French, A., 15.
French Janet, Keddie, 23.
French Revolution, Carlyle, 53; Gardiner, 53.
French traits, Brownell, 81.
Fresco, Wilson, 83. *See also* Decorative arts; Mural painting.
Fresh fields, Burroughs, 108.
Froebel, J., 94; teachings of, Blow, 94; Marenholtz-Bulow, 94; Shirreff, 95.
From dusk to dawn, Woods, 40.
From the cradle to the school, Meyer, 94.
From the tone world, Ehlert, 91.
Fromentin, E., 85.
Frothingham, A. L. *See* Marquand, A., *and* Frothingham, A. L., *jr.*, 86.

Froudacity, Thomas, 50.
Froude, J. A., 43, 50, 51-52, 52.
Frye, A. E., 102.
Fuller, M., Howe, 43.
Fungi, De Bary, 106.
Furniture. *See* House decoration.
Further records, Kemble, 44.
Fyffe, C. A., 52.

Gabriel Conroy, Harte, 18.
Galbraith, A. M., 119.
Games, 133-134; traditional, Gomme, 78.
Gardening, 126-128. *See also* Landscape gardening; Flower garden; Botany.
Gardiner, B. M., 53.
Gardiner, *Mrs.* S. M. H., 15.
Gardiner, S. R., 50. *See* Freeman, E. A., *and* Gardiner, S., 89.
Garland, H., 15.
Garnett, L. M. J., 78.
Garnier, A., 134.
Garrett, R. *and* A., 129.
Gaskell, *Mrs.* E. C., 15.
Gates ajar, Ward, 37.
Gates between, Ward, 37.
Gayley, C. M., 78.
Gayworthys, Whitney, 39.
Geikie, Sir A., 103.
Gentleman of France, Weyman, 38.
Gentleman of leisure, Fawcett, 14.
Gentleman Upcott's daughter, Raymond, 30.
Genung, J. F., 98.
Geoffrey Hamlin, Kingsley, 23.
Geography (department), 102.
Geology (department), 103-105.
Geometry, Bradbury, 98-99; Hill, 99.
George, H., 113.
Gerard, E. D. *See* Laszowska, *Mrs.* E. D. G., 24.
Gerard, J. N. *See* Woman's book, 123.
Germany, Bryce, 53; Henderson, 53; Gould, 53; Sime, 53; Mahaffy *and* Rogers, 57; Millet, 58.
Gervinus, G. G., 74.
Giant's robe, Guthrie, 16.
Gibbon, E., 52-53.
Gibson, L. H., 129.
Gibson, W. H., 109.
Gilchrist, A., 43.
Gilder, J. L. *See* Cone, H. G., *and* Gilder, J. L., 42.
Gilder, R. W., 66.
Gilder, *Mrs.* R. W., 116.
Giles Corey, Wilkins, 39.
Gilman, D. C., 115.
Gilman, N. P., 113, 118.
Girlhood of Shakespeare's heroines, Clarke, 75.
Girls' club with home of its own, 141-143; home constitution for, 143; hints for a literary, 144.
Girls' Friendly Society. *See* Jones, M. C., 122.
Girl's room, A, 129.
Gissing, G. R., 15.
Gladden, W., 113.
Glaister, E., 124.
Glass, Sturgis, 90.
Glimpses of fifty years, Willard, F. E., 46.
God and the man, Buchanan, 6.
God in the car, Hawkins, 19.
Gods (The), some mortals, and Lord Wickenham, Craigie, 9.
Godwin, M. *See* Shelley, *Mrs.* M. G., 33.
Godwin, W., 15.
Goebel, K., 106.
Goethe, C. E., 43.
Goethe, J. W. *von*, correspondence, 43; life of, Grimm, 43.
Golden bells, Francillon, 14.
Golden butterfly, Besant *and* Rice, 4.
Golden dog, Kirby, 24.
Golden justice, Bishop, 4.
Golden wedding, Stuart, 34.
Goldsmith, O., tales, 15; poems, essays, plays, 66; life of, Black, 66, Irving, 68.
Gomme, A. B., 78, 133.
Gomme, G. L., 78.
Gonse, L., 84, 85.
Goodale, G. L., 106.
Good-bye, sweetheart, Broughton, 6.

Goode, G. B., 109.
Goodholme, T. D., 130.
Goodyear, W. H., 82.
Gordon, J. (*pseud.*). *See* Cruger, *Mrs.* J. G., 10.
Gourgaud. *See* Napoleon, 45.
Government, American, 115; British, 115; Canadian, 115. *See also* Municipal government.
Grammar, David, 97.
Grandfather's chair, Hawthorne, 19.
Grandissimes, Cable, 7.
Grant, J., 16.
Grant, J. B., 109.
Grant, R., 16.
Grape culture, Bailey, 126.
Graphic art. *See* Drawing, Painting, Engraving.
Gray, A., 106.
Gray, T., Johnson, 43-44.
Gray days and gold, Winter, 59.
Graysons, Eggleston, 12
Great Britain, antiquities of, Brand, 78.
Great commanders series, 46.
Great Porter Square, Farjeon, 13.
Great remembrance, Gilder, 66.
Great world, Hatton, 18.
Great writers series, 46.
Greece, Myers *and* Allen, 52; Blumner, 52; Fowler, 52; Mahaffy, 53, 57; Oman, 53; Harrison, 85; Redford, 87; Upcott, 87; Sturgis, 90.
Greek studies, Pater, 71.
Greely, A. W., 43, 56.
Green, A. K. *See* Rohlfs, *Mrs.* A. K. G., 31.
Green, J. R., 51.
Green. T. H., 118.
Green fairy book, Lang, 24.
Greene, *Mrs.* S. P. M., 16.
Greenhouse construction, Taft, 127.
Greifenstein, Crawford, 9.
Greiner, T., 126.
Grey, Maxwell *pseud.*). *See* Tuttiett, M. G., 37.
Grif, Farjeon, 13.
Griffis, W. E., 56.
Griffith Gaunt, Reade, 30.
Grimm, H., 43.
Grimm, J., 79.
Griswold, W. M., 1, 54.
Grocutt, J. C., 137.
Grove, Sir G., 91.
Growoll, A., 125.
Growth of a people, Lacombe, 53.
Guardian angel, Holmes, 20.
Guenn, Howard, 20.
Guizot, F., 51, 53.
Gulliver's travels, Swift, 35.
Gurler, H. B., 127.
Guthrie, T. A., 16.
Guy Mannering, Scott, 32.
Gymnastics. *See* Physical culture.

H. H. (*pseud.*). *See* Jackson, *Mrs.* H. M. (F.).
Habberton, J, 16.
Hadley, A. T., 114.
Hadow, W. H., 91.
Haggard, H. R., 16.
Haifa, Oliphant, 58.
Hale, E. E., tales, 17; history, 50.
Hale, H., 98.
Hale, L. P., 133.
Half-century of conflict, Parkman, 48.
Haliburton, T. C., 17.
Hall, F H., 121.
Hall, G. S., 96.
Hallam, H., 51.
Halle, E. v., 114.
Hamerton, P. G., novels, 17; art, 82, 85, 121.
Hamilton. *See* Philosophical classics, 117.
Hamlin, A. D. F., 80.
Hampton, I. A., 120.
Hand and glove, Edwards, 12.
Handel, G. F., Rockstro, 91.
Handicraft and design, Benson, 90.
Handwriting. *See* Penmanship.
Handy Andy, Lover, 25.
Hannah Thurston, Taylor, 35.
Hanslick, E., 92.
Hapgood, I. F., 56.
Hapgood, O. C., 124.
Happy Dodd, Cooke, 8.
Hardinge, E. M., 106.
Hardy, A. S., 17.

Hardy, T., 17.
Hare A. J. C, biography, 43; travel, 57.
Harland, H., 17.
Harland, Marian (*pseud*.). *See* Terhune, *Mrs.* M. V. H.
Harold, Bulwer-Lytton, 6.
Harraden, B., 17.
Harris, J. C., 18.
Harris, *Mrs.* M. (C.), 18.
Harris, W. T., 117.
Harrison, *Mrs.* B. *See* Harrison, *Mrs.* C. C.
Harrison, *Mrs.* C. C., 18, 129. *See also* Woman's book, 123.
Harrison, E., 94.
Harrison, F., 54.
Harrison, J. E., 85.
Harrison, *Mrs.* M., 18.
Harry Blount, Hamerton, 17.
Harry Heathcote, Trollope, 37.
Harry Lorrequer, Lever, 25.
Hart, A. B. *See* Epochs of American history, 47.
Harte, F. Bret, stories, 18; poems, 66-67.
Hartland, E. S., 79.
Hartley, *Mrs.* M., 18.
Hartmann, R., 109.
Harvey, W. H., 114.
Hasse, A. R., annotator, 55.
Hatton, J., 18.
Hauser's Era of the Reformation, 52.
Havard, H., 85.
Hawkins, A. H., 18.
Hawthorne, J., novels, 19; biography, 43; literature, 60.
Hawthorne, N., novels, 19; life of, Hawthorne, J., 43; travels, 57.
Hay, J. *See* Nicolay, J. G., *and* Hay, J., 45.
Hay, M. C., 19.
Haydn, J., Nohl, 92.
Haydn's dictionary of dates, Vincent, 137.
Hayes, Henry (*pseud*.). *See* Kirk, *Mrs.* E. W. O, 24.
Hayne, P. H., 67.
Hazard of new fortunes, Howells, 20.
Hazell's annual, 137.
Head, P. R. *See* Poynter, E. J., *and* Head, P. R., 86.
Head of Medusa, Fletcher, 14.
Heaps of money, Norris, 28.
Hearn, L., tales, 19; travel, 57.
Heart of Midlothian, Scott, 32.
Heart of the world, Haggard, 16.
Hearts and hands, Tiernan, 36.
Heat, Wright, 100.
Heather and snow, MacDonald, 26.
Heaton, *Mrs.* C. S., 85.
Hector, *Mrs.* A. F., 19.
Hector, Shaw, 33.
Hedged in, Ward, 38.
He fell among thieves, Murray, 27.
Hegel, Harris, 117; Wallace, 118. *See also* Philosophical classics, 117.
Heilprin, L., 54.
Heinrich, J., 127.
Heir of Redclyffe, Yonge, 40.
Heir presumptive and heir apparent, Oliphant, 28.
Helbig, H., 82.
Helen's babies, Habberton, 16.
Henderson, C. R., 115.
Henderson, E. F., 53.
Henderson, I., 70.
Henderson, M. F., 130.
Henderson, P., 126, 127.
Henderson, W. J., 91.
Henry, P., Life of, Tyler, 46.
Henry Esmond, Thackeray, 35.
Henry of Guise, James, 22.
Herbart and the Herbartians, De Garmo, 96.
Herbart Society, 96.
Herbert, G., 67.
Her dearest foe, Hector, 19.
Heredity, Weismann, 110; Strahan, 130.
Hereward, Kingsley, 23.
Herman, H., 20.
Herndon, W. H., 43.
Heroes and hero-worship, Carlyle, 63.
Heroes of the nations series, 46, 54.
Herrick, C. T., 130, 130-131.
Herr Paulus, Besant, 6.
Hester Stanley at St. Mark's, Spofford, 33.
Hetty's strange history, Jackson, 21.

Hewitt, A. S., 116.
Hidden path, Terhune, 35.
Higginson, T. W., histories, 47, 51; explorers, 57. *See also* Woman's book, 123.
Hildreth, R., 49.
Hill, A. S., 98.
Hill, G., 132.
Hill, G. A., 99.
Hillyars and Burtons, Kingsley, 23.
Hinsdale, B. A., 48, 54.
His grace, Norris, 28.
His great self, Terhune, 35.
Historic boys, Brooks, 41.
Historic girls, Brooks, 41-42.
History (department), 47-54.
History, ancient, Myers *and* Allen, 52.
History, study of, Keary, 52; Adams, 54; Freeman, 54; Harrison, 54; Hinsdale, 54; Larned, 54, 137; Brewer, 54; Heilprin, 54; Adams, 137; Low *and* Pulling, 137.
History, universal, Fisher, 47.
Hobbes. *See* Philosophical classics, 117.
Hoffmann, *Prof*. (*pseud*.), 133, 134.
Hogan, M P., Hartley, 18.
Holden, E. S. *See* Newcomb, S., *and* Holden, E. S., 99.
Holland, Amicis, 55; Motley, 53-54; Mahaffy *and* Rogers, 57; Havard, 85.
Hollands, Townsend, 36.
Holmes, *Mrs.* M. J. H., 20.
Holmes, O. W., novels, 20; poems, essays, 67; life of Emerson, 66; psychology, 112.
Holy Land. *See* Palestine.
Holy Roman empire, Bryce, 53.
Home influence, Aguilar, 1.
Home occupations, Runtz-Rees, 133.
Home scenes and heart studies, Aguilar, 1.
Homer, Bryant, 69; Morris, 71.
Honorable Peter Stirling, Ford, 14.
Hood, T., 67.
Hoosier schoolmaster, Eggleston, 12.
Hope, Anthony (*pseud*.). *See* Hawkins, A. H., 18.
Horace Chase, Woolson, 40.
Horsemanship for women, De Hurst, 134; Mead, 134.
Horticulture. *See* Orchard and kitchen garden, 126-127.
Houp la!, Stannard, 33.
Hours in a library, Stephen, 76.
House decoration, 129. *See also* Woman's book, 123; Goodholme, 130.
House of a merchant prince, Bishop, 5
House of the seven gables, Hawthorne, 19.
House of the wolf, Weyman, 38.
House of Yorke, Tincker, 36.
House on the marsh, James, 21.
Housekeeping, 130. *See also* Woman's book, 123; Parloa, 131; Terhune, 131.
Houston, E. J., 100, 125.
How like a woman, Lean, 24.
How to win, Willard, 121.
Howadji in Syria, Curtis, 65.
Howard, B. W., 20.
Howard's book of conundrums, 133.
Howe, E. W., 20.
Howe, J. W., 43. *See also* Meyer, 123.
Howells, W. D., 20.
Hoyle, the American, Dick, 134.
Hubbard, C. B., 94.
Hubert, P. G., 123.
Huckleberries gathered from New England hills, Cooke, 8.
Hudson, G., 57, 109.
Hughes, W. S., 99.
Huguenot family, Keddie, 23.
Human intercourse, Hamerton, 121.
Humble romance, Wilkins, 39.
Hume, D., 51. *See* Philosophical classics, 117.
Humorists, English, Thackeray, 77.
Humphrey, F. S., 125.
Humphrey, M. G., 129. *See also* Woman's book, 123.
Hungerford, *Mrs.* M. H., 21.
Hunt, Helen. *See* Jackson, *Mrs.* H. M. F., 21.
Hunt, H. G. B., 92.
Hunt, M. A., 127.
Huntington, E., 95.
Hurst, G. H., 132.

Hutchinson, *Miss* E. M. *See* Stedman, E. C., *and* Hutchinson, *Miss* E. M., 60.
Hutton, L. *See* Clement, C. E., *and* Hutton, L., 84.
Hutton, R. H., 67, 74.
Huxley, T. H., 119.
Hydrostatics, Taylor, 100.
Hygiene, 119-120. *See* Woman's book, 123.
Hypatia, Kingsley, 23.

Ice, Prudden, 120.
Idylls of the king, Tennyson, 76.
Iles, G., 113.
Iliad. *See* Bryant, 62.
Illustration, American, Coffin, 84.
Imaginary conversations, Landor, 69.
Imaginary portraits, Pater, 71.
Immigration, Smith, 115.
Impressions and opinions, Moore, 86.
In direst peril, Murray, 27.
In exile Foote, 14
In memoriam, Tennyson, 76.
In old Virginia, Page, 28.
In silk attire, Black, 5.
In the child's world, Poulsson, 95.
In the golden days, Lyall, 25.
In the heart of the storm, Tuttiett, 37.
In the Tennessee mountains, Murfree, 27.
In the valley, Frederic, 15.
In varying moods, Harraden, 17.
In the vestibule limited, Matthews, 26.
In the wire grass, Pendleton, 29.
India, Dufferin and Ava, 56.
Indian summer, Howells, 21.
Indiscretion of the duchess, Hawkins, 19.
Infelice, Wilson, 39.
Ingelow, J., novels, 21; poems, 67-68.
Inheritance, Ferrier, 14.
Initials, Tautphœus, 35.
Initials and pseudonyms, Cushing, 137.
Inlay, 90.
Insects, Weed, 107; Comstock, 108; Hamilton, 109; Lubbock, 109; Manton, 109; McCook, 109; Packard, 110; Sempers, 127; Butler, 129. *See also* Natural history, 109.
Intellectual life, Hamerton, 82.
Interloper, Peard, 29.
International dictionary, 81, 136.
International episode, James, 22.
Invisible empire, Tourgée, 36.
Ireland, Lecky, 51.
Irish idylls, Barlow, 3.
Irish melodies and songs, Moore, 71.
Irish stories and legends, Lover, 25.
Iron, Ralph (*pseud*.). *See* Schreiner, O., 31.
Irving, W., tales, 21; life of Columbus, 43; Captain Bonneville, Astoria, 48; works, 68.
Ismay's children, Hartley, 18.
Italian popular tales, Crane, 78.
Italy, Symonds, 54; Perkins, 86.
It is never too late to mend, Reade, 30.
Ivanhoe, Scott, 32.

Jack Hinton, Lever, 25.
Jackson, E. P., 118.
Jackson, F. G., 124.
Jackson, *Mrs.* H. H. (F.), stories, 21; poems, 68, 122.
Jackson, J., 97.
Jacobi, A., 120.
Jacobi, Mary P., 116. *See also* Meyer, 123.
Jahn, O., 92.
James, *Mrs.* F. A. P., 21.
James, G. P. R., 21-22.
James, H., 22.
James, W., 112.
Jameson, J. F., 49.
Jamison, *Mrs.* C. V., 22.
Jamison, H., 116.
Jane Eyre, Brontë, 5.
Jan Vedder's wife, Barr, 3.
Janvier, T. A., 22.
Japan, Bacon, 55; Hall, 56; Hearn, 57; Tracy, 50; Morse, 82.
Jean Monteith, McClelland, 26.
Jefferson, J., autobiography, 43.
Jenkin, *Mrs.* H. C. (C.), 22.
Jenks, H. S. *See* Walker, G., *and* Jenks, H. S., 95.

Index.   155

Jerry, Elliott, 13.
Jess, Haggard, 16.
Jevons, W. S., 117-118.
Jewett, S. O., 22.
Jewitt, L., 63.
John, Oliphant, 28.
John-a-dreams, Sturgis, 35.
John Bodewin's testimony, Foote, 14.
John Brent, Winthrop, 39.
John Godfrey's fortunes, Taylor, 35.
John Gray, Allen, 2.
John Halifax, gentleman, Craik, 9.
John Inglesant, Shorthouse, 33.
John Jerome, Ingelow, 21.
John Maidment, Sturgis, 35.
John Needham's double, Hatton, 19.
John Paget, Elliott, 13.
John Ward, preacher, Deland, 10.
Johnson, H K., annotator, 135.
Johnson, A., 48, 116.
Johnson, S., works, 22, 43, 44; life of, Boswell, 41; Stephen, 76.
Johnson, S. W., 126
Johnson's cyclopædia, 136.
Johnston, A., 49.
Johnston, J. F. W., 101.
Johnston, R. M., tales, 23; life of A. H. Stephens, 44.
Jones, M. C., 122. *See also* Woman's book, 123.
Joseph and his friends, Taylor, 35.
Joshua Marvel, Farjeon, 13.
Journalism, Luce, 98, 125. *See also* Hubert, 123; Meyer, 123.
Journal of American Folk-Lore, 79.
Juan and Juanita, Baylor, 4.
Julian Home, Farrar, 13.
Julian, Ware, 38.
Jullien, A., 92.
June, Jennie (*pseud.*). *See* Croly, *Mrs.* J. C., 123.
Jungle book, Kipling, 24.
Junot, *Mme*. *See* Napoleon, 45.
Jupiter lights, Woolson, 40.
Jupiter's daughters, Jenkin, 22.

Kant. *See* Philosophical classics, 117.
Kay, D., 121.
Keary, A. M., 24.
Keary, C. F., 52, 54.
Keats, J., 68; life of, Colvin, 68; Rossetti, 68.
Keddie, H., 23.
Keltie, J. S. *See* Statesman's year-book, 137.
Kemble, F. A., 44.
Kemp, E., 127-128.
Kenelm Chillingly, Bulwer-Lytton, 6.
Kenilworth, Scott, 32.
Kennard, N. H., 44.
Kennelly, A. E., 99.
Kentucky cardinal, Allen, 2.
Kerrigan's quality, Barlow, 3.
Keyser, L. S., 109.
Kidd, B., 115.
Kidnapped, Stevenson, 34.
Kindergarten (department), 94-95. *See also* Jones, 122.
King, Charles, 23.
King, Grace, 23.
Kinglake, A., 44.
King of Schnorrers, Zangwill, 40.
King Solomon's mines, Haggard, 16.
King Tom, Pendleton, 29.
Kingsford, W., 60.
Kingsland, W. G., 62.
Kingsley, C., novels, 23; Roman and Teuton, 53.
Kingsley, H., 23.
King's own borderers, Grant, 16.
Kipling, R., tales, 23-24; poems, 68-69.
Kirby, W., 24.
Kirk, *Mrs.* E. W. O., 24.
Kirkland, J. 24.
Kirkwood, L. J., 124.
Kismet, Fletcher, 14.
Kit and Kitty, Blackmore, 5.
Kitchen and cooking-garden, 95.
Kitchen-garden, 95, 126-127; Hunting-ton, 95.
Kith and kin, Fothergill, 14.
Kitty's conquest, King, 23.
Knickerbocker's history of New York, Irving, 21.
Knight, C., 51.
Knight J., 72.
Knitters in the sun, French, 15.

Knitting, Croly, 124; Rosevear, 124-125; Butterick Pub., 125.
Knox, T. W., 57.
Koehler, S. R., 86.
Krehbiel, H. E., annotator, 91.
Kroeger, A. B., annotator, 133.

Labor. *See* Capital and labor, 113.
Labor arbitration, Lowell, 113.
Labor movement in America, Ely, 49.
Lace, Léfebure, 90, 124; Butterick Pub., 125.
Lacombe P., 53.
Ladd, G. T., 112.
Laddie, 27.
Ladies' gallery, McCarthy and Campbell-Praed, 25.
Lady Audley's secret, Maxwell, 26.
Lady Jane, Jamison, 22.
Lady of Fort St. John, Catherwood, 8.
Lady of the ice, De Mille, 10.
Lady of the lake, Scott, 74.
Lady or the tiger?, Stockton, 34.
La Farge, J., 85.
Laffan, M. *See* Hartley, *Mrs. M.*, 18.
La Grange, F., 119.
Laird of Norlaw, Oliphant, 28.
Lalla Rookh, Moore, 71.
Lamb, C., 24, 69, 75.
Lamb, M., tales, 24; life of, Gilchrist, 43.
Lampadius, W. A., 92.
Lamplighter, Cummins, 10.
Lamson, M. S., 44.
Lanciani, R. *See* Helbig, H., *and* Lanciani, R., 82; Ramsay, W., *and* Lanciani, R., 83.
Land and rent, 113.
Land and the book, Thomson, 58.
Land beyond the forest, Laszowska, 24.
Landor, W. S., 69; life of, Colvin, 69.
Landscape art, Hamerton, 85.
Landscape gardening, 127-128. *See also* Woman's book, 123.
Lanfrey, P. *See* Napoleon, 45.
Lang, A., tales, 24; folk-lore, 79.
Lange, H., 96.
Lange, K., 96.
Langhans, W., 92.
Language, 98; Whitney, 98; Müller, 98.
Lanier, S., 69.
La Plata, Hudson, 57.
Larcom, L., 44, 49; life of, Addison, 41.
Larned, J. N., 54, 137.
La Salle and the discovery of the great west, Parkman, 48.
Las Casas. *See* Napoleon, 45.
Last chronicles of Barset, Trollope, 37.
Last days of Pompeii, Bulwer-Lytton, 6.
Last meeting, Matthews, 26.
Last of her line, Stephenson, 34.
Last of the McAllisters, Barr, 3.
Last of the Mohicans, Cooper, 9.
Last sentence, Tuttiett, 37.
Laszowska, *Mrs.* E. D. G. v., 24.
Laundry work, 132.
Law, practice of. *See* Hubert, 123; Meyer, 123; advice on, *see* Stoddard, 127.
Lawn tennis, Dwight, 134.
Lawton girl, Frederic, 15.
Lay of the last minstrel, Scott, 74.
Lays of ancient Rome, Macaulay, 70.
Lean, *Mrs.* F. M., 24.
Leap in the dark, Southworth, 33.
Leather work, 90.
Leavenworth case, Rohlfs, 31.
Leckey, W. E. H., 51.
Le Conte, J., 103.
Led-horse claim, Foote, 14.
Lee, F., 44.
Lee, *General* R. E., life of, Lee, 44.
Lee, S. (*ed.*). *See* Dictionary of Eng. nat. biog., 41.
Léfebure, E., 90, 124.
Leffingwell, Albert (*pseud.*). *See* Tracy, A., 60.
Legend of Jubal, Eliot, 66.
Legends and lyrics, Hayne, 67; Procter, 72.
Legouvé, E., 121.
Leibnitz. *See* Philosophical classics, 117.
Leland, C. G., 123, 124.

Lemcke, G., 131.
Lemmon, L. *See* Hawthorne, J., *and* Lemmon, L., 60.
Lena Rivers, Holmes, 20.
Lenox Dare, Townsend, 36.
Leon Pontifex, Greene, 16.
Leslie Goldthwaite, Whitney, 39.
Less black than we're painted, Payn, 29.
Lesson of the master, James, 22.
Lester, A. S. E. *See* Name and fame, 32.
Letter-writing, Morton, 98.
Lever, C., 24.
Lewes, G. H., 98, 117.
Lewes, *Mrs.* G. H. *See* Eliot, G.
Lewis, A. J. *See* Hoffman, *Prof.* (*pseud.*), 133.
Lewis, T. H., 89.
Leypoldt, A. H., 119, 121, 123, 129.
Libraries, aid for small, Plummer, 141.
Library schools. *See* Hubert, 123.
Life and death of Jason, Morris, 71.
Life for a life, Craik, 9.
Light, Wright, 100.
Light of her countenance, Boyesen, 5.
Light that failed, Kipling, 24.
Lighthall, W. D., 60.
Lilac sunbonnet, Crockett, 10.
Lincoln, A., life of, Coffin, 42; Herndon *and* Weik, 43; Morse, 45; Nicolay *and* Hay, 45.
Lincoln, *Mrs.* D. A., 131.
Linn, W. A. *See* Sturgis, 129.
Linton, *Mrs.* E. L., 25.
Linton, W. J., 85.
Lion's cub, Stoddard, 76.
Lippincott's biographical dictionary, 44, 136.
Lippincott's gazetteer of the world, 57, 137.
Liquor question, 115.
List, ye landsmen!, Russell, 31.
Liszt, Nohl, 92.
Literary club for girls and women, hints on forming, 144.
Literary curiosities, handbook of, Walsh, 137.
Literature (department), 60-80.
Literature, American Stedman *and* Hutchinson, 60, 75, 135; Hawthorne, 60; Richardson, 61; Tyler, 61.
Literature and dogma, Arnold, 61.
Literature, English, Morley 51: Pancoast, 60; Brooke, 60; Oliphant, 60; Taine, 61; cyclopædia of, Chambers, 136; dictionary of, Adams, 136.
Literature, success in, Lewes, 98.
Little brothers of the air, Miller, 109.
Little Lord Fauntleroy, Burnett, 7.
Little men, Alcott, 2.
Little minister, Barrie, 4.
Little women, Alcott, 2.
Livelihoods for women, 123-125.
Livermore, M. A. *See* Meyer, 123.
Lives of girls who became famous, Bolton, 41.
Lloyd, H. D., 114.
Loan associations, Dexter, 113. *See also* Stoddard, 123; Sturgis, 129.
Locke. *See* Philosophical classics, 117.
Lockhart J. G., 44.
Lockwood, T. D., 125.
Locusts and wild honey, Burroughs, 108.
Lodge, H. C., 44.
Logic, 117-118.
Longfellow, H. W. 69; life of, Longfellow, S., 69; Robertson, 69.
Longfellow, S., 69.
Lonsdale, M., 44.
Looking backward, Bellamy, 4, 114.
Lounus, L. C., 57.
Lord Ormont and his Aminta, Meredith, 27.
Lorna Doone, Blackmore, 5.
Los Cerritos, Atherton, 2.
Lossing, B. J., 44. 49.
Lost heiress, Southworth, 33.
Lost Sir Massingberd, Payn, 29.
Lothair, Disraeli, 11.
Lotus-eating, Curtis, 65.
Loughead, P. H., 26.
Louie's last term at St. Mary's, Harris, 18.
Louis *of Poissy* 117.
Louisiana, Burnett, 7.

Louisiana, folk-tales of, Fortier, 79.
Lounsbury, T. R., 98.
Love and quiet life Raymond, 30.
Love is enough, Morris, 71.
Love me little, love me long, Reade, 30.
Lovel the widower, Thackeray, 36.
Lover, S., 25.
Low, S. J., 137.
Low and Pulling's dict. of Eng. hist., 52.
Lowell, J. R., 70.
Lowell, J. S., 113. *See also* Meyer, 123.
Loyalty George, Parr, 29.
Lubbock, Sir J., 109, 111.
Luce, R., 98, 125.
Lucia, Hugh and another, Needell, 27.
Luck of Roaring Camp, Harte, 18.
Luska, Sidney (*pseud.*). *See* Harland, H., 17.
Lyall, Edna (*pseud.*), 25.
Lytton. *See* Bulwer-Lytton, E. G. E. L., 6.

Mabel Vaughan, Cummins, 10.
Macaulay, T. B., history, 51; essays and poems, 70; life of, Trevelyan, 46, 70; Morison, 70.
McCarthy, J., novels, 25; histories, 51.
McClelland, M. G., 25
McCook, H. C., 109.
MacDonald, G., 26.
Macfarren, G. A., 92.
MacFlecknoe, Dryden, 65.
McGlasson, E. W., 132. *See also* Woman's book, 123.
Machar, A. M., 50.
Mackay, C., 60.
Mackay, M., 26.
Mackenzie, E. C. W., 135.
Mackenzie, R., 124.
Mackintosh, J., 51.
Maclaren, Ian (*pseud.*). *See* Watson, J. M., 38.
Maclehose, S., 75.
Macleod of Dare, Black, 5.
McMaster, J. B., 48.
Macmullen, J. M., 50.
McMurray, C. A., 47.
Macquoid, *Mrs.* K. S., 26.
McVays, Kirkland, 24.
MacVicar, M., 97.
Macy, J., 115.
Madam De Beaupré Jenkin. 22.
Madame Delphine, Cable, 7.
Madame Silva, McClelland, 26.
Mademoiselle, Peard, 20.
Mademoiselle de Mersac, Norris, 28.
Mademoiselle Miss, Harland, 17.
Madison, *Mrs.* D. P., 44.
Magazines, list of, 139-140.
Magic. *See* Conjuring, 134.
Magnetism and electricity, Poyser, 100; Thompson, 100.
Mahaffy, J. P., 53, 57, 121.
Maid Marian, Seawell, 32.
Maine woods, Thoreau, 110
Malet, Lucas (*pseud.*). *See* Harrison, *Mrs.* M., 18.
Mallock, W. H., 113.
Malthus and his work, Bonar, 114.
Mammon of unrighteousness, Boyesen, 5.
Man and wife, Collins, 8.
Man who was guilty, Loughead, 25.
Man without a country, Hale, 17.
Man wonderful in the house beautiful, Allen, 119.
Mann, E. E. *See* Calder, F. L., *and* Mann, E. E., 132.
Manners, Aikman, 126.
Mansfield, J. M., 96.
Mansfield Park, Austen, 3.
Manton, W. P., 109.
Manxman, Caine, 7.
Many inventions, Kipling, 24.
Marble faun, Hawthorne 10.
Marbot, *Baron de*. *See* Napoleon, 45.
Marcella, Ward, 38.
Marching to victory Coffin, 49.
March in the ranks, Fothergill, 14.
Marenholtz-Bulow, B. v., 94.
Margery Daw, Aldrich, 2.
Margery Daw's home confectionery, 130.
Marionettes, Cruger 10.
Marius, the Epicurean, Pater, 71.

Mark Rutherford's deliverance, White, 38.
Marmion, Scott, 74.
Marmont. *See* Napoleon, 45.
Marmorne, Hamerton, 17.
Marquand, A., 86.
Marquis of Carabas, Spofford, 33.
Marriage, Ferrier, 14.
Marriage, Strahan, 170. *See also* Terhune, 120; Ruskin, 121.
Marryat, F. *See* Lean, *Mrs.* F., 24.
Marse Chan, Page, 28.
Martin, *Mrs.* A., 57.
Martin Chuzzlewit, Dickens, 11.
Martineau, G., 124.
Marvel, Ik (*pseud.*). *See* Mitchell, D. G., 129.
Marx, A. B., 92.
Mary Barton Gaskell, 15.
Marzials, F. T., 77.
Marzio's crucifix, Crawford, 9.
Mason, O. T., 111.
Maspero, G., 82.
Massena. *See* Napoleon, 45.
Masson, D., 71.
Master, Zangwill, 40.
Master of Ballantrae, Stevenson, 34.
Master of the mine, Buchanan, 6.
Mathematics, 98-99; Hill, 99; Smith *and* Stringham, 99; Wentworth, 99.
Mathews, F. S., 106, 127.
Matrimony, Norris, 28.
Matter of millions, Rohlfs, 31.
Matthews, B, 26.
Maud, Tennyson, 76.
Maver, W., 125.
Maxwell, *Mrs.* M. E. B., 26.
May, T. E., 51.
Mead, T. H., 134.
Mechanics, Taylor, 100.
Medicine, practice of. *See* Hubert, 123; Meyer, 123; Goodholme, 130.
Meldola, R., 124.
Melito. *See* Napoleon, 45.
Melville, H., 26.
Memoirs of Sherlock Holmes, Doyle, 12.
Memorie and rime, Miller, 70.
Memory, Kay, 121.
Men and women of the time, 44.
Men of achievement series, 46.
Mendelssohn-Bartholdy, F., Lampadius, 92.
Meneval. *See* Napoleon, 45.
Mercy Philbrick's choice, Jackson, 21
Meredith, G., 27.
Merivale, H. T., 77.
Meriwether, L., 57.
Merle's crusade, Carey, 8.
Mermaid, Dougall, 11.
Merriam, F. A., 109.
Merry stories and games, Hubbard, 94.
Meservey, A. B., 99
Metal work, 90; Middleton, 90; Rudler, 90; Sturgis, 90.
Meta's faith, Stephenson, 34.
Meteorology, Russell, 104.
Metternich. *See* Napoleon, 45.
Metzerott, shoemaker, Woods, 40.
Mexico, Hale, 50; Prescott, 50; Appleton, 55.
Meyer, A. N., 123.
Meyer, B., 94.
Meyer, E. v., 101.
Meyer, L., 101.
Micah Clarke, Doyle, 12.
Michaud, J. F., 52.
Microbes, Trouessart, 107. *See also* Bacteria.
Microscopy, Stokes, 110.
Middle Ages, Emerton, 52.
Middlemarch, Eliot, 13.
Middleton, J. H., 82, 86, 89, 90; *and* Morris, 86, 89.
Midge, Bunner, 6.
Miles, H. H., 50.
Mill, H. R., 102.
Mill, J. S., 118; philosophy of, Watson, 117.
Mill mystery, Rohlfs, 31.
Mill on the Floss, Eliot, 13.
Millbank, Holmes, 20.
Miller, C. H., 70.
Miller, E., 106.
Miller, H., 44.
Miller, H. M. *See* Miller, O. T.
Miller, O T., annotator, 108, 109, 122, 145.

Millet, F. D., 58.
Millinery. *See* Hubert, 123.
Millis, J., 90.
Mills of Tuxbury, Townsend, 36.
Milton, J., works, 70-71; life of, Johnson, 43-44; Masson, 71; Pattison, 71.
Mine own people, Kipling, 24.
Mingo and other sketches, Harris, 18.
Minister's wooing, Stowe, 34.
Miot's memoirs. *See* Napoleon, 45.
Mirage, Fletcher, 14.
Miriam, Terhune, 35.
Mischief of Monica, Walford, 37.
Miss Angel, Ritchie, 31.
Miss Carew, Edwards, 12.
Miss Churchill, Tiernan, 36.
Miss Marjoribanks, Oliphant, 28.
Miss Stewart's legacy, Steel, 33.
Miss Toosey's mission, 27
Missing bride, Southworth, 33.
Mr Absalom Billingslea and others, Johnston, 23.
Mr. Isaacs, Crawford, 9.
Mr. Smith, Walford, 37.
Mistress and maid, Craik, 9.
Mrs. Falchion, Parker, 29.
Mrs. Gainsborough's diamonds, Hawthorne, 19.
Mrs. Geoffrey, Hungerford, 21.
Mrs. Harold Stagg, Grant, 16.
Mrs Keats Bradford, Pool, 29.
Mrs. Leicester's school, Lamb, C. *and* M., 24.
Mrs. Lorimer, Harrison, 18.
Mrs. Peixada, Harland, 17.
Mrs Skagg's husbands, Harte, 18.
Mitchell, D. G. *See* Sturgis, 129.
Mitchell, S. W., 120.
Mitford, M, R, 27.
Modelling, Leland, 123.
Modern Aladdin, Pyle, 30.
Modern buccaneer, Browne, 6.
Modern Frenchmen, Hamerton, 85.
Modern guides of English thought, Hutton, 67.
Modern instance, Howells, 20.
Modern painters, Ruskin, 73, 83.
Molesworth, W. N., 51.
Molly Bawn, Hungerford, 21.
Money, 114.
Monsieur Motte, King, 23.
Montagu, *Lady* M. W., letters of, 44-45.
Montcalm and Wolfe, Parkman, 48.
Montgomery, 52, 53.
Montholon. *See* Napoleon, 45.
Moody, F. W., 82.
Moonlight bay, Howe, 20.
Moonstone, Collins, 8.
Moore, G., 86.
Moore, T., 71.
Mopsa, the fairy, Ingelow, 21.
More short sixes, Bunner, 7.
Morgan, C. L., 109, 112.
Morison, J. C., 70.
Morley, H., 51.
Morley, J., 71.
Morris, W., poems, 71; art, 90; *and* Middleton, 86, 89.
Morse, E. S., 82, 110.
Morse, J. T. *Jr.*, 45.
Morton, A. H., 98.
Morton, H., 90.
Mosaic, 90; Middleton, 90; Leland, 123.
Mosses from an old manse, Hawthorne, 19.
Mother play and nursery songs, Froebel, 94.
Mother's recompense, Aguilar, 1.
Motley, J. L., 53-54.
Mozart, Jahn, 92; Nohl, 92.
Muir, M. M. P., 101.
Müller, F., 98.
Müller, H., 106.
Mulock, D. M. *See* Craik, *Mrs.* D. M. M., 9.
Municipal government, 116.
Muntz, E., 90.
Mural painting, Morris *and* Middleton, 86, 89. *See also* Art, Fresco.
Murfree, M. N., 27.
Murray, A. S., 82.
Murray, D. C., 27.
Murray, J. C., annotator, 117.
Murray's handbooks, 18.
Music (department), 91-94.

My enemy's daughter, McCarthy, 25.
My guardian, Cambridge, 8.
My Lady Rotha, Weyman, 38.
My novel, Bulwer-Lytton, 6.
My schools and school-masters, Miller, 14.
My wife and I, Stowe, 34.
Myers, F. W. H., 77.
Myers, P. V. N., 52; *and* Allen, W. F., 52.
Mysteries of Udolpho, Radcliffe, 30.
Mystery of the locks, Howe, 90.
Mystery of the *Ocean Star*, Russell, 31.
Mythology, Cox, 78; Grimm, 79.
Mythology and folk-lore (department), 78-80.
Myths, Baring-Gould, 78; Brinton, 78; Gayley, 78; Lang, 79.

Name and fame, Sergeant *and* Lester, 32.
Nameless nobleman, Austin, 3.
Nansen, F., 58.
Napoleon, lives and memoirs of, 45.
National American Woman Suffrage Association, 116.
National Civil Service Reform League, 116.
National Science Club for Women, 111.
Nations around Israel, Keary, 24.
Native of Winby, Jewett, 22.
Natural history and human evolution (department), 108-112.
Natural science, Buckley, 101.
Naturalist on the river Amazons, Bates, 55, 108; in La Plata, Hudson, 57.
Nature, Emerson, 66.
Nature and human nature, Haliburton, 17.
Nature and man in America, Shaler, 103.
Naulahka, Balestier *and* Kipling, 4, 24.
Nearest and dearest, Southworth, 33.
Needell, *Mrs.* J. H., 27.
Needlework, 124-125.
Neighborly poems, Riley, 73.
Nelly's silver mine, Jackson, 21.
New Arabian nights, Stevenson, 34.
New day, Gilder, 66.
New England girlhood, Larcom, 44.
New England, making of, Drake, 49.
New England nun, Wilkins, 39.
New man at Rossmere, Walworth, 37.
New woman, Linton, 25.
New York family, Fawcett, 14.
Newcomb, S., *and* Holden, E. S., 99.
Newcomer, A. G., 98.
Newcomes, Thackeray, 36.
Newell, J. H., 106.
Newell, W. W., 133.
Newsholme, A., 120.
Next door, Burnham, 7.
Nichol, J., 63.
Nicholas Nickleby, Dickens, 11.
Nicholls, *Mrs.* *See* Brontë, C.
Nicholson, H. A., 110.
Nicolay, J. G., 45.
Niecks, F., 92.
Nights with Uncle Remus, Harris, 18.
Nile notes, Curtis, 65.
Nitsch, H., 130-131.
No gentlemen, Burnham, 7.
No name, Collins, 8.
No new thing, Norris, 28.
Nobody's fortunes, Yates, 40.
Nohl, L., 92.
Nordenskiold, A. E., 58.
Norman conquest, Freeman, 51.
Norris, W. E., 28.
North and South, Gaskell, 15.
Northanger abbey, Austen, 3.
Northern tour, Parkman, 58.
Norway, Boyesen, 54; Keary, 54.
Not all in vain, Cambridge, 8.
Not like other girls, Carey, 8.
Not wisely but too well, Broughton, 6.
Novels, Griswold, 54.
Novum organum, Bacon, 62.
Nursing, 120. *See also* Hubert, 123.

Oblivion, McClelland, 26.
O'Connor, E. M., 137.
Odd women, Gissing, 15.

Odyssey. *See* Bryant, 62; Morris, 71.
Off the Skelligs, Ingelow, 21.
Ohio Valley states, making of, Drake, 49.
Old creole days, Cable, 7.
Old fashioned girl, Alcott, 2.
Old fashioned roses, Riley, 73.
Old Kensington, Ritchie, 31.
Old Mark Langston, Johnston, 23.
Old masters of Belgium and Holland, Fromentin, 85.
Old Mortality, Scott, 32.
Old Myddleton's money, Hay, 19.
Old Northwest, Hinsdale, 48.
Old régime in Canada, Parkman, 48.
Old Town folks, Stowe, 34.
Oldbury, Keary, 24.
Oliphant, L., novels, 28; travel, 58.
Oliphant, *Mrs.* M. O. W., novels, 28; literature, 60.
Oman, C. W. C., 53.
O'Meara. *See* Napoleon, 45.
Omoo, Melville, 27.
On both sides, Baylor, 4.
On Newfound River, Page, 25.
One good guest, Walford, 37.
One hundred days in Europe, Holmes, 67.
One summer, Howard, 20.
One too many, Linton, 25.
Open door, Howard, 20.
Opening of a chestnut burr, Roe, 31.
Operas, Upton, 93.
Oratorios, Upton, 93.
Orchard and kitchen-garden, 126-127.
Orchids, Darwin, 105.
Ordeal of Richard Feverel, Meredith, 27.
Oregon trail, Parkman, 48.
Orford, H. W. *See* Walpole, H., 37.
Origin of species, Darwin, 109.
Original belle, Roe, 31.
Orioles' daughter, Fothergill, 14.
Orley farm, Trollope, 37.
Orr, *Mrs.* S., 62.
Osborne, C. F., 129.
Ostrich farm, life on an, Martin, 57.
Otté, E. C., 54.
Otto the knight, French, 15.
Ought we to visit her?, Edwardes, 12.
Ouida. *See* De la Ramé, 10.
Our home pets, Miller, 109.
Our mutual friend, Dickens, 11.
Our old home, Hawthorne, 57.
Our village, Mitford, 27.
Out at Twinnett's, Habberton, 16.
Out of step, Pool, 29.
Owen, Catherine (*pseud.*). *See* Nitsch, H., 130-131.

Pacific coast, Finck, 56.
Packard, A. S., *jr.*, 110.
Packard S. S., 99.
Pactolus Prime, Tourgee, 36.
Page, A. L., 94.
Page, T. N., 28.
Painter, F. V. N., 97.
Painters, Vasari, 83; Bryan, 84; Erskine *and* Hutton, 84; Huxton, 86; Koehler, 86; Redgrave, 87; Champlin, 136.
Painting, 84-88; Chesneau, 84; Coffin, 85; Hamerton, 85; Havard, 85; Heaton, 95; Middleton, 86; Moore, 86; Morris *and* Middleton, 86; Poynter *and* Head, 86; Smith, 86. Buxton *and* Poynter, 86; Redgrave, 86; Radcliffe, 86; Reid, 87; Stranahan, 87; Van Dyke, 87; Wauters, 88; Norris *and* Middleton, 89; Champlin, 136; on porcelain, Leland, 123; on silk, satin, or plush, 124. *See also* Harrison, 129.
Pair of blue eyes, Hardy, 17.
Palestine, Oliphant, 58; Thomson, 58.
Palgrave, F. T., 83.
Pamela, Richardson, 30.
Pancoast, H. S., 60.
Papworth, W., 89.
Paraguay, Child, 56.
Paris, P., 86.
Paris exposition, 1889, art at, Coffin, 81.
Paris sketch-book, Thackeray, 77.
Parker, G., 28.
Parkin, G. R., 58.
Parkman, F., histories, 48; travel, 58; woman suffrage, 116.

Parliamentary practice, 116; Shattuck, 122.
Parliament of foules, Chaucer, 64.
Parloa, M., 131.
Parr, *Mrs.* L. T., 29.
Parry, C. H. H., 92.
Parsons, S., 128. *See also* Woman's book, 123. *See* Sturgis, 129.
Pasquier, *Chancellor*. *See* Napoleon, 45.
Passe Rose, Hardy, 17.
Passing the love of women, Needell, 27.
Past and present, Carlyle, 63.
Patagonia, Hudson, 57.
Pater, W. H., 71.
Pathfinder, Cooper, 9.
Patricia, Linton, 25.
Pattison, M., 71.
Patty, Macquoid, 26.
Paul Clifford, Bulwer-Lytton, 6.
Paul Massie, McCarthy, 25.
Paul Patoff, Crawford, 9.
Payn, J., 29.
Payne, J., 97.
Peabody, E. P., 94.
Peabody, *Mrs.* H., 94.
Peard, F. M., 29.
Pearls for young ladies, Ruskin, 121.
Peary, *Mrs.* J. D., 58.
Pedagogical seminary, 96.
Pedagogy, Compayré, 96. *See also* Teaching, 96.
Peg Woffington, Reade, 30.
Pelham, Bulwer-Lytton, 6.
Pembroke, Wilkins, 39.
Pendennis, Thackeray, 36.
Penelope's suitors, Byuner, 7.
Pen portraits of literary women, Cone *and* Gilder, 42.
Penhallow, D. P., annotator, 105, 106.
Penmanship, Jackson, 97; Witherbee, 97.
Pendleton, L., 29.
Pepacton, Burroughs, 108.
Perfect fool, James, 21.
Pericles and Aspasia, Landor, 69.
Periodicals, list of, 139-140.
Perkins, C. C., 86.
Perlycross, Blackmore, 5.
Perpetual curate, Oliphant, 28.
Perry, N., 29.
Persia, Benjamin, 55.
Persuasion, Austen, 3.
Peru, Prescott, 50; Markham, 50; Child, 56.
Peter Ibbetson, Du Maurier, 12.
Petric, W. M. F., 83.
Phantom rickshaw, Kipling, 24.
Phelps, E. S. *See* Ward, *Mrs.* E. S. P., 37.
Philanthropy. *See* Charities.
Philip and his wife, Deland, 10.
Philology. *See* Language.
Philosophical classics, 117.
Philosophy (department), 117-118.
Phœbe, junior, Oliphant, 28.
Phonography. *See* Shorthand, 97.
Photography. *See* Hubert, 123, and also 124.
Phyllis, Hungerford, 21.
Phyllis of the Sierras Harte, 18.
Pianoforte. *See* Music.
Piccadilly, Oliphant, 28.
Pickard, S. T., 77.
Pickwick papers, Dickens, 11.
Pictures from Italy, Dickens, 11.
Pictures, how to judge, Van Dyke, 87.
Pierre and his people, Parker, 28.
Physical culture (department), 119.
Physics, Shaw, 100. *See also* Electricity.
Physiography, Mill, 102. *See also* Geography.
Pilgrim's progress, Bunyan, 7.
Pilot, Cooper, 9.
Pioneers, Cooper, 9.
Pioneers of France in the New World, Parkman, 48.
Pitman, I., 97.
Plain tales from the hills, Kipling, 24.
Plants. *See* Botany, 105-108.
Plants, folk-lore of, Dyer, 78.
Plarr, V. G. (*ed.*), 44.
Plastic art. *See* Sculpture.
Plato and Platonism, Pater, 71.
Play actress, Crockett, 10.

Plumbing, Plunkett, 120; Tracy, 120.
  See also Suburban and country homes 129.
Plummer, M. W., 141.
Plunkett, *Mrs.* H. M., 120.
Plutarch's lives, 45.
Poe, E. A., tales, 29; works, 71-72; life of, Woodberry, 46, 72.
Poems here at home, Riley, 73.
Poems of the day, Morris, 71.
Poetry. *See* Literature (department), 60-80.
Poetry, nature and elements of, Stedman, 75; Watts, 84.
Poets, Johnson, 43; Stedman, 75.
Political economy, 113.
Political science. *See* Economic, social and political science, 113-117.
Pollard, J., 133.
Polly Oliver's problem, Wiggin, 39.
Pool, *Mrs.* M. L., 29.
Poole, J., 125.
Poor humanity, Robinson, 31.
Pope, A., works, 72; life of Johnson, 43-44; Stephen, 72, 76.
Pope, F. L., 99.
Poppæa, Cruger, 10.
Porcelain, 90; Sturgis, 90.
Porter, J., 29.
Porter, L. H., 134.
Portrait of a lady, James, 22.
Posse, N., 119.
Potiphar papers, Curtis, 65.
Pot of gold, Wilkins, 39.
Potter's thumb, Steel, 33.
Pottery, Sturgis, 90.
Poulsson, E., 94.
Poultry, 127.
Power through repose, Call, 119.
Poynter, E. J., 86; *and* Buxton, H. J. W., 86; *and* Smith, T. R., 89.
Poyser, A. W., 100.
Praed, *Mrs.* R. M., 29.
Prairie folks, Garland, 15.
Prelate, Henderson, 20.
Prescott, W., 50.
Preserving, Rorer, 131.
Press, writing for the, Luce, 98.
Preston, H. W., 53.
Preyer, W., 112.
Price, B. *See* Sturgis, 129.
Pride and prejudice, Austen, 3.
Primes and their neighbors, Johnston, 23.
Prince and the pauper, Clemens, 8.
Prince Deukalion Taylor, 76.
Prince of India, Wallace, 37.
Princess, McClelland, 26.
Princess (The), Tennyson, 76.
Princess Aline, Davis, 10.
Princess Casamassima, James, 22.
Princess of Thule, Black 5.
Prisoner of Zenda, Hawkins, 19.
Procter, A. A., 72.
Profit sharing, Gilman, 113. *See also* Capital and labor.
Progress and poverty, George, 113.
Prohibition. *See* Liquor question, 115.
Property, care of, Stoddard, 123; Walker, 123.
Prophet of the Great Smoky Mountains, Murfree, 27.
Protection, 114.
Protestant Reformation, Seebohm, 52; Hauser, 52.
Prudden, T. M., 120.
Prudence Palfrey, Aldrich, 2.
Prue and I, Curtis, 10.
Pseudonyms, Cushing, 137.
Psychology (department), 112-113.
Publishers, list of, 146.
Pulling, F. S. *See* Low, S. J., *and* Pulling, F. S., 137.
Puritan in Holland, England, and America, Campbell, 48.
Puritan pagan, Cruger, 10.
Putnam, *Mrs.* H. H., 94.
Put yourself in his place, Reade, 30.
Puzzles, Howard, 133.
Pyle, H., 29-30.

"Q" (*pseud.*). *See* Couch, A. T. Q., 9.
Quaker idyls, Gardner, 15.
Queechy, Warner, 38.
Queen money, Kirk, 24.
Queen of Bohemia, Hatton, 18.
Queen of Sheba, Aldrich, 2.
Queen of the air, Ruskin 73.
Queens of England, Strickland, 51.

Quentin Durward, Scott, 32.
Questions of the day, Smith, 75.
Questions of the day series, 116.
Quick, R. H., 97.
Quinton, A. B. *See* Meyer, 123.
Quits, Tautphœus, 35.
Quotations, dictionaries of, 137.

Radcliffe, A. G., 86.
Radcliffe, *Mrs.* A. W., 30.
Rae, J., 115.
Raiders, Crockett, 10.
Railroads, 114.
Ralph, J., 58.
Ralph Ryder of Brent, James, 21.
Ralph the heir, Trollope, 37.
Ralph Wilton's weird, Hector, 19.
Ramage's quotations, 137.
Rambler's lease, Torrey, 110.
Ramona, Jackson, 21.
Ramsay, W., 83.
Rasselas, Johnson, 72-73.
Ravenshoe, Kingsley, 23.
Rawson W. W., 126.
Raymond, W., 30.
Read, T. B., 72.
Reade, C., 30.
Reader's guide, Bowker *and* Iles, 113.
Reader's handbook, Brewer, 137.
Reading, art of, Legouvé, 121. *See also* Woman's book, 123.
Ready money Mortiboy, Besant *and* Rice, 4.
Realm of nature, Mill, 102.
Rebel queen, Besant, 4.
Reher, v., 89.
Recollections of Geoffrey Hamlyn, Kingsley, 23.
Records of a girlhood, Kemble, 44.
Records of later life, Kemble, 44.
Rector, Oliphant, 28.
Red as a rose is she, Broughton, 6.
Red Cross Association. *See* Meyer, 123.
Red fairy book, Lang, 24.
Red Rover, Cooper, 9.
Redeeming the republic, Coffin, 49.
Redford, G., 87.
Redgrave, G. R., 86.
Redgrave, R. *and* S., 87.
Reflections of a married man, Grant, 16.
Reform Club, N. Y., 114.
Reformation, Protestant. Seebohm, 52; Hauser, 52.
Refugees, Doyle, 12.
Regnault, H., Hamerton, 85.
Reid, Christian (*pseud.*). *See* Tiernan, *Mrs.* F. E., 36.
Reid, G., 87.
Reissman, A., 92.
Remember the Alamo, Barr, 3.
Remsen, I., 101.
Rémusat. *See* Napoleon, 45.
Renaissance, Symonds, 54; Pater, 71; Goodyear, 82; Scott, 87.
Renwick, I. P. A. *See* Statesman's year-book, 137.
Repoussé, work. Leland, 123.
Representative men, Emerson, 42, 66.
Reproach of Annesley, Tuttiett, 37.
Return of the native, Hardy, 17.
Reverberator, James, 22.
Revolution in Tanner's Lane, White, 38.
Reynolds, E. S., 120.
Rhetoric, Genung, 98; Hill, 98.
Rhine, A. H. *See* Meyer, 123.
Rhoda Fleming, Meredith, 27.
Ribot, T., 112.
Rice, J. *See* Besant, W., 4.
Richards, A. G., 131.
Richards, *Mrs.* E. H., 101.
Richardson, *Sir* B. W., 134.
Richardson, C. F., 61.
Richardson, S., 30.
Richelieu, James, 22.
Riding. *See* Horsemanship, 134.
Rienzi, Bulwer-Lytton, 6.
Right honourable (The), McCarthy *and* Campbell-Praed, 25.
Riley, J. W., 72.
Rise of Silas Lapham, Howells, 20.
Ritchie, *Mrs.* A. I., 30-31. *See also* Thackeray, A., 46.
Riverby, Burroughs, 108.
Rives, A. *See* Chanler, *Mrs.* A. R., 8.
Rob Roy, Scott, 32.
Robbery under arms, Browne, 6.

Robert Elsmere, Ward, 38.
Robert Falconer, MacDonald, 26.
Robertson, E. S., 69.
Robin, Parr, 29.
Robinson, F. W., 31.
Robinson, W., 127.
Robinson Crusoe, Defoe, 10.
Roche, R. M., 31.
Rockstro, W. S., 93.
Rodman the keeper, Woolson, 40.
Roe, E. P., 31, 127.
Rogers, J. E. *See* Mahaffy, J. P., *and* Rogers, J. E., 57.
Roget, P. M., 138.
Rohlfs, A. K. G., 31.
Roland, *Mme.*, life of, Blind, 41.
Roland Yorke, Wood, 40.
Roman and Teuton, Kingsley, 53.
Romance of a transport, Russell, 31.
Romance of Dollard, Catherwood, 8.
Romance of the forest, Radcliff, 30.
Romance of two worlds, Mackay, 26.
Romance of war, Grant, 16.
Romanes, G. J., 98, 110.
Roman singer, Crawford, 9.
Rome, Myers *and* Allen, 52; Fowler, 52; Gibbon, 52-53; Preston *and* Dodge, 53; Middleton, 82, 89; Redford, 87.
Romola, Eliot, 13.
Roosevelt, J. W. *See* Woman's book, 123.
Roosevelt, T., 48.
Root, A. I. *See* Terry, T. B., *and* Root, A. I., 127.
Root, J. W. *See* Sturgis, 129.
Root, L. C., 114.
Ropes, A. H. (*ed.*). *See* Montagu, Lady M. W., 44-45.
Ropes, J. C. *See* Napoleon, 45.
Rorer, *Mrs.* S. T., 131.
Rory O'More, Lover, 25.
Rose and the ring, Thackeray, 77.
Rose of paradise, Pyle, 30.
Rosebud garden of girls, Perry, 29.
Rosengarten, A., 83.
Rosevear, E., 124-125.
Rossetti, C. G., 73.
Rossetti, D. G., 73; life of, Knight, 73.
Rossetti, W. M., biography, 68; art, 83.
Rothery, G. C., 132.
Roundabout papers, Thackeray, 77.
Round Robin Reading Club, 145.
Roweny in Boston, Pool, 29.
Rudder Grange, Stockton, 34.
Rude, F., life of, Hamerton, 85.
Rudler, F. W., 90.
Ruskin, J., works, 73, 83, 89, 121; work of, Waldstein, 74.
Russell, H. L., 127.
Russell, T., 104.
Russell, W. C., 31.
Russia, Brandes, 55; Hapgood, 56; Hare, 57; Wallace, 59.
Rutherford, Mark. *See* White, W. H., 38.
Rutledge, Harris, 18.
Ruutz-Rees, J. E., 133.

Sachet. *See* Napoleon, 45.
Sachs, J. v., 107.
St. Elmo, Wilson, 30.
St. Katherine's by the tower, Besant, 4.
St. Philip's, Harris, 18.
St. Winifred, Farrar, 13.
Saintsbury, G., 68.
Salem chapel, Oliphant, 28.
Salmon, D., 97.
Sam Lawson's fireside stories, Stowe, 34.
San Salvador, Tincker, 36.
Sanford, E. C., 112.
Sanitation, 119-120.
Sant' Ilario, Crawford, 9.
Sappho of Green Springs, Harte, 18.
Saracinesca, Crawford 9.
Sartoris, *Mrs.* A. K., 31.
Satchel guide for the vacation tourist, 58.
Satires, Dryden, 65.
Satires and epistles, Pope, 172.
Saxe Holm's stories, Jackson, 21.
Sayce, A. H., 83.
Scandinavia, Otté, 54; Boyesen, 54; Keary, 54.
Seapegoat. Caine, 7.
Scarlet letter, Hawthorne, 19.

Scarlet poppy, Spofford, 33.
Scenes of clerical life, Eliot, 13.
Schiller, F. v., life of, Carlyle, 63.
Schouler, J., 48.
Schreiber, T., 135.
Schreiner, O., 31.
Schuman, Reissman, 92.
Schurman, J. G., 118.
Schurz, C., 45.
Scidmore, *Miss* E. R., 58.
Science of thought, Müller, 98.
Score of famous composers, Dole, 42.
Scotland, Mackintosh, 51; Burton, 51; Winter, 59.
Scott, F. M., 1, 6.
Scott, L., 87.
Scott, M., 32.
Scott, M. E. *See* Newsholme, A., *and* Scott, M. E., 120.
Scott, *Sir* W., novels, 32; life of, Lockhart, 44; Hutton, 74; letters, 45; journal, 45; poems, 74.
Scottish chiefs, Porter, 29.
Scouring, 132.
Scripture, E. W., annotator, 112.
Scudder, H. E., 45
Sculptors, Vasari, 83.
Sculpture, 84–86; Goodyear, 82; Marquand *and* Frothingham, 86; Middleton, 86; Paris, 86; Perkins, 86; Radcliffe, 86; Redford, 87; Scott, 87; Upcott, 87; Waldstein, 87.
Sea change, Shaw, 33.
Seaside studies in natural history. Agassiz, 108.
Seawell, M. E., 32.
Secession, war of, Johnson, 48.
Second cousin Sarah, Robinson, 31.
Sedgwick, H., 118.
Seebohm, F., 52.
Seeley, J. R., art, 83. *See also* Napoleon, 45.
Seelye, E. E., 52.
Seelye, J. H., 118.
Ségur. *See* Napoleon, 45.
Self-culture (department), 121–122.
Sempers, F. W., 127.
Sense and sensibility, Austen, 3.
Sergeant, A., 32.
Serviss, G. P., 99.
Sesame and lilies, Ruskin, 73.
Seth's brother's wife, Frederic, 15.
Seven lamps of architecture, Ruskin, 73, 83.
Sevigné, *Mme.* de, life of, Thackeray, 46.
Sewall, M. W. *See* Meyer, 123.
Sewing. *See* Needlework, 124–125.
Sex in education, Clarke, 119.
Seyffert, O., 135.
Shadow of a crime, Caine, 7.
Shadow of the sword, Buchanan, 6.
Sharp, J. C., 63.
Shakespeare, W., 74–75; works on, Dowden, 74; Abbott, 74; Craik, 74; Gervinus, 74; Corson, 74; Bartlett, 74; Clarke, 74, 75; Adams, 74; Brandram, 75; Faucit, 75; Lamb, 75; concordances to, 137; index to, O'Connor, 137.
Shakespeare's England, Winter, 59.
Shaler, N. S., 103.
Sharp eyes, Gibson, 109.
Shattuck, H. R., 122.
Shaw, A., 116.
Shaw, E. R., annotator, 96, 98, 100.
Shaw, F. L., 33.
She, Haggard, 16.
Shelley, *Mrs.* M. G., 33.
Shelley, P. B., 75.
Sherburne house, Douglas, 12.
Sheridan, R. B., life of, Moore, 71.
Sherwood, *Mrs.* M. E. W., 122, 133.
She's all the world to me, Caine, 7.
Ships that pass in the night, Harraden, 17.
Shirrell, E., 95.
Shirley, Brontë, 5.
Shorthand, Pitman, 97. *See also* Stenography, Hubert, 123.
Shorthouse, J. H., 33.
Short sixes, Bunner, 7.
Siddons, *Mrs.*, life of, Kennard, 44.
Sidney, Deland, 10.
Signor Monaldini's niece, Tincker, 39.
Signs and seasons, Burroughs, 108.
Silas Marner, Eliot, 13.
Silence of Dean Maitland, Tuttiett, 37.

Silent partner, Ward, 38.
Silent witness, Yates, 40.
Sime, J., 53.
Simple adventures of a mem-sahib, Cotes, 9.
Sinner's comedy, Craigie, 9.
Sir Charles Grandison, Richardson, 30.
Sir Percival, Shorthouse, 33.
Sir Roger de Coverley, Addison, 61.
Sister's tragedy, Aldrich, 61.
Sketch-book, Irving, 21.
Skirmishing, Jenkin, 22.
Sladen, D. B. W., 60.
Slater, J. *See* Smith, T. R., *and* Slater, J., 89.
Slaves of the ring, Robinson, 31.
Slick, Sam (*pseud.*). *See* Haliburton, T. C., 17.
Sloane, W. M., 49.
Small house at Allington, Trollope, 37.
Smiley, *Mrs.*, A. E., 133.
Smith, A. T., 58
Smith, C. J., 138.
Smith, C., *and* Stringham, T., 99.
Smith, F. H., 33.
Smith, Goldwin, biography, 45, 64; history, 47, 50, 116; travel, 85; essays, 75.
Smith, G. W., 86.
Smith, J., 107.
Smith, R. M., 115.
Smith, T. R., 89.
Social customs. *See* Etiquette.
Social departure, Cotes, 56.
Social England, Traill, 51.
Social evolution, Kidd, 115.
Social questions, 114–115.
Social science. *See* Economic, social and political science, 113–117.
Social science series, 116.
Socialism, 114–115.
Society to Encourage Studies at Home, 145.
Soldiers three, Kipling, 24.
Somebody's neighbors, Cooke, 8.
Some eminent women, Fawcett, 43.
Some emotions and a moral, Craigie, 9.
Somerville, M. F. G., 45.
Songs and games for little ones, Walker *and* Jenks, 95.
Songs before sunrise, Swinburne, 76.
Songs of summer lands, Miller, 70.
Songs of the Sierras, Miller, 70.
Songs of the springtides, Swinburne, 76.
Sons of Ham, Pendleton, 29.
Soul of Lilith, Mackay, 26.
Sound, Wright, 100.
Sound Currency, 114.
South America, Vincent, 59.
Southworth, *Mrs.* E. D. E. N., 33.
Sowing the wind, Linton, 25.
Spain, Amicis, 55; Borrow, 55.
Spanish America (department), 50.
Spanish-American republics, Child, 56.
Spanish gypsy, Eliot, 66.
Spaulding, V. M., 107.
Spectator, Addison, 61.
Spencer, H., 97, 115, 117, 118; teachings of, Collins, 117; Watson, 117.
Spenser, E., 75; tales from, Maclehose, 75; Towry, 75; life of, Church, 75.
Sphinx's children, Cooke, 8.
Spinoza. *See* Philosophical classics, 117.
Spitta, P., 93.
Splendid spur, Couch, 9.
Spofford, *Mrs.* H. E. P., 33.
Sports, 133–134.
Springhaven, Blackmore, 5.
Springsteed, A. F., 131.
Spy, Cooper, 9.
Squatter's dream, Browne, 6.
Squire's legacy, Hay, 19.
Staël, *Mme.* de, Duffy, 42.
Stainer, *Sir* J., 93.
Standard dictionary, 136.
Standish of Standish, Austin, 3.
Stanley, H. M., 58.
Stanley, M., 122.
Stannard, *Mrs.* H. E. V. P., 33.
Stanton, E. C., *and others*, 116.
Starr, L., 120.
Starr, M. A., 99.
Statesman's year-book, Keltie *and* Renwick, 137.

Steadfast, Cooke, 8.
Stebbins, E., 45–46.
Stedman, E. C., 60, 75, 135.
Steel, *Mrs.* F. A., 33.
Steele, F. M., 112.
Stencilling, Leland, 123.
Stenography, Hubert, 123. *See also* Shorthand, 97.
Stephen, L., 72, 76.
Stephen Ellicott's daughter, Needell, 27.
Stephens, A. H., life of, Johnston *and* Browne, 44.
Stephenson, E. T., 13.
Sterling, J., life of, Carlyle, 64.
Stern necessity, Robinson, 31.
Stevenson, R. L. B., 34.
Stickit minister, Crockett, 10.
Stillwater tragedy, Aldrich, 2.
Stockton, F. R., 34.
Stoddard, R. H., 76.
Stoddard, W. O., 123.
Stokes, A. C., 110.
Stones of Venice, Ruskin, 73, 83, 89.
Stories in song, Emerson *and* Brown, 94.
Stories of New France, Machar, 50.
Story, W. W., 87.
Story of Avis, Ward, 38.
Story of a bad boy, Aldrich, 2.
Story of a child, Deland, 10.
Story of a country town, Howe, 20.
Story of an African farm, Schreiner, 31.
Story of an enthusiast, Jamison, 22.
Story of a New York house, Bunner, 6.
Story of a young designer, Viollet-le-Duc, 87
Story of Babette, Stuart, 34.
Story of Dan, Francis, 14.
Story of Elizabeth, Ritchie, 31.
Story of Kennett, Taylor, 35.
Story of liberty, Coffin, 40.
Story of Margaret Kent, Kirk, 24.
Story of our continent, Shaler, 103.
Story of Patsy, Wiggin, 39.
Story of the nations series, 54.
Story of the states series, 49.
Story of Tonty, Catherwood, 8.
Stowe, C. E., 46.
Stowe, H. E. B., novels, 34; life of, 46.
Strahan, S. A. R., 120.
Stranahan, *Mrs.* C. H., 87.
Strange adventures of a phaeton, Black, 5.
Strange case of Dr. Jekyll and Mr. Hyde, Stevenson, 34.
Strange disappearance, Rohlfs, 31.
Strange story, Bulwer-Lytton, 6.
Strange true stories of Louisiana, Cable, 7.
Street, G. E. *See* Lewis, T. H., *and* Street, G. E., 89.
Strickland, A., 51.
Stringham, I. *See* Smith, C., *and* Stringham, I., 99.
Stuart Glennie, J. S. *See* Garnett, L., *and* Stuart Glennie, J. S., 78.
Stuart, *Mrs.* R. McE., 34.
Studies in the South and West, Warner, 59.
Study at home, Society to encourage, 145.
Study in temptations, Craigie, 9.
Sturgis, J. R., 34.
Sturgis, R., annotator, 80, 83, 87, 90, 129.
Successful man, Cruger, 10.
Sullivan, J. W., 15.
Summer in a cañon, Wiggin, 39.
Sumner, W. G., 114.
Surrender of Margaret Bellarmine, Sergeant, 32.
Sweet bells out of tune, Harrison, 18.
Swift, J., 15; life of, Johnson 43–44; Stephen, 76.
Swinburne, A. C., 76.
Sylvia's lovers, Gaskell, 15.
Symbolic education, Blow, 94.
Symonds, J. A., 54.
Symphonies, Upton, 93.
Synonyms, Fallows, 137; Smith, 138; Roget, 138.

Tableaux, Pollard, 134.
Table talk, Coleridge, 64.
Tait, L. R., 127.

Index

Taine, H. A., 61; art, 83. *See also* Napoleon, 45.
Tainsh, A. C., 77.
Tales of a lonely parish, Crawford, 9.
Tale of Chloe, Meredith, 27.
Tale of two cities, Dickens, 11.
Tales from Shakespeare, Lamb, C. and M., 69, 75.
Tale of a time and place, King, 23.
Tales of a traveler, Irving, 21.
Tales of the Argonauts, Harte, 18.
Talisman, Scott, 32.
Talleyrand, *Prince*. *See* Napoleon, 45.
Tanglewood tales, Hawthorne, 19.
Tapestry, Muntz, 90.
Tautphœus, J. M., 35.
Taylor, B., novels, 35; poems, 76; life of, 76.
Taylor, J. E., 100.
Teacher of the violin, Shorthouse, 33.
Teaching, Fitch, 96. *See also* Hubert, 123; and Pedagogy, 96.
Telegraphy, 125.
Telephony, 125.
Tempera, Middleton, 86.
Temperance. *See* Liquor question, 115.
Tenants of an old farm, McCook, 109.
Tender recollections of Irene Macgillicuddy, Oliphant, 28.
Ten dollars enough, Nitsch, 130.
Tenement tales of New York, Sullivan, 35.
Tennyson, A., 76; works on, Van Dyke, 77; Tainsh, 77; Brooke, 77; Dawson, 77.
Terhune, *Mrs.* M. V. H., 35, 120, 131.
Terrible family, James, 21.
Terry, T. B., 127.
Tess of the D'Urbervilles, Hardy, 17.
Textile fabrics, 90; Lefebure, 90; Middleton, 90; Muntz, 90; Sturgis, 90.
Thackeray, A., 46. *See also* Ritchie, A. T., 30-31.
Thackeray, W. M., novels, 35; lectures, sketches, poems, 77; memoir, Trollope, 77; Merivale *and* Marzials, 77.
Thaddeus of Warsaw, Porter, 29.
Thanet, Octave (*pseud.*). *See* French, A., 15.
That lass o' Lowrie's, Burnett, 7.
Thayer, A. W., 93.
Their wedding journey, Howells, 20.
Thelma, Mackay, 26.
Theological and literary essays, Hutton, 67.
There is no death, Lean, 24.
Thesaurus, Roget, 138.
Thinking, feeling, doing, Scripture, 112.
Thomas, A. C., 47-50.
Thomas, J. (*ed.*). *See* Lippincott's biog. dict., 44.
Thompson, *Sir* H., 131.
Thompson, L. S., 97.
Thompson, M., 110.
Thompson, R. E., 114.
Thompson, S. P., 100.
Thomson, T. A., 110.
Thomson, W. M., 58.
Thoreau, H. D., 110.
Thought, science of, Müller, 98.
Thoughts of busy girls, Dodge, 121.
Thousand miles up the Nile, Edwards, 6.
Three kingdoms, Ballard, 108.
Three Miss Kings, Cambridge, 8.
Three years of Arctic service, Greely, 56.
Throckmorton, Seawell, 32.
Through one administration, Burnett, 7.
Through the long night, Linton, 25.
Through the looking-glass, Dodgson, 11.
Thrown on her resources, Croly, 123.
Thwaites, R. G., annotator, 47. *See also* Epochs of American history, 47.
Tiernan, *Mrs.* F. C., 36.
Time's revenges, Murray, 27.
Timothy's quest, Wiggin, 39.
Tincker, M. A., 36.
Tinkling cymbals, Fawcett, 14.
Tip cat, 27.
Toinette's Philip, Jamison, 22.
Tom Burke of Ours, Lever, 25.
Tom Cringle's log, Scott, 32.
Tom Jones, history of, Fielding, 14.

Tompkins and other folks, Deming, 10.
Tony the maid, Howard, 20.
Tools and the man, Gladden, 113.
Torrey, B., 110, 125.
To the bitter end, Maxwell, 26.
Tourgée, A. W., 36.
Tourmalin's time checks, Guthrie, 16.
Townsend, V. F., 36.
Towry, M. H., 75.
Toynbee, A., 113.
Tracy, A., 59.
Tracy, F., 112.
Tracy, R. S., 120.
Trail of the sword, Parker, 28-29.
Traill, H. D., 51.
Tramp trip, Meriwether, 57.
Translation of a savage, Parker, 29.
Travel and exploration (department), 55-60.
Travel, art of, Bisland, 55; Knox, 57; Loomis, 57; Meriwether, 57. *See also* Woman's book, 123.
Traveller, Goldsmith, 66.
Traveller from Altruria, Howells, 20.
Treasure Island, Stevenson, 34.
Treat, *Mrs.* M., 110.
Trenholm, W. M., 114.
Trespasser, Parker, 29.
Trevelyan, G. O., 46, 70.
Trilby, Du Maurier, 12.
Trollope, A., novels, 36; memoir of Thackeray, 77.
Trollope, *Mrs.* F. E. M., 59.
Troublesome daughters, Walford, 37.
Trouessart, E. L., 107.
Trusts, 114.
Tryon, T. *See* Brunner, A. W., *and* Tryon, T., 129.
Tryphena in love, Raymond, 30.
Turner, J. M. W., Hamerton, 85.
Tuttiett, M. G., 37.
Twain, Mark (*pseud.*). *See* Clemens, 8.
Twice-told tales, Hawthorne, 19.
Two admirals, Cooper, 9.
Two bites at a cherry, Aldrich, 2.
Two Salomes, Pool, 29.
Two worlds, Gilder, 66.
Two years ago, Kingsley, 23.
Two years before the mast, Dana, 56.
Tyler, M. C., biography, 46; literature, 61.
Tylor, E. B., 111.
Typee, Melville, 27.
Typewriting, 125. *See also* Hubert, 123.
Tytler, Sarah (*pseud.*). *See* Keddie, H., 23.

Uffelmann, J., 120.
Uncle of an angel, Janvier, 22.
Uncle Remus and his friends, Harris, 18.
Uncle Tom's cabin, Stowe, 34.
Under fire, Roing, 23.
Under the evening lamp, Stoddard, 76.
Under the red robe, Weyman, 38.
Under two flags, De la Ramé, 10.
United Kingdom (department), 50-52.
United States (department), 47-49; Appleton, 49, 55; Baedecker, 55; Fiske, 47, 48, 68.
University Extension, 96.
Unmarried woman, Chester, 121.
Up and down the brooks, Bamford, 108.
Upcott, L. E., 87.
Ups and downs, Hale, 17.
Upton, G. P., 93.
Uruguay, Chi'd, 56.
Useful arts (department), 123-125.

Vagabond heroine, Edwardes, 12.
Vagabonds, Woods, 40.
Vale of cedars, Aguilar, 1.
Valerie Aylmer, Tiernan, 36.
Van Bibber, Davis, 10.
Van Dyke, H., 77.
Van Dyke, J. C., 87.
Van Rensselaer, *Mrs.* S., 116, 128.
Vanity Fair, Thackeray, 36.
Vasari, G., 83.
Vashti, Wilson, 39.
Vathek, Beckford, 4.
Venable, F. P., 101.
Vendetta, Mackay, 26.

Vengeance of James Vansittart, Needell, 27.
Venice, Hare, 57; Freeman, 89.
Vernon's aunt, Cotes, 9.
Verse, science of English, Lanier, 69.
Very hard cash, Reade, 30.
Vestigia, Fletcher, 14.
Vesty of the Basins, Greene, 16.
Vicar of Wakefield, Goldsmith, 15-16.
Vice versa, Guthrie, 16.
Vico. *See* Philosophical classics, 117.
Victoria, *Queen*, Wilson, 46.
Vignettes of Manhattan, Matthews, 26.
Village on the cliff, Ritchie, 31.
Village tragedy, Woods, 40.
Villette, Brontë, 5-6.
Vincent, B., 137.
Vincent, F., 59.
Vines, S. H., 107.
Viollet-le-Duc, E. E., 87, 90.
Virgil, Morris, 71.
Virginia, making of, Drake, 49.
Virginians, Thackeray, 35-36.
Vivian Grey, Disraeli, 11.
Voyage of the *Vega*, Nordenskiold, 58.

Wages of sin, Harrison, 18.
Wagner, R., Finck, 91; Jullien, 92; Nohl, 92.
Wagoner of the Alleghanies, Read, 72.
Wake robin, Burroughs, 108.
Walden, Thoreau, 110.
Waldstein, C., 74, 87.
Walford, *Mrs.* L. B. C., 37.
Walker, A., 123.
Walker, F. A., 49, 113.
Walker, G., 95.
Walks and talks in the geological field, Winchell, 104.
Wallace, A. R., 110.
Wallace, D. M., 59.
Wallace, L., 37.
Wallace, W., 118.
Walpole, H., novels, 37; life of, Morley, 71.
Walsh, W. S., 137.
Walworth, *Mrs.* J. R. H., 37.
Ward, A. W., 64.
Ward, *Mrs.* E. S. P., 37.
Ward, *Mrs.* Mary Augusta, 38.
Ward, May Alden, 46.
Ward, T. H. (*ed.*); English poets, 60.
Warden, Florence, (*pseud.*). *See* James, *Mrs.* F. A., 21.
Warden, Trollope, 36.
Ware, W., 38.
Waring, G. E., 126.
Warner, A. W., 115.
Warner, C. D., 59.
Warner, J. De W., 114.
Warner, S., 38.
War-time wooing, King, 23.
Washington, G., life of, Lodge, 44; Scudder, 45; Seelye, 45; Irving, 68; writings of, Ford, 46.
Washington, Mary *and* Martha, Lossing, 44.
Wasps. *See* Insects.
Water, Prudden, 120.
Water babies, Kingsley, 23.
Waterdale neighbors, McCarthy, 25.
Water ghost, Bangs, J. K., 3.
Waters of Hercules, Laszowska, 24.
Water-witch, Cooper, 9.
Watson, B. M., annotator, 126.
Watson, J., 117.
Watson, J. M., 38.
Watts, T., 84.
Wauters, A. J., 88.
Waverley, Scott, 32.
Way of the world, Murray, 27.
We all, French, 15.
We and our neighbors, Stowe, 34.
We two, Lyall, 24.
Wealth against commonwealth, Lloyd, 114.
Web of gold, Woods, 40.
Webb, H. L., 99.
Webb, S., 114.
Weber, F. v. Benedict, 91.
Webster's international dictionary, 81, 136; academic, 136.
Wedding garment, Pendleton, 29.
Weed, C. M., 107.
Week in a French country house, Sartoris, 31.

Weik, J. W. *See* Herndon, W. H., *and* Weik, J. W., 41.
Weismann, D. A., 110.
Weitzman, C. F., 93.
Wells, D. A., 114.
Wenderholme, Hamerton, 77.
Wentworth, G. A, 90.
West Indies (department), 50; Fronde, 50; Hearn, 57.
West, winning of the, Roosevelt, 48; making of the, Drake, 49; our great west, Ralph, 58; studies in the, Warner, 59.
Wetherell, E. (*pseud.*). *See* Warner, S., 38.
Westward ho !, Kingsley, 23.
Wetzler, J., 99.
Weyman, S. J., 38.
What dreams may come, Atherton, 2.
What he cost her, Payn, 29.
What necessity knows, Dougall, 11.
What shall we do to night ? 113.
What will he do with it?, Bulwer-Lytton, 6.
Wheeler, C., 129.
Wheeler, W. A., 136-137, *and* C. G., 135.
When a man's single, Barrie, 4.
Where the battle was fought, Murfree, 27.
Which shall it be ?, Hector, 19.
Whist, Coffin, 133; modern whist, 134.
White, G., 124.
White, Horace, 114.
White, S. J., 123, 131-132.
White, W. H., 38.
White cockade, Grant, 16.
White company, Doyle, 12.
White heron, Jewett. 22.
White jacket, Melville, 27.
White ladies, Oliphant, 28.
Whiting, M. C. *See* Miller, E., *and* Whiting, M. C., 106.
Whitney, *Mrs.* A. D. T., 39.
Whitney, W. D., 98.
Whittier, J. G., 77; life of, Pickard, 77.
Who breaks, pays, Jenkin, 22.
Who was lost and is found, Oliphant, 28.
Wide, wide world, Warner, 38.
Widow Guthrie, Johnston, 23.
Wieland, Brown, C. B., 6.
Wiggin, K. D., 39. *See also* Woman's book, 123.
Wilfred Cumbermede, MacDonald, 26.

Wilkins, M. E., 39.
Willard, F. E., 46, 121. *See also* Meyer, 123.
Willcox, M. A., 110.
Williams, W. M., 132.
Wilson, *Mrs.* A. J. E., 39.
Wilson, C. H., 88.
Wilson, R., 46.
Wilson, W. *See* Epochs of American history, 47.
Wiltse, S. E., 95.
Winchell, A., 104.
Wind of destiny, Hardy, 17.
Window - gardening. *See* Flower-garden.
Window in Thrums, Barrie, J. M., 4.
Wing and wing, Cooper, 9.
Winifred Bertram, Charles, 8.
Winners in life's race, Buckley, 108.
Winsor, J., biography, 46; histories, 50.
Winter, John Strange (*pseud.*). *See* Stannard, *Mrs.* H. E. V. P., 33.
Winter, W., 59.
Winter sunshine, Burroughs, 108.
Winthrop, T., 39.
Witherbee, J. V., 97.
Within an ace, Jenkin, 22.
Within the capes, Pyle, 30.
With my friends, Matthews, 26.
Without blemish, Walworth, 37.
Withrow, W. H., 50.
Wives and daughters, Gaskell, 15.
Wolfert's Roost, Irving, 21.
Woman in white, Collins, 8.
Woman of the century, 46.
Woman suffrage, *pro* and *anti*, 116.
Woman's book, 122, 123, 138.
Woman's club, a literary, 144; hints on forming, 145.
Woman's share in primitive culture, Mason, 111.
Woman's work in America, Meyer, 123.
Women, Bacon, 55; Garnett *and* Stuart Glennie, 78; Lange, 96; Bissell, 119; Davis, 119; Galbraith, 119; Chester, 121; Dodge, 121; Ruskin, 121; Miller, 122; Stanley, 122; Shattuck 122; Jones, 122; biographies of, Bolton, 41; Cone *and* Gilder, 42; Fawcett, 43; men and women of the time, 44; woman of the century, 46.
Women, livelihoods for, 123-125.
Women's Christian Temperance Union, work of. *See* Meyer, 123.
Women's exchanges. *See* Hubert, 123.

Won by waiting, Lyall, 25.
Wonder-book, Hawthorne, 19.
Wood, *Mrs.* E. P., 39.
Wood, H., 114.
Wood, J, 137.
Woodberry, G. E., 46, 72.
Wood-carving, Middleton, 86; Leland, 123; Martineau, 124; Harrison, 129
Woodlanders, Hardy, 17.
Woods, K. P., 40.
Woods, *Mrs* M. L., 40.
Wooing o't, Hector, 19.
Woolman, M. S., 125.
Woolson, C. F., 40.
Worcester's dictionary, 136.
Wordsworth, W., 77; Myers, 77.
Work, Alcott, 2.
Works of reference (department), 135-137.
World's fair, Chicago; 1893, art at, Coffin, 81.
World well lost, Linton, 25.
World went very well then, Besant, 4.
Wormwood, Mackay, 26.
Wrecker, Stevenson, 34.
Wreck of the *Grosvenor*, Russell, 31.
Wright, L., 127.
Wright, M. O., 110.
Wright, M. R., 100.
Wundt, W., 112.
Wuthering heights, Brontë, E., 6.
Wyman, L. B. C. *See* Meyer, 123.

Yates. E. A., 40.
Yellow fairy-book, Lang, 24.
Yesterdays with authors, Fields, 43.
Yoke of the Thorah, Harland, 17.
Vonge. C. M., 40.
York and a Lancaster Rose, Keary, 24.
Youma, Hearn. 19.
Young, C. A.. 99.
Young maids and old, Burnham, 7.

Zachary Phips, Bynner, 7.
Zadoc Pine, Bunner, 6.
Zaehnsdorf, J. W., 124.
Zangwill, I., 40.
Zanoni, Bulwer-Lytton, 6.
Zenobia, Ware, 38.
Zeph, Jackson, 21.
Zoölogy, Morse, 110; Nicholson, 110.
Zury, Kirkland, 24.

www.ingramcontent.com/pod-product-compliance
Lightning Source LLC
Chambersburg PA
CBHW022117160426
43197CB00009B/1058